John Wood

**Hardy Perennials and old-fashioned Garden Flowers**

Describing the most desirable Plants for Borders, Rockeries, and Shrubberies

John Wood

**Hardy Perennials and old-fashioned Garden Flowers**
*Describing the most desirable Plants for Borders, Rockcries, and Shrubberies*

ISBN/EAN: 9783337070212

Printed in Europe, USA, Canada, Australia, Japan

Cover: Foto ©ninafisch / pixelio.de

More available books at **www.hansebooks.com**

# HARDY PERENNIALS

AND

Old=Fashioned Garden Flowers:

DESCRIBING

THE MOST DESIRABLE PLANTS FOR BORDERS,
ROCKERIES, AND SHRUBBERIES,

INCLUDING

FOLIAGE AS WELL AS FLOWERING PLANTS.

By JOHN WOOD.

ILLUSTRATED.

LONDON:
L. UPCOTT GILL, 170, STRAND, W.C.
1884.

LONDON: PRINTED BY A. BRADLEY, 170, STRAND, W.C.

# PREFACE.

At the present time there is a growing desire to patronise perennial plants, more especially the many and beautiful varieties known as "old-fashioned flowers." Not only do they deserve to be cultivated on their individual merits, but for other very important reasons; they afford great variety of form, foliage, and flower, and compared with annual and tender plants, they are found to give much less trouble. If a right selection is made and properly planted, the plants may be relied upon to appear with perennial vigour and produce flowers more or less throughout the year. I would not say bouquets may be gathered in the depth of winter, but what will be equally cheering may be had in blow, such as the Bluet, Violet, Primrose, Christmas Rose, Crocus, Hepatica, Squills, Snowdrops, and other less known winter bloomers. It does not seem to be generally understood that warm nooks and corners, under trees or walls, serve to produce in winter flowers which usually appear in spring when otherwise placed.

There are many subjects which, from fine habit and foliage, even when flowerless, claim notice, and they, too, are described.

Many gardens are very small, but these, if properly managed, have their advantages. The smaller the garden the more choice should be the collection, and the more highly should it be cultivated. I shall be glad if anything I say tends in this direction. From my notes of plants useful memoranda may be made, with the object of adding a few of the freest bloomers in each month, thus avoiding the error often committed of growing such subjects as mostly flower at one time, after which the garden has a forlorn appearance. The plants should not be blamed for this; the selection is at fault. No amount of time and care can make a garden what it should be if untidy and weedy plants prevail. On the other hand, the most beautiful species, both as regards foliage and flowers, can be just as easily cultivated.

The object of this small work is to furnish the names and descriptions of really useful and reliable Hardy and Perennial Plants, suitable for all kinds of flower gardens, together with definite cultural hints on each plant.

Perhaps flowers were never cultivated of more diversified kinds than at the present time; and it is a legitimate and not uncommon question to ask, "What do you grow?" Not only have we now the lovers of the distinct and showy, but numerous admirers of such species as need to be closely examined, that their beautiful and interesting features may gladden and stir the mind. The latter class of plants, without doubt, is capable of giving most pleasure; and to meet the growing taste for these, books on flowers must necessarily treat upon the species or varieties in a more detailed manner, in order to get at their peculiarities and requirements. The more we learn about our flowers the more we enjoy them; to simply see bright colours and pretty forms is far from all the pleasure we may reap in our gardens.

If I have not been able to give scientific information, possibly that of a practical kind may be of some use, as for many years, and never more than now, I have enjoyed the cultivation of flowers with my own hands. To be able to grow a plant well is of the highest importance, and the first step towards a full enjoyment of it.

I have had more especially in view the wants of the less experienced Amateur; and as all descriptions and modes of culture are given from specimens successfully grown in my own garden, I hope I may have at least a claim to being practical.

I have largely to thank several correspondents of many years' standing for hints and information incorporated in these pages.

J. WOOD.

WOODVILLE, KIRKSTALL,
*November*, 1883.

# ERRATA.

For the placing of capital letters uniformly throughout this Volume to the specific names at the cross-headings, and for the omission of many capitals in the body of the type, the printer is alone responsible.

Numerous oversights fall to my lot, but in many of the descriptions other than strictly proper botanical terms have been employed, where it seemed desirable to use more intelligible ones; as, for instance, the flowers of the Composites have not always been termed "heads," perianths have sometimes been called corollas, and their divisions at times petals, and so on; this is hardly worthy of the times, perhaps, but it was thought that the terms would be more generally understood.

Page 7, line 8. For "lupin" read "Lupine."
Page 39, line 31. For "calyx" read "involucre."
Page 40, line 27. For "calyx" read "involucre."
Page 46, line 1. For "corolla" read "perianth."
Page 47, lines 3 and 6. For "corolla" read "perianth."
Page 48, last line. For "lupin" read "Lupine."
Page 60, line 16. For "pompon" read "pompone."
Page 64, line 36. For "corolla" read "perianth."
Page 102, line 27. For "Fritillaries" read "Fritillarias."
Page 114, cross-heading. For "Ice-cold Gentian" read "Ice-cold Loving Gentian."
Page 213. For "*Tirolensis*" read "*Tyrolensis.*"
Page 214, cross-heading. For "*Cashmerianum*" read "*Cashmeriana.*"
Page 215, cross-heading. For "*Cashmerianum*" read "*Cashmeriana.*"
Page 275, line 26. For "corolla" read "perianth."
Page 284, line 25. For "calyx" read "involucre."
Page 285, line 1. For "calyx" read "involucre."

JOHN WOOD.

*November 14th, 1883.*

# HARDY PERENNIALS

AND

## OLD-FASHIONED GARDEN FLOWERS.

### Acæna Novæ Zealandiæ.
*Otherwise* A. MICROPHYLLA; *Nat. Ord.* SANGUISORBEÆ,
*or* ROSE FAMILY.

THE plant, as may be seen by the illustration (Fig. 1), is small, and its flowers are microscopic, hardly having the appearance of flowers, even when minutely examined, but when the bloom has faded there is a rapid growth, the calyces forming a stout set of long spines; these, springing from the globular head in considerable numbers, soon become pleasingly conspicuous, and this is by far the more ornamental stage of the plant. It is hardy, evergreen, and creeping. It seldom rises more than one or two inches from the ground, and only when it approaches a wall, stones, or some such fixed body, does it show an inclination to climb; it is, therefore, a capital rock plant. As implied by its specific name, it comes from New Zealand, and has not long been acclimatised in this country.

The flowers are produced on fine wiry stems an inch or more long, being nearly erect; they are arranged in round heads, at first about the size of a small pea; these, when bruised, have an ammoniacal smell. Each minute flower has four green petals and brownish seed organs, which cause the knob of flowers to have a rather grimy look, and a calyx which is very hard and stout, having two scales and four sepals. These sepals are the parts which, after the seed organs have performed their functions, become elongated and of a fine rosy-crimson colour; they form stiff and rather stout spines, often ¾in. long; they bristle evenly from every part of the little globe of seed vessels, and are very pretty. The spines are produced in great abundance, and they may be cut freely; their effect is unique when used for table decoration, stuck in tufts of dark green selaginella. On the plant they keep in good form for two months. The leaves are 1in. to 2in. long, pinnate; the leaflets are of a dark bronzy colour on the upper side and a pale green underneath, like

FIG. 1. ACÆNA NOVÆ ZEALANDIÆ.
(One-half natural size.)

maidenhair, which they also resemble in form, being nearly round and toothed. They are in pairs, with a terminal odd one; they are largest at the extremity, and gradually lessen to rudimentary leaflets; the foliage is but sparingly produced on the creeping stems, which root as they creep on the surface.

The habit of the plant is compact and cushion-like, and the brilliant spiny balls are well set off on the bed of fern-like but sombre foliage. During August it is one of the most effective plants in the rock garden, where I find it to do well in either moist or dry situations; it grows fast, and, being evergreen, it is one of the more useful creepers for all-the-year-round effect; for covering dormant bulbs or bare places it is at once efficient and beautiful. It requires light soil, and seems to enjoy grit;

nowhere does it appear in better health or more at home than when carpeting the walk or track of the rock garden.

It is self-propagating, but when it is desirable to move a tuft of it, it should be done during the growing season, so that it may begin to root at once and get established, otherwise the wind and frosts will displace it.

It blooms from June to September, more or less, but only the earliest flowers produce well-coloured spines.

## Achillea Ægyptica.

EGYPTIAN YARROW; *Nat. Ord.* COMPOSITÆ.

THIS is an evergreen (though herb-like) species. It has been grown for more than 200 years in English gardens, and originally came, as its name implies, from Egypt. Notwithstanding the much warmer climate of its native country, it proves to be one of the hardiest plants in our gardens. I dare say many will think the Yarrows are not worthy of a place in the garden; but it should not be forgotten that not only are fine and useful flowers included in this work, but also the good "old-fashioned" kinds, and that a few such are to be found amongst the Yarrows is without doubt. Could the reader see the collection now before me, cut with a good piece of stem and some foliage, and pushed into a deep vase, he would not only own that they were a pleasing contrast, but quaintly grand for indoor decoration.

*A. Ægyptica* not only produces a rich yellow flower, but the whole plant is ornamental, having an abundance of finely-cut foliage, which, from a downy or nappy covering, has a pleasing grey or silvery appearance. The flowers are produced on long stems nearly 2ft. high, furnished at the nodes with clean grey tufts of smaller-sized leaves; near the top the stems are all but naked, and are terminated by the flat heads or corymbs of closely-packed flowers. They are individually small, but the corymbs will be from 2in. to 3in. across. Their form is that of the common Yarrow, but the colour is a bright light yellow. The leaves are 6in. to 8in. long, narrow and pinnate, the leaflets of irregular form, variously toothed and lobed; the whole foliage is soft to the touch, from the nappy covering, as already mentioned. Its flowers, from their extra fine colour, are very telling in a cut state. The plant is suitable for the borders, more especially amongst other old kinds. Ordinary garden loam suits it, and its propagation may be carried out at any time by root division.

Flowering period, June to September.

live in the most reeky towns, only mentioned here to introduce
*A. P. fl.-pl.*, which is one of the most useful of border flowers. I
am bound to add, however, that only when in flower is it more
presentable than the weedy and typical form; but the grand
masses of pure white bachelors'-button-like flowers, which are
produced for many weeks in succession, render this plant
deserving of a place in every garden. It is a very old flower in
English gardens. Some 250 years ago Parkinson referred to the
double flowering kind, in his "Paradise of Pleasant Flowers,"
as a then common plant; and I may as well produce Gerarde's
description of the typical form, which answers, in all respects,
for the double one, with the exception of the flowers themselves:
"The small Sneesewoort hath many rounde and brittle braunches,
beset with long and narrowe leaues, hackt about the edges like a
sawe; at the top of the stalkes do grow smal single flowers like
the fielde Daisie. The roote is tender and full of strings,
creeping farre abroade in the earth, and in short time occupieth
very much grounde." The flowers of this plant are often, but
wrongly, called "bachelors' buttons," which they much resemble.

For cutting purposes, this plant is one of the most useful; not
only are the blooms a good white, but they have the quality
of keeping clean, and are produced in greater numbers than
ever I saw them on the single form. Those requiring large
quantities of white flowers could not do better than give the
plant a few square yards in some unfrequented part of the
garden; any kind of soil will suit it, but if enriched the bloom
will be all the better for it. The roots run freely just under the
surface, so that a large stock may soon be had; yet, fine as are
its flowers, hardy and spreading as the plant proves, it is but
seldom met with. Even in small gardens this fine old flower
should be allowed a little space. Transplant any time.

Flowering period, June to August.

## Aconitum Autumnale.

AUTUMN MONK'S-HOOD; *Nat. Ord.* RANUNCULACEÆ.

HARDY, perennial, and herbaceous. This is one of the finest
subjects for autumn flowering. The whole plant, which stands
nearly 3ft. high, is stately and distinct (Fig. 2); the leaves are
dark green, large, deeply cut and veined, of good substance, and
slightly drooping. The flowers are a fine blue (a colour somewhat scarce in our gardens at that season), irregularly arranged
on very stout stems; in form they exactly resemble a monk's
hood, and the manner in which they are held from the stems
further accords with that likeness. These rich flowers are
numerously produced; a three-year-old plant will have as many
as six stout stems all well furnished, rendering the specimen very
conspicuous.

FIG. 2.
ACONITUM AUTUMNALE.
(About one-tenth natural size.)

This is one form of the Monk's-hood long grown in English gardens, and is called "old-fashioned." *A. japonicum*, according to some, is identical with it, but whether that is so or not, there is but a slight difference, and both, of course, are good.

I find it likes a rich deep soil. It is propagated by division of the roots after the tops have turned yellow in autumn or winter.

It flowers from August until cut down by frosts.

### Allium Moly.

LARGE YELLOW GARLIC; *Nat. Ord.* LILIACEÆ.

A HARDY bulbous perennial, of neat habit, with bright golden flowers, produced in large heads; they endure a long time and are very effective; it is by far the best yellow species. Where bold clumps of yellow are desirable, especially if somewhat in the background, there can be few subjects more suitable for the purpose than this plant; both leaves and flowers, however, have a disagreeable odour, if in the least bruised. It is a very old plant in English gardens, and is a native of the South of Europe. Its chief merits are fine colour, large head, neat habit, and easy culture. The flowers are 1in. across, borne in close heads, having stalks over an inch long springing from stout scapes; the six long oval petals are of a shining yellow colour; the seed organs also are all yellow and half the length of petals; the scape is about a foot high, naked, round, and very stout; the leaves are nearly as broad as tulip leaves, and otherwise much resemble them.

Flowering period, June to August.

### Allium Neapolitanum.

NEAPOLITAN ALLIUM; *Nat. Ord.* LILIACEÆ.

THIS has pure white flowers arranged in neat and effective umbels, and though not so useful in colour as the flowers of *A. Moly*, they are much superior to those of many of the genus.

Flowering period, June to August.

Both of the above Alliums may be grown in any odd parts which need decorating with subjects requiring little care; any kind of soil will do for them, but if planted too near the walks the flowers are liable to be cut by persons who may not be aware of their evil odour. The bulbs may be divided every three years with advantage, and may be usefully planted in lines in front of shrubs, or mixed with other strong-growing flowers, such as alkanets, lupins, and foxgloves.

## Alyssum Saxatile.

ROCK MADWORT, *or* GOLDEN TUFT; *Nat. Ord.* CRUCIFERÆ.

THIS pleasing and well-known hardy, evergreen, half-woody shrub is always a welcome flower. From its quantity of bloom

FIG. 3. ALYSSUM SAXATILE.
(One-third natural size).

all its other parts are literally smothered (see Fig. 3). When passing large pieces of it in full blow, its fragrant honey smell reminds one of summer clover fields.

Its golden yellow flowers are densely produced in panicles on procumbent stems, 12in. to 18in. long. The little flowers, from distinct notches in the petals, have a different appearance from many of the order *Cruciferæ*, as, unless they are well expanded, there seem to be eight instead of four petals. The leaves are inversely ovate, lanceolate, villose, and slightly toothed. A specimen will continue in good form during average weather for about three weeks. It is not only seen to most advantage on rockwork, where its prostrate stems can fall over the stones, but the dry situation is in accordance with its requirements; still, it is not at all particular, but does well in any sunny situation, in any soil that is not over moist or ill drained. It is easily and quickly propagated by cuttings in early summer.

Flowering period, April and May.

## Anchusa Italica.

ITALIAN ALKANET; *Nat. Ord.* BORAGINACEÆ.

A HARDY herbaceous perennial of first-class merit for gardens where there is plenty of room; amongst shrubs it will not only prove worthy of the situation, but, being a ceaseless bloomer, its tall and leafy stems decked with brilliant flowers may always be relied upon for cutting purposes; and let me add, as, perhaps, many have never tried this fine but common flower in a large vase, the stems, if cut to the length of 18in., and loosely placed in an old-fashioned vase, without any other flowers, are more than ornamental—they are fine.

FIG. 4. ANCHUSA ITALICA (Flower Spray).
(One-third natural size.)

Its main features are seen in its bold leafy stems, furnished with large, dark blue, forget-me-not-like flowers, nearly all their length. The little white eyes of the blossoms are very telling (see Fig. 4). The flowers are held well out from the large leaves of the main stem by smaller ones (from 1in. to 8in. long), at the ends of which the buds and flowers are clustered, backed by a pair of small leaflets, like wings. Just before the buds open they are of a bright rose colour, and when the flowers fade the leafy calyx completely hides the withered parts, and other blooms take their places between the wing-like pair of leaflets; so the succession of bloom is kept up through the whole summer. The leaves of the root are very large when fully grown during summer—over a foot long—those of the stems are much less; all are lance-shaped and pointed, plain at the edges, very hairy, and of a dark green colour. The stems are numerous, upright, and, as before hinted, branched; also, like the leaves, they are covered with stiff hairs, a characteristic common to the order. Well-established plants will grow to the height of 3ft. to 5ft.

Flowering period, May to September.

## Anchusa Sempervirens.
### *Nat. Ord.* BORAGINACEÆ.

THIS is a British species, and, as its name denotes, is evergreen; not, let me add, as a tall plant, for the stems wither or at least become very sere, only the large leaves of the root remaining fresh; and though it has many points of difference from *A. Italica*, such as shorter growth, darker flowers and foliage, and more oval leaves—these form the distinctions most observable. By its evergreen quality it is easily identified in winter. There is also an important difference from the axillary character of the flower stems. With these exceptions the description of *A. Italica* will fairly hold good for this native species.

This Alkanet has various other names, as *Borago sempervirens*, *Buglossum s.*, and with old writers it, together with allied species, was much esteemed, not only for the flowers, but for its reputed medicinal properties. To those who care to grow these good old plants I would say, well enrich the soil; when so treated, the results are very different from those where the plants have been put in hungry and otherwise neglected situations; this favourable condition may be easily afforded, and will be more than repaid. Strong roots may be transplanted at any time, and propagation is more quickly carried out by division of the woody roots, which should be cut or split so that each piece has a share of bark and a crown. Just before new growth has begun, as in January, is the best time for this operation, so that there is no chance of rot from dormancy.

Flowering period, May to September.

## Andromeda Tetragona.

*Syn.* CASSIOPE TETRAGONA; *Nat. Ord.* ERICACEÆ.

A DWARF hardy evergreen shrub, which comes to us from Lapland and North America; though a very beautiful subject for either rockwork or border, it is rarely seen. It is not one of the easiest plants to grow, which may, to some extent, account for its rarity. Still, when it can have its requirements, it not only thrives well, but its handsome form and flowers repay any extra trouble it may have given. In the culture of this, as of most plants of the order *Ericaceæ*, there is decidedly a right way and a wrong one, and if the species now under consideration has one or two special requirements it deserves them.

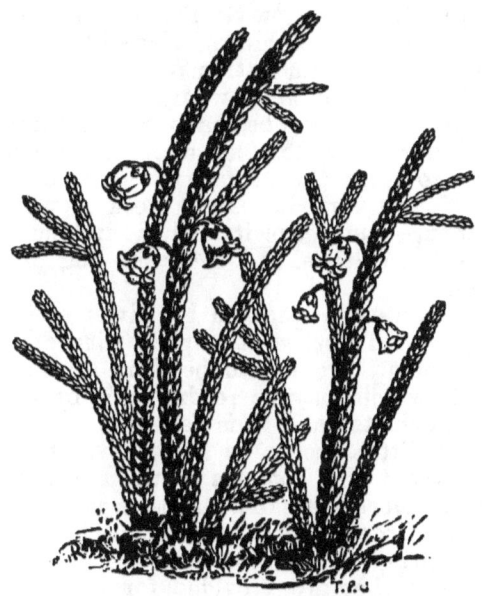

FIG. 5. ANDROMEDA TETRAGONA.
(One-half natural size).

With me it never exceeds a height of 6in. or 7in., is much branched, and of a fine apple green colour; the flowers are small but very beautiful, bell-shaped, pendent, and springing from the leafy stems of the previous year's growth. The leaves are small as well as curious, both in form and arrangement, completely hiding their stems; their roundish grain-shaped forms are evenly arranged in four rows extending throughout the whole length of the branches (whence the name *tetragona*), giving them a square appearance resembling an ear of wheat, but much less stout (see Fig. 5); the little leaves, too, are frosted somewhat in the way of many of the saxifrages. It is next to impossible to describe this pretty shrub; fortunately, the cut will convey a proper idea at a glance. All who possess more select collections of hardy plants and shrubs should not fail to include this; it is fit for any collection of fifty choice species.

I struggled long before finding out the right treatment, as presumably I now have, yet it is very simple, in fact, only such as many other plants should have; but, unlike them, *A. tetragona* will take no alternative; it must have partial shade, sandy peat or leaf soil, and be planted in a moist or semi-bog situation. On the raised parts of rockwork it became burnt up; planted in loam, though light, it was dormant as a stone; in pots, it withered at the tips; but, with the above treatment, I have flowers and numerous branchlets. Many little schemes may be improvised for the accommodation of this and similar subjects. Something of the bog character would appear to be the difficulty here; a miniature one may be made in less than half an hour. Next the walk dig a hole 18in. all ways, fill in with sandy peat, make it firm; so form the surface of the walk that the water from it will eddy or turn in. In a week it will have settled; do not fill it up, but leave it dished and put in the plant. Gentians, *pyrolas*, calthas, and even the bog pimpernel I have long grown so.

*A. tetragona* can be propagated by division of the roots, but such division should not be attempted with other than a perfectly healthy plant. It should be done in spring, just as it begins to push, which may be readily seen by the bright green tips of the branchlets; and it is desirable, when replanting, to put the parts a little deeper, so as to cover the dead but persistent leaves about the bottoms of the stems which occur on the parts four or more years old. After a year, when so planted, I have found good roots emitted from these parts, and, doubtless, such deeper planting will, in some way, meet its requirements, as in this respect they are provided for in its habitats by the annual and heavy fall of leaves from other trees which shade it.

Flowering period, April and May.

## Anemone Alpina.

ALPINE WINDFLOWER; *Nat. Ord.* RANUNCULACEÆ.

FROM Austria, the foliage closely resembling that of *A. sulphurea*, but the flowers are larger and of various colours. It is said to be the parent of *A. sulphurea*.

It flowers in June. See *A. sulphurea*.

## Anemone Apennina.
MOUNTAIN WINDFLOWER; *Nat. Ord.* RANUNCULACEÆ.

THIS is one of the "old-fashioned" flowers of our gardens—in fact, a native species, having a black tuberous root, which forms a distinct, though invisible characteristic of the species. As the old names are somewhat descriptive, I give them—viz., Geranium-leaved Anemone, and Stork's-bill Windflower.

The appearance of a bold piece of this plant when in flower is exceedingly cheerful; the soft-looking feathery foliage forms a rich groundwork for the lavish number of flowers, which vary much in colour, from sky-blue to nearly white, according to the number of days they may have been in blow, blue being the opening colour. The flowers are produced singly on stems, 6in. high, and ornamented with a whorl of finely-cut leaflets, stalked, lobed, and toothed; above this whorl the ruddy flower stem is much more slender. During sunshine the flowers are 1½in. across the tips of sepals, becoming reflexed. The foliage, as before hinted, is in the form of a whorl, there being no root leaf, and the soft appearance of the whole plant is due to its downiness, which extends to and includes the calyx. The lobes of the leaves are cupped, but the leaves themselves reflex until their tips touch the ground, whence their distinct and pleasing form.

This plant is most at home in the half shade of trees, where its flowers retain their blue colour longer. It should be grown in bold patches, and in free or sandy soil. The tubers may be transplanted soon after the tops have died off in late summer.

Flowering period, April and May.

## Anemone Blanda.
FAIR WINDFLOWER, or BLUE GRECIAN ANEMONE;
*Nat. Ord.* RANUNCULACEÆ.

THIS is a lovely winter flower, of great value in our gardens, from its showiness. It is a recent introduction from the warmer climes of the South of Europe and Asia Minor; and though it is not so vigorous under cultivation in our climate as most Windflowers, it proves perfectly hardy. A little extra care should be taken in planting it as regards soil and position, in order to grow it well. It belongs to that section of its numerous genus having an involucrum of stalked leaflets.

The flowers are produced on stalks, 4in. to 6in. high; they are nearly 2in. across, of a fine deep blue colour; the sepals are numerous and narrow, in the way of *A. stellata*, or star anemone. The leaves are triternate, divisions deeply cut and acute; the leaves of the involucrum are stalked, trifid, and deeply cut. The whole plant much resembles *A. Apennina*. Where it can be established, it must prove one of the most useful flowers, and to possess such charming winter blossom is worth much effort in affording it suitable conditions. The soil should be rich, light, and well drained, as sandy loam, and if mixed with plenty of leaf soil all the better. The position should be sheltered, otherwise this native of warm countries will have its early leaves and flowers damaged by the wintry blast, and the evil does not stop there, for the check at such a period interferes with the root development, and repetitions of such damage drive the plants into a state of "dwindling," and I may add, this is the condition in which this plant may frequently be seen. Many of the Anemones may be planted without much care, other than that of giving them a little shade from sunshine. The present subject, however, being so early, is not likely to obtain too much bright weather, but rather the reverse. If, then, it is planted in warm quarters, it may be expected to yield its desirable flowers in average quantity compared with other Windflowers, and in such proportion will its roots increase. The latter may be divided (providing they are of good size and healthy) when the leaves have died off.

Flowering period, February and March.

## Anemone Coronaria.

POPPY-LIKE WINDFLOWER; *Nat. Ord.* RANUNCULACEÆ.

HARDY and turberous. The illustration (Fig. 6) is of the double form, in which it may frequently be seen; also in many colours, as blue, purple, white, scarlet, and striped; the same colours may be found in the single and semi-double forms. There are many shades or half colours, which are anything but pleasing, and where such have established themselves, either as seedlings or otherwise, they should be weeded out, as there are numerous distinct hues, which may just as easily be cultivated. The great variety in colour and form of this Anemone is perhaps its most peculiar characteristic; for nearly 300 years it has had a place in English gardens, and came originally from the Levant. Its habit is neat; seldom does it reach a foot in height, the flowers being produced terminally; they are poppy-like, and 2in. to 3in. across, having six sepals. The leaves are ternate, segments numerous; each leaf springs from the tuber, with the exception of those of the involucre.

In planting this species, it should be kept in mind that it neither likes too much sunshine nor a light soil; under such conditions it may exist, but it will not thrive and scarcely ever flower. When the tuberous roots have become devoid of foliage they may be lifted, and if they have grown to a size exceeding 3in. long and 1in. in diameter, they may be broken in halves with advantage; the sooner they are put back into the ground the better; slight shade from the mid-day sun and good loam will be found to suit them best. When the various colours are kept separate, bold clumps of a score or so of each are very effective; mixed beds are gay, almost gaudy; but the grouping plan is so much better, that, during the blooming period, it is worth the trouble to mark the different colours, with a view to sorting them at the proper time.

Fig. 6. ANEMONE CORONARIA FLORE-PLENO.
(One-third natural size.)

The nutty roots are often eaten by earth vermin, especially wireworm. Whenever there is occasion to lift the roots it is a good plan to dress them, by repeated dips in a mixture of clay and soot, until they are well coated; they should be allowed to dry for a short time between each dip; this will not only be found useful in keeping off wireworm and similar pests, but will otherwise benefit the plants as a manure.

Flowering period, May and June.

## Anemone Decapetala.
*Nat. Ord.* RANUNCULACEÆ.

NEW, from North America; has a deteriorated resemblance to *A. alpina* and *A. sulphurea* (which see). The foliage is much less; the flower stems are numerous, close together, stout, and 9in. to 12in. high; they are also branched, but not spreading. The flowers have seven to ten sepals, are an inch across, and of a creamy white colour. The heads of seed are more interesting than their flowers; they form cotton-like globes, 1½in. diameter, and endure in that state for a fortnight. I was inclined to discard this species when I first saw its dumpy and badly-coloured flowers, but the specimen was left in the ground, and time, which has allowed the plant to become more naturally established, has also caused it to produce finer bloom, and it is now a pleasing and distinct species of an interesting character.

The same treatment will answer for this species as for *A. sulphurea*. All the Anemones may be propagated by seeds or division of the roots. The latter method should only be adopted in the case of strong roots, and their division will be more safely effected in early spring, when they can start into growth at once.

Flowering period, May to June.

## Anemone Fulgens.
SHINING WINDFLOWER; *Nat. Ord.* RANUNCULACEÆ.

THIS is a variety of *A. hortensis* or *A. pavonina*, all of which much resemble each other. This very showy flower is much and deservedly admired. In sheltered quarters or during mild seasons it will flower at Christmas and continue to bloom for several months. It will be seen by the illustration (Fig. 7) to be a plant of neat habit, and for effect and usefulness it is one of the very best flowers that can be introduced into the garden, especially the spring garden, as there is scarcely another of its colour, and certainly not one so floriferous and durable. Though it has been in English gardens over fifty years, it seems as if only recently its real worth has been discovered. It is now fast becoming a universal favourite. The flowers are 2in. across, and of a

FIG. 7. ANEMONE FULGENS.
(Plant, one-eighth natural size.)

most brilliant scarlet colour, produced singly on tall naked stems, nearly a foot high. They vary in number of sepals, some being semi-double. The foliage is bright and compact, more freely produced than that of most Windflowers; it is also richly cut.

It may be grown in pots for conservatory or indoor decoration. It needs no forcing for such purposes; a cold frame will prove sufficient to bring out the flowers in winter. Borders or the moist parts of rockwork are suitable for it; but perhaps it is seen to greatest advantage in irregular masses in the half shade of trees in front of a shrubbery, and, after all, it is impossible to plant this flower wrong, as regards effect. To grow it well, however, it must have a moist situation, and good loam to grow in. It is easily propagated by division of strong healthy roots in autumn.

Flowering period, January to June, according to position and time of planting.

### Anemone Japonica.

JAPAN WINDFLOWER; *Nat. Ord.* RANUNCULACEÆ.

THIS and its varieties are hardy perennials of the most reliable kinds; the typical form has flowers of a clear rose colour. *A. j. vitifolia* has larger flowers of a fine bluish tint, and seems to be the hybrid between the type and the most popular variety, viz., *A. j. alba*—Honorine Jobert—(see Fig. 8). So much has this grown in favour that it has nearly monopolised the name of the species, of which it is but a variety; hence the necessity of pointing out the distinctions. Frequently the beautiful white kind is sought for by the typical name only, so that if a plant were supplied accordingly there would be disappointment at seeing a somewhat coarse specimen, with small rosy flowers, instead of a bold and beautiful plant with a base of large vine-shaped foliage and strong stems, numerously furnished with large white flowers, quite 2in. across, and centered by a dense arrangement of lemon-coloured stamens, somewhat like a large single white rose. This more desirable white variety sometimes grows 3ft. high, and is eminently a plant for the border in front of shrubs, though it is very effective in any position. I grow it in the border, on rockwork, and in a half shady place, and it seems at home in all. It will continue in bloom until stopped by frosts. The flowers are among the most useful in a cut state, especially when mingled with the now fashionable and handsome leaves of heucheras and tiarellas; they form a chaste embellishment for the table or fruit dishes.

The plant is sometimes much eaten by caterpillars; for this the remedy is soapy water syringed on the under side of the leaves. Earwigs also attack the flowers; they should be trapped by a similar plan to that usually adopted for dahlias.

To those wishing to grow this choice Anemone, let me say, begin with the young underground runners; plant them in the autumn anywhere you like, but see that the soil is deep, and if

FIG. 8. ANEMONE JAPONICA ALBA (A. HONORINE JOBERT).
(About one-twelfth natural size.)

it is not rich, make it so with well-decayed leaves or manure, and you will have your reward.

Flowering period, August to November.

## Anemone Nemorosa Flore-pleno.

DOUBLE WOOD ANEMONE, or WINDFLOWER; *Nat. Ord.* RANUNCULACEÆ.

THIS is the double form of the common British species; in every part but the flower it resembles the type. The flower, from being double, and perhaps from being grown in more exposed situations than the common form in the shaded woods, is much more durable; an established clump has kept in good form for three weeks.

The petals (if they may be so called), which render this flower so pleasingly distinct, are arranged in an even tuft, being much shorter than the outer or normal sepals, the size and form of which remain true to the type. The pure white flower—more than an inch across—is somewhat distant from the handsome three-leaved involucrum, and is supported by a wiry flower stalk, 3in. to 5in. long; it is about the same length from the root, otherwise the plant is stemless. The flowers are produced singly, and have six to eight petal-like sepals; the leaves are ternately cut; leaflets or segments three-cut, lanceolate, and deeply toothed; petioles channelled; the roots are long and round, of about the thickness of a pen-holder. This plant grown in bold clumps is indispensable for the choice spring garden; its quiet beauty is much admired.

It enjoys a strongish loam, and a slightly shaded situation will conduce to its lengthened flowering, and also tend to luxuriance. Soon after the flowers fade the foliage begins to dry up; care should, therefore, be taken to have some other suitable flower growing near it, so as to avoid dead or blank spaces. Pentstemons, rooted cuttings of which are very handy at this season for transplanting, are well adapted for such use and situations, and as their flowers cannot endure hot sunshine without suffering more or less, such half-shady quarters will be just the places for them.

The double white Wood Anemone may be propagated by divisions of the tubers, after the foliage has completely withered.

Flowering period, May.

## Anemone Pulsatilla.

PASQUE FLOWER; *Nat. Ord.* RANUNCULACEÆ.

A BRITISH species. This beautiful flower has long been cultivated in our gardens, and is deservedly a great favourite. It may not be uninteresting to give the other common and ancient names of the Easter Flower, as in every way this is not only an old plant, but an old-fashioned flower. "Passe Flower" and "Flaw Flower" come from the above common names, being only derivations, but in Cambridgeshire, where it grows wild, it is called "Coventry Bells" and "Hill Tulip." Three hundred years ago Gerarde gave the following description of it, which, together with the illustration (Fig. 9), will, I trust, be found ample: "These Passe flowers hath many small leaues, finely cut or iagged, like those of carrots, among which rise up naked stalks, rough and hairie; whereupon do growe beautiful flowers bell fashion, of a bright delaied purple colour; in the bottome whereof groweth a tuft of yellow thrums, and in the middle of the thrums thrusteth foorth a small purple pointell; when the whole flower is past, there succeedeth an head or knoppe, compact of many graie hairie lockes, and in the solide parts of the knops lieth the seede flat and hoarie, euery seed having his own small haire hanging at it. The roote is thick and knobbie of a finger long, and like vnto those of the anemones (as it doth in all other parts verie notablie resemble) whereof no doubt this is a kinde."

This flower in olden times was used for making garlands, and even now there are few flowers more suitable for such purpose;

Fig. 9. Anemone Pulsatilla.
(One-half natural size.)

it varies much in colour, being also sometimes double. It may be grown in pots for window decoration or in the open garden; it likes a dry situation and well-drained soil of a calcareous nature. In these respects it differs widely from many of the other species of Windflower, yet I find it to do well in a collection bed where nearly twenty other species are grown, and where there are both shade and more moisture than in the open parts of the garden. It may be propagated by division of the strong root-limbs, each of which should have a portion of the smaller roots on them. Soon after flowering is a good time to divide it. Flowering period, March to May.

## Anemone Stellata.

STAR WINDFLOWER; *Nat. Ord.* RANUNCULACEÆ.

THIS gay spring flower (Fig. 10) comes to us from Italy, but that it loves our dull climate is beyond doubt, as it not only flowers early, but continues for a long time in beauty. *A. hortensis* is

FIG. 10. ANEMONE STELLATA.
(One-half natural size.)

another name for it, and there are several varieties of the species, which mostly vary only in the colours of the flowers, as striped, white and purple. The typical form, as illustrated, is seen to be a quaint little plant; its flowers are large, of a shining light purple colour, and star-shaped; the dwarf foliage is of the well-known crowfoot kind. When grown in bold clumps it is richly effective, and, like most other Anemones, is sure to be admired.

OLD-FASHIONED GARDEN FLOWERS. 21

It thrives well in a light loam and in slight shade; I have tried it in pots kept in cold frames, where it flowers in midwinter. It would doubtless make a showy appearance in a cool greenhouse. To propagate it, the roots should be divided after the tops have died down in summer.

Flowering period, February to June, according to position and time of planting.

## Anemone Sulphurea.

SULPHUR-COLOURED WINDFLOWER; *Syn.* A. APIIFOLIA; *Nat. Ord.* RANUNCULACEÆ.

THIS is a grandly beautiful Windflower from Central Europe. The names, combined with the illustration (Fig. 11), must fail to

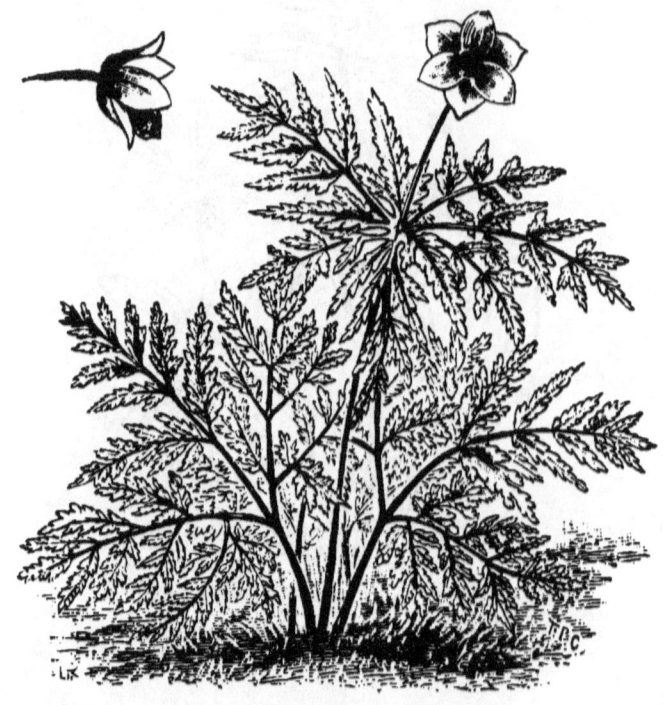

FIG. 11. ANEMONE SULPHUREA.
(One-fourth natural size.)

give the reader a proper idea of its beauty; the specific name in reference to the colour falls far short, and cannot give a hint of its handsome form and numerous finely-coloured stamens; and the drawing can in no way illustrate the hues and shell-like substance of the sepals; there is also a softness and graceful habit about the foliage, that the name, *apiifolia* (parsley-leaved), does not much help the reader to realise. It may be parsley-like foliage in the comparative sense and in relation to that of other Anemones, but otherwise it can hardly be said to be like parsley. It is said by some to be only a variety of *A. alpina*; if so, it is not only a distinct but an unvarying form, so much so that by others it is held to be a species; the line of difference in many respects seems so far removed, even granting it to be a variety (as in hundreds of similar cases), as to warrant a specific title. It may be more interesting to state that it is a lovely and showy flower, and that the shortest cut to an enjoyment of its beauties is to grow it.

The flowers are 2in. to 2½in. across when expanded, but usually they are cup-shaped. The six sepals are egg-shaped but pointed, of much substance, and covered with a silky down on the outside, causing them to have changeable hues according to the play of wind and light. The stamens are very numerous, the anthers being closely arranged and of a rich golden colour; the flower stems grow from 9in. to 18in. high, being terminated by one flower; it carries a large and handsome involucre of three leaves, a little higher than the middle of the stem, and just overtopping the radical leaves, umbrella fashion; the leaves of the involucre are like those of the root, but stalkless. The radical leaves are stalked, well thrown out, drooping, and over 1ft. long, ternate and villous; the leaflets are pinnatfiid and deeply toothed.

This desirable plant is of the easiest culture, thriving in common garden soil, but it prefers that of a rich vegetable character and a situation not over dry. The flowers are persistent under any conditions, and they are further preserved when grown under a little shade, but it should only be a little.

For propagation see *A. decapetala*.

Flowering period, May and June.

There are two other allied kinds which not only much resemble this, but which flower at or near the same time—viz., *A. alpina* and *A. decapetala*, which see.

## Anemone Sylvestris.

SNOWDROP A.; *Nat. Ord.* RANUNCULACEÆ.

THIS hardy herbaceous species comes from Germany, but it has been grown nearly 300 years in this country, It is distinct, showy, and beautiful; it ranks with "old-fashioned" flowers. Of late this Windflower has come into great favour, as if for a time it had been forgotten; still, it is hard to make out how such a fine border plant could be overlooked. However, it is well and deservedly esteemed at the present time; and, although many have proved the plant and flowers to be contrary to their expectations in reference to its common name, "Snowdrop Anemone," the disappointment has been, otherwise, an agreeable one. It only resembles the snowdrop as regards the purity and drooping habit of its flowers.

Well-grown specimens have an exceedingly neat habit—the foliage spreads and touches the ground, rounding up to the flower stems (which are about a foot high) in a pleasing manner. The earliest flowers are very large—when fully open quite 1½in. across—but they are more often seen in the unopen state, when they resemble a nutmeg in shape. Whether open or shut, they are a pure white, and their pendent habit adds not a little to their beauty, as also does the leafy involucre. The leaves are three-parted, the two lower lobes being deeply divided, so that at a first glance the leaves appear to be five-parted; each of the five lobes are three-cleft, and also dentate, downy, and veined; the leaf stalks are radical, red, long, slightly channelled, and wiry; in all respects the leaves of the involucre resemble those of the root, excepting the size, which is smaller, and the stalks are green, like the flower stems.

In a cut state, the pure satin-white blossoms are fit for the most delicate wreath or bouquet; they have, morever, a delicious clover-scent. It enjoys a light vegetable soil in a slightly shaded and moist situation; if it could be allowed to ramble in the small openings of a front shrubbery, such positions would answer admirably.

The roots are underground-creeping, which renders this species somewhat awkward to manage when grown with others in a collection of less rampant habit. On the other hand, the disposition it has to spread might very well be taken advantage of by providing it with a good broad space, than which nothing could be more lovely for two months of the year.

It is needless to give directions for its propagation, as the runners spring up all round the parent plant. Slugs are very fond of it, and in early spring, especially when the new growths are appearing, they should be kept in check, otherwise they will eat down into the heart of the strongest plant; a dose of clear lime water will be found effective and will not hurt the new leaves; if this is followed up with a few sprinklings of sand, the slugs will not care to occupy such unpleasant quarters.

Flowering period, May and June.

## Anemone Vernalis.

SHAGGY WINDFLOWER; *Nat. Ord.* RANUNCULACEÆ.

A CURIOUS but pretty alpine species, from the Swiss Alps, consequently very hardy. It is not a showy subject, but its distinctions are really beautiful, and commend it to those who love to grow plants of a *recherché* character.

The illustration (Fig. 12) will give some idea of it, but no description can convey even an approximate notion of its flowers, which are produced singly, on short, stout, hairy stems, about 5in. high. For so small a plant the flower is large, more than an inch across when expanded, but usually it keeps of a roundish, bell-shaped form. Its colour is a bluish-white inside, the outside being much darker. It would be violet, were not the hairs so long and numerous that they form a brownish coat which is, perhaps, the most remarkable trait of this species.

FIG. 12. ANEMONE VERNALIS (SHAGGY ANEMONE).
(One-half natural size).

The leaves, too, are very hairy—twice, and sometimes thrice, divided, rather small, and also few.

This little plant is most enjoyed when grown in pots. It may be plunged in sand or ashes in an open space, but it should never be allowed to suffer for moisture. When so grown, and just before the flowers open, it should be removed to a cool, airy frame, where it should also be plunged to keep its roots cool and moist; it will require to be very near the glass, so as to get perfect flowers. Such a method of growing this flower affords the best opportunity for its close examination; besides, it is so preserved in finer and more enduring form. It thrives well in lumpy peat and loam, but I have found charcoal, in very small lumps, to improve it, as it does most plants grown in pots, especially such as require frequent supplies of water. The slugs are very fond of it; a look-out for them should be kept when the plants are growing, and frequent sprinklings of sharp ashes will be found useful.

Flowering period, April and May.

## Anthericum Liliago.

### St. Bernard's Lily; *Nat. Ord.* Liliaceæ.

This may be grown as a companion to St. Bruno's Lily, though not so neat in habit or rich in bloom. In all respects it is very different. It is taller, the flowers not half the size, and more star-shaped, foliage more grassy, and the roots creeping and jointed.

All the Anthericums named by me will do in ordinary soil, but prefer a fat loam of considerable depth. If, therefore, such conditions do not exist, there should be a good dressing of well-rotted stable manure turned in, and a mulching given in early spring.

Anthericums are propagated by division of the roots, which should be carefully performed during the autumn. After such mutilation they should not be disturbed again for three years, or they will deteriorate in vigour and beauty.

Flowering period, June and July.

## Anthericum Liliastrum.

### St. Bruno's Lily; *Nat. Ord.* Liliaceæ.

This charming plant is a native of Alpine meadows, and is known by other names, as *Paradisia* and *Cyackia*, but is more commonly called St. Bruno's Lily. It is emphatically one of the most useful and handsome flowers that can be grown in English gardens, where, as yet, it is anything but as plentiful as it ought to be. Not only is it perfectly hardy in our climate, but it seems to thrive and flower abundantly. It is fast becoming a favourite, and it is probable that before long it will be very common, from the facts, firstly, of its own value and beauty, and, secondly, because the Dutch bulb-growers have taken it in hand. Not long ago they were said to be buying stock wherever they could find it. The illustration (Fig. 13) shows it in a small-sized clump. Three or four such specimens are very effective when grown near together; the satin-like or shining pure white flowers show to greater advantage when there is plenty of foliage. A number planted in strong single roots, but near together, forming a clump several feet in diameter, represent also a good style; but a single massive specimen, with at least fifty crowns, and nearly as many spikes of bloom just beginning to unfold, is one of the most lovely objects in my own garden.

The chaste flowers are 2in. long, six sepalled, lily-shaped, of a transparent whiteness, and sweetly perfumed; filaments white, and long as the sepals; anthers large, and thickly furnished with bright orange-yellow pollen; the stems are round, stout, 18in. high, and produce from six to twelve flowers, two or three of which are open at one and the same time. The leaves are long, thick, with membranous sheaths, alternate and stem-clasping, or semi-cylindrical; the upper parts are lanceolate, dilated,

FIG. 13. ANTHERICUM LILIASTRUM.
(Plant, one-sixth natural size; blossom, one-fourth natural size.)

subulate, and of a pale green colour. The roots are long, fleshy, brittle, and fasciculate.

This plant for three or four weeks is one of the most decorative; no matter whether in partial shade or full sunshine, it not only flowers well, but adorns its situation most richly; the flowers, in a cut state, are amongst the most useful and effective of hardy kinds—indeed, they vie with the tender exotics.

Flowering period, June and July.

*A. l. major* is a new variety in all its parts like the type, with the exception of size, the flowers being larger by nearly an inch. The variety is said to grow to the height of 8ft.

## Anthyllis Montana.
MOUNTAIN KIDNEY VETCH; *Nat. Ord.* LEGUMINOSÆ.

FOR rockwork this is one of the most lovely subjects. It is seldom seen, though easy to grow, perfectly hardy, and perennial. It is classed as an herbaceous plant, but it is shrubby, and on old specimens there is more wood than on many dwarf shrubs. It is of a procumbent habit, and only 4in. to 6in. high in this climate. It comes from the South of Europe, where it probably grows larger.

In early spring the woody tips begin to send out the hoary leaves; they are 3in. to 6in. long, and from their dense habit, and the way in which they intersect each other, they present a pleasing and distinct mass of woolly foliage.

The leaves are pinnatifid, leaflets numerous, oval, oblong, and very grey, nearly white, with long silky hairs.

The flowers are of a purple-pink colour, very small, and in close drumstick-like heads. The long and numerous hairs of the involucre and calyx almost cover over the flowers and render them inconspicuous; still, they are a pretty feature of the plant; the bloom stands well above the foliage on very downy, but otherwise naked stalks.

When planted in such a position that it can rest on the edge of or droop over a stone, strong specimens are very effective. It seems to enjoy soil of a vegetable character, with its roots near large stones. I have heard that it has been found difficult to grow, but that I cannot understand. I fear the fault has been in having badly-rooted plants to start with, as cuttings are very slow in making an ample set of roots for safe transplanting. Its increase by division is no easy matter, as the woody stems are all joined in one, and the roots are of a tap character. Seed seldom ripens; by cuttings appears to be the readier mode of propagation; if these are taken off in early spring, put in a shady position, and in leaf soil, they will probably root as the seasons get warmer.

Flowering period, June and July.

## Apios Tuberosa.
*Syn.* GLYCINE APIOS; *Nat. Ord.* LEGUMINOSÆ.

THIS is a pretty climber, or, more strictly speaking, a twiner; it is hardy, tuberous, and perennial  The tubers resemble potatoes, but incline to pear-shape, as implied by the generic name. 240 years ago it was introduced from North America; still, it is seldom met with, notwithstanding its good habit and colour. It is one of those happy subjects which most conduce to the freshness and wild beauty of our gardens; the dark and glossy verdure is charmingly disposed in embowerments by means of the delicate twining stems; and though it grows apace, there is never an unsightly dense or dark mass, so commonly seen in many climbers, but, instead, it elegantly adorns its station, and the outlines of its pretty pinnate leaves may easily be traced against the light.

FIG. 14. APIOS TUBEROSA.
(One-twelfth natural size; a, flower, natural size.)

As may be seen by the illustration (Fig. 14), it is in the way of a climbing bean. The flowers are purple and borne in small clusters from the axils of the leaves, and, of course, as indicated by the order to which it belongs, they are like pea flowers; they are produced a long time in succession, providing the frosts do not occur; they have the scent of violets. The leaves are distantly produced on fine wiry stems, which grow to the length of 12ft.; they are pinnate, the leaflets being of various sizes, oval, smooth, and of a dark shining green colour.

The roots are not only peculiar in the way already mentioned,

but the tubers have the appearance of being strung together by
their ends. They are edible, and where they grow wild they are
called "ground nuts." From the description given it will be easy
to decide how and where it should be planted.

There should be provision made for its twining habit, and it
may have the liberty of mixing its foliage with that of less
beautiful things during autumn, such, for instance, as the bare
*Jasmine nudiflora*; its spare but effective leaves and flowers will
do little or no harm to such trees, and after the frosts come the
jasmine will be clear again. It may also be grown with happy
results as shown in the illustration, needing only a well-secured
twiggy bush. Cut as sprays it is very serviceable for hanging or
twining purposes.

It most enjoys a light soil, also a sunny situation. Sometimes
it has been found slow at starting into growth when newly
planted; this, however, can hardly be the case with newly lifted
tubers. I may add that it is no uncommon thing for these to be
out of the ground for weeks and months together, when they not
only become hard and woody, but when suddenly brought in
contact with the damp earth rot overtakes them. There is no
difficulty whatever with fresh tubers, which may be lifted after
the tops have died off. Beyond securing fresh roots, there is
nothing special about the culture of this desirable climber.

Flowering period, August to October.

## Arabis Lucida.

SHINING ROCK CRESS; *Nat. Ord.* CRUCIFERÆ.

THIS member of a well-known family of early spring flowers
is desirable, for its neat habit and verdancy. There is not a
particle of sere foliage to be seen, and it has, moreover, a glossy
appearance, whence the specific name. The flowers are not of
much effect, though, from their earliness, not without value;
they are in the way of the flowers of the more common species,
*A. alpina*, but less in size; they are also more straggling in the
raceme; these two features render it inferior as a flower; the
stalks are 3in. to 6in. high. The leaves are arranged in lax
flattened rosettes, are 1in. to 3in. long, somewhat spathulate,
notched, fleshy, of a very dark green colour, and shining. The
habit is dense and spreading, established tufts having a fresh
effect. Though an Hungarian species, it can hardly have a more
happy home in its habitat than in our climate. Where verdant
dwarf subjects are in request, either for edgings, borders, or
rockwork, this is to be commended as one of the most reliable,
both for effect and vigour. In the last-named situation it proves
useful all the year round, but care should be taken that it does
not overgrow less rampant rock plants.

*A. l. variegata* is a variety with finely-marked leaves. The bloom resembles that of the type, but is rather weaker. It is better to remove the flowers of this kind, as then the rather slow habit of growth is much improved, as also is the colour of the foliage. The leaves being more serviceable and effective than the bloom, the uses should be made of it accordingly. They are broadly edged with yellow, the green being lighter than that of the type, but equally bright; the ends of the leaves are curled backwards, but, with the exception of being a little smaller, they are similar in shape to the parent form. This is a gem for rockwork, and, if it did not belong to a rather ordinary race of plants, it would, perhaps, be more often seen in choice collections. This, however, does not alter its worth. Seen in crevices of dark stone on rockwork, or in bold tufts near the walks, or planted with judgment near other dwarf foliaged subjects, it ever proves attractive. It is much less rampant, and, perhaps, less hardy than the type. It has only been during the recent very severe winters, however, that it has been killed. The Arabis is easily propagated by slips or rootlets, which should be taken after flowering. The variegated form is better for being so propagated every year. If bold patches are desired, they should be formed by planting a number together, 3in. or 4in. apart.

Flowering period, February to June.

## Aralia Sieboldi.

SIEBOLD'S ARALIA; *Nat. Ord.* ARALIACEÆ.

THE present subject (see Fig. 15)—beautiful, hardy, and evergreen—is a species of recent introduction; still, it has already become well known and distributed, so much so that it scarcely needs description; but there are facts in reference to it which would seem to be less known. It is seldom seen in the open garden, and many amateurs, who otherwise are well acquainted with it, when they see it fresh and glossy in the open garden in the earliest months of the year, ask, "Is it really hardy?" Not only is such the case, but the foliage, and especially the deep green colour, are rarely so fine when the specimens have indoor treatment, and, on this account, the shrub is eminently suitable for notice here.

The order *Araliaceæ* is nearly related to *Umbelliferæ*, from which fact an idea may be had of the kind and arrangement of the flowers. Many of the genera of the order *Araliaceæ* are little known; perhaps the genus *Hedera* (ivy) is the only one that is popular, and it so happens to immediately follow the genus *Aralia*. To remember this will further assist in gleaning an idea of the form of blossom, as that of ivy is well known. *Aralia Sieboldi*, however, seldom flowers in this climate, either in or out of doors. When it does, the white flowers are not of much value; they are small, like ivy blossom in form, but more spread in the arrangement. There are five sepals, five petals, five styles, and five cells in the berries. The flowers are produced on specimens 2ft. to 5ft. high during winter,

Fig. 15. Aralia Sieboldi.
(One-tenth natural size.)

when favourable. The leaves, when well grown, are the main feature of the shrub, and are 12in. or more across. This size is not usual, but a leaf now before me, and taken from an outside specimen, measures over a foot, with a stout round stalk, 13in.

long; the form of leaf is fan-shaped, having generally seven lobes, each supported by a strong mid-rib; the lobes are formed by divisions rather more than half the diameter of the leaf; they are slightly distant, broadly lance-shaped, waved at the edges, toothed near the ends, the teeth being somewhat spiny; the substance is very stout and leather-like to the touch; the upper surface is a dark shining bronzy-green, beautifully netted or veined; the under surface is a pale green, and richly ornamented by the risen mid-ribs and nerves of the whole leaf; the leaf-stalks are thick, round, bending downwards, and 6in. to 18in. long, springing from the half woody stem.

The habit of the shrub is bushy, somewhat spreading, causing the specimens to have a fine effect from their roundness, the leaf arrangement also being perfect. Without doubt this is one of the most distinct and charming evergreens for the ornamental garden, sub-tropical in appearance, and only inferior to palms as regards size; it is effective anywhere. It need not be stated that as a vase or table decoration it ranks with the best for effect and service, as it is already well-known as such. In planting this subject outside, young but well-rooted examples should be selected and gradually hardened off. At the latter end of May they should be turned out of the pots into a rich but sandy loam. The position should be sunny, and sheltered from the north. Some have advised that it should be grown under trees, but I have proved that when so treated the less ripened foliage has suffered with frost, whilst the specimens fully exposed to the sun have not suffered in the least; they would droop and shrivel as long as the frost remained, but as soon as the temperature rose they became normal, without a trace of injury. When planted as above, young specimens will soon become so established and inured to open-air conditions, that little concern need be felt as regards winter; even such as were under trees, where they continued to grow too long, and whose tender tops were cut away by frost, have, the following summer, made a number of fresh growths lower down the stems. I should like to say that on rockwork this shrub has a superb effect, and I imagine the better drained condition of such a structure is greatly in favour of its health and hardiness. The propagation is by means of cuttings; slips of half-ripened wood, taken during the warmest months, if put in sandy loam in a cucumber frame, will root like willow. As soon as roots have formed, pot them separately and plunge the pots in the same frame for a week or two, then harden off. For the first winter the young stock ought to be kept either in a greenhouse or a cold frame, and by the end of the following May they will be ready to plant out. A well-drained position is important.

Flowering period, November to March, in favourable or mild seasons.

## Arisæma Triphyllum.

*Syns.* A. ZEBRINUM *and* ARUM TRIPHYLLUM; *Common Names,*
THREE-LEAVED ARUM *and* JACK-IN-THE-PULPIT; *Nat.
Ord.* ARACEÆ.

A HARDY tuberous-rooted perennial from North America. I will at once explain that the above leading name is not the one generally used here, but in America, where the species is common, botanists have adopted it; besides, it is, as will be seen from the following description, very distinct from other Arums. The Syn. *Arisæma zebrinum*, as given, belongs really to a variety of *A. triphyllum*, but the type is marked in its flowers zebra-like, and there are many shades and colours of it, therefore both or either of the names may be used for the different forms, with a fair degree of propriety, as in fact they are.

There is a doubt with some as to the hardiness of this plant; in my mind there is none whatever. It is no stranger to frosts in its habitats, but I do not found my conviction on anything but my experience of it. It has been grown fully exposed for two winters, and sometimes the frosts must have gone as far down as the roots.

There is nothing showy about this plant, but there is something which stamps it as a fitting subject for a garden of choice plants; its bold, dark green foliage and quaint-looking flowers render it desirable on the score of distinctness. It has, moreover, a freshness upon which the eye can always linger. The flowers are in general form like the calla-lily; the upper part of the spathe, or sheathing leaf, which is really the calyx, is, however, more elongated, pointed, and hooked; otherwise the spathe is erect, slightly reflexed just above the folded part, giving the appearance of a pair of small lobes; this—the calyx—is really the most conspicuous part of the flower; in the belly it is beautifully striped with broad lines of a purplish-brown colour, which shade off to an inch of green in the middle, when they form again, and continue to the tip of the spathe, which will be 4in. to 6in. long, and nearly 2in. broad at the widest part; these lines run between the ribs, and, as before hinted, they are of various colours, such as brown, purple, pink, and green. The ribs are nearly white, and the green parts are very pale. The spadix is over 3in. long, club-shaped, spotted with brown, very much so near the end. The anthers at the base of the spadix are curious, and should be examined. They are invisible until the folded part of the spathe is opened; they are numerous, arranged in a dense broad ring, sessile, and nearly black. This curious flower is produced on a stout, round scape, a foot or more in height. The leaves are radical, having a stalk a foot long. They are, as the specific name implies, divided into three parts, each being of equal length, entire, wavy, and pointed.

D

The whole plant has a somewhat top-heavy appearance (see Fig. 16), but I never saw it broken down by the weather. It makes quick growth in spring, the scape appearing with the leaves; in late summer it dies down. It looks well in quiet nooks, but it also forms a good companion to showy flowers in more open situations; in a cut state, for dressing "old-fashioned" vases, nothing could be in better character, a few leaves of yarrow, day lily, flag, or similar foliage being all it will require.

FIG. 16. ARISÆMA TRIPHYLLUM.
(One-fourth natural size.)

It may be transplanted, any time from September to the end of January, into good light loam or leaf soil, 4in. or 6in. deep; if there should be a dry season during the period of growth, the plant should be well watered. To increase it, the tubers may be divided every third year, providing the growth has been of a vigorous tone. I may add, that, from its tall and not over-dense habit, there may with advantage, both to it and the plants used, be a carpet grown underneath—ivy, vincas, or sweet woodruff for some situations, and brighter subjects for more conspicuous parts of the garden, such as the finer kinds of mimulus, ourisia, alpine aster, and dwarf iris.

Flowering period, June and July.

## Arum Crinitum.

HAIRY ARUM, *or* DRAGON'S MOUTH; *Nat. Ord.* ARACEÆ.

As may be seen by the illustration (Fig. 17), this is a most singular plant. It proves hardy in this climate if its position is selected; in other words, it is not hardy in all kinds of soils and situations, but if planted four or five inches deep, in sandy or half decayed vegetable mould, facing the south, there is little to fear either as regards hardiness or its thriving. I think, therefore, it may be called hardy. It is far more interesting than handsome, but there is at the present time an evident desire amongst amateurs to grow the various Arums, and more especially has this one been sought after; I have, therefore, introduced it amongst more beautiful flowers, and given an enlarged drawing of the entire plant, together with the spathe in its unopened state.

The plant is a native of Minorca, and was imported in 1777. In this climate it grows to the height of 18in., developing the flower with the foliage. It is produced on a stout scape nearly 1ft. high, of a pale green colour, marked with dark short lines and spotted with delicate pink dots. The folded spathe is of leather-like substance, rough, almost corky in texture; also variously marked and tinted. At the base there are a number of green lines arranged evenly and longitudinally on a nearly white ground. A little higher—the belly part—the lines are less frequent, irregular, and mixed with pink dots. Still higher, the ground colour becomes pale green, the lines dark green, and the pink spots are changed to clouded tints; the remainder of the folded spathe—to the tip—is a mixture of brown and green dots, the total length being fully 9in. When the spathe opens, it does so quickly, bending more than half its length outwards, the division looking upwards. To those who have not before seen the plant at this stage, it will prove an interesting surprise; the odour, however, is repulsive. The spathe at its widest part is 6in. broad, and tapers off to a blunt point. It is of a dark purple colour and covered with long bent dark hairs, whence the specific name. They are curiously disposed, and remind one of some hairy animal that has been lifted out of the water the wrong way as regards the direction of the hair. The spadix is comparatively small, black, and also covered with hairs. The flower should be closely watched if its peculiarities are to be fully noted, as it not only opens quickly but soon begins to wither. During the short period that the flower in open the lower part of the spathe or belly becomes filled wits all kinds of flies, being held by the spear-like hairs.

The leaves have long stalks, marked and tinted in a similar manner to that of the scape. They are curiously formed and twisted, pedate or bird-foot shaped, the outer segments twice

D 2

FIG. 17. ARUM CRINITUM.
(One-fourth natural size.)

cut, lance-shaped, and turned inwards or over the main part of the leaf; the leaves are of a deep green colour, and of good substance; they seldom exceed four in number to each plant or tuber.

This curious species should, as above indicated, have a warm situation, where it will also be comparatively dry in winter. Its propagation may be effected by division of the roots of strong specimens.

Flowering period, June and July.

## Asters.

MICHAELMAS DAISIES, or STARWORTS ; *Nat. Ord.* COMPOSITÆ.

HARDY, perennial, and herbaceous. These are a numerous family, and many of them have an ungainly habit and insignificant flowers—in fact, are not worth growing, save as wild flowers in unfrequented places. I will mention a few of the finer sorts, which are mostly species : *A. diversifolius*, *A. ericoides*, *A. grandiflorus*, *A. pendulus*, and *A. Dumosus*, these are all good, both in habit and flowers ; *ericoides* and *pendulus* make really handsome bushes, but the very beautiful *A. amellus*, and its more dwarf variety (*A. Mdme. Soyance*), have tempted me to write of these old-fashioned plants, which may be said to be wholly distinct, as their flowers are so very much brighter (dark purple, with a clear yellow centre), and the rays so much more evenly and compactly furnished. Their stems are 2ft. to 3ft. high, and flowered half their length with clusters of bloom about the size and form of full-grown field daisies. These wand-like spikes in a cut state are bright and appropriate decorations. In vases they are very effective, even when used alone. The flowers are very lasting, either cut or otherwise; the plants will bloom six or eight weeks.

These subjects will thrive in almost any kind of soil or position, opening their flowers during the dullest weather, and though they like sunshine, they will not wait for it. It is scarcely needful to further describe these well-known flowers, but, as well as the species, there are some bright and beautiful varieties which merit further notice All the Starworts are easily increased by root division any time.

Flowering period, August to November.

## Aster Alpinus.

ALPINE STARWORT, or BLUE DAISY; *Nat. Ord.* COMPOSITÆ.

AN exceedingly beautiful and very much admired alpine plant, which does not die down like most of the Starworts, but has woody stems; it is seldom seen more than a foot high, and its large bright purple flowers seem disproportionate. This is one of the plants which should have a place in every garden, and more especially in rock gardens. There cannot well be a more neat and telling subject; the form and size of its flowers are not often seen on such dwarf plants, and it also has the merit of being a "tidy" subject when not in bloom. The illustration (Fig. 18) will give a fair idea of its main features. Its purple flowers, which are fully 2in. across, have for many days an even and well-expanded ray, when the florets curl or reflex;

FIG 18 ASTER ALPINUS.
(One-third natural size.)

the disk is large, and numerously set with lemon-yellow florets; the flowers are well lifted up on stout round stems, covered with short stiff hairs, and furnished with five or six small leaves; the main foliage is of compact growth, lance-shaped, entire, spathulate and covered with short hairs.

Considering that this plant has been in English gardens for 220 years, and that its merits must be seen by anyone at a glance, it is hard to say why it is not better known; even in choice and large collections it always proves attractive when in flower. The blooms in a cut state are very durable; they not only hold together, but also keep a good colour. Under cultivation it is in no way particular; it will endure anything but being deprived of light; from its dwarf, stout, and shrubby character, it would form a useful and a handsome edging to the larger walks; and by growing it so extensively an enviable supply of flowers for cutting would be at hand.

A stock of young plants may soon be got up by division of strong roots after the flowering season; such pieces as have roots may be planted at once in their permanent quarters; the rootless parts should be dibbled into light sandy loam and shaded with branches for a week or two.

Flowering period, June and July.

*A. a. albus* is a white-flowered variety, blooming about the same time. There does not appear to be that vigour about it which characterises the type; this, however, is not the only shortcoming; when compared with the rich purple flower, the white one, with its large yellow disk, appears, to say the least, a questionable improvement.

## Aster Ptarmicoides.

BOUQUET STARWORT; *Nat. Ord.* COMPOSITÆ.

THIS Starwort is a very recently-imported species from North America. Like many other things which have proved worthless as decorative flowers, this was highly praised, but for a while its weedy-looking foliage caused suspicion; after becoming well established, it flowered, and, I am glad to say, proves a most distinct and useful Starwort. Its small white flowers much resemble the field daisy, but they are borne on densely-branched stems in hundreds; in fact, the plant, which grows nearly 2ft. high, seems to be nearly all flowers. Each one has a single ray of shining white florets, narrow and separate. Those of the disk are of a canary-yellow colour; the imbricated calyx is pear-shaped; pedicels slender, bent, wiry, and furnished with very small leaves; main stems hispid, woody, and brittle. The leaves of the root are 2in. to 4in. long, smooth, entire, linear, almost grass-like; those of the stems much less, becoming smaller as they near the flowers; they are somewhat rough, partaking of the quality of the stems. The habit of the plant is much branched, the spreading clusters of flowers being six or ten times the size of the plant, so that it becomes top-heavy; it blooms for many weeks, and is not damaged by coarse weather. Amongst other Asters it shows to advantage, flowering earlier than most of them, but lasting well into their period of bloom. It is sure to prove a useful white autumnal flower; small sprays when cut look better than on the plant, as they are then seen to be well spread and rigidly held by means of their wiry stalks;

they have the scent of Southernwood. It grows well with me in ordinary garden loam, the situation being well exposed to the sun. It may be readily propagated by root division. Flowering period, August to October.

## Bellis Perennis.
COMMON PERENNIAL DAISY; *Nat. Ord.* COMPOSITÆ.

THIS native plant, the commonest flower of the field and wayside, and the weed of our grass-plots, is the parent form of the handsome and popular double kinds seen in almost every garden. Well known as these flowers are, it may prove interesting to learn a little more about the fine large double crimson and white kinds—their treatment, for instance—in order to have abundance of flowers during the earliest months of the year; and the uses to which they may be most advantageously put; for, common as are the Daisies, they are, without doubt, amongst the most useful flowers we possess. First, I will briefly give the names and descriptions of the more distinct varieties.

*B. p. aucubifolia* is the Double Daisy, having a beautifully variegated foliage, mottled with golden-yellow in the way of the aucuba.

*B. p. fistulosa.*—This is the double crimson or pink Daisy, having its florets piped or quilled (see Fig. 19).

*B. p. hortensis* embraces all the double forms raised and cultivated in gardens, no matter what colour, and so distinguished from the typical form of the fields.

*B. p. prolifera* is that curious and favourite kind called "Hen and Chickens." The flowers are double, and from the imbricate calyx of the normal flower there issue a number of smaller Daisies having straggling florets; the whole on one main stalk presenting a bouquet-like effect.

These kinds, the specific names of which are not only descriptive, but amply embrace the group, are much added to by flowers having other names and minor distinctions, the latter, for the most part, being only shades or mixtures of colour—as crimson, pink, white, and bicolours. The florets in many kinds are exceedingly pretty, from the way in which they are tipped and shaded; notably, a new variety that was sent me under the name of Dresden China. These sorts having different tints are usefully named with "florists'" names—as Pearl, Snowball, Rob Roy, Sweep, Bride, &c. I may say that I have long grown the Daisy largely, Bride and Sweep being the favourite kinds; both are robust growers, very hardy and early. Bride is the purest white, with florets full, shining, and well reflexed; rather larger than a florin, and when fully developed has a half globular appearance; another good point is its flower stalks being 4in.

to 5in. long, which renders it serviceable as cut bloom. Sweep is not quite so large, though a good-sized Daisy, it also opens more flat; its colour, however, is first rate, it is the darkest crimson Daisy I ever saw, is of a quilled form and very full.

Fig. 19. Bellis Perennis Fistulosa.
(One-third natural size.)

Its chief point is its constant colour; if the florets are examined, they are the same deep crimson underneath as on the face of the flower; this, together with its long stalks, renders it useful, too, in a cut state.

To grow this useful flower well and render it doubly valuable by having it in bloom in mid-winter, requires three things: First, timely transplanting; secondly, rich soil; thirdly, partial shade; these conditions will be more briefly and, perhaps, clearly explained, if I state my method. At the end of May or fore part of June, plenty of good rotten stable manure is wheeled into the bush-fruit quarters; it is worked in with a fork, so as to do as little damage as possible to the bush roots. A line is drawn, and the old Daisy roots which have just been taken up are trimmed by shortening both tops and roots. They are severely divided, and the pieces planted 6in. apart in rows 8in. asunder. In such a cool, moist situation they soon form good tufts, and I need scarcely say that the dressing of manure has also a marked effect on the fruit crop. A planting so made is not only a cheerful carpet of greenery during winter, but is well dotted over with bloom. The plants being well established in rich soil, and having the shelter of the bushes during summer and winter, are the conditions which have conduced to such early flowers. This is the method I have adopted for years, and both Daisies and fruit have been invariably good crops. I ought, however, to say that beds more exposed, together with the fact that the Daisy roots have to be transplanted in October or November, never flower so early, from which it will be seen that the treatment explained hardly applies to such bedding; but where a breadth of bloom is required, say, for cutting purposes, I know no better plan. As cut bloom the daisy is charming in glass trays on a bed of moss, or even in small bouquets, mixed with the foliage of pinks, carnations, and rosemary. Such an arrangement has at least the merit of sweet simplicity, and somehow has also the effect of carrying our thoughts with a bound to spring-time.

The ancient names for this "old-fashioned" flower were "Little Daisies" and "Bruisewoorte." The latter name, according to Gerarde, was applied for the following reasons: "The leaues stamped, taketh away bruses and swellings proceeding of some stroke, if they be stamped and laide thereon, whereupon it was called in olde time Bruise-woorte. The iuice put into the eies cleereth them, and taketh away the watering;" and here is a dog note: "The same given to little dogs with milke, keepeth them from growing great."

Flowering period, February to July.

## Bocconia Cordata.
*Syn.* MACLEAYA CORDATA; *Nat. Ord.* PAPAVERACEÆ.

A HARDY herbaceous perennial from China. It is a tall and handsome plant; its fine features are its stately habit, finely-cut foliage, and noble panicles of buds and flowers; during the whole progress of its growth it is a pleasing object, but in the autumn, when at the height of 7ft. it has become topped with lax clusters of flowers, over 2ft. long, it is simply grand. There are other names in trade lists, as *B. japonica* and *B. alba*, but they are identical with *B. cordata*; possibly there may be a little difference in the shades of the flowers, but nothing to warrant another name. Having grown the so-called species or varieties, I have hitherto found no difference whatever; and of the hardy species of this genus, I believe *B. cordata* is the only one at present grown in English gardens. During spring and early summer this subject makes rapid growth, pushing forth its thick leafy stems, which are attractive, not only by reason of their somewhat unusual form, but also because of their tender and unseasonable appearance, especially during spring; it is rare, however, that the late frosts do any damage to its foliage. It continues to grow with remarkable vigour until, at the height of 5ft. or more, the flower panicles begin to develop; these usually add 2ft. or more to its tallness.

The flowers are very small but numerous, of an ivory-white colour; they are more beautiful in the unopened state, when the

OLD-FASHIONED GARDEN FLOWERS. 43

two-sepalled calyx for many days compresses the tassel-like cluster of stamens. Each half of the calyx is boat-shaped, and before they burst they have the form and colour of clean plump groats; as already hinted, the stamens are numerous, and the anthers large for so small a flower, being spathulate. As

FIG. 20. BOCCONIA CORDATA.
(About one-twentieth natural size; blossom, one-half natural size.)

soon as the stamens become exposed, the calyx falls, and in a short time—a few hours—the fugacious anthers disappear, to be followed only a little later by the fall of the filaments; there is then left a naked but headed capsule, half the size of the buds, and of the same colour; they may be traced on the panicle in the illustration (Fig. 20). From the fading quality of the above-named parts, the buds and capsules chiefly form the ornamental portion of the compound racemes.

The leaves are from 8in. to 10in. in diameter, the largest being at the base of the tall stems; their outline, as the specific name implies, is heart-shaped, but they are deeply lobed and dentate, in the way of the fig leaf, but more profusely so; they are stalked, of good substance, glaucous, nearly white underneath, which part is also furnished with short stiff hairs. The glaucous hue or farina which covers the leaf-stalks and main stems has a metallic appearance, and is one of its pleasing features as a decorative plant. For many weeks the flowers continue to be developed, and from the deciduous quality of the fading parts, the panicles have a neat appearance to the last. In a cut state the long side branches of flowers, more than a foot long, are very effective, either alone or when mixed with other kinds, the little clusters of white drop-like buds being suitable for combination with the choicest flowers.

As a decorative specimen for the more ornamental parts of the garden, and where bold subjects are desired, there are few herbaceous things that can be named as more suitable; from the day it appears above the ground, to and throughout its fading days in the autumn, when it has pleasing tints, it is not only a handsome but distinct form of plant; as an isolated specimen on the lawn, or by frequented walks, it may be grown with marked effect; if too nearly surrounded with other tall things, its beauty is somewhat marred; but wherever it is planted it should have a good fat loam of considerable depth. I ought not to omit saying that it forms a capital subject for pot culture; plants so treated, when 12in. or 18in. high, no matter if not then in flower, are very useful as window or table plants; but of course, being herbaceous, they are serviceable only during their growing season; they need not, however, be a source of care during winter, for they may with safety be plunged outside in a bed of ashes or sand, where they will take care of themselves during the severest weather.

It may be propagated by cuttings taken from the axils of the larger leaves during early summer; if this method is followed, the cuttings should be pushed on, so that there are plenty of roots before the winter sets in. I have found it by far the better plan to take young suckers from established plants; in good rich soil these are freely produced from the slightly running roots; they may be separated and transplanted any time, but if it is done during summer they will flower the following season. Tall as this subject grows, it needs no supports; neither have I noticed it to be troubled by any of the garden pests.

Flowering period, September to August.

## Bulbocodium Trigynum.

*Syns.* COLCHICUM CAUCASICUM *and* MERENDERA CAUCASICUM; *Nat. Ord.* MELANTHACEÆ.

THIS pretty miniature bulbous plant is very hardy, flowering in winter. It is a scarce flower, and has recently been represented as a new plant. As a matter of fact, it is not new, but has been known under the above synonymous names since 1823, when it was brought from the Caucasus. In general appearance it is very different from the *Colchicum* (Sprengle), as may be seen by the drawing (Fig. 21), and *Merendera* (Bieberstein) is only another Spanish name for *Colchicum*. The new name, authorised by Adams, may have been the cause, all or in part, of its

FIG. 21. BULBOCODIUM TRIGYNUM.
(Full size.)

being taken for a new species. The specific name may be presumed to be in reference to either its deeply-channelled, almost keeled leaves, which have the appearance of three corners, or in allusion to the triangular way in which they are disposed. It is a desirable flower for several reasons—its earliness, durability, rich perfume, and intrinsic beauty.

The little plant, at the height of 2in., produces its rather large flowers in ones and twos in February, and they last for many days in perfect form. The scent reminds one of the sweet honey smell of a white clover field during summer. The colour is very pale lilac, nearly white; the tube takes on a little greenness; it is also divided, though the slits are invisible until the bloom begins to fade. The corolla, of irregular segments, is 1½in. across when expanded; the stamens are half the length of the petal-like segments, and carry anthers of exquisite beauty, especially when young, then they are orange colour, divided like a pair of half-opened shells, and edged with chocolate; the styles are a delicate pale green, and rather longer than the stamens. The leaves, as already stated, are channelled, broadest at the base, tapering to a point, which is rather twisted; they are 2in. long during the blooming period, of a deep green colour, stiff, but spreading, forming a pretty accurate triangle. This description, together with the cut, will suggest both the uses and positions in which it should be planted; if a single blossom, when brought indoors, proves strongly fragrant, it is easy to imagine what a clump must be in the garden. Like those of the colchicum, its flowers are quickly developed; the leaves grow longer afterwards, and die off in summer.

It thrives in a sandy loam or leaf soil, in a sunny part, and increases itself at the roots like the saffrons.

Flowering period, February and March.

## Bulbocodium Vernum.

SPRING BULBOCODIUM, or SPRING SAFFRON; *Nat. Ord.*
MELANTHACEÆ.

IN mild winters, sheltered positions, and light vegetable soil, this bulbous plant may be seen in blossom from January to March. The flowers appear before the leaves, and may, at the first glance, be taken for lilac-coloured croci. Up to a certain stage, however, the colour gradually improves in the direction of purple, and where there are established patches it is no inconsiderable part of the effect caused by this desirable winter flower to see it a mass of bloom in many shades, ranging from white (as in the bud state) to a lively purple. It is an old plant in English gardens, and is largely found wild in mid-Europe. It came from Spain as early as 1629. Still, it is not generally known or grown; but within the last few years it has come to the fore, with a host of other hardy and early-flowering subjects. The natural order in which it is classed includes many beautiful genera, both as regards their floral effect and anatomical structures. *Veratrum, Uvularia,* and *Colchicum* are, perhaps, the more familiar, and the last-mentioned genus is a very nearly allied one. A feature of the genus *Bulbocodium* is implied by the name itself, which means "a wool-covered bulb." This quality, however, will be more observable when the bulb is in a dormant state; it exists under the envelope. The crocus or saffron-like flowers are aptly named "Spring Saffron," though there is a great botanical difference to be seen between this genus and that of *Colchicum* when the flower is dissected. The bloom is produced from the midst of an ample sheath and overlapping leaves, which are only just visible in the early season of this year; the corolla of six petal-like divisions is 2in. to 3in. across when expanded, and of various shades and colours, as already stated; the segments are completely divided, being continued from the throat of the corolla to the ovary by long tapering bases, called nails, claws, or ungues. The leaves are stout, broadly strap-shaped, channelled, and of a deep green colour. The bulb is rather small; its form resembles that of the autumn crocus, as also does its mode of growth and reproduction.

The early blossoms of this bulb soon disappear, and though the roots are all the better for being well ripened, a thin patch of some of the finer annuals sown in spring amongst their withering leaves will not do much harm, and will prove useful as gap-stoppers. Another good way is to grow these dwarf bulbous flowers with a carpet of creepers, of which there are scores in every way suitable; and where nothing else is available or to be grown with success, the small-leaved ivy will answer well. The dwarf phloxes, however, are more useful; their browned spreading branches form a neutral but warm-looking ground to the purple blossoms; besides, by the time all trace of the Bulbocodium has shrivelled up, they begin to produce their sheets of bloom. All such prostrate forms not only preserve dwarf winter flowers from the mud, but otherwise give effect to the borders. This bulb thrives best in light soil, well drained; in sheltered nooks it may be had in flower a month earlier than in exposed parts. Under such conditions it increases very fast, and the bulbs may be transplanted with advantage every other year after the tops have died off. In stiff or clay-like soil it dwindles and dies.

Flowering period, January to March.

## Calthus Palustris Flore-pleno.

DOUBLE MARSH MARIGOLD; *Old Common Name*, "MEADOW BOOTES"; *Nat. Ord.* RANUNCULACEÆ.

THE typical, or single-flowering variety of this plant is a British species, and a rather common one; but the pleasing habit and bright, finely-formed, orange-yellow flower of this double kind renders it a suitable plant for any garden. It is herbaceous and perennial, and loves boggy situations. It is, however, very accommodating, and will be found to do well in ordinary garden soil, especially if it be a stiffish loam; clayey land is well adapted for it. No matter what kind of weather prevails, it has always a neat and fresh appearance. By the illustration (Fig. 22) the reader will doubtless recognise its familiar form. As already stated, its flowers are orange-yellow, very full, with petals evenly arranged; they are 1in. across, and produced on round, short, hollow stems, seldom more than 9in. high. The forked flower stalks are furnished with embracing leaves, differing very much from the others, which are stalked, heart-shaped, nearly round, and evenly-toothed. All the foliage is of a rich dark shining green colour. Strong specimens produce flowers for a long time, fully two months, and frequently they burst into blossom again in the autumn. Individual flowers are very lasting, and, moreover, are very effective in a cut state. It is a robust grower, providing it is not in light dry soil; it seems with me to do equally well fully exposed to sunshine and in partial shade, but both positions are of a moist character.

It has long fleshy roots, which allows of its being transplanted at any time, early spring being the best, to increase it. The crowns should be divided every three years, when there will be found to be ample roots to each one.

Flowering period, April to June.

FIG. 22. CALTHUS PALUSTRIS FLORE-PLENO.
(One-half natural size.)

## Calystegia Pubescens Flore-pleno.
*Nat. Ord.* CONVOLVULACEÆ.

THIS double Convolvulus is a somewhat recent introduction from China; it is hardy and perennial. So distinct are its large flesh-coloured flowers that they are often taken at the first glance, when cut, for double pyrethrums or chrysanthemums, but, seen in connection with the plant, the form of foliage and climbing or twining habit of the bindweed soon enable the most casual observer of flowers to recognise its genus.

The flowers are 2in. to 3in. across, petals long, narrow, wavy, and reflexed; these are well held together by the five-parted calyx, further supported by a bract of two small but stout leaves. The flower stalks are round and wiry, 3in. or 4in. long; they are produced all along the twining stems, which are only of the moderate length of 5ft. or 6ft. The leaves are of the well-known Convolvulus form.

I find it a good plan to grow this subject amongst tall and early flowering plants, such as lupins, foxgloves, and lilies, the old stems of which form ample supports for the climber; moreover, they are rendered less unsightly from being thus furnished anew with leaf and flower, even though not their own. Another method is in early summer to place a short twiggy branch over the pushing growths; it will soon become covered, and if not too large, the ends of the shoots will slightly outgrow the twigs and hang down in a pleasing manner. The plant should be started in light sandy loam and have a warm situation, otherwise flowers will be scarce and the whole specimen have a weedy appearance. When once it becomes established, it will be found to spread rapidly by means of its running roots, which, unless checked, will soon become a pest. I simply pull out all growths except such as shoot up in the desired position, and so continue to treat them as weeds throughout the growing season. Stems furnished with flowers a yard or more long, in a cut state, make rich festoons; single blooms (the smaller ones) look well as "button-holes," being neat and effective, without gaudiness. I ought to state that a succession of flowers is kept up for fully three months; this fact adds not a little to the value of this handsome flesh-coloured bloomer. Roots may be transplanted at any time; the smallest piece will produce a blooming plant the first season, if put into a proper soil and situation.

Flowering period, July to September.

## Campanula Grandis.

GREAT BELLFLOWER; *Nat. Ord.* CAMPANULACEÆ.

A HARDY herbaceous perennial from Siberia, growing to a height of 3ft. Its flowers are large, bright, and numerous; well-established clumps will present masses of bloom for more than a month with average weather. As a large showy subject there are few plants more reliable, or that can in any way excel it, more especially for town gardens. It is a rampant grower, quickly covering large spaces by means of its progressive roots; in gardens or collections where it can only be allowed a limited space, the running habit of the roots will doubtless prove troublesome, and often such free growers, however handsome they may be otherwise, are esteemed common, which should not be. The proper thing to do would be to give these vigorous and fine flowering subjects such quarters as will allow them their natural and unrestrained development.

The flowers of *C. grandis* are more than 1in. across the corolla, the five segments being large and bluntly pointed, of a transparent purple-blue colour, and very enduring; they are arranged on short stalks, which issue from the strong upright stems. They form little tufts of bloom at every joint for a length of nearly 2ft.; the succession, too, is well kept up. Buds continue to form long after the earliest have opened. The leaves are 4in.

E

to 8in. long and ¾in. wide, lance-shaped, stalkless, and finely toothed. They are arranged in round tufts on the unproductive crowns, and they remain green throughout the winter.

As regards soil, any kind will do; neither is the question of position of any moment beyond the precaution which should be taken against its encroachments on smaller subjects. In the partial shade of shrubs it not only flowers well but proves very effective. Useful as this plant is in the garden, it becomes far more so in a cut state. When it is needful to make up a bold vase or basket of flowers for room decoration, it can be quickly and effectively done by a liberal use of its long, leafy, but well-bloomed spikes; five or six of them, 2ft. to 3ft. long, based with a few large roses, pæonies, or sprays of thalictrum, make a noble ornament for the table, hall, or sideboard, and it is not one of the least useful flowers for trays or dishes when cut short. Propagated by division at any time, the parts may be planted at once in their blooming quarters.

Flowering period, June and July.

## Campanula Latifolia.

BROAD-LEAVED BELLFLOWER; *Nat. Ord.* CAMPANULACEÆ.

A BRITISH species, very much resembling *C. grandis*, but somewhat taller, and flowering a little earlier; the latter quality has induced me to mention it, as it offers a fine spike for cutting purposes before the above is ready.

Culture, uses, and propagation, the same as for *C. grandis*.

Flowering period, June and July.

## Campanula Persicifolia.

PEACH-LEAVED BELLFLOWER; *Old Common Names*, "PEACH-BELS" *and* "STEEPLE-BELS"; *Nat. Ord.* CAMPANULACEÆ.

THIS good "old-fashioned" perennial has had a place in English gardens for several hundred years; it is still justly and highly esteemed. It is a well-known plant, and as the specific name is descriptive of the leaves, I will only add a few words of Gerarde's respecting the flowers: "Alongst the stalke growe many flowers like bels, sometime white, and for the most part, of a faire blewe colour; but the bels are nothing so deepe as they of the other kindes, and these also are more delated and spred abroade then any of the reste." The varieties include single blue (type) and white, double blue, and different forms of double white.

In all cases the corolla is cup or broad bell shaped, and the flowers are sparingly produced on slightly foliaged stems, 18in. to 3ft. high; there are, however, such marked distinctions belonging to *C. p. alba* fl.-pl. in two forms that they deserve special notice; they are very desirable flowers, on the score of both quaintness and beauty. I will first notice the kind with two corollas, the inner bell of which will be more than an inch deep, and about the same in diameter. The outer corolla is much shorter, crumpled, rolled back, and somewhat marked with green, as if intermediate in its nature between the larger corolla and the calyx. The whole flower has a droll but pleasing form, and I have heard it not inaptly called "Grandmother's Frilled Cap." The other kind has five or more corollas, which are neatly arranged, each growing less as they approach the centre. In all, the segments are but slightly divided, though neatly formed; this flower is of the purest white and very beautiful, resembling a small double rose. It is one of the best flowers to be found at its season in the borders, and for cutting purposes I know none to surpass it; it is clean and durable. So much are the flowers esteemed, that the plant is often grown in pots for forcing and conservatory decoration, to which treatment it takes kindly.

In the open all the above varieties grow freely in any kind of garden soil, but if transplanted in the autumn into newly-dug quarters they will in every way prove more satisfactory; this is not necessary, but if cultivation means anything, it means we should adopt the best-known methods of treatment towards all the plants we grow, and certainly some of the above Bellflowers are deserving of all the care that flowers are worth.

Flowering period, July to September.

## Campanula Pyramidalis.
PYRAMIDAL or CHIMNEY CAMPANULA; *Nat. Ord.*
CAMPANULACEÆ.

THIS herbaceous perennial is a very old flower in this country; it came from Carniola in the year 1594. It is very hardy, and for several months together it continues to produce its large lively blue flowers, beginning in July and lasting until stopped by frosts. At no time is it in finer form than in September; at the height of from 5ft. to 7ft. it proves richly effective amongst the blooming hollyhocks, where, as regards colour, it supplies the "missing link" (see Fig. 23).

The flowers are a light bright blue colour, and 1in. to 1½in. across. The corolla is bell-shaped, the five divisions being deeply cut, which allows the flower to expand well; the calyx is neat and smooth, the segments long and awl-shaped; the flower stalks are short, causing the numerous erect branches to be closely furnished with bloom during favourable weather. The leaves of the root are very large and stalked, of irregular shape, but for the most part broadly oval or lance-shaped. The edges are slightly toothed, having minute glands; those of the stems are much smaller, sessile, and long egg-shaped; all the foliage is smooth, and of a dark green colour; the main stems are very stout, and sometimes grow to the height of 7ft. Vigorous plants will send up several of these, from which a great number of small ones issue, all assuming an erect habit; blooming specimens are hardly anything else than a wand-like set of flowered stems, and though it is advisable to stake them, I have seen them bend and wave during high winds without damage.

In the borders and shrubbery this is a very effective subject; it is amongst herbaceous plants what the Lombardy poplar is

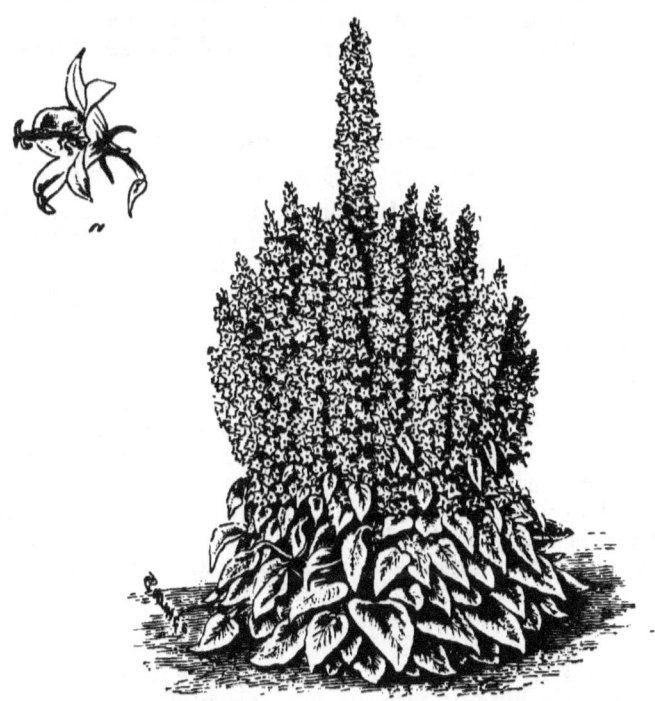

FIG. 23. CAMPANULA PYRAMIDALIS.
(One-twentieth natural size; a, one-half natural size.)

amongst forest trees—tall, elegant, and distinct. Its use, however, is somewhat limited, owing to the stiffness of the stems and the shortness of the flower stalks; but when grown in pots—as it often is—for indoor decoration, it proves useful for standing amongst orange and camellia trees. It has very strong tap roots, and enjoys a deep rich loam. Not only does it look well among trees, but otherwise the partial shade of such quarters seems conducive to finer bloom.

Flowering period, July to October.

*C. p. alba* is a white flowering variety of the above species; its other points of distinction are its smaller-sized leaves and much paler green colour, by which alone the plants may be easily recognised from the type. This variety may be grown with good effect in pots or the border; it scarcely gets so tall as the blue form, but looks well by the side of it.

The readiest way to increase these plants is to take the young and dwarf growths from the woody crown of the roots, paring off a little of the bark with each. If these are put in sandy loam during the warm growing season and kept shaded for a few days, they will very soon make plenty of roots; this method in no way damages the flowers. Another way is by seed, but seedlings are two years before they bloom.

## Campanula Speciosa.

SHOWY HAREBELL; *Nat. Ord.* CAMPANULACEÆ.

A COMPARATIVELY new species, brought from Siberia in 1825, and sometimes called *C. glomerata dahurica*. It is a good hardy plant, perennial and herbaceous, and one of the earliest to flower. It has a distinct appearance; it nearly resembles *C. aggregata*, but the latter does not flower until several weeks later. Apart from its likeness to other species of the genus, it is a first-class border flower, having large bells of a fine deep purple colour, and, unlike many of the Harebells, is not over tall, but usually about a foot high, having a neat habit. The flowers are arranged in dense heads, whorl fashion, having very short stalks; they are nearly 2in. long and bell shaped. The leaves (radical) are oval heart-shaped and stalked; those of the stems are sessile; the whole plant is hairy and robust. This is one of the flowers which can hardly be planted out of place in any garden, excepting amongst the rare and very dwarf alpines; it is not only true to its name, "showy," but handsome. It will grow and flower well in the worst soil and needs no sort of care; it would be fine in lines by a shrubbery, and is effective in bold clumps; and though a new kind, it belongs to a race of "old-fashioned" flowers, amongst which it would mix appropriately. Increased by division in autumn.

Flowering period, June and July.

## Campanula Waldsteiniana.

*Nat. Ord.* CAMPANULACEÆ.

A RARE and distinct alpine species from Carinthia. It proves perfectly hardy in this climate. For the rock garden it is a gem of the first water, its habit being dwarf, dense, and rigid; floriferous as many of the Bellflowers are, I know none to excel this one. As may be observed in the following description, there are

not a few distinctive traits about it, which, more or less, go to
make it a desirable subject for rare and choice collections.

The flowers are a glistening bluish-lilac, erect, and ¾in. across
when fully expanded. The corolla can hardly be said to be bell-
shaped, as the five divisions are two-thirds of its depth, which
allows it, when full blown, to become nearly flat, and as the
segments are equal, sharply cut, and pointed, the flower has a
star-like appearance. The little calyx is cup-shaped, angular,
and has small, stout, horn-like segments, which are bent downwards. Each flower has a pedicel about 1in. long, which
springs from the axils of the main stem leaves; the stems
seldom exceed the height of 4in. or 5in., and they are exceedingly fine, thready, as also are the pedicels; they are, moreover, of zig-zag form, from node to node. The leaves are ¾in.
long, and less than ½in. wide, ovate or nearly cordate, partially
folded, and sometimes reflexed at the ends, nearly stalkless,
slightly toothed, smooth, of good substance and a peculiar grey-
green colour. The foliage for two or three weeks is completely
hidden by the large number of flowers, during which time it is
a most attractive subject.

I grow it with other dwarf Campanulas in a collection bed,
where it compares well with the finest, such as *C. pulla*, *C.
muralis*, and *C. Zoysii*, for effectiveness. Having proved it to
thrive well in light sandy soil of a vegetable character, I have
not tried it otherwise; it enjoys a sunny situation. The site
should be well drained; it will endure nothing like stagnant
moisture—its peculiar roots would indicate this fact, they are
not only tender and fleshy, but thick and of a pith-like nature,
and, as I have never been able to gather any seed, and the propagation has to be carried out by root division, there requires to
be a careful manipulation of these parts, for not only do they
split and break with the least strain, but when so mutilated they
are very liable to rot. I have found it by far the better plan to
divide this plant after it has begun to grow in March or April,
when its fine shining black shoots, which resemble horse hairs
in appearance, are about ½in. high. Slugs are fond of this plant;
a dressing once a week of sand and soot, when it begins to grow,
will keep them off.

Flowering period, July and August.

## Centaurea Montana.

MOUNTAIN KNAPWEED; *Nat. Ord.* COMPOSITÆ.

THIS is an "old-fashioned" and favourite flower. Every one
must be familiar with its thistle-like formed flowers; it is sometimes called the large or perennial Cornflower and also the
Large Bluebottle. The blue variety has been grown in English
gardens since 1596. There are now white and pink coloured

varieties, all rampant growers, very hardy and perennial. They are in every way superior to the annual kind, which is so largely grown, the flowers being more than twice the size, and produced two months earlier; the blooming period is maintained until late autumn.

The flowers, as before hinted, are thistle-shaped; the pericline or knob just under the florets is cone-shaped, covered with evenly set and pointed scales, green, edged with a brown margin, set round with short bristle-like teeth. The florets of the outer ring are 1½in. long, tubular half their length, the wider portion being five to seven cut; the centre florets are short and irregular, richly tinted with pink at their bases; the whole flower or ray, when expanded, is 3in. across. They are produced on stems over 2ft. long and of a somewhat procumbent habit, angular and branched near the tops; the leaves are 3in. to 6in. long, lance-shaped, entire and decurrent, giving the stems a winged appearance. They are of a greyish colour—nappy—whence the name Knapweed.

This vigorous species, with its white and pink varieties, may be grown in any kind of soil. It requires plenty of room; a two-year-old plant will form a specimen a yard in diameter under favourable conditions. The effect is good when all the three colours are grown near each other in bold pieces. They yield an unfailing supply of flowers, which are of a very useful type; in fact, the more they are cut the more they seem to bloom, and it is a good plan to cut short half the stems about June. They will (in a week or two) produce new shoots and large flowers in abundance, the gain being flowers of extra size during autumn.

Propagated by division of the roots any time.

Flowering period, June to September.

## Centranthus Ruber.
*Syn.* VALERIANA RUBER—RED VALERIAN; *Nat. Ord.*
VALERIANACEÆ.

THIS is a strong and vigorous garden plant, with a somewhat shrubby appearance; it is herbaceous, perennial, and sometimes classed as a British species, therefore hardy; but though its classification among British plants is justifiable, it is only so on the ground of its being a naturalised subject, its original habitats being in the South of Europe. It is a favourite and "old-fashioned" flower, and it fully justifies the estimation in which it is held, the flowers being produced in large bunches of a fine rich colour, which are very durable. Its shrubby habit is not one of its least recommendations; seen at a distance—which it easily can be—it might be taken for a ruby-coloured rhododendron, to which, of course, it has no resemblance when closely inspected. It grows 2ft. high or more.

The flowers are a bright ruby colour, very small, but closely massed in great numbers, borne in corymbs, terminal and much branched; "the calyx-limb, at first revolute, afterwards expanded into a feather-like pappus;" the corolla is tubular, long, slender, and spurred; the segments or petals are small and uneven, both in form and arrangement; the germen is long; anther prominent and large for so small a flower, viz., ¾in. long and hardly ⅓in. in diameter. The stems are stout, round, hollow, and glaucous; they are furnished with leaves of various shapes at the nodes, as lance-shaped, long oval, heart-shaped and plain, elliptical and pointed, wavy and notched, and arrow-shaped, lobed, and toothed. The root leaves are mostly ovate, lanceolate, and entire. The whole plant is smooth and glaucous. From the description given, it may readily be seen that when in flower it will be effective—massive heads of ruby flowers topping a shrub-like plant of shining foliage and glaucous hue. It is eminently fitted for lines or borders where other strong growers are admitted. In a cut state the flowers are very useful; they are strongly scented, something like the lilac, with just a suspicion of Valerian in it. I ought not to omit mention of its extra brightness as seen by gaslight—this fact adds much to its value for indoor decoration.

It may be grown in any kind of garden soil, needing nothing at any time in the way of special treatment; but if it is supplied with a little manure it will pay back with interest, in the form of extra-sized bunches and brighter flowers.

*C. r. albus* is a white-flowering kind of the above; its main points of difference are its paler green foliage, smaller sized corymbs, shorter growth, and rather later season of bloom.

*C. r. coccinea* is another kind; the specific name is misleading. It is not scarlet, but nearer a rose colour, and when compared with the typical colour it appears much inferior; still, it is a good variety. All the three colours, when grown side by side, are very showy when in bloom.

This species, with its varieties, may be easily propagated by root divisions at any time from late summer to spring; the long fleshy roots should not be broken more than can be helped; every piece with a crown on it will make a flowering plant the first season.

Flowering period, June to September.

## Cheiranthus Cheiri.

COMMON WALLFLOWER; *Nat. Ord.* CRUCIFERÆ.

THIS well-known evergreen shrub (see Fig. 24) is more or less hardy in our climate, according to the conditions under which it is grown. Although a native of the South of Europe, it rarely happens, however severe the winter may be in this country, that we are totally deprived of the favourite bouquet of Wallflowers in winter or early spring, while it is equally true that, during the hard weather of one or two recent winters, in numerous gardens every plant was killed. In favourable seasons its blooms are produced throughout winter, but the full blow comes in April. Three hundred years ago it was known by its present name; in this respect it is a rare exception, as most flowers have many and widely different names, especially the "old-fashioned" sorts, so that often the varied nomenclature hinders the identification of the species. At one time the Wallflower was called the "Gillyflower," but the name is now only applied to a biennial and single-flowered variety of the stock—a near relation of the Wallflower. More than 200 years ago Parkinson wrote, "Those Wallflowers that, carrying beautiful flowers, are the delights and ornaments of a garden of pleasure."

Of its well-known beauties, as regards its form, colour, varieties, and delicious perfume, description is needless, though I may say, in passing, that its fragrance renders it of value to those whose olfactory nerve is dead to the scent of most other flowers.

Two errors are frequently committed in planting the Wallflower; first, at the wrong time, when it is nearly a full-grown specimen and showing its flowers; next, in the wrong way, as in rows or dotted about. It should be transplanted from the seed beds when small, in summer or early autumn, and not in ones and twos, but in bold and irregular groups of scores together; anything like lines or designs seems out of harmony with this semi-wildling. There is another and very easy method which I should like to mention, as a suggestion—that of naturalisation; let those near ruins, quarries, and railway embankments and cuttings, generously scatter some seed thereon during the spring showers, when the air is still; in such dry situations this flower proves more hardy than in many gardens. Moreover, they serve to show it to advantage, either alone or in

Fig. 24. CHIERANTHUS CHEIRI. (One-fourth natural size.)

connection with other shrubs, as the whin, which flowers at the same time; here, too, it would be comparatively safe from being "grubbed up."
Flowering period, January to June.

## Cheiranthus Marshallii.
MARSHALL'S WALLFLOWER; *Nat. Ord.* CRUCIFERÆ.

A DISTINCT and very hardy hybrid, being shrubby and tree-like in shape, but withal very dwarf. From the compact habit, abundance and long duration of its flowers, it is well suited for showy borders or lines. It is not yet well known, but its qualities are such that there can be no wonder at its quickly coming to the front where known.

It differs from the common Wallflower in being more dwarf and horizontally branched, while the leaves are more bent back, hairy, and toothed; immediately below the floriferous part of the stem the leaves are more crowded, the stems more angular, the flowers much less, not so straggling, and of a dark orange colour. Other hybrids in the same way are being produced, differing mostly in the colour of the flowers, as lemon, greenish-yellow, copper, and so on.

Plants a year old are so easily raised from cuttings, and form such neat specimens, that a stock cannot be otherwise than very useful in any garden; besides, they lift so well that transplanting may be done at any time. My finest specimens have been grown from their cutting state, on a bed of sifted ashes liberally mixed with well-rotted stable manure; in such light material they have not only done well, but, when a few roots were required, they lifted large balls without leaving any fibre in the ground. To have good stout stock before winter sets in, slips should be taken from the old plants as soon as they have done flowering; dibble them into light but well enriched soil, and give water in droughty weather only.

I ought to mention that this dwarf Wallflower, and also its allied kinds, are capital subjects for very dry situations; on old walls and the tops of outhouses they not only do well, but prove decorative throughout the year. In such places plants will live to a great age, and sow their own seed freely besides.

Flowering period, May and June.

## Chionodóxa Luciliæ.
SNOW GLORY; *Nat. Ord.* LILIACEÆ.

A HARDY bulbous perennial, from Asia Minor. It has only been cultivated about four years in English gardens; still it has been proved to be as hardy as the squills, which it very much resembles. Mr. Maw, who discovered and introduced it, found it "near the summit of the mountain," which (though it is a native of a much warmer climate than ours) may account for its hardy character. That it is a most beautiful flower is beyond doubt, but there are those who think it has been overpraised. It should not, however, be forgotten that Mr. Maw's description of it was from a sight of it in masses, a state in which it can hardly have been judged yet in this country, as until very recently the bulbs were very expensive. It has, however, taken kindly to our climate, and is likely to increase fast, when it may be seen to greater advantage.

It grows to the height of 6in. or 8in.; the flower scapes, which are rather slender, are somewhat shorter than the foliage, the flowers being longer in the petals than the squills, almost star-shaped, and nearly 1in. across; later on they reflex. Their colour is an intense blue, shading to white in the centre of the flower. The flowers are produced in numbers, from three to six on a stem, having slender pedicels, which cause the flowers to hang slightly bell fashion. The leaves, from their flaccidness and narrowness, compared with the squills, may be described as grassy. The bulbs are a little larger than the kernel of a cob nut, nearly round, having satiny skins or coats.

It may be grown in pots, and forces well if allowed first to make good roots, by being treated like the hyacinth. It should be kept very near the glass. It has also flowered fairly well in the open border fully exposed, but in a cold frame, plunged in sand and near the glass, it has been perfection. Single bulbs so grown in "sixties" pots have done the best by far.

All the bulbs hitherto experimented with have been newly imported; very different results may possibly be realised from "home-grown" bulbs. It is also probable that there may be varieties of this species, as not only have I noticed a great difference in the bulbs, but also in the flowers and the habit of plant. This I have mentioned to a keen observer, and he is of the same opinion; be that as it may, we have in this new plant a lovely companion to the later snowdrops, and though it much resembles the squills, it is not only sufficiently distinct from them, but an early bloomer, which we gladly welcome to our gardens. It seems to do well in equal parts of peat, loam, and sand, also in leaf soil and sand.

Flowering period, March and April.

## Chrysanthemum.
### *Nat. Ord.* COMPOSITÆ.

THE flowers to which I would now refer the reader are of no particular species, but, like several other genera, this genus has been considerably drawn upon or utilised by the hybridiser, and the species, looked upon from a florist's point of view, have been much improved upon by their offspring. Not only are Japan and China the homes of the finer flowering species, but in these countries the Chrysanthemum has been esteemed and highly cultivated for centuries; in fact, such a favourite is this flower with the Chinese, that they have treated it with many forms of their well-known art in matters horticultural, and when the flower was brought to this country it would doubtless be in a form improved by them. It reached this country nearly 100 years ago, and was known by the names *C. indicum* and *C. sinense*; about the same time a species from the East Indies was called *C. indicum*. This flower, from the time of its introduction, has been justly appreciated; and by the skill of several cultivators we have a largely increased number of forms and colours. Still, there are certain distinctions kept up amongst the varieties, and they are commonly known by such names as "large-flowering," "pompon, or small-flowered," "early flowering," "anemone-flowered," and "Japanese." These names, besides being somewhat descriptive, are otherwise useful to the amateur who may wish to grow a representative collection, and where there is convenience it is desirable to do so in order to observe their widely different forms and colours, as well as to enjoy a long succession of bloom.

So well is the Chrysanthemum known that little could be usefully said of it by way of description; but well as it is known and easy as its culture is, there are few things in our gardens that show to greater disadvantage. This should not be with a subject which offers such range of habit, colour, and period of blooming; and when such is the case, there must be some radical mistake made. The mistake I believe to be in the selection, and that alone. If so, the remedy is an easy matter. Let me ask the reader to remember three facts: (1) Many sorts grown in pots and flowered under glass are unfitted for the borders or open garden. (2) The later flowering varieties are of no use whatever for outside bloom. (3) Of the early blooming section, not only may the finest varieties be grown with marked effect, but they, as a rule, are of more dwarf habit, and will afford abundance of bloom for cutting purposes for nearly two months. Selections are too often made from seeing the fine sorts in pots; let it be understood that all are perfectly hardy, but owing to their lateness, their utility can only be realised under artificial conditions. I am not now considering pot, but garden kinds, and no matter what other rules may be observed, if this is overlooked it will be found that though the plant may grow finely and set buds in plenty, they will be so late as to perish in their greenness by the early frosts; on the other hand, of the early section, some will begin to bloom in August, and others later, each kind, after being covered with flowers for several weeks, seeming to finish naturally with our season of flowers.

There is nothing special about the culture of this very hardy and rampant-growing plant, but I may add that, though it will stand for many years in one place, and flower well too, it is vastly improved by division of the roots in autumn or early spring every second year. The earth of its new site should be deeply dug and well enriched with stable manure; it will not then matter much what sort of soil it is—the more open the situation the better. How grandly these decorate the borders when in masses! and as a cut flower I need hardly say that there are few to excel the Chrysanthemum, either as an individual bloom or for bouquet and other work.

I do not frequently make mention of many florists' flowers by name, but in this case I think I may usefully name a few varieties: Andromeda, cream coloured, Sept.; Captain Nemo, rosy purple, Aug.; Cassy, pink and white, Oct.; Cromatella, orange and brown, Sept.; Delphine Caboche, reddish mauve, Aug.; Golden Button, small canary yellow, Aug.; Illustration, soft pink to white, Aug.; Jardin des Plantes, white, Sept.; La Petite Marie, white, good, Aug.; Madame Pecoul, large, light rose, Aug.; Mexico, white, Oct.; Nanum, large, creamy blush, Aug.; Précocité, large, orange, Sept.; Sœur Melaine, French white, Oct.; St. Mary, very beautiful, white, Sept. These, it will be seen, are likely to afford a variety and succession of bloom.

Flowering period, August to November.

## Cichorium Intybus.

*Syns.* C. PERENNE *and* C. SYLVESTRE—WILD SUCCORY or CHICORY; *Nat. Ord.* COMPOSITÆ.

THIS herbaceous perennial is a native plant, in many parts being very common. Not only, however, do many not know it as a wild flower, but we have the facts that under cultivation it is a distinct and showy plant, and that of late it has come into great request. Its flowers are a pleasing blue, and produced on ample branches, and for mixing with other "old-fashioned" kinds, either in the borders or as cut blooms, they are decidedly telling; for blending with other Composites it has its value mainly from the fact that blues are rare in September; the China asters are too short in the stalk for cutting purposes, and many of the tall perennial starworts are neither bright nor well disposed. I may also mention another proof of its decorative quality—it is not common (*i.e.*, wild) in my district, and a plant being cultivated in my garden for its flowers has been so much admired that it is likely to have other patrons, and in many instances it is being introduced into gardens where the choicest flowers are cultivated. I am bound, however, to say that when not in flower it has the appearance of the commonest weed.

Its flowers are produced when 2ft. to 6ft. high. They are of a fine glistening blue colour, 1in. to 1½in. across, and in the way of a dandelion flower, but stalkless individually, being disposed in ones, twos, and threes, somewhat distantly in the axils of the leaves, and all over the numerous and straggling branches. The leaves are rough, of a dingy green colour, and variously shaped, Gerarde's description being as follows: "Wilde Succori hath long leaues, somewhat snipt about the edges like the leaues of sow thistle, with a stalke growing to the height of two cubits, which is deuided towarde the top into many braunches. The flowers grow at the top blewe of colour; the roote is tough and woodie, with many strings fastened thereto."

I find this plant not only enjoys a half shady place, but if it is so placed that its quick growing branches can mix with those of other subjects in a trellis or other supports, its coarser parts will not only be partially hidden, but the rich coloured flowers will show to advantage. I may mention that mine is mixed with Virginian creeper on wires, and the effect may easily be imagined. It will do in any kind of garden soil, but if deeply dug and well manured the flowers are vastly improved. Propagated by seed or division of the stout tap roots.

Flowering period, August to September.

## Clethra Alnifolia.

ALDER-LEAVED CLETHRA; *Nat. Ord.* ERICACEÆ.

A HARDY deciduous shrub, and mentioned in connection with herbaceous perennials because of its rich flowers and dwarf habit. It is a native of North America, having been grown in this country for 150 years; it is not so often met with as it ought to be, though much esteemed. It becomes very productive of flowers when only 2ft. high, but grows somewhat taller when well established; it is more valuable than common from its floriferousness during late summer to the end of the season.

Let me at once state that its winning point is the delicious scent of its pure white flowers; it is very powerful, and like that of the lilac and alder combined; the racemes are 2in. or 3in. long, and compactly formed of short-stalked flowers less than ½in. across; they are of good substance, and in form resemble the lilac flower minus the tube; the flower stems are somewhat woody, and foliaged to the base of the spike or raceme. The leaves are of varying sizes, oval, lance-shaped, and short-stalked, distinctly veined and slightly wrinkled, sharp but finely toothed, of a dark shining green colour on the upper and a greyish-green on the under side. The whole shrub is somewhat rough to the touch; the habit is bushy and branching, increasing in size from suckers; the numerous twiggy side shoots of the previous year's growth produce the flowers.

It enjoys a light soil and sunny situation, and it may be planted anywhere in the shrubbery or borders as a first-class flowering subject. Its scent loads the air for some distance around, and pleasantly reminds one of spring flowers. Such sweet-smelling flowers are not too plentiful in September, and I know not a better one than this amongst hardy flowers for the late season. Its odour is fine and full; a single sprig now by me proves almost too much for the confinement of a room. This quality is invaluable in small flowers that can be freely cut, which, moreover, as in this case, are otherwise suitable for bouquet work. Propagated by cuttings and division of the suckers, taken when growth has ceased; if put in sandy loam and a warm situation, they will become rooted during the following spring.

Flowering period, August and September.

## Colchicum Autumnale.

MEADOW SAFFRON; *Common Name*, AUTUMNAL CROCUS; *Nat. Ord.* MELANTHACEÆ.

A NATIVE bulbous perennial (see Fig. 25). The Colchicums are often confounded with the autumn-flowering species of croci, which they much resemble when in bloom; the similarity is the more marked by the absence, from both, of their leaves in that season, otherwise the leaves would prove to be the clearest mark of difference. Botanically they are far removed from each other, being of different orders, but there is no need to go into such distinctions, not, at any rate, in this case.

The flowers are well known and they need not be described further than by saying they are in form crocus-like, but much longer in the tubes and of a bright mauve-purple colour. The bulbs have no resemblance to the crocus whatever, being often four times the size of the crocus corms. Moreover, they are pear-shaped and covered with flaky wrappers of a chestnut brown colour; if examined, these coverings will be found, near the neck of the bulb, to be very numerous

FIG. 25. COLCHICUM AUTUMNALE (about one-sixth natural size).

and slack fitting, extending above the ground, where they have the form of decayed or blackened foliage; a singular fact in connection with the roots is, they are not emitted from the base of the bulb, but from the side of the thickened or ovate part, and are short and tufty. In early spring the leaves, which are somewhat like the daffodil, but much broader and sheathed, are quickly grown; at the same time the fruit appears. In summer the foliage suddenly turns brown, and in the autumn nothing is seen but blackened foliage, which is very persistent, and which, a little later, acts as sheaths for the long-tubed flowers. Unless the weather be very unfavourable, these flowers last a long time —fully two weeks. The double variety, which is somewhat scarce, is even more lasting, and I may add, it is a form and colour so softly and richly shaded that it is nothing short of exquisite; but the single variety, now more especially under notice, is also capable of agreeably surprising its friends when used in certain ways, for instance, as follows: A tray of the bright green and nearly transparent selaginella, so common in all greenhouses, should form the ground for twos or threes of these simple but elegant Saffron flowers; no other should be placed near—their simplicity forms their charm. It will be seen that the robust but soft-coloured flower of the meadows harmonises finely with the more delicately grown moss. In other ways this fine autumnal flower may be used with pleasing effect in a cut state, and it blends well with the more choice exotics. This is more than can be said of many hardy flowers, and it is fortunate that during dull weather, when we are driven from our gardens, there are still some flowers which may be hastily gathered and so arranged indoors as to give us all the pleasure which only such flowers can yield at such a season.

I find this subject to do well in any situation, but I think the blooms are a richer colour if grown under partial shade. The bulbs should not be disturbed if abundance of flowers are wanted; but if it is found desirable to propagate them, the bulbs may be lifted every two or three years, when the tops have withered, and when there will probably be found a goodly crop of young tubers.

Flowering period, September and October.

## Colchicum Variegatum.
*Nat. Ord.* MELANTHACEÆ.

THIS comes from Greece, nevertheless it is perfectly hardy; it is not only peculiarly pretty when closely examined, but a truly handsome flower, either as cut bloom or seen in groups in a growing state. Compared with *C. autumnale*, it is shorter in the tube, or more dwarf; still, it is a larger flower, and its rosy purple petals, or divisions of the corolla, are more spear-shaped, and each from 2in. to 3in. long; they have a stout and almost white mid-rib, the other parts of the segments being distinctly and beautifully chequered with white and rosy purple; the tube is stout, and of transparent whiteness; the foliage less than that of the British species, and more wavy. The habit of the flowers is erect, and during sunshine they become flatly expanded, when they will be 4in. to 5in. across, being 3in. to 4in. high. It is a very durable flower, lasting at least a fortnight, and many are produced from one bulb, appearing in succession, so that the blooming period is well extended; it braves the worst weather with little or no damage. Unlike the longer-tubed varieties, it is never seen in a broken state, and it is this which mainly renders it superior. Either as a cut flower, or a decorative subject for the borders or rockwork, it is a first-rate plant, being neat and showy.

It enjoys a sandy loam in a moist but warm situation; at the base of a small rockwork having a southern aspect it flourishes to perfection; it can hardly be planted wrongly provided there is no stagnant moisture. Propagated like *C. autumnale*, than which it is of slower increase.

Flowering period, September and October.

## Coreopsis Auriculata.

EAR-LEAVED COREOPSIS;
*Nat. Ord.* COMPOSITÆ.

THE oldest species of the genus grown in English gardens; its flowers are yellow, but dotted at the base of the ray florets. The leaves, as implied by the name, are dissimilar to other species, being lobed and having ear-like appendages; but this feature is far from constant, and otherwise the leaves differ, being sub-sessile and oval-lance-shaped (see Fig. 26). It came from North America as long ago as 1699. Slugs are very fond of these plants, and in winter more especially, when the

FIG. 26. COREOPSIS AURICULATA.
(One-fourth natural size.)

F

dormant eyes are not only in a green, but exposed state; they should be watched after, or during one mild night the whole may be grazed off, to the great injury of the plant.

Its habit, uses, culture, and propagation are the same as for *C. tenuifolia*.

## Coreopsis Grandiflora.
LARGE-FLOWERED COREOPSIS; *Nat. Ord.* COMPOSITÆ.

IN many parts this resembles *C. lanceolata*, its main distinction being implied by its name. The flowers are larger and the ray florets more deeply cut; it is also bolder in the foliage, and the stems grow nearly as strong as willows. It is an abundant bloomer, and a good specimen is a' glorious object during the autumn. It comes from North America, but my experience of it is that it is not so hardy as *C. lanceolata* and *C. auriculata*.

Habit, uses, culture, and propagation, as for *C. lanceolata*.

## Coreopsis Lanceolata.
SPEAR-LEAVED COREOPSIS; *Nat. Ord.* COMPOSITÆ.

THIS form of bright yellow flower is in great favour during August, but that is not all. The various kinds of this genus are plants of the easiest culture, and their rich flowers are produced in great quantities from midsummer to the time the frosts begin. This species has been said to be only of a biennial character; it is, however, understood generally to be perennial, though not quite so hardy as others which come from the colder climates of America. It was imported from Carolina in 1724, and in this country proves hardy in selected situations, where its roots are comparatively dry in winter, and I may add that it proves a true perennial.

When the plant has attained the height of a foot it begins to flower; each bloom has a long pedicel, nearly naked, also round and smooth. The flowers are a shining yellow colour, and nearly 3in. across; the florets of the ray are flatly arranged, shield-shaped, pleated, and four-toothed, the teeth being sometimes jagged; the disk is small for so large a flower; the florets brown and yellow. The double involucrum, common to the genus, has its upper set of bracteoles rolled outward; they are of a brownish colour; the lower set are green and wheel-shaped during the period of a perfect ray, and they alternate with the upper ones. The leaves, as may be inferred from the specific name, are lance-shaped, 2in. to 6in. long, smooth and entire; they are attenuated to the stems, which they more or less clasp. The habit of the plant is much branched, but only slightly at base; it becomes top-heavy from the numerous shoots near the top, which cause it to be procumbent; otherwise this subject would rank with tall growers. It is one of the most useful flowers, both in the garden and when cut, the long stalks in both cases adding much to its effectiveness; its form and brightness are sure to commend it, no matter whether it happens to be a fashionable flower or otherwise. It is at once a bold and delicate form, and one that harmonises with any other kinds and colours.

It should be grown in deeply-dug and well-enriched earth, and, as already hinted, the drier the situation the more safely will it winter. Not only that, but on raised beds or banks sloping to the full sunshine it will also flower to perfection. All its family, so far as I have proved them, hate excessive moisture. Its propagation may be by division, as in this damp climate it does not seem to ripen seed, but I have found sometimes not a little difficulty in dividing the woody roots, as frequently there is only one stem below the surface with roots. When there are more the difficulty is lessened, but I have noticed that the stronger branches which are weighted to the ground form rudimentary roots where in contact with the earth. These may either be pegged and covered with soil, or cut off and made into cuttings, removing most of the tops. If the latter is done during August they will become well rooted before the frosts appear.

Flowering period, July to October.

## Coreopsis Tenuifolia.

SLENDER-LEAVED COREOPSIS; *Nat. Ord.* COMPOSITÆ.

HARDY, herbaceous, and perennial; a native of North America, and a distinct species, from its finely-cut foliage and small, dark, orange-yellow flowers. For several weeks it has a few flowers, but during September it literally covers itself with bloom, so that it is one of the most pleasing objects in the garden.

It grows 2ft. high; each flower has a long nearly nude stalk, slender but wiry; the flowers are 1½in. across, and of a deep yellow colour; the florets of the ray are more distant from each other than is the case with many of the genus; the disk is small, dark brown, but changing from the appearance and disappearance of the yellow seed organs. The foliage, as may be seen by the illustration (Fig. 27), is deeply and finely cut, of a dark green colour, and so arranged that each node has a nearly uniform dressing; the main stems are slender, and bend gracefully with the least breeze, and otherwise this plant proves a lively subject. Its habit is bushy and very floriferous, and it is well worth a place in every garden. It cannot fail to win admiration; even when growing, and before the flowers appear, it is a refreshing plant to look upon. In a cut state, the bloom, if taken with long stems, is well adapted for relieving large and more formal kinds. Tastes differ, and in, perhaps, nothing more than floral decorations; all tastes have a right to a share of indulgence, and in claiming my privilege in the use of this flower, I should place two or three sprays (stems) alone in a glass or bright vase, but there might be added a spike of the cardinal flower or a pair of single dahlias and a falling spray of the Flame nasturtium (*Tropæolum speciosum*).

This plant should have a rich soil, sunny aspect, and a raised

FIG. 27. COREOPSIS TENUIFOLIA.
(One-sixth natural size; a, half natural size.)

or well-drained site, and this is all it needs; it is not a subject to increase fast; not only, however, may it be easily divided, but if properly done after the tops have died down, the smallest pieces will make good blooming stock the first season.

Flowering period, August and September.

## Cornus Canadensis.

CANADIAN CORNELL, *or* DOGWOOD; *Nat. Ord.* CORNACEÆ.

THIS pretty herbaceous plant is sometimes said to be a British species; its specific name, however, somewhat forbids that opinion. *C. suecica*, which is British, is very similar in all its parts, and the two may have been confounded. They flower, however, at very different dates, *C. Canadensis* beginning in June and continuing until well into autumn; during the month of August the flowers are in their finest form and greatest numbers. It grows 6in. to 8in. high, and notwithstanding its dwarfness, it proves a most attractive object, being not only conspicuous for so small a plant, but chastely beautiful.

The flowers are exceedingly small, strictly speaking, and are arranged in a minute umbel in the midst of a bract of four white pink-tinted leaves; these latter are commonly taken for the

FIG. 28. CORNUS CANADENSIS.
(One-half natural size.)

petals, and, as may be seen in the illustration (Fig 28), the real flowers will only appear as so many stamens; but at their earlier stage these are of a yellowish colour; later the purplish style becomes prominent and imparts that colour to the umbel, and, in due time, small fruit are formed. All the while the bract of pleasing white leaves remain in unimpaired condition; they are arranged in two pairs, one of larger size than the other, somewhat heart-shaped and bluntly-pointed, richly tinted at their edges and tips with a bright pink colour, and forming a flower-like bract 1½in. across the broadest part. The bract and pedicels of the umbel all spring from the extremity of a peduncle 1½in. long, square, but of wiry character; this grows from the midst of a whorl of six leaves, and sometimes only four. They are in pairs, one pair being larger than their fellows, and are from 1½in. to 2in. long, elliptical-oblong, entire, smooth, waved, distinctly veined, tinted with pink at the tips and edges, and of a pale apple-green colour. On the stem, below the whorl of leaves, there is one pair more, varying only in size, being rather less. The habit of the species is neatness itself. From the slightly creeping roots, the perennial stems are produced separately, forming compact colonies of bright foliage, topped with its lively bracts.

It is a suitable plant for the moist parts of rockwork, where it may be grown with such things as *Cardamine trifolia, Galax aphylla, Pyrola rotundifolia,* and *Salix reticulata,* and it would form a rich edging to choice dwarf plants, more especially if the position were gutter-formed, as it loves moisture in abundance. In such positions as those just mentioned, together with a light vegetable soil, this plant will grow to perfection, and that it is worth a proper place is evidenced by its long-continued blooming. Many flowers come and go during its period of attractiveness, and, after the summer flush, it is one to remain, braving alike the hot sunshine and heavy rain. Its propagation is by division of the roots in autumn or very early spring.

Flowering period, June to October.

## Corydalis Lutea.
YELLOW FUMITORY; *Nat. Ord.* FUMARIACEÆ.

A NATIVE herbaceous perennial, though somewhat rare in a wild state. As grown in gardens, where it seems to appreciate cultural attentions, it proves both useful and effective, especially when placed in partial shade (when its foliage has an almost maiden-hair-like appearance), or as an edging it proves both neat and beautiful.

It seldom exceeds a foot in height. The flowers are small, a yellow, white and green mixture, the yellow predominating; they are produced in loose spare racemes, on well-foliaged diffuse stems, which are also angular; the calyx is composed of two leaves; the petals are four, forming a snapdragon-like flower. The leaves are bipinnate, leaflets wedge-shape, trifoliate, and glaucous; the foliage very dense, having a pretty drooping habit. It flowers all summer, and is one of the most useful plants in a garden to cut from, the foliage being more valuable than the flowers.

Its native habitats are said to be old walls and ruins, but I

OLD-FASHIONED GARDEN FLOWERS. 71

have proved it for years to do grandly in ordinary garden soil, both exposed and in the shade of fruit trees. When once established it propagates itself freely by seed. I ought to add that it answers admirably grown in pots for window decoration, the rich foliage nearly hiding the pot.

Flowering period, May to October.

## Corydalis Nobilis.
NOBLE or GREAT-FLOWERED CORYDALIS; *Nat. Ord.*
FUMARIACEÆ.

A HARDY tuberose perennial, imported from Siberia in 1783. It is one of that section of the Fumitories called "Hollowe Roote,"

FIG. 29. CORYDALIS NOBILIS.
(One-half natural size; blossom, natural size.)

the appropriateness of which name is most amply illustrated in the species now under consideration. If, in the first or second month of the year, a strong specimen is examined, the long and otherwise stout tuberous root will be found, immediately under the healthy and plump crown, to be not only hollow, but so decayed that the lower and heavy fleshy parts of the root, which are attached to the crown by a narrow and very thin portion of the root bark, in such a way as to suggest that the lower parts might as well be cut off as useless—but, let me say, do not cut it. If it is intended to replant the specimen, let it go back to "Mother Earth" with all its parts, deformed as some may seem to us; otherwise *Corydalis nobilis* will be anything but a noble plant at the flowering season; it may not die, but it will probably make for itself another "hollowe roote" before it produces any flowers. The habit and form of this plant are perfect (see Fig. 29), and there are other points of excellence about it which cannot be shown by an engraving, in the way of the arrangements of colours and shades. Seldom does the little plant, so full of character, exceed a height of 8in. The specimen from which the drawing was made was 7in., and grown fully exposed in a pot plunged in sand. Another plant, grown on rockwork, "high and dry," is about the same size, but it looks better fed. Probably the long roots are short of depth in pots, and the amount of decay may soon poison the handful of mould contained therein. Be that as it may, the specimens grown in pots have a hungry appearance compared with those less confined at the roots.

The flowers are a pleasing mixture of white, yellow, brown, and green. The four petals are of such a shape and so arranged as to form a small snapdragon-like flower. These are densely produced in a terminal cluster in pyramid form on the stout and richly-foliaged stem; dense as is the head of flowers, every floret is alternated with a richly-cut leaf, both diminishing in size as they near the top. The older flowers become yellow, with two petals tipped with brown, the younger ones have more white and green, and the youngest are a rich blend of white and green; the head or truss is therefore very beautiful in both form and colour, and withal exquisitely scented, like peach blossom and lilac. The leaves are stalked bipinnate; leaflets three-parted, cut, and glaucous; there are few plants with more handsome foliage, and its beauty is further enhanced by the gracefully bending habit of the whole compound leaf. The flowers are too stiff for cutting, and otherwise their fine forms, colours, and perfume cannot well be enjoyed unless the plants are grown either in pots or at suitable elevations on rockwork, the latter being the more preferable way. The long blooming period of this plant adds not a little to its value, lasting, as it does, quite a month, the weather having little or no effect on the flowers.

Any kind of sweet garden soil seems to do for it, and its propagation is carried out by careful root division.

Flowering period, April to June.

## Corydalis Solida.
*Common Name,* FUMITORY; *Nat. Ord.* FUMARIACEÆ.

THIS is said to be a British species, but it is a doubtful, as well as somewhat scarce one. Though but a small plant of the height of 6in. or 8in., it is very effective, being compact with finely-cut foliage of a pale glaucous green, and the stems pleasingly tinted. For some weeks in early spring it forms a graceful object on rockwork, where it seems to thrive well.

The flowers, which are purple, are not showy; still, they are effective from the way in which they are borne, as the illustration (Fig. 30) will show. Its specific name is in reference to its

FIG. 30. CORYDALIS SOLIDA.
(One-half natural size.)

root, which is bulbous and solid. Many of the Fumitories have remarkably hollow roots, and one of the old names of this genus is written "Hollowe roote." When the flowers fade the whole plant withers, nothing being left but the bulbous roots to complete their ripening; still, this should not hinder its extensive cultivation, because it not only appears in its best form when flowers are rare, but also because it is so pleasingly distinct.

I find it to do well on rockwork, also in well-drained borders of

light loam. It should be allowed to increase until it forms good-sized tufts, which it soon does. To propagate it, it is only necessary to divide the tubers any time from July to October.
Flowering period, February to May.

## Crocus Medius.
*Nat. Ord.* IRIDACEÆ.

THIS is a charming kind, seldom seen and, perhaps, little known; the name would imply that it is a variety having equal traits of two other forms. It blooms in January and the flowers appear without any foliage. So well is the Crocus known, it will only be needful to state the more striking features of the one under notice.

The flowers are produced on tubes 3in. to 5in. long, and stoutly formed; the colour is a shaded lilac-purple, striped with darker lines; the petals or divisions of the perianth are 1½in. long and ½in. broad, shining or satiny, and become well expanded during the short moments of winter sunshine; the stamens are half the length of perianth, of a fine deep orange colour, and covered with a thick coat of pollen all their visible length. In rich contrast with these is the style, with its tuft of filaments of a bright orange scarlet colour. From this description it will be seen that the flower is a rather small Crocus, but from the soft tints of the perianth, and more pronounced and bright colours of the seed organs, it is one of much beauty. These features, added to the facts of the bloom appearing in winter and having the scent of wild roses, are sure to render it a favourite kind wherever grown. The leaves are short and narrow, almost grassy.

It enjoys a light but rich loam and sunny aspect, and increases itself freely by offsets of the matured corms, clumps of which may be divided after the foliage has withered.
Flowering period, January.

## Cyananthus Lobatus.
*Nat. Ord.* POLEMONACEÆ.

A SMALL plant with a large flower, a veritable gem; no collection of choice alpines can be complete without this species. A native of Chinese Tartary, brought to this country in 1844, where it proves perfectly hardy in the most exposed parts of the open garden; it is herbaceous and perennial; its large and brilliant flowers are very beautiful, but all its other parts are small, as may be seen in the illustration (Fig. 31). It is seldom met with except in collections of rare plants, but there is no reason why it should not be more commonly grown, as its requirements are now well understood. It is not a showy subject, but, when examined, it proves of exquisite beauty.

The flowers are of a bright purple-blue colour, over an inch across, the petals being of good substance, tongue-shaped, and falling backwards, when the china-like whiteness about the top of the tube becomes more exposed; the calyx is very large, nearly egg-shaped, having five finely-pointed and deeply-cut segments; the bulky-looking part, which has an inflated appearance, is neatly set on a slender stem, and densely furnished with short black hairs of even length; this dusky coat has a changeable effect, and adds not only to the character, but also to the beauty of the flower. The small attenuated leaves

FIG. 31. CYANANTHUS LOBATUS.
(Natural size.)

are alternate and laxly arranged on the flower stems, which are 6in. to 12in. long, round, and nearly red. Each leaf is less than 1in. long, distinctly lobed with five or more lobes, and all the edges are turned back, causing the foliage to appear thick and well finished; the foliage of the stems not bearing flowers is more closely set. The habit of the plant is procumbent; stems contorted, and producing solitary flowers.

It should be grown on rockwork, where its stems can nestle between the stones and its roots find plenty of moisture, as in a dip or hollowed part; the long and fleshy roots love to run in damp leaf mould and sand. The position should be open and sunny, in order to have flowers. Cuttings may be taken during summer, and struck in sandy peat kept moist, or strong roots may be divided. The latter method is the less desirable, not only because of jeopardising the parent stock but also because strong roots show to greater advantage when not separated.

Flowering period, September and October.

## Cypripedium Calceolus.

ENGLISH LADY'S SLIPPER; *Nat. Ord.* ORCHIDACEÆ.

THIS well-known terrestrial orchid is a rare British plant, very beautiful, and much admired, so much so, indeed, that many desire to grow it. It happens, however, that it seldom thrives under cultural treatment, and seems to prefer a home of its own selection, but its habitats are said now to be very few in Great Britain, it having been hunted out and grubbed up everywhere. Fortunately, it can be grown in gardens, and in good form, though rarely seen thus. To see well-grown flowers of this orchid either makes us feel more contented with our own climate or strongly reminds us of others where the most gorgeous varieties of flowers and fruit grow wild. It is large and striking, fragrant, and very beautiful; no one can see it, especially in a growing state, without being charmed by its freshness and simplicity; it also forms one of the finest specimens for the student in botany, and in every way it is a plant and flower of the highest merit (see Fig. 32). It should be in all collections of choice plants, and every amateur should persevere until he succeeds in establishing it.

FIG. 32. CYPRIPEDIUM CALCEOLUS. (One-third natural size.)

Under cultivation it flowers in early May, at a height of 9in. to 12in.; the flowers are composed of a calyx of three brownish-purple sepals, which have only the appearance of two, from the fact of the lower two being joined or grown together, and even so combined they are somewhat less than the upper sepal. The division may be observed at the tips, though in some specimens it is microscopic—in the one now by me it is hardly the eighth of an inch. Two petals; these are cross-form in relation to the sepals, of the same colour, and a little longer—about 2in.— narrow, drooping, pointed, and slightly twisted when a few days old; lip, "blown out like a slipper," shorter than the sepals, compressed, richly veined, and lemon yellow. The seed organs are curious, the stigma being foot-stalked, peltate, and placed between and above the anthers. The leaves are pale green, very hairy, many-ribbed, stem-clasping, alternate, ovate, and slightly wavy; the lower ones are 5in. or 6in. long and 2in. to 3in. wide, and pointed. The root is creeping, the fibres stout, long, wiry, and bent. During spring the plant makes rapid growth, and seldom bears more than one flower; for the first time a plant produced two with me in 1882. They are sweetly scented, like the primrose.

Many amateurs, who have otherwise proved their knowledge of the requirements of plants by growing large and choice collections, have failed to establish this after many trials; and were it not for the fact that with me it is growing in various positions and under different modes of treatment, and that it has so grown for several years, I think I should not have ventured to give hints to experienced horticulturists. In my opinion, four conditions are strictly necessary in order to establish this native orchid in our garden: (1) A strong specimen with a goodly portion of the rhizoma attached; (2) Firm or solid planting during autumn; (3) Moist situation; (4) Shade from the mid-day sun. Further information may be best given by stating the *modus operandi*: Several years ago a number of good roots were planted in sandy loam of a calcareous nature. They were put in somewhat deeply, the roots carefully spread out, and the soil made solid by repeated waterings, the position being shaded by an apple tree. They are now well established, and only receive a top dressing of leaves and manure to keep them cool and moist in summer. At the same time a number were potted deeply in loam, peat, and broken oyster shells; when filling in the compost, it, too, was washed to the roots, so as to make all solid by frequent applications; the pots have always been kept in cool and shady quarters, and plunged; they bloom well every season. I have likewise found another plan to answer well. In a moist corner make up a low-lying bed of sand and peat, mostly sand, plant 9in. deep, and make all solid, as before, by water. When the growths appear on the surface, water with weak liquid manure, and if shade does not exist from the mid-day sun, some should be provided; in this way I am now growing my finest specimens; but if once the roots become dry, the plants will suffer a serious check. I feel equally confident that the roots enjoy a firm bed, but it should be of such material that they can freely run in it.

Flowering period, May and June.

## Daphne Cneorum.

TRAILING DAPHNE; *Common and Poetical Name*, GARLAND FLOWER; *Nat. Ord.* THYMELACEÆ.

AN alpine shrub from Austria; dwarf, evergreen, and having a tendency to creep. It is deservedly a great favourite; it wins admiration by its neat and compact form and its dense and numerous half-globular heads of rosy pink flowers, which are exceedingly fragrant, in the way of the old clove carnation, but more full.

The flower buds are formed during the previous season of growth, like those of the rhododendron; for many days before the flowers open the buds have a

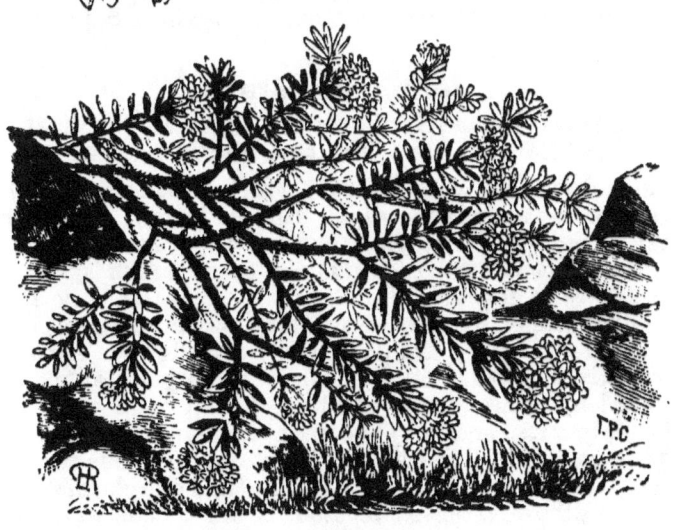

FIG. 33. DAPHNE CNEORUM.
(One-fourth natural size; (1) flower, full size.)

very pleasing appearance, being closely packed and coral-like; when all the florets are expanded they form a half-globular head 1in. to 1½in. across, being of a lively pink colour. The flowers are composed of a tubular calyx, four-parted; leaves inversely ovate, lanceolate, pointed, and entire; about an inch long, and narrow; of a dark green colour and much substance, being arranged in circular form on the round and somewhat wiry, tough stems, which in time become very long and bare.

In order to grow this shrub well, three conditions are needful, viz., a moderately pure atmosphere, exposure to full sunshine, and plenty of moisture; it also prefers peat or vegetable soil, but this is not strictly needful if the other conditions are present. I have grown the specimen, from part of which the illustration (Fig. 33) was drawn, for four years in rich loam, without a particle of peat, but the roots have been protected against drought by large stones at the base of small rockwork. Doubtless, peat, where it is plentiful, used in addition to the above compost, would prove beneficial. After a few years' growth in one position, bushes which have become long and bare in the stems may be transplanted with advantage, laying in the stems to a moderate depth, from which new roots will issue the first season; this is also the readiest way of propagation. February or September would be suitable months for such operation, but the latter would probably interfere with its flowering at that time, when frequently a second but spare crop is produced.

Flowering periods, April and May, and again in September.

## Daphne Mezereum.

MEZEREON; *Old Names*, SPURGE-FLAX, GERMAN OLIVE-SPURGE, and DWARF BAY; *Nat. Ord.* THYMELACEÆ.

THIS is a dwarf deciduous shrub, which produces its welcome flowers in great abundance whilst bare of leaves; it is a British species, though not occurring generally, yet it is pretty well known from its extensive cultivation as a garden shrub. The flowers are very desirable, from the way in which they are produced in knotted clusters on the long stems; they appear in winter; moreover, they are of a hardy and durable nature and very sweetly scented. As a shrub it is very suitable for any sized garden, being dwarf—2ft. to 4ft. In some parts it is a general favourite, and may be seen in almost every garden; such patronage is well merited, as it not only enlivens the garden at a dead season, but it heralds spring time and furnishes long sprigs of wallflower-scented blossom as cut bloom, which shows to advantage by gaslight.

There are interesting facts in connection with this shrub that add to its charm. It was esteemed of old of great virtue; all its parts are hot and biting, more especially the berries, of which it was said that "if a drunkard do eate—he cannot be allured to drinke any drinke at that time: such will be the heate of his mouth and choking in the throte." Its wood is very soft and tough, and cannot easily be broken; this, however is a quality common to the genus. The berries are poisonous to man, but birds are so fond of them that they are rarely allowed to become ripe, at least, such is the case near towns. The seeds of this and allied species are used in the South of Europe as a yellow dye for wool. From its importance, the shrub has been long and widely known, and both its botanical and common names are numerous; for these, however, the reader may not care. It is seldom called by any other than its specific name, Mezereon, which Gerarde describes as English-Dutch.

Its flowers, which are purple, come on the otherwise naked stems of last season's growth, lateral fashion, in threes mostly, and sometimes the blossomed stems will be over a foot in length; the flowers are ½in. long, sessile and funnel-shaped; the limb four-cut; sweet smelling and very durable. The berries are the size of a small pea, bright green at first, then turning to red, and ultimately to a nearly black colour. The leaves—lance-shaped, smooth, and deciduous—appear after the flowers. The habit is branched and erect, forming neat bushes. In a wild state it flowers in March and April, but under cultivation it is much earlier.

In the garden it may be planted under other trees, where it proves one of a scarce class of shade-loving flowering shrubs; it also does well in open quarters. In gardens, where its fruit is unmolested, it is, perhaps, more attractive than when in blossom, as then the foliage adds to its beauty. The flowers in a cut state are serviceable, pretty, and desirable from their sweetness; long sprigs mixed with lavender or rosemary form a winter bouquet not to be despised; or, it may be placed in a vase, with a few small-leaved ivy trails and a spray of evergreen bamboo (Metake). Gerarde's description of this shrub will, doubtless, be read with interest: "The braunches be tough, limber, and easie to bend, very soft to be cut; whereon do grow long leaves like those of priuet, but thicker and fatter. The flowers come foorth before the leaves, oftentimes in the moneth of Januarie, clustering togither about the stalks at certain distances, of a whitish colour tending to purple, and of a most fragrant and pleasant sweet smell. After come the smal berries—of an exceeding hot and burning taste, inflaming the mouth and throte of those that do taste thereof, with danger of choking."

Flowering period, February to April.

There is a variety called *D. M. album*; the only difference from the typical form is implied by the name, the flowers being white. It also is in bloom at the same time as the species.

*D. M. autumnale* is another variety, which, however, blooms in the autumn; the flowers are red; it is a native of Europe.

These shrubs enjoy a light but moist soil of a vegetable nature, but they also thrive in a sandy loam. They may be increased by seed, or, more quickly, by grafting on stocks of spurge laurel; cuttings may be rooted, but are uncertain.

## Dentaria Digitata.
TOOTHWORT; *Nat. Ord.* CRUCIFERÆ.

A HARDY, tuberous perennial, native of Switzerland, but long cultivated in British gardens, and decidedly "old-fashioned."

Imagine a spray of pale purple wallflower, and that will give some idea of the form and colour of its flowers, which are produced on round wiry stems, nearly a foot high, in terminal racemes. The leaves, which are produced mostly in threes on a stem, have a channelled petiole, and, as the specific name denotes, are spread out like fingers, mostly of five parts; a five-cut leaf of a Christmas rose will give a fair notion of the form, but the Toothwort leaves are less, not so thick, and more herb-like than the hellebore; they are also finely, deeply, but irregularly toothed. The roots are of singular form, almost like human teeth, arranged as scales, whence the name Toothwort. Its first appearance above ground is in February, when the young growths are bent or folded like those of the anemone, and in genial seasons it will flower early in March.

It loves both a little shade and moisture. I grow it at the base of a bit of rockwork, in black or leaf mould; the aspect is south-east, but an old sun-dial screens it from the midday sun. The whole plant has a somewhat quaint appearance, but it has proved a great favourite. When the tops have died down the roots can safely be lifted, cut in lengths of one or two inches, and then replanted. It also produces seed freely, but from the easy method of increase by root division, I have not had occasion to experiment with seed.

Flowering period, March to May.

## Dianthus Deltoides.
MAIDEN PINK; *Old Names,* "WILD GILLOFLOWER," "VIRGIN-LIKE PINKE," "MAIDENLY PINKE"; *Nat. Ord.* CARYOPHYLLACEÆ—SILENACEÆ.

A BRITISH species of perennial character, never failing to bloom for a long period when it meets with a suitable home in our gardens—as in positions similar to those described for *Erysimum pumilum.* Seen either wild or in gardens it is much admired; it bears but simple flowers, but therein consists its beauty.

As Gerarde says, "Virgin-like Pinke is like unto the rest of the garden pinkes in stalkes, leaves, and rootes. The flowers are of a blush colour, whereof it tooke his name, which sheweth the difference from the other." It is about the most simple form of the Pink tribe. The flowers are a little over $\frac{1}{2}$in. across, of a rose colour or pleasing blush. It grows nearly a foot high in some soils, but in a poor compost it is more dwarf and floriferous. The flower stems are much divided near the tops, and capable of producing a good effect from their numbers of bright flowers.

The leaves are small, scarcely 1in. long, linear, lance-shaped, and of a dark green colour; they are closely arranged on decumbent stems, which sometimes are more than 1ft. long. The habit is compact, both as regards leaves, stems, and flowers.

For all such places as afford dryness at the roots this is a suitable plant as a constant bloomer of effective colour. When once it has become established it seeds freely, and the young plants may be seen in the walks for yards around the parent stock. It is one of those happy subjects that can take care of themselves, either braving its enemies or having none.

In its wild state it blooms from the sixth to the tenth month, both inclusive; but with cultural attention and during favourable winters, it has been seen in flower to the end of the year.

Flowering period, June to October.

## Dianthus Hybridus.
*Syn.* D. MULTIFLORUS; MULE PINK; *Nat. Ord.* CARYOPHYLLACEÆ.

HARDY and evergreen. The specific name of this variety is not at all descriptive, and it may be better to at once give its common name of Mule Pink, of which there are various colours, as bright scarlet, rose and pure white, all very double and neat flowers.

It is the double rose kind which has induced me to speak of this section of the Pink and Sweetwilliam family. I dare say many will be surprised when I state that my strongest plant of this has been in flower more than two years. Severe as the 1881 winter was, when the plant was clear of snow it was seen to have both flowers and buds—in fact, for two years it has flowered unceasingly; the other varieties are not such persistent bloomers. The genus to which these hybrids belong is very numerous, and includes Carnations, Picotees, garden and alpine Pinks and Sweetwilliams. They are all remarkable for their fresh green and glaucous foliage and handsome flowers. Some species or varieties are amongst the "old-fashioned" garden plants of Parkinson's time, and all are characterised by an exquisite perfume. The Latin name of this genus is a very happy one, meaning "divine flower," in reference to its fragrance. Nearly every form and colour of Dianthus are popular favourites, and hardly any garden is without some of them.

The Mule Pink is supposed to have been produced from *D. barbatus* and *D. plumarius*; be that as it may, the features of both are distinctly seen in it: the colour and partial form of the foliage, the form of stems, and clustered arrangement of the buds much resemble *D. barbatus* or Sweetwilliam; whilst the stout reflexed and pointed features of the leaves, and the general form of the small but double flowers resemble *D. plumarius*, or the garden Pink. To this description of *D. hybridus* I will only add that in both foliage and flowers there is more substance than in either of its reputed parents, and the habit of the plant is semi-trailing or procumbent, as seen in specimens three years old. It is rather more difficult to grow than the common Pink. Any position or soil will not answer; it does well on rockwork, where it can hardly suffer from damp, so much disliked by all the genus; but if thus planted, it should be where its thickly-foliaged stems cannot be turned over and wrenched by strong winds. It may be grown in borders in sandy loam; and if such borders are well drained, as they always should be for choice flowers, there will be little to fear as to its thriving. Such an excellent flower, which, moreover, is perpetually produced, deserves some extra care, though, beyond the requirements already mentioned, it will give very little trouble.

To increase it, the readiest way is to layer the shoots about midsummer, half cutting through the stems, as for Carnations; thus treated, nice plants will be formed by October, when they may be lifted and transplanted to their blooming quarters; and I may here state that a line of it, when in flower, is richly effective. A good style also is to make a bold clump by setting ten or twelve plants 9in. apart. Another mode of propagation is to take cuttings at midsummer and dibble them into boxes of leaf soil and sand. Keep them shaded and rather close for a week or more. If the boxes could be placed in a cucumber frame, the bottom heat and moisture would be a great help to them. The object to aim at should be not only to root the cuttings, but to grow them on to fair-sized plants for putting out in the autumn. To do this, when the cuttings are rooted they should be planted 6in. apart in a bed made up of well decayed manure and sand, in which it will be seen that they will make plenty of roots and become sturdy plants. The wireworm and slugs are both very fond of Pinks and Carnations. Slugs should be trapped, but the wireworm, unfortunately, has often done the mischief before we become aware of its presence, and even then it is a troublesome pest to get rid of. I find nothing more useful than stirring and digging the soil as soon as there is room to work with a spade or fork; the worm cannot endure frequent disturbance, and such operations are otherwise beneficial to the plants.

Flowering period, May to September

### Dodecatheon Jeffreyanum.
*Nat. Ord.* PRIMULACEÆ.

THIS is a distinct and noble species. The older leaves are more spoon-shaped, at least a foot long, rather narrow, not toothed, of a reddish colour at the base, and the mid-rib pale green, almost straw-colour; the flower scape is also reddish, but the flowers are fewer. As a foliage plant this species is very effective.

All the Dodecatheons make a rapid growth in spring, their scapes being developed with the leaves; the genus will continue in flower for two months, after which time, however, their foliage begins to dry up. They should, therefore, be planted with other subjects of later growth and blooming, so as to avoid blank spaces. The overshading foliage of other things will do them no harm, as it will be only for a season. The position should be moist and somewhat sheltered from high winds, or the stout and tender flower stems will be snapped off. The soil should be of a vegetable character and retentive of moisture. My specimens are grown in leaf soil and loam, in a dip of small rockwork. All the kinds were planted that a large flat stone, which we had ready, would so fit to, or over, them as to secure their roots against drought. This I find a good plan with moisture-loving subjects, where suitable positions are not otherwise readily offered. Besides, the varieties so grown have a pleasing appearance, and for purposes of comparison are very handy. Their propagation is easy. The crowns may be divided either in spring or autumn, the latter being the best time, as then probably each piece will flower the following spring.

Flowering period, April to June.

## Dodecatheon Meadia.

SHOOTING STAR, or AMERICAN COWSLIP; Nat. Ord. PRIMULACEÆ.

A DISTINCT and pretty herbaceous perennial, very hardy and floriferous. Those who do not readily recognise it by any of the above names, may do so by the illustration (Fig. 34). It has long been grown in English gardens—nearly 150 years—its habitat being North America. Not only does it do well in this climate, but since its introduction several improved varieties of this species have been produced, which are both good and distinct. A brief notice of them will not be out of place here, but first the general description may as well be given.

FIG. 34. DODECATHEON MEADIA.
(One-sixth natural size.)

The flowers much resemble the Cyclamen, but they are only

about one-fourth the size; the calyx is five-parted; the corolla has five stout petals inserted in the tube of calyx; they are well reflexed and rather twisted; their colour is purplish-lilac, but at the base of the petals there is a rich blending of maroon and yellow. The seed organs are very long, compact, and pointed, giving the appearance of shooting stars. The flowers are arranged in fine clusters on a scape more than a foot high, each flower having a rather long, wiry, and gracefully bending pedicel; all of them spring from one centre. The leaves are radical, oblong, smooth, dented, and wavy, about 8in. long and nearly 3in. broad.

*D. M. albiflorum* I do not grow, but from what I remember of it, it differs from the above only in being less vigorous and in having white flowers.

*D. M. elegans.*—Shorter and broader in leaf, and roundly toothed; flower stems shorter, umbels more numerously flowered, bloom deeper in colour.

*D. M. giganteum* has a very large leaf, much larger than the typical form of the species, and of a pale green colour, and in all other respects it is larger, being also more than a week earlier in flower.

Flowering period, April to June.

## Dondia Epipactis.

*Syns.* ASTRANTIA EPIPACTIS *and* HACQUETIA EPIPACTIS;
*Nat. Ord.* UMBELLIFERÆ.

THIS is a little gem, perhaps rather overdone with too many big names; still, this choice, hardy, herbaceous perennial is worth knowing by all its titles. Never more than 6in. high, its singular flowers are very attractive; they spring from the ground almost abruptly, are greenish-yellow and leafy in appearance—in fact, what at first sight might seem to be the petals are really but whorled bracts, which embrace the tiny umbels of flowers. Soon after the flowers the leaves begin to appear, unfolding like many of the anemones, each one springing from the root only; they also are of a peculiar colour and shape, being three-lobed and finely notched.

It will stand any amount of rough weather, always having a fresh appearance when above ground. It forms a choice specimen for pot culture in cold frames or amongst select rock plants; it should be grown in mostly vegetable mould, as peat or leaf mould, and have a moist position. Not only is it a slow-growing subject, but it is impatient of being disturbed; its propagation should therefore only be undertaken in the case of strong and healthy clumps, which are best divided before growth commences in February.

Flowering period, April and May.

## Doronicum Caucasicum.

LEOPARD'S-BANE; *Syn.* D. ORIENTALE; *Nat. Ord.* COMPOSITÆ.

THE specific name denotes sufficiently whence this comes. It is hardy, herbaceous, and perennial, and one of those plants which deserves to be in every garden; its general appearance is that of a tender plant, from the pale but fine delicate green of its foliage, a somewhat uncommon shade for so early a season. It begins to flower in March in a warm situation in the garden, when only a few inches high, and it goes on growing and flowering until summer, when it is nearly 2ft. high. A glance at Fig. 35 will give a fair idea of its habit.

FIG. 35. DORONICUM CAUCASICUM.
(One-third natural size.)

The flowers, which are bright yellow, are 2½in. across, produced one at a time, though the leafy stems are well supplied with buds in various stages of development. The leaves, besides being so rich in colour, are of handsome forms, being variously shaped, some having long stalks, others none; all are finely toothed and heart-shaped; the radical ones come well out and form a good base, from which the flower stems rise, and they in their turn serve to display the richly veined and ample foliage which clasps them to near their tops. Although this species is not a very old plant in English gardens, it belongs to a genus, several species of which are very "old-fashioned," and, consequently, it shares the esteem in which such subjects are held at the present time.

If left alone, after being planted in fairly good soil, it will soon grow to a bold specimen. Plants three years old are 2ft. across: rockwork or ordinary borders are alike suitable for it, but if planted on the former, it should be of a bold character, so as to harmonise. I have observed that neither grubs nor slugs seem to meddle with this plant, which is certainly a rare recommendation. Its propagation may be carried out at almost any time.

Flowering period, March to July.

## Echinacea Purpurea.

*Syn.* RUDBECKIA PURPUREA; PURPLE CONE-FLOWER; *Nat. Ord.* COMPOSITÆ.

IN the autumn season one is almost confined to Composites, but in this subject there is, at any rate, a change as regards colour. Yellows are indispensable, but then predominate too strongly. The flower under notice is a peculiar purple with greenish-white shadings. This will doubtless sound undesirable, but when the flower is seen it can hardly fail to be appreciated. It is much admired; in fact it is stately, sombre, and richly beautiful—not only an "old-fashioned" flower, but an old inhabitant of English gardens, coming, as it did, from North America in the year 1699. In every way the plant is distinct; it does not produce many flowers, but they individually last for several weeks, and their metallic appearance is a fitting symbol of their durability. They begin to expand in the early part of September, and well-established plants will have bloom until cut off by frost.

The flowers are borne at the height of 2ft. to 3ft., and are produced singly on very thick, rigid stalks, long, nearly nude, grooved, furnished with numerous short, bristle-like hairs, and gradually thickening up to the involucrum of the flower. Said involucrum is composed of numerous small leaves, a distinguishing trait from its nearest relative genus *Rudbeckia*. The receptacle or main body of the flower is very bulky; the ray is fully 4in. across, the florets being short for so large a ray; they are set somewhat apart, slightly reflexed, plaited, and rolled at the edges, colour reddish-purple, paling off at the tips to a greyish-green; the disk is very large, rather flat, and furnished with spine-like scales, whence the name *Echinacea,* derived from *echinus* (a hedgehog). In smelling this flower contact should therefore be avoided; it is rather forbidding; the disk has changeable hues of red, chocolate, and green. The leaves of the root are oval, some nearly heart-shaped, unevenly toothed, having long channelled stalks; those of the stems are lance-shaped, distinctly toothed, of stouter substance, short stalked, and, like those of the root, distinctly nerved, very rough on both sides, and during September quickly changes to a dark, dull, purple colour. The habit of the plant is rather "dumpy;" being spare of foliage, thick and straight in the stems, which are drum-stick like; it is for all that a pleasing subject when in flower; I consider the blooms too stiff for cutting, more especially as they face upwards.

Unlike many species of its order, it is somewhat fickle. I have lost many plants of it; it likes neither shade nor too much moisture; latterly I have found it to do well in a sunny situation, in deep rich loam and vegetable soil mixed. If planted with other ray flowers it forms a fine contrast, and when once it has found suitable quarters the more seldom it is disturbed the better. It may be propagated by division, which may be more safely done after growth has fairly started in spring, or it may be done at the sacrifice of the flowers in late summer or early autumn, before growth or root action has ceased.

Flowering period, September to end of October.

## Edraianthus Dalmaticus.
### *Nat. Ord.* CAMPANULACEÆ.

A RARE and beautiful alpine species, from Dalmatia and Switzerland. At the end of July it is one of the most distinct and charming flowers in the rock garden, where it not only finds a happy home, but, by its neat and peculiar habit, proves a decorative subject of much merit. This desirable plant (see Fig. 36) is quite hardy in this climate, being herbaceous and perennial; it has, however, the reputation of being difficult to manage, but, like numerous other things, when once its requirements and enemies are found out, the former supplied and protection from the latter afforded, it proves of easy management. In some instances these conditions may, though stated in such few words, prove comprehensive; but in this case it is not so. The position and soil it most seems to enjoy may be readily afforded in any garden, as we shall shortly see; but, so far as my experience goes, the slugs are its most persistent enemies. Especially when in flower do they make long journeys to reach it; they go over sand and ashes with impunity, and often the beautiful tufts of bloom are all grazed off in one night. I had occasion to fetch in from the garden the specimen now before me, and, when brought into the gas-light, a large slug was found in the midst of the grassy foliage, and a smaller one inside one of the bell flowers. The "catch and kill 'em" process is doubtless the surest remedy, and three hours after sunset seems to be the time of their strongest muster. Not only does this plant suffer from slugs when in flower, but perhaps equally as much when in its dormant state, especially if the winter is mild; then I have noticed the somewhat prominent crowns eaten entirely off, and it is not unlikely that this plant has come to have the name of a fickle grower, from being the favourite prey of slugs.

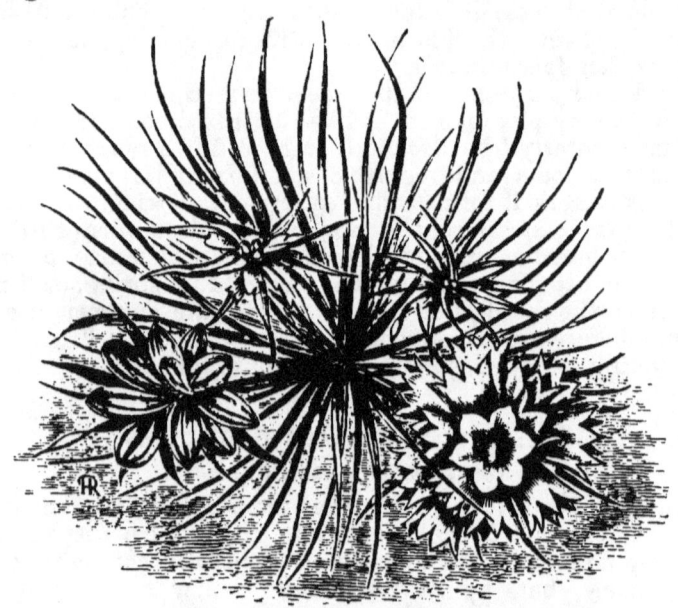

Fig. 36.  Edraianthus Dalmaticus.
(One-half natural size.)

It is not more than 4in. high under any conditions in this climate, and more often only 3in. in height. From the thrift-like tufts of foliage there radiates a set of stout round flower stalks, which are 3in. to 4in. long, and rest on the ground; the large heads of flowers are erect; the stalks are red, and furnished with short stout hairs and short foliage, the latter becoming sere long before the bloom fades. The crowded heads of "bells" are of pale purple colour, in the style of the bell-flower; they are an inch in length, the corolla being somewhat deeply divided; eight to twelve form the terminal cluster, and they have a fleshy calyx, with very long and persistent segments; the lower part can scarcely be seen for the ample and somewhat peculiar bract which closely embraces the whole cluster; said bract springs from the much thickened stalk and is composed of half leaf and half scale-like forms, arranged in two or more circles; the scales feather off with the leaf-like appendage, the latter being reflexed, but the whole is furnished with spines. The foliage of a well-grown specimen is arranged in tufts, the whole having a grass-like appearance. The leaves are 2in. to 4in. long, rough and hairy on the upper side, smooth and shining underneath, the edges having rather long hairs their whole length; the main root is long, thick, and somewhat woody.

To grow this plant well, it requires a good deep loam for its long roots, and a surfacing of grit will be of benefit, as the crowns should be clear of the damp loam. This elevation of the crowns is natural to the plant, and should be provided for. The position cannot well be too exposed, provided the deep searching roots can find plenty of moisture. On rockwork this subject may be planted with considerable effect. If put between large stones in upright positions, the plant will show its pretty form to advantage. The spoke-like flower stalks, radiating from the rich dark green tufts of foliage, are very pleasing. It may be propagated by offsets from strong and healthy plants. Care should be taken not only to have all the roots possible with each crown, but the young stock should be carefully established in pots before planting in the open. Shade and careful watering will be needful; too much of the latter will render rot inevitable. Soon as the flowering period is past is the best time to divide the roots, which should not be done too severely.

Flowering period, July and August.

## Epigæa Repens.

CREEPING or GROUND LAUREL; *Nat. Ord.* ERICACEÆ.

A HARDY evergreen creeper, long since imported into this country from North America (1736), but only within the last few years has it won much favour. At the present time it is much sought after. It has the reputation of being a ticklish subject to grow. Many have had it and lost it, and those who still retain a specimen are loth to mutilate it for increase. This may to some extent account for the present demand for and difficulty experienced in obtaining it. For the last three years, hard as the seasons have been within that time, its flowers have been produced in great abundance on my specimen.

Usually it flowers in this climate in April, but when winter has continued open and genial, its blooms are produced as early as the middle of March, and they are in their full beauty in early April. They are white, delicately tinged with pink, of much substance and wax-like appearance. They are small, not unlike in form the lilac flower, but rather more open at the corolla and shorter in the tube. They are arranged in one-sided, elongated bunches, which rest on the ground, the blossoms peeping through the foliage. I must not omit to mention perhaps the most desirable property of this species—viz., the perfume of its flowers; which is strong, aromatic, and refreshing. The leaves are cordate, ovate, and entire, nearly 2in. long, slightly drawn or wrinkled, and covered with stiffish hairs. They are arranged on procumbent branches, all, like the flowers, facing upwards. To see the clusters of waxy flowers these branches must be raised, when it will be seen that the flower stalks issue from the axils of the leaves all along the branches. In a cut state the flowers are more than useful; they are, from their delicious scent, a great treat. The plant is a suitable companion to the ledums, kalmias, gaultherias, and other genera of its own order.

Its culture, in this climate at least, has, from all accounts, proved rather difficult, so that it may be said to require special treatment; such, at any rate, has been my experience of it. Suitable soil, aspect, shelter, moisture, and position, all seem necessary for the well-doing of this plant. It deserves them all, and, let me add, they may all be easily afforded. The list of requirements may seem formidable on paper, but to put them into practice is but a trifling affair. My specimen is grown in leaf mould, a little loam mixed in with it, and fine charcoal instead of sand, but sand will answer nearly as well; the aspect is east, it is sheltered from the west by a wall, the north by rhododendrons, and the south by a tall andromeda. Moreover, its position is one that is sunken between small mounds, where moisture collects, and is never wanting; and when the specimen was first planted a large sandstone was placed over its roots to further secure them against drought; under these conditions it has thriven and flowered well, and afforded many offshoots. I attribute its well-doing mainly to the sheltered aspect and even state of moisture, but doubtless all the conditions have helped its growth. Its propagation is best carried out by earthing up about the collar, so as to induce the branches to become rooted, or they may be pegged near the extremities like carnation layers, but they will be two years, probably, before they can be safely lifted.

Flowering period, middle of March to end of April.

## Eranthis Hyemalis.

*Syn.* HELLEBORUS HYEMALIS; WINTER ACONITE; *Nat. Ord.* RANUNCULACEÆ.

THIS, though well known and a general favourite, is not seen in the broad masses which ought to characterise its culture.

It is nearly related to the Christmas roses, and, like them, flowers in winter, the bright golden blossoms suddenly appearing during sunshine close to the earth. A little later the involucrum becomes developed, and is no unimportant feature. It forms a dark green setting for the sessile flower, and is beautifully cut, like the Aconite. There are other and very interesting traits about this little flower that will engage the study of botanists.

It enjoys a moist soil, somewhat light; also a little shade. In such quarters not only do the tubers increase quickly, but the seed germinates, and if such positions are allowed it, and garden tools kept off, there will soon be a dense carpet of golden flowers to brighten the wintry aspect of the open garden. Many things in the way of deciduous flowering shrubs may be grown with them, their bareness in winter and shade during summer favouring their enjoyment and growth. Early in the summer they die down. From that time the tubers may be lifted and transplanted. Such work should be finished in early autumn, or the roots will not have time to establish themselves for the first winter's bloom.

Flowering period, December to February.

## Erica Carnea.
WINTER HEATH; *Nat. Ord.* ERICACEÆ.

A WELL-KNOWN, hardy, evergreen shrub, belonging to a genus comprising many hundreds of species and varieties, which, for the most part, however, are not hardy in this country, being natives of the Cape. The genus is most numerously and beautifully illustrated in *Loddige's Botanical Cabinet*. This might be thought to have no claim to consideration in this book, but I introduce it because of its great value in the spring garden, and because in all respects it may be cultivated like an ordinary border plant, which is saying a deal for one of the Heath family.

*Erica carnea* comes to us from Germany, but it has so long been grown in this country that it would appear to have become naturalised in some parts. In the latter part of March it is to be seen in its full beauty; the flowers are reddish-purple, abundantly produced on short leafy stems, and arranged in racemes, drooping; the foliage is of the well-known Heath type; the whole shrub has a procumbent habit, rarely growing more than a foot high; its fine deep green foliage, compact habit, and bright enduring flowers are its chief recommendations; the latter often last six weeks in good form and colour, so that little more needs to be said in its praise.

It can hardly be planted in a wrong position—on rockwork, in borders, or shrubberies, fully exposed, or otherwise, it proves a cheerful object, whilst as an edging shrub it is second to none, excelling box by the additional charm of its flowers. Not long since I was struck by the way in which the common vinca had interlaced itself with a few bushes of this Heath, both being in full bloom at the same time; the effect was truly fine, the red of the Heath and pale blue flowers of the periwinkle being so numerous and set on such a fine bright green carpet, of two distinct types of foliage, that to my mind they suggested a most pleasing form of spring bedding, and also one of semi-wildness, which, for quiet beauty, more laboured planting could certainly not excel. Most Ericas require peaty soil; in the case of this, however, it is not necessary. Doubtless it would do well in peat, but I have ever found it to thrive in ordinary loam or garden soil, so that I have never planted it otherwise, except where peat has been the most handy. It is also easily propagated, carrying, as it does, plenty of root as well as earth with each rooted stem; these only need to be carefully divided and transplanted in showery weather, just before the new growths commence being the best time. An annual top dressing of leaf mould is very beneficial.

Flowering period, February to April.

## Erigeron Caucasicus.

CAUCASIAN FLEABANE; *Nat. Ord.* COMPOSITÆ.

HERBACEOUS and perennial. This species is a somewhat recent introduction compared with some of the same genus which may be called old varieties, from having been introduced as early as 1633, as in the case of *E. graveolens*. Moreover, the genus is represented by such British species as *E. acris*, *E. alpinus*, and *E. uniflorus*. The variety now under notice is, as its specific name implies, a native of the Caucasus, first brought into this country about sixty years ago. It is a pleasing subject when in flower, and is certainly worth growing.

Its daisy-shaped flowers are less than an inch across, and when fully matured of a rosy purple colour; but, perhaps, the most interesting and attractive features about this plant are the various forms and colours of its flowers at their different stages of development; just before opening, the buds are like miniature birds' nests formed of white horsehairs, all arranged in the same way, *i.e.*, round the bud, but the points are turned into the centre—these are the unexpanded florets; the next stage of development may be seen in buds, say, two days older, when a few of the florets have sprung from the nest form, and have the appearance of mauve-coloured spiders' legs laid over the bud; gradually they (being dense and numerous) expand in a similar manner, outgrowing their angularity, and at the same time deepening in colour, until at length we see the rosy-purple, daisy-shaped, and feathery flower with a yellowish centre. These pleasing flowers are borne in loose masses on stems nearly 2ft. high, and remain in bloom all the summer through.

About the middle of August a large plant was divided, and the flowers were then cut away. The young stock so propagated were in flower in the following June. I may here appropriately name an experiment I tried on this species two years ago. It was sent to me as the dwarf *Aster dumosus*, which it much resembles in the leaves, these being spoon-shaped from the roots, the others tongue-shaped and stem-clasping, but rougher and lighter green. I also saw it was not woody enough in the stem for the Michaelmas daisy. It was then near flowering, and the winter was just upon us, so, in order to get the flowers out, I covered it with a bell glass, slightly tilted. It flowered, and continued to flower throughout the winter with such shelter, and doubtless many of our fine late-blooming perennials, by such simple contrivances, might have their flowers protected or produced at a much later date than otherwise.

Flowering period, June to October.

## Erigeron Glaucum.
*Syn.* CONYZA CHILENSIS; GLAUCOUS FLEABANE, *or* SPIKENARD; *Nat. Ord.* COMPOSITÆ.

THIS very beautiful species is far from common. There are many facts in connection with it which render it of more than ordinary value and interest. It is sometimes classed as an alpine; probably that is only an inference, or it may be so considered by some, from its dwarf habit and suitable association with alpines. It is not an alpine; it comes from South America, and though that climate differs so widely from ours, the plant grows and winters to perfection in this country.

One of its main distinctions is its somewhat shrubby and evergreen character; of the whole genus, so far as it is at present comprehended, it is the only species with such traits; its foliage, too, is of leathery substance, and compares oddly with the herb-like leaves of its relatives; it is, moreover, as indicated by its specific name, of a glaucous hue; and otherwise, as may be seen in the following description, there exist well marked dissimilarities. But, what is of more importance, when viewed as a garden subject or an ornamental flower, it is one of the most useful as well as distinctly beautiful, as much from the fact that it produces its flowers in two crops, which extend over six or seven months of the year, as from their numbers and showiness.

The flowers are nearly 2in. across the ray, the florets being of a pleasing lilac-purple, and rather short, owing to the large size of the disk, which is often nearly an inch in diameter; this part of the flower is more than usually effective, as the disk florets become well developed in succession, when they have the appearance of being dusted with gold; the scales, which are set on the swollen stem, are of a substantial character; the numerous imbricate parts, which are covered with long downy hairs pointing downwards, give the body of the flower a somewhat bulky appearance. It will be observed that I have made no mention of the Conyza traits of divided ray florets and reflexed scales, simply because they do not exist in this species, and though there are other Conyza traits about the plant, notwithstanding its almost isolating distinctions from other Erigerons, it would seem to have more properly the latter name, and which is most often applied to it. The flower stems, which produce the flowers singly, seldom exceed a height of 12in.; they are stout, round, and covered with soft hairs, somewhat bent downwards. They spring from the parts having new foliage, and for a portion—about half—of their length are furnished with small leaves, which differ from those on the non-floriferous parts of the shrub, inasmuch as they have no stalks. The leaves are produced in compact tufts on the extremities of the old or woody parts of the shrub, which become procumbent in aged specimens; the leaves vary in length from 2in. to 4in. long, and are roundly spoon-shaped, also slightly and distantly toothed, but only on the upper half; they are stout, ribbed, clammy, and glaucous. The habit of the shrub is much branching, dense, and prostrate; its foliage has a pleasant, mentha-like odour, and the flowers have a honey smell.

This subject may occupy such positions as rockwork, borders of the shrubbery, or beds of "old-fashioned" flowers. Its flowers, being, as taste goes at the present time, of a desirable form, will prove very serviceable as cut bloom. A good loam suits it to perfection, and no flower will better repay a good mulching of rotten manure. Its propagation, though easy, is somewhat special, inasmuch as its woody parts are stick-like and bare of roots, until followed down to a considerable depth, therefore the better plan is either to take advantage of its prostrate habit by pegging and embedding its branches, or, as I have mostly done, take cuttings with a part of the previous season's wood to them, put them well down in deeply-dug light soil, and make them firm. If this plan is followed, it should be done during the summer, so that the cuttings will have time to root before winter sets in. The layering may be done any time, but if in spring or summer, rooted plants will be ready for the following season.

This subject begins to flower in June, and, as already hinted, it produces two crops of flowers; the first are from the parts which have been green and leafy through the winter, the second from the more numerous growths of the new season, and which are grandly in bloom in August; not only are the latter more effective as regards numbers and colour, but the fuller habit or more luxuriant condition of the shrub render the specimens more effective in late summer.

## Eryngium Giganteum.

GREAT ERYNGO; *Nat. Ord.* UMBELLIFERÆ.

THIS hardy species was brought from the Caucasus in 1820. The genus, though not commonly patronised as garden subjects, are, nevertheless, highly ornamental, and when well grown much admired. Specimens are of various heights, according to position and nature of the soil; under ordinary conditions they will be 2ft. to 3ft. high at the blooming period.

As will be inferred from the order to which the Eryngium

FIG. 37. ERYNGIUM GIGANTEUM.
(One-tenth natural size.)

belongs, the flowers are aggregate, of a changeable blue, and arranged in cone-shaped heads 1½in. long; the heads are neatly embraced by an ample bract of prickly leaves; the main flower stem is well and evenly branched (see Fig. 37), each node being furnished with leaves which clasp the stems; they are, like those of the flower bract, deeply cut and prickly; the radical leaves are very different, long stalked, large heart-shaped and toothed, of good substance and a glossy green colour. The whole plant has a rather stiff appearance, the flower stems, together with the stem leaves, are of a pleasing hue, nearly the colour of blue note paper; this is characteristic of several of the genus, and adds greatly to their effect. Specimens look well with a grassy foreground or in borders.

Their culture is easy, provided the soil is of a light nature; a sunny position is needful, in order to have the tops well coloured. Propagate by division of strong and healthy clumps when dormant. Wireworm and grub are fond of the roots; when the plants appear sickly, these pests should be looked for.

Flowering period, August and September.

## Erysimum Pumilum.
FAIRY WALLFLOWER, *or* DWARF TREACLE-MUSTARD;
*Nat. Ord.* CRUCIFERÆ.

ONE of the alpine gems of our rock gardens, not in the sense of its rarity, because it grows and increases fast. It came from Switzerland about sixty years ago, and for a long time was esteemed as a biennial, but it is more—it is perennial and evergreen; at any rate its new branches take root, and so its perennial quality is established. Let the reader imagine a shrub, 3in. high, much branched, and densely furnished with pale green foliage, which hides all its woody parts, forming itself into cushions, more or less dotted over with minute canary-yellow flowers, and he will then only have a poor idea of the beauty of this pretty alpine. It flowers in summer, autumn, and winter, and in certain positions both its habit and flowers show to most advantage at the latter season. At no other time during the year have my specimens looked so fresh and beautiful as in January. This I have proved repeatedly to be the result of position, shortly to be explained.

The flowers are produced in terminal racemes, are scarcely ½in. across, cruciform in the way of the Wallflower, greenish-yellow, and delicately scented. The leaves vary in shape on the various parts of the branches, some being lance-shaped and others nearly spoon-shaped; the lower ones being all but entire, and the upper ones, which are arranged in rosettes, distinctly toothed. They seldom exceed an inch in length, more often they are only half that size, but much depends on the position and soil. In summer the foliage is greyish-green; later it is almost a bright or clear green, the latter being its present colour. The habit is branching and compact, by which it adapts itself to crevices and uneven parts in a pleasing manner; and not only does it best adorn such places, but from the fact of their dryness, they are better suited to the requirements of this little shrub.

A sandy loam, such as will not bake, suits, and if mixed with a few stones all the better—this will be found ample food for it; poor soil and a dry situation grow this subject in its finest form. I may perhaps usefully give the method by which my specimen is grown, after experimenting with it in various parts of the garden, and also the substance of a few notes I made of it. In pots the fine roots soon formed a matted coat next the sides, when the foliage would turn sickly and yellow, so that, useful as the practice is of growing alpines in pots, it does not answer in this case. On rockwork, in vegetable soil, this low shrub grew taller, being less woody, and was killed by severe weather. On the flat, in borders, in rich soil, it did well for a season, then damped off, a branch or two together. On the flat, in sand alone, it does well, also on the top of a wall, such being a position especially provided for hardy sempervivums and a few cacti. A bit of the Fairy Wallflower was tried there in a thin layer of sandy loam, and for two years my finest specimen has occupied that position, flowering more or less throughout the winter. Where there are old walls or rockwork it should be introduced. A ready and effective way of planting it is to get a sod of grass 3in. thick; measure with the eye the size of the interstice in the side of a wall, partly cut through the sod on the earthy side, open it by bending, and insert the roots of a small specimen; close up, and cram the planted sod tightly into the selected opening. In one season the shrub so planted will have a snug and pretty appearance. It is self-propagating, from the fact of its lower branches rooting where they touch the soil. These may be taken any time and planted separately.

Flowering period, April to winter.

## Erythronium Dens-canis.

DOG'S-TOOTH VIOLET; *Nat. Ord.* LILIACEÆ.

A HARDY bulbous perennial. There are several varieties of this species, and all are very handsome.

The variety shown at Fig. 38 is the large white-flowering kind; others have yellow, pale purple, and lilac-coloured blooms. All are produced singly on stems 4in. or 5in. long, and gracefully bending. During bright weather the divisions of the lily-like flowers become reflexed and otherwise show themselves to advantage. Their foliage forms a rich setting for the flowers, being variously coloured with red, brown, and different shades of green, all charmingly blended or marbled. The leaves are broad and oval, and open out flatly, so that their beauties can be well seen; if they are grown amongst the very dwarf sedums or mosses, they look all the better and are preserved from splashes. Two leaves, one stem, one flower, and one bulb constitute a whole plant; both flowers and foliage remain in beauty for a long time.

I have them growing in various positions and soils, and I think they most enjoy a vegetable mould, with full exposure to the sun, but they should not lack moisture; they seem to increase

Fig. 38. ERYTHRONIUM DENS-CANIS.
(Large white variety. One-half natural size.)

more rapidly in peat than in any other compost. They should not be disturbed more than necessary, and when they are, autumn is the best time to transplant.
Flowering period, March and April.

## Euonymus Japonicus Radicans Variegata.
VARIEGATED ROOTING SPINDLE TREE;
*Nat. Ord.* CELASTRACEÆ.

IT is probable that the genus *Euonymus* is more generally known than that of *Celastrus*, from which the order takes its name;

besides, the latter is composed of unfamiliar genera, so it is more likely that the reader will not care about any reference to them; it may concern him more to know that the above somewhat long name belongs to a very dwarf hardy evergreen shrub, having a neat habit and very beautiful foliage. This variety is one of many forms which come under the name *E. japonicus*, none of which, however, have long been cultivated in this country, the date of the introduction of the type being 1804. The genus is remarkable for the number of its species having ornamental foliage, and not less so, perhaps, for the insignificance of their flowers. The species under notice (*E. japonicus*) in cultivation has proved sportive, which habit has been taken advantage of, whence the numerous forms, including the one I have selected for these remarks. Some of the Spindle Trees do not flower in this climate, and others, which do, produce no seed; these facts are in connection with the more finely leaf-marked sorts, and it may be inferred that such unfruitfulness arises from their hybrid nature or abnormal tendency, as seen in " sports."

The typical form is a tree growing 20ft. high, producing small white flowers, but of the variegated kind under notice established specimens have ever failed to show the least sign of flowering, though otherwise well developed and of good habit. The leaves are nearly oval, ½in. to 1½in. long, sometimes oblong, sharply serrulated, of stout leathery substance, smooth, and much variegated in colour. The markings are mostly on and near the edges, and take the form of lines and marblings. The tints are a mixture of white, yellow, and pink, inclining to purple; these are variously disposed on a dark green ground. The arrangement of the leaves is crowded and panicled on the recent shoots, which are twice and thrice branched; from the shortness and twisted shape of the leaf stalks, the branchlets have a compressed appearance. The old stems are round, wiry, 9in. to 18in. long, prostrate, and emit roots like the ivy when they come in contact with suitable surfaces, whence the name "*radicans*." The habit of the shrub, from its dense and flattened foliage, fine colour, and persistent nature, together with its dwarfness and rooting faculty, all go to render it one of the finest rock shrubs for winter effect. The wetness of our climate only seems to make it all the brighter, and it is also without that undesirable habit of rooting and spreading immoderately.

It enjoys a sunny situation and enriched sandy loam. Where such conditions exist it may be planted with good effect as a permanent edging to walks or beds; as such it may be clipped once or twice a year, but I may add that it is worth the extra time required for pruning with a knife, as then the leaves are not cut in two and the outline is left less formal. By such treatment the foliage is kept thick to the base of the shrub. The summer prunings may be pricked into sandy loam in a shady part, where they will root and become useful stock for the following spring, or strong examples may be pulled to pieces of the desired size.

## Festuca Glauca.
BLUE GRASS; *Nat. Ord.* GRAMINEÆ.

THIS comes from the warm climate of Southern Europe, but is a perfectly hardy grass in this country; it is highly ornamental, irrespective of its flowers, and is useful in several ways. With me it is grown somewhat largely, and both professional and amateur gardeners have quickly appreciated its effectiveness, but it has been amusing to see their want of faith when told that "it stands out all winter." It belongs to a section of grasses of fine quality as fodder for cattle, all enjoying good soil of a light and rich nature. Its main features as a garden subject are its distinct blue colour and dense graceful habit; these qualities, however, are greatly dependent on the quality of soil, which must be positively rich. Its bloom is of no value ornamentally, being much like that of some of our common meadow grasses, and it will be as well to remove it in order that the grass may be all the brighter and more luxuriant. The blades, if they can be so called, are reed-like, but very fine, 6in. to 12in. long, densely produced, and gracefully bending. The glaucous quality is most pronounced, and quite justifies the common name Blue Grass. More need not be said to show that this must be effective in a garden, especially where bedding and the formation of bold lines are carried out; as single tufts, on rockwork, or in the borders, it looks well; whilst as an edging to taller grasses and bamboos it shows all to advantage. It is also often grown in pots in greenhouses, where it proves useful for drooping over the edges of the stage; but if it once obtains a place in the garden and is well grown, the amateur will see in it a suitable subject for many and varied uses.

Wherever it is planted the soil should be made sandy and fat with manure; in this the long roots are not only warmer, but they amply support a rapid growth and metallic lustre. As the roots can easily be lifted from the light soil without damage, this grass may be divided any time when increase is needful.

Flowering period, summer.

## Fritillaria Armena.
*Nat. Ord.* LILIACEÆ.

A CHARMING little hardy bulbous perennial, which, although as yet a comparative stranger in this country, bids fair to find a place not only in our gardens, but in the list of the choicest spring favourites, such as lily of the valley, snowdrops, snowflake, and squills, being of the same or nearly allied order, as well as of corresponding stature. Its yellow flowers, too, highly commend it, as, with the exception of the yellow crocus, we have not a very dwarf spring flower of the kind, and, as may be seen by the illustration (Fig. 39), it differs widely from the crocus in every way.

This is a really charming species; its dark yellow flowers are large for so small a plant, being more than an inch across when expanded by sunshine, but its more common form is bell-shape; one, and sometimes more flowers are produced on the upright, smooth, leafy stem, which is less than 6in. high. The leaves are alternate linear, sharply pointed, smooth, and glaucous. Such dwarf flowers always show to most advantage, as well as keep cleaner, where carpeted with suitable vegetation; the dark green *Herniaria glabra* would be perfection for this glaucous plant.

FIG. 39. FRITILLARIA ARMENA.
(One-half natural size.)

It seems happy where growing fully exposed in ordinary garden soil, but it is not unlikely that it may require more shade, in common with other Fritillaries, for, as before hinted, it is yet in its trial stage. I am, however, pretty certain of its hardiness, but not about the best mode of culture and propagation.

Flowering period, April and May.

## Funkia Albo-marginata.
*Common Name*, WHITE-EDGED PLANTING-LEAVED LILY;
*Nat. Ord.* LILIACEÆ.

A HARDY herbaceous perennial from Japan, of but recent introduction, than which there are few more useful subjects to be found in our gardens. It combines with its wealth of foliage a bold spike of pleasing lilac flowers, the former, as implied by the specific name, being edged with a white line, which is broad and constant, this quality being all the more commendable from the fact that many variegations are anything but reliable. Speaking of this as a decorative plant for the garden, it may be said to be one of the best; however placed, it has a neatness and beauty which are characteristic, especially when used in lines, and has become well established; from early spring, when the fresh young leaves appear, until the autumn is well advanced, this plant upholds a fine appearance independent of its flowers; they are,

however, not wanting in beauty, produced as they are on stems nearly 2ft. high, and nude with the exception of one or two very small leaves. The floral part of the stem will be 8in. or more in length; the flowers are numerous, 2in. long, trumpet-shaped, drooping, and so arranged that all fall in one direction; the colour is lilac, with stripes of purple and white; each flower is supported by a bract, which, like the foliage, is margined with white. The leaves are 6in. to 8in. long, oval-lanceolate, waved and ribbed, of a dark green colour, margined with white; the leaf stalks are stout, 6in. long, and broadly channelled.
Flowering period, June to August.

## Funkia Sieboldii.

SIEBOLD'S PLANTING-LEAVED LILY; *Nat. Ord.* LILIACEÆ.

THIS is a grand plant; the lily-like flowers alone are sufficient to commend it, but when we have them springing from such a glorious mass of luxuriant and beautiful foliage, disposed with a charming neatness rarely equalled, they are additionally effective. The illustration (Fig. 40) gives a fair idea of the form and dimensions of a specimen three years ago cut from the parent plant, when it would not have more than two or three crowns, so it may be described as very vigorous; and, as if its beauties were not sufficiently amplified by flowers and form of foliage, the whole plant is of a rich glaucous hue, rendering it still more conspicuous and distinct. It is herbaceous and perfectly hardy, though it comes from the much warmer climate of Japan, whence are all the species of *Funkia*. It is a comparatively new plant in English gardens, having been introduced into this country only about fifty years; still, it is pretty widely distributed, thanks, doubtless, to its exceptionally fine qualities. I know no plant more capable of improvement as regards size than this; if set in rich deep soil, it will in a few years grow to an enormous specimen. One so treated in my garden is 4ft. to 5ft. in diameter, and about the same height when the flower-stems are fully developed. I should, however, add that this is an unusual size, but it, neverthelesss, indicates what may be done by high culture.

The flowers are produced on nude stems, 2ft. or 4ft. high, being arranged in somewhat short and irregular one-sided spikes; they spring singly from the axils of rather long bracts (see Fig. 40) and have long bending pedicels, which cause the flowers to hang bell fashion; their colour is a soft pale lilac, nearly white. Size, 1in. to 2in. long, and bell or trumpet shaped. They are of good substance, and last a long time in fine form. The leaves have radical stalks, nearly 2ft. long in well-grown specimens, gracefully bending and deeply channelled; they are from 8in. to 12in. long, and about half as wide, long heart-shaped, somewhat hooded, waved, distinctly ribbed, and evenly wrinkled; glaucous and leathery. The outer foliage is so disposed that the tips touch the ground; it is abundantly produced, forming massive tufts.

FIG. 40. FUNKIA SIEBOLDII.
(One-eighth natural size.)

The long fleshy roots denote its love of a deep soil; a moist but well-drained situation suits it, and manure may be used—both dug in and as a top dressing—with marked advantage. The natural beauty of this subject fits it for any position—the lawn, shrubbery, borders, beds, or rockwork can all be additionally beautified by its noble form; grown in pots, it becomes an effective plant for the table or conservatory. The flowers in a cut state are quaint and graceful, and the leaves are even more useful; these may be cut with long stalks and stood in vases in twos and threes without any other dressing, or, when desired, a few large flowers may be added for a change, such as a panicle of *Spiræa aruncus*, a large sunflower, or a spike or two of gladioli. Leaves so cut may be used for weeks; after they have become dusty they may be sponged, when they will appear fresh, like new-cut ones.

In the propagation of this plant certain rules should be observed, otherwise the stock of young plants will prove stunted and bad in colour. Do not divide any but strong and healthy clumps, taking care not to damage more roots than can be helped; do not divide too severely, but let each part be a strong piece of several crowns, and after this they should be allowed to make three years' growth in a good, rich, deep soil before they are again disturbed, and thereby the stock will not only be of a vigorous character, but always fit for use in the most decorative parts of the garden.

Flowering period, July to September.

## Galanthus Elwesii.

ELWES'S GALANTHUS or SNOWDROP; *Nat. Ord.*
AMARYLLIDACEÆ.

THIS is a splendid species or variety, whichever it may be, said to be the finest of all the Snowdrops; it is a new kind and not yet much known. My impressions of it last spring were not in accordance with such reports, but I ought to add that, though the bulbs were fresh when sent me, they had only been planted less than a year, when they flowered somewhat feebly.

Flowering period, February and March.

All the Snowdrops may be propagated by seed or division of crowded clumps—after all the tops have died off is the proper time; the longer the delay, the worse for next season's bloom, as new root action sets in about that period.

## Galanthus Imperati.

IMPERIAL SNOWDROP; *Nat. Ord.* AMARYLLIDACEÆ.

I HAVE only recently flowered this kind. It is said by Mr. W. Robinson to be double the size of *G. nivalis*, which estimate is probably correct, judging from the blooms which I have obtained. With me the bulbs seem either not to have a happy home, or they may have suffered from the vicissitudes of transport from the genial climate of Italy. The publisher of this book informs me that he flowered *G. imperati* the first year in the open borders, from some bulbs procured from Messrs. Collins Bros., and that the blossoms were highly scented, as of elder flowers.

Flowering period, February and March.

## Galanthus Nivalis.

COMMON SNOWDROP, EARLY BULBOUS VIOLET, *and* FAIR MAIDS OF FEBRUARY; *Nat. Ord.* AMARYLLIDACEÆ.

ONE of the most charming members of the British flora; a native of our fields and orchards, so beautiful as to be beyond description, and, fortunately, so common as to need none (see Fig. 41). It belongs to a noble order of bulbous plants, the

FIG. 41. GALANTHUS NIVALIS.
(One-half natural size.)

genera of which are numerous, as are the species too, in perhaps an increased proportion. Comparatively few are hardy in our climate, and very few indeed are natives of this country, so that in this respect the Snowdrop, if not a rare flower, is a rare representative in our flora of the order *Amaryllidaceæ*.

It may be useful to give a few of the better-known genera to which *Galanthus* is so nearly related: *Amaryllis, Nerine, Crinum, Vallota, Pancratium, Alstrœmeria,* and *Narcissus.* The last-named genus is more nearly allied than any of the other genera mentioned; not only does it resemble the Galanthus in style, early period of bloom, and habit of becoming double, but also for the general hardiness of its species, a feature not usual in their order.

The literal meaning of the generic name is "Milk Flower." The title with such a pleasing reference was given by Linnæus. The specific name—meaning white—may, for two reasons, seem unnecessary; first, because milk is white, and again, because no other than white-flowered species are known. All the three common names are happy ones: "Snowdrop" and "Fair Maids of February" are appropriate both to the season and a pretty flower; "Bulbous Violet" pleasantly alludes to its sweetness; all are poetical, as if this lovely flower had the same effect on the different minds of those (including Linnæus) who first gave them. A dropped name for the Snowdrop was that of "Gilloflower"; Theophrastus, the father of natural history, gave it the name of "Violet" (*Viola alba* or *V. bulbosa*)—that would be 2100 years ago! The bulbs should be planted by thousands; they will grow anywhere and in any kind of soil; the demand for their blossom is ever increasing, and Snowdrops, as everybody knows, are always in place, on the grass, border, or window sill, or for table; they may be used as emblems of either grief or joy; they are sweetly pure and attractive, without showiness.

Flowering period, February to April.

## Galanthus Plicatus.

FOLDED GALANTHUS; *Nat. Ord.* AMARYLLIDACEÆ.

A SPECIES from the Crimea; compared with our native kind, it is larger in the grass, having also other, but very slight, points of difference. The main one is implied by its name, "plicatus," or folded; its leaves are furrowed, which causes it to have a folded appearance.

Culture and flowering period, the same as for the other species.

## Galanthus Redoutei.

REDOUTE'S GALANTHUS; *Nat. Ord.* AMARYLLIDACEÆ.

THIS is by far the most distinct form, having broad grass-green foliage. It is somewhat late in flowering (during March and April), and not so free as others.

## Galax Aphylla.

*Syn.* BLANDFORDIA CORDATA; HEART-LEAVED GALAX;
*Nat. Ord.* PYROLACEÆ.

NEARLY 100 years ago this charming little plant was imported from North America; still, it is rarely seen, notwithstanding that rock-gardens have long been popular. On rockwork it not only thrives well, but appears to great advantage. No rock-garden should be without it. It is a rare and beautiful subject, remarkably distinct and pleasing; it is perfectly hardy, also

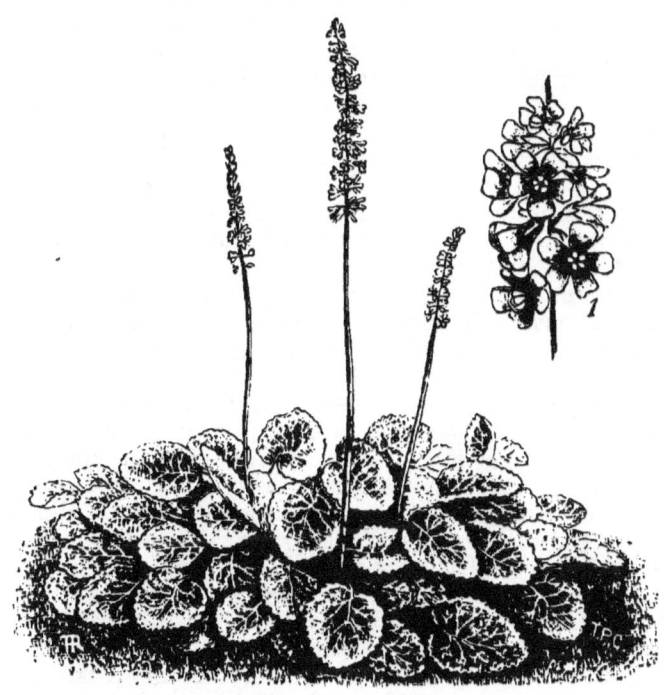

FIG. 42. GALAX APHYLLA.
(One-sixth natural size; 1, natural size.)

perennial and herbaceous; but its last-named characteristic should be qualified, inasmuch as the old leaves remain in good form and colour until long after the new ones are fully grown, so that there are always two sets of foliage. Viewed in this light, it may be called an evergreen plant; moreover, it is one of those plants which the artist can scarcely do justice to, for though the illustration (Fig. 42) depicts faithfully its neat habit and handsome foliage, the living plant makes a better impression. I said it was rare, but this is less in the sense of scarcity than because it is little known and seldom seen; it is also quite distinct from any other plant, and the only species of the genus.

Its milk-white flowers, which, though very simple, are richly effective, are produced on tall, nude stems, 18in. high, round, wiry, and nearly amber-coloured. They are arranged in a dense spike, 6in. to 8in. long.; the corolla is $\frac{1}{4}$in. across, and composed of five petals; the calyx has a short tube and five sepals; the leaves are heart-shaped, nearly round, evenly toothed, and sometimes glandular; of leathery substance, and somewhat stiff, smooth, shining, and richly veined or nerved. The leaves of various ages differ in colour; the old ones are dark green, conspicuously reticulated; the new, but perfectly-developed ones, are pale green, with a ray of yellowish-green next the edges; the growing ones are nearly red, and all the serrated edges are hemmed with a nearly scarlet line, always brightest at the points of the teeth. This finely-tinted foliage is elegantly disposed by means of the stalks, which bend in various ways; they vary in length from 4in. to 8in., and are all radical; they are round, wiry, and once grooved. The bloom lasts for several weeks in good form, and the foliage is always beautiful, more especially in the autumn, when it glows like polished mahogany. Such a plant can hardly fail to please when well grown, but it must be so developed.

This lovely plant certainly requires a little special treatment, but that is easy and simple; in fact, it scarcely can be called special. It may be put in a few words—damp, but not sour vegetable soil, and very slight shade. My specimen, from which the drawing was taken, is growing in a little dip at the base of a small rockery, below the level of the walk, which acts as a watershed; the soil is nearly all leaf mould—a small portion of loam, and I ought to add that there is a moderate quantity of small charcoal incorporated with it, which will doubtless assist in keeping the soil sweet. There cannot, therefore, be much difficulty in setting up these conditions; the charcoal may not be necessary, but an annual top-dressing with it will meet the case of such plants as grow in low damp situations. The propagation of this species is very easy in the case of well-grown clumps, which, when dug up in the autumn and thoroughly shaken, will come asunder into many small and well-rooted crowns; these only require to be replanted separately, under similar conditions to those by which they were produced. No attempt should be made to divide other than perfectly healthy clumps.

Flowering period, July and August.

## Galega Officinalis.
OFFICINAL GOAT'S-RUE; *Nat. Ord.* LEGUMINOSÆ.

A GRAND "old-fashioned" flower. It is 314 years since this plant was brought from Spain; it is perfectly hardy and herbaceous. Both it and its varieties are among the most useful subjects of the flower garden; they grow to shrub-like bushes, have elegant foliage, and an abundance of bloom, which continues until late autumn. Specimens have a clean and healthy appearance, and though they grow to the height of 4ft., they give no trouble, requiring neither tying nor supports. From their large quantities of flowers they are exceedingly gay; but it is for the handsome stems in a cut state that they should be most prized. These, cut 18in. long, and placed singly in pots or vases, are truly noble, more especially by gaslight.

As will be inferred from the order to which *Galega* belongs, the flowers are pea-flower-shaped, about ½in. or more long, and the same broad. They are of a pleasing, but undecided blue colour, arranged in long conical racemes, on stout, round stalks, as long as the leaves, which are pinnate, having a terminal odd one. The leaflets are evenly arranged in pairs, mostly in six pairs; they are each about 2in. long, lance-shaped, mucronate, entire, smooth, and glaucous. The floriferous character of the plant may be inferred from the fact that, after the raceme fades, there pushes from the axil a peduncle, which, in a short time, produces many other racemes.

*G. o. alba*, a variety of the above, grows 4ft. high, and is an abundant bloomer; flowers superb for cutting purposes. For culture, see *G. Persica lilacina*.

Flowering period, July to September.

## Galega Persica Lilacina.
*Nat. Ord.* LEGUMINOSÆ.

THIS is a lovely species of *Galega* imported little more than fifty years ago from Persia. Perfectly hardy; in general form it corresponds with *G. officinalis*. The following are its distinctions: More dense racemes of lilac flowers, a foot less tall, leaflets shorter and broader—in fact, oval, oblong, somewhat twisted or edged up in the arrangement, and often without the terminal leaflet.

The above Goat's-rues are of the simplest culture; they will do in any soil, but if they are liberally treated they will repay it. A fat loam and sunny situation are what they delight in. They may remain year after year in one position, but I find them to do better in every way if they are divided the second year; it should be done in summer, so that they can make a little growth in their new quarters before winter sets in. In order to carry out this, the older plants (I divide half my stock one year, the other half the year following) should be cut over near the ground, though they may be in full bloom. Divide the roots into several strong pieces, and replant them in soil deeply dug and where they are intended to flower; they will bloom finely the following season.

Flowering period, July to September.

## Gentiana Acaulis.
GENTIANELLA; *Nat. Ord.* GENTIANACEÆ.

A HARDY, evergreen creeper, its creeping stems running immediately under the surface. This is a remarkably beautiful plant, and the wonder is that it is not grown in every garden. The most attractive features, when in flower, of this dwarf Gentian are its immensely large blooms and neat shining green foliage (see Fig. 43). It is easily identified, there being not another

FIG. 43. GENTIANA ACAULIS.
(One-fourth natural size.)

species like it, and certainly very few to equal it for beauty and service; it forms one of the best edgings for beds and borders. Many report that it is difficult to grow, which may be the case in some gardens from one cause or other, whilst in many places it runs like quick-grass.

Flowers, dark bright blue, large, long bell-shaped, but not drooping; tube, five-angular, nearly 3in. long; corolla, five-limbed, and an inch or more wide; the stems are seldom more than 3in. long, square, furnished with small opposite leaves, and terminated with one flower on each. That part of the foliage which sends up the flower is arranged in rosette form, the leaves being stout, flat, and acutely lance-shaped. Anywhere or everywhere may this subject be planted; it is always bright, even in winter, and when there are no flowers upon it it forms a rich covering for the otherwise bare ground; its blooms will each keep good a week. They are rarely produced in great numbers at one time, but the plants will continue for a long while to yield them sparingly.

I find *G. acaulis* to thrive well at the base of rockwork, as an edging to a flat bed, and in the gutters of the garden walks—it likes moisture. To me this is clearly proved by other plants, which, in all respects but one, are treated the same, the exceptional condition being that they are planted on the sloping face of rockwork, where they scarcely grow and never bloom. With reference to soil, rich or silky loam is best for it, but any kind, if sweet and retentive, will do. Its propagation may be effected by division of the rooted creeping stems after they have made four leaves. Very early in spring is a good time to do this, but neither these nor the old plant, if it has been much disturbed, will flower the same season after being so mutilated.

Flowering period, May to July.

## Gentiana Asclepiadea.

SWALLOW-WORT-LEAVED GENTIAN; *Nat. Ord.* GENTIANACEÆ.

A TALL and beautiful alpine species from Austria, very hardy and herbaceous. It has long had a place in English gardens—fully 250 years—and is described by Parkinson in his "Paradise of Flowers." The tall stems are very showy, having an abundance of shining dark green foliage, amongst which nestle the large and bright purple-blue flowers; it is a subject that looks well at a distance, and, as a rule, flowers with that quality are of the greatest value for borders and cutting purposes.

It grows nearly 2ft. high; the stems are round, erect, short-jointed, and very leafy; the flowers are produced on a third of their length, they are stalkless, and spring from the axils of the leaves in pairs; the calyx is ½in. long, tubular, angled, and having fang-shaped segments; the corolla is also tubular and angled, somewhat bellied, the divisions being deeply cut and reflexed; the whole flower will be fully 1½in. long. The inside of the corolla is striped with white and various shades of blue and purple. The leaves are 2in. long, oval, lance-shaped, distinctly ribbed, somewhat lobed at the base, and stem-clasping, which gives the pair of leaves a joined or perfoliate appearance; the nodes are short, or near together, the lower ones being the more distant, where also the leaves are much smaller; the foliage is a glossy dark green colour, the whole plant having a sombre but rich effect.

From the fact that the long stems are top-heavy and of a brittle character, a sheltered position should be given to this plant, or the wind will snap them off. It ought not to have stakes, as they would mar its good form. A fat loam and a moist situation will suit this Gentian to perfection, and it may be planted with other strong herbaceous things in the borders, where it should be allowed to grow to large specimens. It is one of the quickest growers of its genus, few species of which can be grown in too large quantities. When it is needful to increase this subject, it may be done more readily than the propagation of some Gentians—the roots are more easily separated. It should, however, be carefully done, and early spring is the best time; or if the autumn should be a dry season and the tops die off early, it may be done then.

Flowering period, July and August.

## Gentiana Burseri.
BURSER'S GENTIAN; *Nat. Ord.* GENTIANACEÆ.

A HARDY perennial species, of a bold but neat habit, while the flowers and foliage combine in rendering it a first-class decorative subject. It is a recent introduction, having been brought from the Pyrenees in 1820; it is seldom seen in flower gardens, where it certainly deserves to be.

Its flowers are not brilliant, but they are effective from their size, number, and persistency; they are produced in whorls on stout round stems 18in. high, but only on the three or four upper joints. Each flower is 1½in. long, lemon-yellow, tubular, angular, having four to six segments, widely separated, and furnished with a membrane at each separation. The segments, and also the tube, are dotted with dark brown spots; each flower is tightly folded in a somewhat one-sided membranous calyx and borne erect. They occur in pairs mostly, but with several pairs in a whorl. They have very short pedicels, and the whorl is supported by a bract of stem-clasping leaves, cupped, and variously shaped, as ovate and beaked; there are also supplementary bracteoles. The leaves of the root very much resemble the plantain leaf, also that of *G. lutea*, having longish ribbed and grooved petioles or stalks; they are 5in. to 6in. long, and over 3in. broad, egg-shaped, entire, veined longitudinally, and slightly wrinkled; they are of a dark green colour, shining, and of good substance. The leaves of the stems, as already stated, are stem-clasping, and differ in shape. The flowers keep in good form for two or three weeks, and otherwise this rigid bright-foliaged Gentian proves very ornamental.

I find it to do well in vegetable soil in a moist quarter. Most of the members of this genus enjoy plenty of moisture at their roots, and this specimen is no exception. A flat stone will form a good substitute for a damp situation if placed over the roots; besides, such a method of growing this and others of the tall Gentians will allow of their being planted on

I

rockwork, or otherwise, near the more frequented walks, where they must always prove pleasing from their bold and shining foliage, to say nothing of their striking flowers. The propagation of this species should be effected by division of the roots, which are very strong. Each crown should have as much of the more fibrous roots retained as possible, and the parts to be severed should be cut with a very sharp knife; it also ripens seed plentifully.

Flowering period, June to August.

## Gentiana Cruciata.

CROSS-LEAVED GENTIAN; *Nat. Ord.* GENTIANACEÆ.

AN interesting species from Austria, and one of the "old-fashioned" plants of English gardens, having been cultivated in this country for nearly 300 years. Gerarde gives a faithful and full description of it, which I will quote: "Crossewoort Gentian hath many ribbed leaues spred upon the ground, like unto the leaues of sopewroot, but of a blacker green colour; among which rise vp weak iointed stalks, trailing or leaning towarde the grounde. The flowers growe at the top in bundels, thicke thrust togither, like those of sweete Williams, of a light blew colour. The roote is thicke, and creepeth in the grounde farre abroade, whereby it greatly increaseth." Its height seldom exceeds 10in., and it is to be commended because it is one of the Gentians that are easily grown, and is handsome withal. It may be planted in either vegetable or loamy soil—the common border seems to suit it; it spreads much faster than any of the other Gentians I know, with the exception of *G. acaulis*, and it is in broad masses one sees it to greatest advantage. Propagated by division any time.

Flowering period, June and July.

## Gentiana Gelida.

ICE-COLD GENTIAN; *Nat. Ord.* GENTIANACEÆ.

THIS species comes from Siberia, and has been grown in this country for nearly eighty years. It is a very beautiful species, the whole plant being handsome; it grows nearly a foot high.

The flowers are produced in terminal clusters, one large flower being surrounded by a whorl of smaller ones; they are of a rich purplish-blue inside the corolla, which is rotate; the segments (mitre-shaped) and the spaces between are prettily furnished with a feathery fringe; the wide tube is also finely striped inside; the calyx is tubular, having long awl-shaped segments; the stems are procumbent, firm (almost woody), short jointed, and thickest near the top. The leaves are of a dark shining green colour, from 1½in. to 2in. long, smallest at the root end, and finishing next the flowers with the largest, which are lance-

shaped, the lower ones being heart-shaped; they are closely
arranged in pairs, are sessile, and at right angles with the stem.
It seems to enjoy a shady damp corner in rockwork, where its
distinct forms and neat habit appear to advantage. It should be
planted in vegetable soil, such as peat or well-decayed leaves
mixed with sand. It cannot endure drought at the roots. It is
a slow-growing plant, but very floriferous; the flowers last fully
a fortnight in good form, the weather, however rough or wet,
seeming to have no effect on them. In a cut state it is exquisite,
but those who properly value the Gentians, especially the slow
growers, will hardly care to cut away the stems, as, by doing so,
not only will the plant be checked, but next year's growth will
prove reduced in both number and vigour. It is propagated by
root division when in a dormant state. I have also successfully
transplanted this kind after it has made considerable growth,
but the roots have been carefully guarded against dryness.
Flowering period, June to August.

## Gentiana Verna.

SPRING ALPINE FELWORT; *Nat. Ord.* GENTIANACEÆ.

A NATIVE evergreen creeper. This plant has many synonymous names in old books. It is now, however, well known by
the above Latin name. Let me at once say that it is a matchless
gem. Its flowers are such as to attract the notice of any but a
blind person. It is said to be rare now in this country, still, I
think it is far from being extinct in its wild state. Be that as it
may, it is fortunate that it can be easily cultivated, and nothing
in a garden can give more pleasure. Its flowers are blue—but
such a blue! the most intense, with a large and sharply defined
white eye, and though only ½in. across, one on each stem, and
3in. high, they are grandly effective. It has a tubular, angled
calyx; corolla five-cut. The leaves are oval, nearly 1in. long, and
half as broad; dark shining green and of leathery substance.
The radical leaves are crowded into a nearly rosette form.

By many this Gentian is considered difficult to grow, but if a
proper beginning is made it proves to be of the easiest management. Very suitable places may be found for it in, not *on*, rockwork, where good fat loam forms the staple soil; little corners,
not *above* the ground level, but on, or better still, *below* the
ground level, are sure to meet its requirements; on the edge of
a border, too, where moisture collects in the small gutter, has
proved a suitable position for it. But, perhaps, the most suc-
cessful way of growing it is in pots, for, as with *Trientalis
Europa* and other root creepers, when so treated more compact
specimens are obtained. It is important to begin with properly-
rooted plants, the crowns of which are often 2in. to 3in. below
the surface; from these spring the numerous, bare, yellow, wiry

stems, too often taken for roots, whereas the main roots are still deeper, very long for so small a plant, and furnished with silky feeders. Good crowns potted in rich fibrous loam and plunged in sand, fully exposed, with an unstinted supply of water, is the substance of the simple treatment my plants receive the year round; they are still in the 3in. and 4in. pots in which they were placed three years ago, and during spring they are covered with flowers. When a pot is lifted out of the sand in which it is plunged, the fine long silky roots are seen to have made their way through the hole. Spring is the best time to plant.

Flowering period, April to June.

## Geranium Argenteum.

SILVERY CRANE'S-BILL: *Nat. Ord.* GERANIACEÆ.

A HARDY perennial alpine from the South of Europe, introduced in 1699. It is, therefore, an old plant in this country, and is one

FIG. 44. GERANIUM ARGENTEUM.
(One-half natural size.)

of the gems of the rock garden; very dwarf, but effective, as may be seen by the illustration (Fig. 44). The foliage is of a distinct and somewhat conglomerate character, besides being of a silvery-grey colour. Well-grown specimens of this charming Crane's-bill look remarkably well against dark stones. Its flowers are large for so small a plant, and wherever it finds a suitable home it cannot fail to win admiration. In borders of rich soil it is grown to the height of about six inches, but in drier situations, as on the upper parts of rockwork, it is more dwarf.

The flowers are fully an inch in diameter when open, cup-shaped, and striped in two shades of rose colour; the unopened flowers are bell-shaped and drooping; they are borne on long naked pedicels, bent and wiry, oftentimes two on a stem; calyx five-cleft, segments concave; petals five, equal and evenly arranged. The leaves are produced on long, bent, wiry stalks, the outline is circular, but they are divided into five or seven lobes, which are subdivided and irregular, both in size and arrangement; they have a silky appearance, from being furnished with numerous fine hairs or down. The plant continues to flower for many weeks, but, as may be judged, it is, otherwise than when in flower, highly attractive. To lovers of ornamental bedding this must prove a first-rate plant. As an edging to beds or borders of choice things it would be pleasingly appropriate, and, indeed, anywhere amongst other dwarf flowers it could not be other than decorative.

It thrives well in a good depth of loam, its long tap-roots going a long way down. If, therefore, it is planted on rockwork, suitable provision should be made for this propensity. The propagation of the plant is not so easy, from the fact that it makes large crowns without a corresponding set of roots, and its seed is scarce and often taken by birds before ripened. Moreover, the seedlings do not always come true; still, it seems the only mode of propagation, unless the old plants have plenty of time allowed them to spread and make extra roots. Latterly I have gathered the seeds before the capsules burst—in fact, whilst green —and, after carrying them in the waistcoat pocket for a few days, they have been sown in leaf soil and sand, and germinated freely. When the seedlings have made a few leaves the deteriorated forms may be picked out readily.

Flowering period, May to July.

## Gillenia Trifoliata.

*Syn.* SPIRÆA TRIFOLIATA *and* S. TRILOBA—THREE-LEAVED GILLENIA; *Nat. Ord.* ROSACEÆ.

A HARDY herbaceous perennial from North America, imported in 1713. The main features about this plant are its elegant form and rich tints. The illustration (Fig. 45) may give some idea of the former quality, but to realise the latter the reader should see a living specimen in the form of a bold clump. There is a wild beauty about this subject which it is not easy to describe; as a flower it is insignificant, but the way in which the flowers are disposed on the slender stems, blending with a quaintly pretty foliage, neither too large nor dense, renders them effective in their way. It is, however, only as a whole that it can be considered decorative, and it should be well grown.

Although most nearly related to the spiræas the distinctions from that genus are very marked, notably the very slender stems

FIG. 45. GILLENIA TRIFOLIATA.
(One-sixth natural size; blossom, full size.)

and large flowers, which are produced singly on rather long-bending pedicels, almost as fine as thread, and, like the stems, of a bright brown (nearly ruddy) colour. The flowers form a lax panicle, interspersed with a little foliage. The calyx is a bright brown colour, rather large and bell-shaped. It contrasts finely with the five long, narrow petals, which are white, tinted with red; they are also irregular in form and arrangement, somewhat contorted. The leaves, as implied by the specific name, are composed of three leaflets; they have very short stalks, and the leaflets are all but sessile, lance-shaped, finely toothed or fringed, ribbed, and somewhat bronzed. Perhaps it is most useful in a cut state; the sprays, even if they have but one or two flowers on them, are charming for vase work. I may say the calyx is persistent, and after the petals have fallen they not only increase in size, but turn a fine red colour, and so render the sprays additionally effective.

To grow this plant well it should have a deep soil; it also loves moisture, and, as already hinted, partial shade; it is a steady grower, far from rampant, like the spiræas. This is a capital subject to grow near or under "leggy" shrubs and trees, where, in semi-shade, it is not only at home, but proves very attractive. It may be propagated by division, the best time being early in the year, just before growth commences.

Flowering period, June to August.

## Gynerium Argenteum.

PAMPAS or SILVERY GRASS; *Nat. Ord.* GRAMINEÆ.

THIS handsome grass is well known, at least, its feathery plumes are, from the fact of their being imported largely in a dry state for decorative purposes. It has not been grown long in this country, and, perhaps, it is not generally known that it endures our climate as an outdoor plant; in most parts of Great Britain, however, it proves hardy. As far north as Yorkshire I have seen it in the form of specimens 8ft. high; my own examples are yet young—two and three years old—and are only just beginning to flower, at the height of 3ft. to 4ft., diameter about the same. It is a native of South America, occurring mostly on the prairies; it is also found in other parts where there are swamps and high temperatures. This would lead us to have doubts as to its suitableness for English gardens, but facts prove it to have elastic qualities in this respect. It proves at all times to be a noble ornament in gardens of moderate size.

In its growing or green state it is a distinct and pleasing object, but it is at its greatest beauty when it has ripened its tall and silky plumes, which glisten in the sunshine and are of a silvery-grey colour, and when also the very long and narrow grass has become browned and falls gracefully, more or less curling under the tufts. All its parts are persistent, and, as a specimen of ripe grass, it is not only ornamental in itself, but it gives a warm effect to its surroundings during winter. Under favourable conditions it will grow 10ft. or 12ft. high, but it is seldom that it attains a height of more than 8ft. or 9ft. As an illustration (Fig. 46) is given, further description is not needed. I may add that if it is not "laid" by heavy snows, it keeps in good form until the new grass begins to grow in the following spring.

I find it to do well in light earth, well enriched with stable manure, the soil having a more than ordinary quantity of sand in it; the position is such as can have a good supply of moisture, being near walks that drain to it. In stiffish loam a strong clump was planted three years ago, but it has never looked

Fig. 46. Gynerium Argenteum.
(One-twentieth natural size.)

healthy. The best positions for it are well-prepared shrubbery borders; there it contrasts finely with the greenery, and receives some protection from the high winds. It may be increased by division of healthy roots, when the grass is ripe, but it ought not to be cut off.

The plumes appear in August, and will keep in good condition till the weather changes to a wintry character.

## Harpalium Rigidum.
*Syn.* HELIANTHUS RIGIDUS—RIGID SUNFLOWER;
*Nat. Ord.* COMPOSITÆ.

ONE of the most effective and beautiful flowers to be seen in autumn; it would be hard to mention another at any period of the year that gives more satisfaction and pleasure than this does, either as a decorative plant or a cut flower. A bold specimen, 4ft. through, is truly fine, and not only those who seldom visit a garden, but amateurs well versed in flowers, are alike charmed with its rich and stately blossoms. Most people know what a Sunflower is; many of them are coarse and almost ugly; but though the present subject is of the family, it is supremely distinct; it is without the formal character in its ray, and also the herby leafiness of many of its genus, its large, clean, shining, golden flowers, mounted on slender, ruddy, long, and nearly nude stalks, not only render it distinct, but impart an elegance to this species, which is all its own. It grows 4ft. high, is a comparatively new kind in English gardens, and comes from North America; still, it has become widely known and appreciated, in fact a universal favourite, so much so that, although it increases fast, the demand for it is not yet satisfied; it is, doubtless, a flower for every garden.

The flowers are 4in. across, glistening golden yellow, and formed of a deep ray and small disk; the florets of the ray are 1½in. long and more than ½in. broad, they are incurved at their points, but reflexed at their edges, and are handsomely ribbed or pleated; they are arranged in two or three rays in each flower, and irregularly disposed; the florets, being well apart, not only seem to give the bloom body, but also an artistic informality and lightness. The florets of the disk are chocolate colour, whence issue twirled filamentary forms, which impart to the centre of flower the appearance of being netted with a golden thread. The scaly involucre is formed of numerous small members of a dark olive-green colour, neatly arranged and firmly clasping the whole flower. The pedicels are long, round, covered with short stiff hairs, and thickened at the involucre; the stems are very rough, rigid, hard, and brown or ruddy on the sunny side, sometimes twisted and nude, with the exception of a solitary rudimentary leaf. The main stems have many axillary branches. The leaves of the root are few, 5in. or 6in. long, and oval. Those of the stems more lance-shaped, sessile, and slightly dentate, or toothed, lessening in size as they get higher; all the leaves are very thick, three-veined, and remarkably hispid, being almost as coarse as sandpaper to the touch. I have also observed another peculiarity about the leaves, when they have been taken from the plant for an hour or more, *i.e.*, they have a most elastic property. Very often the leaves may be seen in trios, whence spring three side branches, surrounding the upright and central one. The habit of the whole specimen is very rigid, with the exception of the flowers, which are slightly nodding; the tallest growths need no stakes, and the species enjoys a happy immunity from insect pests, probably by reason of its hispid character. As already stated, as a garden subject this is one of the most useful; it shows grandly in front of evergreens, and associates well with lilies. In borders of tall perennials, or in conspicuous but distant situations, such as are visible from the doors or windows of the house, or as isolated clumps, on or near the lawn, this fine Sunflower may be planted with satisfactory results; in fact, it cannot be planted wrong, provided it is kept away from small subjects. In a cut state it is of such value that it cannot be overpraised—a branch with four fully blown flowers and others nearly out, requires no assistance as a table decoration. Its blooms have the quality of keeping clean, doubtless from the smoothness of the florets.

The cultural requirements are few. Any garden soil will do for it, but if deeply dug and well enriched with stable manure, so much the better; it should have a fairly open situation; it is not only a Sunflower in name and form, but it enjoys sunshine. It is self-propagating, and runs freely at the roots, immediately under the surface; the thick stolons form knobby crowns at their extremities, out of and from under which the roots issue, going straight and deep down, and so forming an independent plant.

Flowering period, August and September.

## Hedera Conglomerata.

CONGLOMERATE IVY; *Nat. Ord.* ARALIACÆ.

I DO not introduce this as a flowering subject, but as a dwarf ornamental shrub; it differs so much from all other species and varieties of Ivy, and is so beautiful withal, that I trust no further apology is needed for giving it a place amongst decorative plants and shrubs. I have not been able to learn its habitat or origin; its stunted tree-like shape, together with other peculiarities, would indicate that it is a species; be that as it may, it has long had a place in English gardens, and yet it is seldom met with—it would be hard to explain why. On a bit of rockwork I have grown a specimen for nearly five years, and it was an old shrub when planted, yet it is not more than 2ft. in diameter and 1ft. high. It is much admired, and many notes have been taken of it. For rockwork, it is one of the best dwarf evergreen shrubs I know.

It has very small leaves, densely arranged in flat or one-sided wreaths. They seldom exceed 1in. in diameter, and are of various forms, as heart-shaped, sagittate, oval, tri-lobed, and so on. Some are notched, others slightly toothed, but many are entire. All are waved or contorted, wrinkled and thickened at the edges, where the younger leaves show a brown line; the under sides are pale green, and furnished with short stiff brown hairs, as also are the stout leaf stalks. The upper side of the foliage is a dark glossy green, with shadings of brown. In substance the leaves are leathery, inclining to stiffness. The stunted branches have a cork-like appearance as regards the bark, are diffuse, curiously bent, and sometimes twisted loosely together. It is of slow growth, more especially in the upward direction, and though provision may be made for it to cling and climb, and it has also well-formed roots on the branchlets, still, it assumes more the tree-shape. I never saw or heard of its flowering, much less that it ever produced seed; if it does not seed we are not only deprived of an ornamental feature belonging to the genus from the absence of berries, but it proves that it is only a variety of some species.

It may be grown in any kind of sandy soil, and nothing special whatever is needed. An open sunny situation will favour its form and colour of foliage; under trees I have found it to produce larger leaves of plainer shape and more even colour. During the winter it becomes a conspicuous object on rockwork, where it seems most at home. It may be propagated by cuttings, and spring is a suitable season to lay them in; in well dug light soil they soon make plenty of roots.

## Helianthus Multiflorus.

MANY-FLOWERED SUNFLOWER; *Nat. Ord.* COMPOSITÆ.

THIS fashionable flower is glaringly showy. Still, it is not wanting in beauty; moreover, it belongs to an " old-fashioned" class, and is itself a species which has been grown for nearly 300 years in English gardens. It was brought from North America in the year 1597, and during the whole of its history in this country, it can hardly ever have been more esteemed than it is to-day; it is very hardy, and in every way a reliable subject. Everybody knows the Sunflower, therefore no one will care to read a description of it; still, one or two remarks may, perhaps, be usefully made in the comparative sense, as this is a numerous genus. Many of the Sunflowers are annuals, to which this and others of a perennial character are much superior, not only in being less trouble and not liable to be out of season from mismanagement in sowing and planting, as with the annual sorts, but from the fact that their flowers are of better substance and far more durable; they are also less in size and more in number —two points of great gain as regards their usefulness as cut bloom. They are, besides, better coloured, and the flowering season more prolonged. Well-established specimens, two or three years old, will, in average weather, last in good form for fully six weeks. The colour (yellow) is common to the Sunflowers. This species has flowers which vary much in size, from 2in. to 6in. across, and they are produced on stems 3ft. to 6ft. high, well furnished with large heart-shaped leaves of a herb-like character, distinctly nerved, toothed, and rough.

Flowering period, August and September.

*H. m. fl.-pl.* is, of course, the double form of the above, the disk being represented by a mass of florets considerably shorter than those of the ray proper. The flowers are not produced in such large numbers as with the typical form, neither does the plant grow so tall, but the foliage is a little larger; these constitute all the points of difference which I have noticed. These forms of Sunflower are very effective—nowhere, perhaps, so much as amongst shrubs. The plants lift well, carrying a good ball that facilitates their being placed in pots even when in bloom, when, as I have lately seen, they may be used in a most telling manner with potted shrubs in large halls, corridors, and public buildings. In such places they get no sun to make them droop, and a good watering keeps them as fresh as if they had not been disturbed. Of the usefulness of this flower in a cut state nothing whatever need be said—who has not tried it? Doubtless, when it becomes unfashionable it will have fewer patrons, but it will be the same flower, richly beautiful—æsthetic. No special culture is needed, any kind of garden soil will suit it; if well enriched, all the better. Any situation will do but one too densely shaded. Propagated by splitting the roots after the plants have done flowering, or in spring.

Flowering period, August and September.

## Helianthus Orygalis.

GRACEFUL SUNFLOWER; *Nat. Ord.* COMPOSITÆ.

YET another Sunflower, and one, too, of the common yellow colour, and not otherwise attractive, as may be seen by the illustration (Fig. 47)—of course, I am now referring to the flower only. There are, however, features about this species which all must admire; stems 7ft. high, furnished with bright foliage, in the manner indicated, are not mean objects, even if topped with but a common yellow composite. This is a native of North America, and of recent introduction; it is a distinct species, and for foliage a prince among its fellows. I know not another to nearly approach it, *H. angustifolius* being perhaps the nearest, but that species has never with me proved of more than a biennial character, and its leaves, though long and narrow, are irregular and herby.

The flowers need not be further described beyond saying that they are borne on short side shoots, near the top of the main stems, but they harmonise with the general arrangement of foliage, and, indeed, from their bract-like leafiness, somewhat enrich it. This is one of the latest-blooming Sunflowers. The leaves are 5in. to 8in. long, and ½in. to 1in. wide, the lower half on the stems droop, though they are of good substance; the upper half bend gracefully, and, from their close arrangement, all but hide the stem. At the axils of the larger leaves, tufts of

FIG. 47. HELIANTHUS ORYGALIS.
(One-eighth natural size; flower, one-fourth natural size.)

smaller (much smaller) leaves appear, causing the long stems to be top-heavy. Still, they wave and bend during the strongest winds without supports or damage. It will be seen that the usefulness of this plant consists in its distinct form and tallness, and that it is effective is without doubt. Among low shrubs, or with other tall things, will prove suitable quarters for it.

Any kind of soil will do, shelter from the wind being the most important, and perhaps the only point to study when planting. It is propagated by root divisions when the tops have withered.

Flowering period, September and October.

## Helleborus Abchasicus.

ABCHASIAN HELLEBORE; *Nat. Ord.* RANUNCULACEÆ.

THIS is a native of the Caucasus, and in this climate, where it has been cultivated about fifteen years, it retains its foliage through the winter in a green state. It is a free grower, and flowers well, having a somewhat slender habit. It is sometimes described as having green flowers, but more often as having purple ones. It may be useful to remember that there are varieties, and it is likely that, even in the so-called green flowers, traces of purple will be seen. Not only is it a fact that this species, like *H. purpurascens* and *H. niger*, is far from fixed as regards depth of colour, but it is said to be one of the parent forms of some of the fine hybrids. These considerations may help to reconcile the apparently conflicting descriptions as regards bloom colour.

The flower stems are 12in. to 18in. high, distantly forked twice, and of a purplish colour. The flowers are produced in threes and fours on each of the branchlets, are inclined to purple, over 2in. across, and nodding; sepals oval, waved, and set well apart at the outer ends; petals scale-like, green, and numerous; anthers a beautiful delicate yellow; leaves of the flower stems few, small, and of irregular form, notched, finely serrate, and of a purplish-green shade; in their young state more especially does the purple prevail on the under surface—they are, in fact, nearly the colour of the flowers. The radical leaves are many, nearly a foot in diameter, of a dark green colour, and leathery substance; the leaflets are rather distant from each other, forming a noble pedate leaf; they are somewhat one-sided, slightly waved, sharply and regularly toothed nearly all their length. From this description it will be inferred that this is one of the most distinct species, and such is truly the case. Moreover, it has a bold and rich effect. The older radical foliage, with its long stalks, is for the most part spread on the ground, when the new erect flower stems, furnished with small leaves and nodding buds and blossoms, all of a shining purplish colour, form a peculiar but pleasing contrast, not nearly so marked in any other species with which I am acquainted. There is a variety called

*H. A. purpureus*, in allusion to the colour of the flowers being a little more purple.

This Abchasian species and its varieties are not widely distributed; they are to be obtained, and need no longer be found only in rare collections. It is desirable in every way for the garden, where it forms a most ornamental object during winter. Its flowers last for four or five weeks, and in a cut state they form rich companion bloom to the white Christmas Rose.

A good fat loam suits them; the position should be rather

shady and moist, but by all means well drained. A top dressing of good rotten manure, after all have done blooming, about the end of March, is a great help to them. All the Hellebores may be easily increased by root divisions, but the stock should be strong and healthy. Roots affected with the least rot or canker should be discarded, as from their slowness of growth they will not be worth garden space. Seed may also be raised, but unless sown as soon as it is ripe germination is less certain, and always slower in proportion to the length of time it has been kept dry. I may add that, in February (1883), I noticed a pot, sown with Hellebore seed in February of 1880; a few were just pushing through the mould. The seed was sold to me as the produce of 1879. Since 1880 I have sown seed ripened on plants that were bloomed for indoor decoration, it being ready about February. From this I had nice little plants in less than twelve months. But by seed the process of propagation is slow, and not advisable unless the object is to obtain new varieties—a very easy matter, by the way, with this family, if the simple rules of cross-hybridising are applied.

All the Christmas Roses should be so planted that they may be conveniently shaded during their blooming time. They mostly flower during the dullest part of the year, and the blossom, more especially the white kinds and those with metallic hues, unless protected, become damaged with mud splashes. Hand-lights or bell-glasses should be freely used.

Flowering period, January to March.

## Helleborus Antiquorum.

ANCIENT HELLEBORE; *Nat. Ord.* RANUNCULACEÆ.

IN what sense this specific name is applied, or which meaning of the word is supposed to be exemplified in this plant, I have no means of being certain. It is very probable that the name is in reference to its " old-fashioned," but beautiful, flowers; that they are " worthy," " dearer, more acceptable," and of " more esteem and account," is likely to be the verdict of every amateur who grows this kind sucessfully, for a more lovely flower could hardly be desired—large, white, softly toned with pink and grey. Sepals very large, incurved, overlapping each other, having the appearance of being semi-double, and being of good substance. The petals are small, short, of a lively green, and numerous. It is a bold and effective flower, but to see it in its full beauty it should be gathered spotlessly clean, as grey and pink tints are ugly when soiled. The leaves accompanying the flowers are of the previous season's growth, and are produced on slender round stalks, 1ft. to 1½ft. long, and much thickened at their junction with the leaves. The latter are nearly a foot across, pedate, or palm-shaped; the segments or leaflets are sub-divided and of irregular form, but mostly ovate, lance-shaped, finely and sharply toothed, and of a dull green colour. In a rich and free loam this kind proves a good grower, and when, in January, it is putting up its flower stalks, the buds being well developed and coloured from the time they appear above the earth, furnished with "floral leaf," in which respect it differs from the common Christmas Rose, it causes a pleased surprise that such a pure and delicate looking blossom can develop and mature in the depth of winter. As a cut flower by many it would be preferred to the better-known *H. niger*, not only for its antique tints, but for the fine cup form, which is constant, and the overlapping, incurved edges of the sepals. Altogether, its form is distinct, and when used in small glasses as single specimens, or, at most, accompanied only by a fern frond or a few blades of grass, it is a charming object.

Cultivation, as for *H. Abchasicus*.

Flowering period, January to April.

## Helleborus Bocconi.

BOCCON'S HELLEBORE; *Nat. Ord.* RANUNCULACEÆ.

THIS, by many, is believed to be a species, but as such is unauthenticated. It is classed as a variety of *H. purpurascens*, compared with which, however, there are some well-marked distinctions. It is sometimes called *H. multifidus*, a name that suits it well, as being descriptive of its irregularly slashed foliage. It has but recently been brought under cultivation, and was found a native of the Apennines of Etruria. It proves perfectly hardy in this climate, and flowers in midwinter unless the season is very severe. As will be inferred from its near relationship to *H. purpurascens*, like that species it has non-persistent foliage, and the flower stems with their floral leaves appear before the leaves of the root. As a species or variety, whichever it may be, its more marked features are to be seen in the form or cut of the leaves.

As a garden flower it is not showy, yet it stands out well in a group; the nodding cup-shaped bloom is a bright green colour, and, for a time, the outer sides of the sepals only are seen; but when the flowers are more fully expanded, the numerous and somewhat long stamens (which are a creamy-white) seem to nearly fill the cup; to my mind, its greatest charm is in the fragrant odour which it yields, resembling that of elder flowers. A single blossom, if plucked dry and when in its prime, scents a small room; at such a stage, the anthers are loaded with pollen, and the tubular petals are richly charged with nectar. True, these last-named qualities are common to the genus, but when they are coupled with that of a sweet perfume, and produced by an open-air plant in winter, such a plant, be its blossoms green or red, is too valuable to be neglected. The flowers are borne on stems 6in. to 12in. high, which are twice and thrice branched or forked, having six to twelve blossoms on a stem. The flowers are bright green, nearly 2in. across, cup-shaped, and drooping. The sepals are somewhat oval, concave, and overlapping; petals very short, pale green, and evenly arranged; stamens creamy-white; styles green. The flowers are supported by floral leaves, which are much divided, in the way of those of *H. purpurascens*, but the segments are more irregular in shape. The radical leaves have long stems, and are palmate; divisions lobed. It dies down entirely during the autumn. Being a vigorous grower and free bloomer, and the flowers very durable withal, it should be largely grown for the sake of its sweet-scented blossoms for cutting purposes. There is an allied variety cultivated under the name of

*H. B. angustifolia* (narrow-leaved). Assuming that *H. Bocconi* is a species, this is a variety but slightly removed from the typical form, inasmuch as the latter is not only much cut in the floral and radical leaves, but the shape is uncertain. This form, then, which, at least by its name, claims a specific feature in the cut of leaf, may be somewhat difficult to identify, more especially as there are no other dissimilarities of note. Seen, however, as a well-grown specimen, the feature of narrow foliage is not only manifest, but the plant is very effective.

Cultivation and flowering period, the same as with *H. Abchasicus*.

## Helleborus Colchicus.

COLCHICAN HELLEBORE; *Nat. Ord.* RANUNCULACEÆ.

A NEW species from Asia Minor. This is a strong grower and blooms well. The flowers vary in size and shade, but it may be said to be distinct in form and pronounced in colour, the latter being an uncommon feature with the Hellebores; either growing or cut it is indispensable to a group. Moreover, it is one of the best flowers of the genus, and would stand high even in a selection of the best six; it is one that should have a place in every collection.

It flowers amongst the previous season's foliage on branched stems; the sepals are somewhat round and flat, which gives the flower a stiff appearance. Still, from their unusual deep purple colour and the yellow stamens, together with the manner in which the sepals overlap each other, the flower is a most effective one; the petals are a bright green, and blend harmoniously with the yellow and purple parts. The leaves are very large, pedate, dentate, and distinctly veined. In a young state the foliage is richly coloured or tinted with "bloom." It enjoys a rich sandy loam and summer shade.

Cultivation, the same as for *H. Abchasicus.*
Flowering period, January to March.

## Helleborus Cupreus.
COPPERY HELLEBORE; *Nat. Ord.* RANUNCULACEÆ.

NOTWITHSTANDING its peculiar colour, as implied by the name, this is a pleasing border flower; moreover, the somewhat large flowers are also numerous; blossoms 3in. across, arranged in clusters of four and six, and handsomely furnished with new foliage, are no mean things in the depth of winter. The specific name of this Hellebore, though applicable, is not so definite as some, inasmuch as the colour to which it refers is that of several other species and varieties; there may be rather more of the metallic hue in our subject, but it is so slight as to be outside the pale of notice to the florist. The Coppery Hellebore is a native of mid-Europe, and is one of recent introduction into this country, where it proves hardy but annually dies down. It grows and flowers freely in January, the flower stalks appearing before the radical foliage, and attaining a height of nearly a foot.

The flower stems are a palish green, with purplish markings, are twice branched and furnished with floral leaves; the latter have ample stipules and seven longish divisions, which are well spread out, distinctly veined underneath, and coarsely toothed. The flowers are 2in. to 3in. across, sepals pointed, overlapping for about half their length, and well expanded; their outsides are of a purplish colour, which extends along the stalk; the inner surface of the sepals is a yellowish green, the whole being suffused with a metallic hue or "bloom"; the stamens and anthers are a creamy white, the petals short and apple-green. The flowers droop gracefully, and are rendered all the more pleasing by the floral leaves which immediately support them. The leaves of the root are large and pedate, the divisions wide apart and unevenly toothed; the under sides are distinctly veined with purplish-brown when in a young state. The habit is robust, and the bloom is produced well above the radical foliage. There is a peculiar beauty about a strong flowering specimen which would hardly be expected from the above description, and it is even more difficult for me to do it justice.

In a cut state a whole stem, with its flowers in different stages of development, is fine. The youngest rosy-purple buds, about the size of a cob nut; the more opened bell-shaped forms, just showing both the inner and outer colours of the sepals; these surmounted by the longer-stalked, fully expanded, but drooping flower, with its tassel-like bunch of stamens, and all finely interspersed with young leaves of two distinct colours, according to the side which meets the eye—all go to make it a charming decoration for indoors, and if cut clean it deserves a place for the whole week or more during which it remains in good form.

Cultivation, as for *H. Abchasicus*.

Flowering period, January to March.

## Helleborus Dumetorum.

BUSHY HELLEBORE; *Nat. Ord.* RANUNCULACEÆ.

ONE of the less showy species. It comes from Hungary, and has been grown in this country about seventy years. It entirely renews its foliage yearly, the flower stems appearing before the radical leaves. The flowers are small, green, and drooping; the sepals are roundish. The flower stems are twice branched, full-flowered, and furnished with the "cut floral leaf," which is nearly stalkless and palmate. The root leaves are very smooth and pedate. The bright green flowers mix well with others, but where Hellebores are grown in limited varieties this may be omitted without loss as regards floral beauty.

Cultivation, as for *H. Abchasicus.*

Flowering period, February and March.

## Helleborus Fœtidus.

STINKING HELLEBORE; *Nat. Ord.* RANUNCULACEÆ.

THIS is a native species, distinct, ornamental, and evergreen. Its name may, with some, prevent its being planted in the pleasure garden, but its fœtid odour is not perceptible unless sought for. It is mostly found wild in this country in chalky districts, and it occurs largely in the southern parts of Europe. Though poisonous, it is a valuable herb. Its value as a garden subject consists in its dark evergreen foliage, good habit, and handsome panicles of bloom. The latter is produced under cultivation in midwinter. It never fails to flower then if the position is a sheltered one. In its wild state the flowers appear in March. It belongs to that section of the Hellebores which have leafy stems and many flowers; its grows 2ft. high, and never seems to rest, but goes on making new leaves throughout winter.

The flowers are produced in clusters larger than a man's hand, and are of a green colour, the sepals edged with brown, which turns to a purplish tint; they are nearly an inch across, well cupped, and mostly hang bell-fashion; the leaves are much smaller than those of most Hellebores, pedate, smooth, of stout substance and dark green colour; the divisions of the leaves are narrow and numerous. The foliage is persistent, and keeps green until after the new has appeared; it bends downwards in a pleasing manner, and the leafy stems have a palm-like appearance. These, when topped with panicles of flowers, though they be green ones, are worthy objects for any garden. It is a suitable plant for mixing with deciduous shrubs; bold specimens of it enliven such borders by their shining greenery, and they are of greatest service when most needed, for in such sheltered quarters they are pretty sure to flower during winter; and

the summer shade, if not too dense, will prove more beneficial to them than otherwise.
Cultivation, ordinary garden soil.
Flowering period, December to April.

## Helleborus Guttatus.
SPOTTED HELLEBORE; *Nat. Ord.* RANUNCULACEÆ.

THIS is one of the newer species or varieties; its main distinction is well implied by the specific name. The flowers are fully 2in. across, and white; the sepals are spotted with purple; the petals are more constant than in some species, and of a rich green colour; flowers are produced on stems having the floral leaf; the buds are a greenish white, but very beautiful. The foliage is smaller than that of most kinds; the leaves are radical, rather short-stalked, pedate, and divisions narrow; they are of a leathery substance and a dark green colour. This is a free bloomer, a fact which, together with those of its winter-blooming habit and distinct flowers, renders it a valuable acquisition to the open garden. Either cut or growing, it is very lasting.
Cultivation, as for *H. Abchasicus.*
Flowering period, January to March.

## Helleborus Niger.
BLACK HELLEBORE, *or* CHRISTMAS ROSE;
*Nat. Ord.* RANUNCULACEÆ.

A HARDY, herbaceous perennial. It came from Austria in 1597. In favoured situations it proves evergreen; there is nothing black to be seen about a growing plant, and it has often puzzled its admirers as to the cause of its specific name, which is in reference to the black roots of a year or more old. It would appear, moreover, that this is not the true "Black Hellebore" of the ancients (see remarks under *H. Orientalis*). This "old-fashioned" flower is becoming more and more valued. That it is a flower of the first quality is not saying much, compared with what might be said for it; and, perhaps, no plant under cultivation is capable of more improvement by proper treatment (see Fig. 48). Soil, position, and tillage may all be made to bear with marked effect on this plant, as regards size and colour of flowers and season of bloom. We took its most used common name—Christmas Rose—from the Dutch, who called it Christmas Herb, or Christ's Herb, "because it flowereth about the birth of our Lord Iesus Christ," and we can easily imagine that its beautiful form would suggest the other part of its compound name, "rose." In sheltered parts, where the soil is deep and rich, specimens will grow a foot high and begin to bloom in December, continuing until March.

## OLD-FASHIONED GARDEN FLOWERS. 133

The individual flowers last a long time in perfection, either on the plant or in a cut state; they vary somewhat in their colour, some being more brown on the outer side of the sepals, and others much suffused with pink; but under glass, whether in the shape of a bell glass in the open garden, or a greenhouse, they mature to a pure white; their form is somewhat like that of a single rose, but may be more properly compared to a flower of its own order—the single pæonia. It is composed of five sepals, and is 2in. to 3in. across, being white or rose-coloured; these sepals form a corolla-like calyx; the petals are very short and tubular, nestling down amongst the tassel-like bunch of

FIG. 48. HELLEBORUS NIGER.
(One-quarter natural size.)

stamens; the flowers are produced on stout leafless scapes, having one or two bracteæ; for the most part the flowers are in ones or pairs, but sometimes there may be seen three, and even four, on a scape. The leaves are radical, having stout, round stalks; they are large and pedate in shape, stout, and of leathery substance. The habit of the plant is neat, growing into rounded tufts.

In suitable quarters it proves a quick grower, whilst in ungenial situations it will hardly increase, though it is seldom killed. As it happens that its flowers are produced at a most unfavourable time for keeping them clean, they should be covered with some kind of glass shelters, or, where the soil is retentive, the roots may be lifted with large balls of earth to them, and be placed in a cool greenhouse well up to the light. It would, however, be a mistake to adopt this plan where the soil is loose, and during the lifting operation will fall from the roots; and it is also a mistake to expect flowers from newly-planted roots. Where its fine bloom is required at Christmas, good roots should have been planted fully a year previously. Doubtless many an amateur will herein recognise his failing point when expecting Christmas Roses from roots planted only a month before, and sometimes less. True, the buds are there, and fine ones, too, perhaps, but the plants, unless transferred with a good ball, suffer a check which it will take at least a year to outgrow. It is a good plan to grow this flower in good-sized pots, which should be plunged in a shady part of the garden all the year, with the exception of the blooming period; but even with pots well grown and showing plenty of buds, the mistake is often made of suddenly placing them in heat, immediately over hot pipes or flues, the heat from which shrivels the buds and foliage too. Though the Hellebores are amongst our best flowers for forcing, it should be done gently in an atmosphere constantly kept humid.

As a cut bloom, the Christmas Rose vies with the eucharis and pancratium. For vase work, or used about the person, it is a flower that wins the greatest admiration, and it is no unusual thing for cut flowers to last indoors quite a fortnight.

*H. n. angustifolius* (narrow-leaved Hellebore) has smaller flowers than the type. The divisions of the leaves or leaflets are narrower, whence its name. The foliage is of a pale or apple green, whereas that of the type is very dark. It was introduced in the same year as its reputed parent. As a foliage plant it is very handsome, the leaves bending gracefully, and the whole specimen having a neat appearance.

*H. n. maximus* is the largest Christmas Rose, and is a truly grand variety; the flowers are 4in. and 5in. across. The illustration (Fig. 49) is one-fourth natural size. The scapes are very stout, and produce several flowers, which are held well above the foliage; like those of the type, they, too, are tinted with a pink colour, which passes away when the flowers are a week or so old. The foliage is remarkably bold, having thick, round, and beautifully marked stalks. Well-established specimens have a shrub-like effect, being nearly 2ft. high, and richly furnished to the ground. The half-blown buds of this variety are exquisitely beautiful, and vary somewhat in form according to their age; some resemble a nearly blown tulip, and others a rosebud. As buttonholes, backed with a frond of maidenhair, they are charming. A whole scape, having one fully-blown flower and several buds, is the most perfect and beautiful decoration imaginable for a lady's hair. This variety is at its best in the month of December, being a little earlier than the typical form.

All these kinds should be grown in moist and rather shady quarters; under trees not too densely foliaged will suit them; the soil should be a deep rich loam. I may mention that all my Hellebores are grown under "nurses," *i.e.*, suitable small trees. I use walnut. About eighteen species and varieties are planted under six small trees, 4ft. high. The reasons why I use walnut are, that they leaf late in spring and lose their leaves early in

FIG. 49. HELLEBORUS NIGER MAXIMUS.
(One-quarter natural size.)

autumn, so affording the greater amount of light during the flowering time of the Hellebores, and screening them in summer from the sun with their ample but not over thick foliage; a cut under the trees once a year with a sharp spade keeps them dwarf and prevents their making too many strong roots. Without saying that Hellebores should be grown in this way, it will serve to show how they may be conveniently shaded. Nothing could well look more happy under such treatment, and, once properly planted, they give no further trouble than a mulching of rotten manure in spring, when all the kinds have finished flowering. Christmas Roses are easily raised from seed, provided it is sown as soon as ripe, but plants so raised are two or three years before they flower. The quicker method of increase is by division of the roots. This can only be done successfully when the old stock is in robust health. Pieces of roots taken from old and unhealthy specimens will remain in the ground for twelve months as immovable as stones, whereas the least bits of clean young growths will form nice blooming plants the first year.

Flowering period, December to March.

## Helleborus Odorus.

SWEET-SCENTED HELLEBORE; *Nat. Ord.* RANUNCULACEÆ.

LIKE all the Hellebores, excepting the white-flowered *H. niger* and its varieties, this has, until very recently, been much neglected, notwithstanding that its name implies the rare and desirable quality of a sweet odour; moreover, it is of easy culture, very hardy, and a free bloomer. It is a native of Hungary, and was introduced to English gardens in 1817. It is like *H. purpurascens*, only its flowers are green; it even more strongly resembles our native *H. viridis*. All its foliage is renewed annually. It belongs to the section having stems few-flowered, forked, and bearing floral leaves. It grows 9in. to 12in. high.

The flowers are green, small, nodding, and scented. The sepals are nearly round, and overlap each other. The flowers are produced at long intervals on the twice-branched, stout, pale green stems; they are supported by prettily-cut leaves, having lance-shaped segments, finely serrated, also having large stipules. The radical leaves are palmate, covered with a fine down on the under surface. The segments are oblong, undivided, and at the base quite entire, but finely toothed near the top. The bloom lasts a long time, either cut or in the growing state. There is nothing very distinct to the eye about this species, but it is to be commended for the sweetness of its flowers.

Like other Hellebores, it should be grown in a shady place, where there is a good depth of rich sandy loam. Propagated by division of healthy stock at almost any period.

Flowering period, February to March.

## Helleborus Olympicus.

OLYMPIAN HELLEBORE; *Nat. Ord.* RANUNCULACEÆ.

THIS comes from a Grecian habitat, as the specific name denotes; still it is perfectly hardy in this climate, and it deserves a place in every garden. It is not so old in English gardens as some kinds, and may not be much known; at any rate, it is seldom

met with; but, from the fact of its coming into bloom in the
first month of the year, and having finely-formed purple flowers,
it is a desirable companion to the white Christmas Rose; it is
variously stated to have white and purple flowers; both state-
ments being authorised; they are produced in spare clusters on
stems a foot high; the buds are charming objects, of a ruddy-
brown colour, and the size of a big filbert; they are rather
close together, and supported by a "cut floral leaf." The leaves
are well divided and almost palm-shaped, the leaflets being
ovate and toothed. It is a free grower, and never fails to bloom
well too.

Cultivation and flowering period, the same as with *H. niger*.

## Helleborus Orientalis.
EASTERN HELLEBORE; *Nat. Ord.* RANUNCULACEÆ.

SOMETIMES also called the Lenten Rose, as it may often be
seen in flower during Lent, though it is no uncommon thing
for it to bloom in January in favoured situations and mild
winters. This is a very old species which has long been known
to botanists, but it has only recently been introduced into this
country. It is a native of the Levant, is plentiful on
mountains and near Thessalonica and Constantinople. It has
gone under the name of *H. officinalis*, and as such was, as it still
is, the shop Hellebore of the East. As a garden flower it is to be
recommended as one of the best of the genus; the colour is
often a fine rose variously tinted, and the blooms are of good
size. It is, however, a species respecting which there is still
considerable misconception. One authority says the leaves die
off and again appear with the flowers; another classes it with
the group "leaves not annually dying"; then one says, "the
greenish-white blossoms are tinted at the margin with purple";
another, that the flowers are "rose-coloured"; whilst botanical
descriptions, usually so taunting to the florist as regards
blossom-colour, are no exceptions in this case. "Sepals oval,
coloured," does not point out very clearly the information desired.
Many of the species of Hellebore are known to produce flowers
varying more or less in colour; and we also know that an
individual blossom, during the long period in which the sepals
keep good, often changes its tints and colours, but we are
scarcely prepared to hear that a species has greenish-white
flowers, whilst we have always seen a rosy or rosy-purple one
produced. Still, the information from another source, that *H.
orientalis* is a species intermediate between *H. niger* and *H.
viridis*, would seem to favour the greenish-white as the typical
colour; be that as it may, it is most likely that the more desirable rosy-flowered variety will prevail in flower gardens, that
being the general recognised colour of the type, and moreover,

one which renders it pleasingly distinct in the whole genus. There are hybrid kinds which have been raised from this species crossed with *H. viridis* and, perhaps, others, and some of them have greenish-white flowers; but they should not be confounded with the species under notice. These varieties have received such names as *H. orientalis elegans*, *H. o. viridescens*, and *H. o. punctatus*. If hybrids are to be honoured with specific names, it will require much care to avoid confusion, and it is just possible that some such causes have led to the various descriptions above referred to. The type under notice is fairly distinct, and the amateur having a slight acquaintance with the Hellebore family will have little difficulty in making it out.

The flowers are produced on forked stems, and are accompanied by finely-cut floral leaves, nearly sessile and palmate; the radical leaves are large, pedate, downy underneath, having long stalks, and remaining green throughout winter. The habit is to push the stout flower stems well up above the foliage, sometimes as high as 18in.; the flowers are very durable, at least the major parts—as the sepals—are, the stamens and petals falling somewhat sooner than those of most species; if different positions are given to a few specimens, flowers may be had from Christmas to Lent, according to amount of shelter or exposure therein obtained for the plants.

There are facts connected with this plant, as other than a garden subject, which can hardly fail to be generally interesting. "This is the Black Hellebore of the ancients," so that, though *H. niger* bears the name and is known to be largely possessed of properties similar to those of the oriental species, it is proved to be wrongly applied. So much was claimed by ancient doctors for the Black Hellebore as a medicine in mania, epilepsy, dropsy, and other ills to which mortals are heirs, that naturally the true plant was sought with much zeal. Dr. Woodville laments the want of proper descriptions of plants and the consequences, and in his "Botany," p. 51, points out some ridiculous errors made in reference to the Black Hellebore previous to 1790; he gives the names of many plants which had been mistaken for it and actually employed, and he assumes that at the time of his writing all such errors had not only been discovered, but corrected, by what he then described as, and we now call by the name of, *H. niger*, being the true Black Hellebore; and after all, the potent herb of the ancients has been identified in a plant (a near relation, it is true) other than the white Christmas Rose —it may be some time before we come to think of our present subject as the true Black Hellebore, especially when an otherwise popular species bears the name.

Cultivation, as for *H. niger*.
Flowering period, December to April.

## Helleborus Purpurascens.

PURPLISH HELLEBORE; *Nat. Ord.* RANUNCULACEÆ.

A NATIVE of Podolia and Hungary, introduced sixty to seventy years ago. It belongs to the section whose flowers appear before the root leaves, having branched flower stalks and the cut floral leaf. It is a dwarf kind, and varies very much; I have now an established specimen in bloom at the height of 3in., and others at 8in. or 9in. It also differs in the depth of bloom-colour; some of its flowers may be described as purplish-green and others as greenish-purple, slaty and dove-coloured; others have a tinge of red more visible. The flowers are few, on twice-forked stems, are 2in. or more across, and commonly, as the name implies, of a purplish colour; the inner surface of the sepals is a slaty shade, the purple prevailing on the outer surface; the form of the flower is nearly round and slightly cupped, from the nearly round or kidney shaped sepals, which neatly overlap each other, and are also incurved at the edges; the petals are very short and green; the stamens and anthers of a creamy white; the floral leaf is nearly stalkless; segments unevenly toothed. The radical leaves are "pubescent on the under surface, palmate, with the segments cuneated at the base, and from three to five lobed at the apex." The habit is robust and free blooming; the flowers slightly droop, and, though the colours are not showy, they are attractive from the way in which they are borne on the straight stems and the absence of the larger leaves. It is a desirable species for the garden; a few specimens grown amongst a mass of the "winter aconite" are enough to make one forget that it is winter.

Cultivation, as for *H. niger*.

Flowering period, February to April.

## Hepatica Angulosa.

*Nat. Ord.* RANUNCULACEÆ.

THIS is a very distinct species. It comes from North America, and is twice the size of *H. triloba* in all its parts; the leaves are more cut, and very woolly; the flowers are bright mauve, and 1½in. across. All the Hepaticas are slow growers, but *H. angulosa* is the more vigorous. Some say they should be grown in peat, but I never saw them so fine in peat as in strong loam, well drained and manured; they are the better with slight shade. I do not object to peat, as possibly it may be more suitable than the natural soil of some gardens. Still, if I had to make up a compost for Hepaticas, I should freely use strong loam on a well-drained site. With me they have been in flower nearly three months, commencing in February.

It seems desirable to increase these fine spring flowers, but they are most impatient of being disturbed, and, after all, the increase can exist in no finer form than in big clumps, though when they are to be propagated the roots should be divided before the new leaves are produced, which is during the blooming period. A deeply-dug and well-manured plot should be prepared for them, and their long roots should not be doubled up in the least; they both need and deserve great care.

Flowering period, February to April.

## Hepatica Triloba.
*Syns.* ANEMONE TRILOBA *and* ANEMONE HEPATICA;
*Nat. Ord.* RANUNCULACEÆ.

THE well-known common Hepatica, of which there are so many beautiful varieties. It is a hardy perennial, one of the "old-fashioned" flowers of English gardens, and is said by some to be a British species; anyhow, it was well known and admired in this country 300 years ago. Well-established specimens form

FIG. 50. HEPATICA TRILOBA.
(One-third natural size.)

neat tufts of three-lobed leaves on long stems, which are not evergreen in this climate, though the Hepaticas are known to be so in North America, one of their most extensive habitats. Here, under cultivation, they produce much finer flowers, and more of them. The cut (Fig. 50), however, shows the foliage in more perfect form than it is commonly seen to be in this climate during the period of bloom, when the old is usually sered, and the new scarcely visible. The varieties of *H. triloba* differ only in the colour and form of their flowers, there being blue, purple, white, and pink. Of the first and last named there are double varieties as well.

Cultivation, the same as for *H. angulosa*.

Flowering period, February to April.

*H. t. splendens* is a charming Windflower, and one which, from its extra brilliancy, is sure to become a favourite, as, indeed, the whole genus *Anemone* is. It is a new variety of *H. triloba*, and is yet somewhat scarce, differing from the more generally known kinds of the same species in only two points, so that, beyond the mention of them, no other description is needful: (1) Its flowers are single red, but so much deeper in colour, brighter, and of better substance, as to be quite distinct, and merit the name "*splendens*." (2) It flowers earlier than the commoner red kind. This handsome seedling of the common Hepatica is very suggestive of what can be done by raising seed from carefully-selected sorts, and within the last few years something has been done in that direction, so that in a little time we may expect to see other good varieties. I may add that seedlings are three years before they bloom, and even longer before a proper idea can be formed of their qualities.

Cultivation, the same as for *H. angulosa*.

Flowering period, February to March.

## Hesperis Matronalis Flore-pleno.
DOUBLE SWEET ROCKET, *or* DAMES' VIOLET; *Nat. Ord.*
CRUCIFERÆ.

THERE are several double forms of this very popular old flower, such as purple, ruby, and pure white, the last named being by far the greatest favourite. A few years ago it was said to be very scarce, and in some parts of the country it certainly was so, but when the present taste for the good old flowers became general, it was not only found, but quickly propagated, so that now the double white Sweet Rocket may be had everywhere, and certainly no more beautiful flower can occupy the garden borders, its perfume being strong and deliciously fragrant. The parent plant of these double kinds is widely distributed over Europe; all are perfectly hardy.

They vary in height from 12in. to 18in., branching candelabra-like, the flowers being produced in terminal spikes, arranged in the way of, and very much resembling, the double stocks—in fact, the Hesperis used to be called "Queene's Gilloflower." The leaves may be briefly described as oval, lance-shaped, toothed, and veined; dark green, and often spotted or blotched. Gerarde's description, too, may be given, as it is always pleasant to recognise the old plants of 300 years ago: "Dames' Violets hath great large leaues of a darke greene colour, somewhat snipt about the edges; among which spring up stalks of the height of two cubites, set with such like leaues; the flowers come foorth at the toppe of the branches—like those of the Stock Gilloflower, of a verie sweete smell."

These desirable flowers have a long blooming period, and their cultivation is simple; there is, however, one special point to be observed, otherwise these double kinds will die off. It should be remembered that they produce no seed, and propagation must be carried out by divisions of the roots and cuttings; old plants, too, have a habit of forming their perennial crowns nearly out of the soil, so that the roots going down from them are often bare and unestablished; the older parts, too, are frequently attacked by ground vermin. No doubt these causes would tend greatly to the former scarcity of the finer kinds, but all the difficulties, if they can be called such, may be overcome by the very simple process of either putting in cuttings like wallflower slips during summer, or, as soon as the old plants are past their best bloom, dividing and replanting the various parts deeper, whereby all of them, however small, will make good plants the following season.

This mode of keeping up the stock will be found to make the plants vigorous and free blooming, and also will prove a remedy for the complaint so often given expression to in such words as "I lost all my double Sweet Rockets; I cannot keep them above two years."

Flowering period, June to August.

## Heuchera.
ALUM-ROOT; *Nat. Ord.* SAXIFRAGACEÆ.

THIS is a small genus of hardy perennials suitable for the decoration of the English garden from their bold and finely-shaped leaves, which are well marked with various pleasing tints, also because of their perpetual verdure and neat habit. It takes its name from J. H. de Heucher, a botanist. The species, as many of them as are known, are from American habitats; nearly all have been introduced within the last sixty years; the well-known *H. Americana*, however, is an old plant in English gardens, having been cultivated for 223 years. The order, as given above, together with the illustration figuring one of the species (see Fig. 51), will give some idea of the usefulness of the genus, especially when it is remembered that in the depth of winter the foliage is fresh, and even in a growing state.

The flowers are of little value for ornamental purposes; they are very small and numerous, and are arranged in panicles or racemes, on rather tall and mostly leafless stems, round, and somewhat wiry; calyx, petals, and stamens have a mixed appearance, the whole flower being of a dingy colour, often resembling some of the panicled bloom of meadow grass, when seen at a short distance; the calyces, however, are persistent, they crown the capsules; these and the naked stems, from their durable nature, mar the beauty of the foliage for several weeks, unless cut off. The plants are more ornamental without the flowers, as they impart a seedy appearance; at no time does the foliage show to more advantage than in January, when most herbaceous plants are dormant, and when their handsome tufts are alike beautiful, either bedewed with fogs, crystallised with hoar-frost, or glittering in the sunshine. As a genus, *Heuchera* is sometimes placed after *Saxifraga* and before that of *Tiarella*; the latter it much resembles, as well as the genera *Mitella* and *Tellima*. Anyone knowing these will at once admit the usefulness of the plants under notice.

Not only do they make good edgings or lines to borders, but the leaves in a cut state are of great service for table decoration, doing duty repeatedly around dishes, &c., either with or without flowers; after being so used, if placed in water, they may be kept a fortnight in good form. I am told that the leaves are sold in Covent Garden Market for similar purposes. I have seen them used in the autumn with the large white anemone, and in winter with the Christmas rose, one flower arranged and tied on the face of a single leaf. These placed round dishes, &c., have a pretty effect.

They grow freely in any kind of soil, excepting stiff clay, and are readily increased by division of the crowns. This may be done any time, but, perhaps, spring is the best.

The Heucheras bloom from May to August.

## Heuchera Americana.

AMERICAN HEUCHERA; *Nat. Ord.* SAXIFRAGACEÆ.

THE flowers of this species are a dull or reddish purple. The foliage is rough and clammy; the form of leaf resembles that of *H. glabra* (see Fig. 51), but the colour is a lighter green. All the genus are of an astringent nature, but this species is remarkably so, and in its native country has earned for the family the name of "Alum-root."

For cultivation and flowering period see *Heuchera*.

## Heuchera Cylindrica.

CYLINDRICAL-SPIKED HEUCHERA; *Nat. Ord.* SAXIFRAGACEÆ.

THIS is much in the way of *H. Richardsoni*, with the distinction indicated by the name, the flowers being arranged evenly round the spike like a cylinder.

For cultivation and flowering period see *Heuchera*

## Heuchera Drummondi.

DRUMMOND'S HEUCHERA; *Nat. Ord.* SAXIFRAGACEÆ.

A TALL kind, with leaves of handsome shape (heart-shaped and lobed) and greener than most varieties.

Cultivation and flowering period are described under *Heuchera*.

## Heuchera Glabra.

SMOOTH HEUCHERA; *Nat. Ord.* SAXIFRAGACEÆ.

THIS was introduced in 1824 from North America. The foliage is bold and abundant; the illustration (Fig. 51) not only gives a

FIG. 51. HEUCHERA GLABRA.
(One-sixth natural size.)

good idea of the form and habit of foliage, but fairly represents the whole genus, as seen during the late (1882) season. This species has dull pinkish flowers; the scapes have a few leaves; root leaves are 2in. to 5in. in diameter, heart-shaped, lobed, toothed, smooth, and of a dark bronzy-green colour. The leaf stalks are long and slender; the habit very neat.

Cultivation and flowering period are described under *Heuchera*.

## Heuchera Lucida.

SHINING-LEAVED HEUCHERA; *Nat. Ord.* SAXIFRAGACEÆ.

A VERY dwarf species, not more than 3in. or 4in. high; the foliage a clear bright green, nearly kidney-shaped, lobed, and roundly toothed. The fresh appearance of its prostrate leaves, which are 2in. across, forms a pleasing object in mid-winter.

Cultivation and flowering period, as given under *Heuchera*.

## Heuchera Metallica.
*Nat. Ord.* SAXIFRAGACEÆ.

THIS was presented to me in 1881 by a lady, who informed me that it was introduced by the late Miss Hope. It is a beautiful plant; the hues somewhat justify the name, but to the touch the leaves are more like a soft fabric, as cloth or velvet. The flowers are of no value, but the foliage is bloom of no mean order, so much so, that everyone stops to admire this handsome plant.

Cultivation and flowering period, as given under *Heuchera*.

## Heuchera Micrantha.
SMALL-FLOWERED HEUCHERA; *Nat. Ord.* SAXIFRAGACEÆ.

FROM Columbia. Flowers a yellowish-green; leaves nearly round, bluntly lobed, crenate or round toothed, the teeth horned or pointed; the colour is inclined to auburn during autumn, but it varies, and for a botanical description it would be hard to state a particular colour. The gardener, however, will find in this a most useful plant, where different forms and tints of foliage are desirable. Into the sub-tropical garden it may be introduced with good effect. I may add that the leaf stalks are 9in. to 12in. long, also of a rich brown colour, and the leaves are 3in. to 5in. across.

Cultivation and flowering period, as described under *Heuchera*.

## Heuchera Purpurea.
*Nat. Ord.* SAXIFRAGACEÆ.

THIS seems to be a less known or newer variety. If the name has reference to the colour of the foliage, it is not inappropriate. The bold leaves are a dark green, shading to a bronze, then a purple, the whole having a soft downy effect. It is a charming kind.

Cultivation and flowering period, the same as for the *Heuchera*.

## Heuchera Ribifolia.
CURRANT-LEAVED HEUCHERA; *Nat. Ord.* SAXIFRAGACEÆ.

THIS is another dwarf kind, producing such leaves as the name denotes. Of this species the only useful feature for a garden seems to be its habit of neatly carpeting the ground under deciduous trees. It has also a remarkably fresh appearance during winter.

Cultivation and flowering period, as for other *Heucheras*.

L

## Heuchera Richardsoni.

RICHARDSON'S HEUCHERA; *Nat. Ord.* SAXIFRAGACEÆ.

A TALLER variety than *H. Drummondi*. The most striking distinctions are the pale green colour of the young leaves contrasting with the bronzed appearance of the older ones, and the larger size of its flowers, which, however, are green.

Cultivation and flowering period, as for other species.

## Houstonia Cœrulea.

BLUETS; *Nat. Ord.* GENTIANACEÆ.

HARDY and evergreen. This pretty little shining plant never exceeds a height of 3in. Like most species of this order, both flowers and foliage have much substance and endure for a long time in perfection, but its neat form and bright parts most commend it—it almost sparkles in both leaf and flower. This species,

FIG. 52. HOUSTONIA CŒRULEA.
(Natural size.)

as implied by the specific name, bears a blue flower, but there is a variety (*H. c. alba* or *H. albiflora*) which bears white flowers, from a specimen of which the illustration (Fig. 52) is drawn, and, as the colour of the flower is the only dissimilarity, a description of the typical form will in all other respects apply to both.

The flowers, which are produced singly on slender stems 2in. high, are composed of a four-toothed calyx; corolla, four petals, or four-toothed and funnel-shaped; when fully expanded each flower is ½in. across, and shows a distinct yellow eye. The leaves of the root are spathulate, those of the stems opposite and lanceolate; all the parts are shown of the natural size in the illustration.

All the known Houstonias are natives of North America; still, our winters seem to kill strong plants. From an impression that the plants were destroyed by insects amongst their roots and foliage, I had several tufts lifted, well shaken out, and divided in the autumn; they were replanted in leaf soil and sand and kept rather moist. When planting them, all amongst the roots was thickly strewn with dry silver sand, so as to leave no space for the lodgment of vermin; the results were fine, fresh, green tufts throughout the following winter, which, however, was not severe; still, the plants not so treated dwindled and were unhealthy, whereas the others were finely in bloom, the subject of the drawing being one of them. These minute plants do well and look well wedged between large stones on rockwork, where they flower nearly all the year round; they also form pretty pot specimens under cold frame treatment; and they may be used with good effect for surfacing the pots in which other hardy but tall and bare stemmed things—such as lilies—are grown.

The mode of propagation has been indicated by the above autumnal treatment.

Flowering period, April to July.

## Hutchinsia Alpina.

*Syn.* LEPIDIUM ALPINUM; *Nat. Ord.* CRUCIFERÆ.

AN alpine species, from South Europe, which may be said to be evergreen in this climate, and, according to my experience of it, flowering throughout the year. Though found in some gardens to be difficult to establish, when it finds a suitable home it becomes a pretty addition.

This alpine seldom exceeds 2in. in height. The flowers are a glistening white and very small, produced in numerous heads, and they are very enduring; the calyx is concave and falls off; the four petals are inversely ovate; the little leaves are deeply lobed, of a pale shining green colour, with plenty of substance; its habit is spreading or creeping. Neither slugs nor any other pests seem to meddle with it. It may be transplanted at any time, and the mode of propagation may be gathered from the following remarks.

Probably because its name implies its alpine character, some may be misled to plant it on rockwork; whether that be so or not, I so tried it, and found it would not grow in such a situation. A bed of dwarf and moisture-loving subjects was being planted, in which a bit of this Hutchinsia was dibbled, and it found a home in the moist vegetable soil. For two or three years I do not remember to have seen it, or the seedlings, without flowers; its pretty, dwarf, rue-like foliage grew so thickly that it threatened to kill the edging of gentianella and such things as *Polemonium variegatum*, the double cuckoo-flower, and the little *Armeria setacea*; it also filled the walks, and its long wiry roots have been eradicated with difficulty. From this it will be seen how much depends, with some plants, on the position in which they are placed.

## Hydrangea Paniculata Grandiflora.

LARGE-PANICLED HYDRANGEA; *Nat. Ord.* SAXIFRAGACEÆ.

THIS dwarf shrub is perfectly hardy and deciduous; it comes from Japan, and is one of the best hardy things I have come across for some time. It is quite a new introduction, and has many fine qualities; the fact of its producing immense clusters of white flowers, 12in. long and 12in. in circumference, as well-established plants, is enough to induce its extended cultivation; but when it is stated that its clusters are numerous and durable, that the shrub begins to flower in summer and continues in great beauty until damaged by frosts, it will doubtless be recorded on the lists of desiderata of those who do not possess it. The usefulness of such a subject is notable not only to the gardener who has a keen eye to artistic effect, but to the lover of showy flowers (see Fig. 53).

The flowers are male and female kinds, and, as is usual with the genus, the fruitful ones are interspersed with unfruitful, being shorter in the stalks and nearly covered over by the latter, which are much larger; in fact, they are not the true flowers from a botanist's point of view, but with the florist it is exactly the opposite; their colour is white, more or less tinted with pink, which, if the autumn season proves fine and dry, becomes purple. As the name denotes, the bloom is arranged in massive panicles, pyramidal form, 6in. to 12in. long, and 4in. to 8in. in diameter. They slightly bend with the great weight, but are otherwise well supported by the woody stems. The latter are somewhat short, seeing they carry such large clusters. The leaves are oval, subcordate (varying), distinctly ribbed, and finely toothed, also varying much in size. The habit of the shrub is much branched, of strong growth, and very floriferous. The flowering shoots issue from the hard wood of the previous season's growth. In the shrubbery it is very attractive, its flowers out-numbering, out-measuring, and out-lasting most of its neighbours. Kept dwarf, what a grand bedder it would make! Grown in pots it is a first-class indoor subject. It has that rare quality, even when in small pots, of being adapted for the company of large ferns, palms, &c., from the great size of its panicles, and I need scarcely say that for cutting purposes it is valuable, more especially in decorations which are not closely viewed.

The culture of this shrub is very simple; it does best in rich loam. The situation should be sunny, that it may well ripen its wood. In order to have clusters of large size, it should be

FIG. 53. HYDRANGEA PANICULATA GRANDIFLORA.
(One-tenth natural size; blossom, natural size.)

closely pruned, like roses, by which treatment the bush may also be kept in the desired form. Its propagation is by cuttings; they should be of fairly well-ripened wood of the last season's growth. The degree of ripeness, like that of such things as roses and fuchsias, may vary according to the method by which the cuttings are to be treated. Half-ripened shoots will root well in a little heat; the harder wood will root equally well, but more slowly, in the open in sandy loam.

Flowering period, July to end of September.

## Hypericum Calycinum.

LARGE-CALYXED ST. JOHN'S WORT, or ROSE OF SHARON; *Nat. Ord.* HYPERICACEÆ.

A VERY ornamental deciduous shrub, but often green throughout the winter. This I claim the privilege of introducing amongst herbaceous perennials; it is a well-known and favourite "old-fashioned" flower, in fact, a native of Ireland. The old name for it was "Cup St. John's Wort." In July it is in splendid form, and, familiar as we are with it, it never fails to win admiration. How charming are its large, shining, golden blossoms, nestling amongst the bright but glaucous foliage! the bundled tassels composed of numerous filamentary stamens glistening like threads of gold; and though often seen one can never tire of it. As a flower, it is distinct in form, showy, and richly effective.

It grows to the height of 1ft. or 18in.; the flowers are 4in. across, of a rich golden-yellow colour, and produced singly on the very leafy stems which, at the base or at their more woody parts, are square, the upper parts being nearly round. Short flower-stalks issue from the side and near the top, a small new growth being produced in juxtaposition with the blossom, the said growth being composed of half-a-dozen or so smaller-sized leaves of a pale apple-green, charmingly suffused with a glaucous hue. The calyx of five sepals is very large, whence the specific name, and each sepal is nearly round and cupped, whence the old common name, "Cup St. John's Wort"; the five petals are 2in. long and widely apart; stamens very numerous, long, thready, and arranged in tufts. These are very beautiful, and form the most conspicuous part of the flower; like the other seed organs, and also the petals, they are of a rich, glistening, yellow colour. The leaves are closely arranged in pairs, opposite, and nearly sessile; they are 2in. to 3in. long, and about 1in. broad, oval-oblong, blunt, smooth, and leathery. When young, they are as above described, but when older, they are of a dark, shining green colour, and somewhat reflexed. The under sides are finely reticulated or veined, and sometimes the foliage is spotted with brown. The habit of the shrub is neat, the short stems being numerous and semi-prostrate, forming dense, even masses of verdant foliage.

Such a subject as this cannot be too highly esteemed on the score of the merits already set forth; but there are other good qualities which I will briefly refer to presently. There can be little doubt that the fine parts and many uses, decorative and otherwise, of most of the "old-fashioned" flowers have much to do with the high and continued esteem in which they are held. Not one of the least recommendations of this St. John's Wort is that it can be grown with great success under the shade of trees. It is one of the very few subjects that will bloom freely in such situations. It is, therefore, very valuable; besides, as regards its period of flowering, it comes in nicely after the vincas are over. These two genera are, perhaps, the best hardy flowering shrubs we possess for planting in the shade of trees. I scarcely need add that for more open situations, as rockwork and borders, it is in every way suitable.

To the lover of cut flowers this must prove one of the most satisfactory, not only because of its beauty, but also because they are produced for fully three months — into September — and they are sweetly scented, like wallflowers. A flower-topped stem forms a perfect and unique decoration for a lady's hair; sprays in small vases are exquisite, whilst a bowlful for the table (without any other flower) is very fine indeed—let the reader try these simple styles of decoration. Also, mixed with other flowers, it is one of the most telling; none of the yellow exotics can excel it. It is now before me, with a few sprays of the pink sweet pea and a bold spike of the white variety of goat's-rue; the blend is both delicate and effective. As a cut flower it can hardly be misused, provided it is not crowded.

Its culture is simple. Any sort of garden soil suits it, but it prefers a sandy loam. A winter top dressing of stable litter will help to produce greater luxuriance and a longer succession of flowers. It quickly and broadly propagates itself by means of its creeping roots; these may be at any time chopped off, with a sharp spade, in strong pieces, which, if planted in deeply-dug loam, will make blooming specimens for the following season.

Flowering period, July to September.

## Iberis Correæfolia.
### Nat. Ord. CRUCIFERÆ.

THIS is a hybrid and much improved variety of the well-known evergreen and shrubby Candytuft, often called "Everlasting Candytuft." A more pronounced remove from its parents could hardly be found in any plant or shrub than is this. There are evident improvements in colour, size, and habit, both in foliage and flowers. It is also a robust grower and perfectly hardy, in these respects being very different from *I. Gibraltarica*. None of the shrubby Candytufts can compare with this for usefulness and beauty; it comes into flower in May, and is in its greatest beauty in early June. It remains in fine form for fully four weeks. At first the flowers seem small, but later they form broad masses of dazzling whiteness, the corymbs being the size of a crown piece. Not only is this wholly distinct from its relatives, but it is one of the most useful flowers and evergreen shrubs which can be introduced to a garden. It cannot be planted wrong as regards either soil or situation. It forms a rich surfacing subject, all the year round, to other tall plants, as lilies, &c. It looks well as a front specimen in the shrubbery, makes an effective and neat appearance at the angles of walks, or as an edging it may be cut and trimmed as a substitute for a grass verge; it thrives on sunny or almost sunless outhouse tops, and on rockwork it is superb; moreover, it grows fairly well in reeky towns, and though its white flowers may be soiled the day they open, its bright green leaves and dense habit render it a pleasing object.

The flowers are arranged in flat heads at first, but as the stems become elongated and the succession of buds open, a long round cluster is formed by the old flowers remaining (as they do for weeks), such heads or spikes sometimes being 3in. long. There is much substance in the petals, which causes them to glisten in strong light; the flower stems are produced 5in. or 6in. above the foliage, their total height rarely exceeding a foot. The leaves are numerous, of a dark shining green colour; in length $1\frac{1}{2}$in., and over $\frac{1}{4}$in. broad near the ends; their shape is spathulate, obtuse, entire, and smooth; the new set of foliage contrasts pleasingly with the old, and its growth is completed during the flowering period; the woody and slender branches are numerous and procumbent.

Besides the positions already mentioned, in which this shrub may usefully be planted, there is none more so, perhaps, than that of rough or unsightly corners, where, if it is provided with a little loam, it will soon adapt its form to the surroundings. The flowers in a cut state are not only sweet-smelling, but very useful where white bloom is needed in quantity, as for church decorations. *I. correæfolia* can scarcely be said to need cultural treatment, but it is useful to bear in mind that it may be much more finely bloomed if generously treated, which simply consists in nothing more than giving it a sunny place and sandy loam, well enriched with old manure. Specimens so treated, which were cuttings only two years ago, are now 2ft. in diameter, and covered densely with large flowers; and how lovely some of the pretty weeds which have sprung up amongst the bushes, and mingle their flowers among the masses of white, appear — such as Spring Beauty (Claytonia), pink flowers; the Maiden Pink (*Dianthus deltoides*), rose; Self-heal (*Prunella pyrenaica*), purple; and the forget-me-nots! This comparatively new Candytuft is as easily increased as grown, by either layers or cuttings; the latter may be put in almost any time, early spring being the best; if put in in June, no better quarters can be given than under the shade of shrubs, where the soil is sandy loam.

Flowering period, middle of May to middle of June.

## Iris Fœtidissima.

GLADDON, GLADWIN, *or* SPURGE-WORT; *Nat. Ord.* IRIDACEÆ.

A BRITISH species, occurring largely in some parts, in shady woods and swampy places near the sea. It is evergreen and of a pleasing form throughout the year. Its flowers are of a dull colour, and not likely to be much esteemed, more especially when in midsummer there are so many beautiful kinds around; still, it merits a place in our gardens. Its handsome berry-like seeds, which are so attractively conspicuous in December, are much more desirable than its flowers, ready as they are for our use at Christmas time.

It grows 2ft. high, and is a water-loving plant, but may be easily grown in the more moist parts of the garden. The large pod is three-cornered; the husks having turned brown, become divided, and expose to view the large, orange-coloured seeds, which, later, turn to a reddish-brown. They are held in the husks for many weeks and strong winds do not displace them; they are very effective amongst the dark green foliage, and may be cut if desired, as they often are, for indoor decoration They may be used in a hundred different ways, but never do they show to more advantage than when cut with long stems and placed in a vase with some of their own dark green sword-shaped leaves; these last-named, by the way, may be appropriated throughout the winter as a dressing for other flowers. There need be no difficulty in growing this species, for if the soil is not naturally moist in summer, a thick dressing of rotten stable manure will meet the case. As a matter of fact, my specimen is grown in a bed fully exposed to the sun; the soil is well drained, and stone-crops are grown in the next bed to it; no water is ever given to established plants, and still the Gladwin is well fruited; the soil is deeply tilled, and there is a thick covering of manure. It is easily propagated by division of the roots in autumn or early spring.

Flowering period, June to August.

## Isopyrum Gracilis.

SLENDER ISOPYRUM; *Nat. Ord.* RANUNCULACEÆ.

THIS is a hardy herbaceous plant, of great beauty. The flowers are not showy, but their great numbers and arrangement render them of importance in what may be termed a fine-foliaged subject. The Isopyrums are very nearly related to the thalictrums or rues, and this one greatly resembles the maidenhair-like section, one of which it is often taken for. There is, however, an important botanical difference between the two genera: the thalictrums have no calyx, and the Isopyrums have. Still, as the flowers of both are very small, that feature is not very observable. As a decorative plant it may be classed with the maidenhair-like rues, and the illustration may be said to give a fair idea of three or four species.

The Isopyrum under notice grows 12in. or 15in. high, and produces its dark brown flowers on slender, well-branched stems, forming feathery panicles, which have a graceful appearance. The flowers are very small, and composed of a five-cleft calyx, five equal petals, and numerous long, pendent seed-organs; the stems are elegantly furnished with the fine-cut foliage. The leaves are large, but the leaflets small, as may be seen by the one given, full size, in the drawing (Fig. 54), being somewhat

FIG. 54. ISOPYRUM GRACILIS.
(One-eighth natural size; 1, leaflet, full size.)

cordate, lobed, and dentate; they have hair-like stalks, which add to their elegance of arrangement, and their glaucous colour further enhances their effectiveness.

This light and diffuse subject may be usefully planted to relieve other kinds; in beds or lines it looks well, having a lace-like effect; as a cut flower or spray it nearly equals maiden-hair, and for mixing with large flowers, it perhaps excels. Either cut or in the growing state it is very durable. It may be grown in average garden soil, but to have it fine, it should be given vegetable soil and a moist situation, not shaded. It is propagated by seeds or division of the roots in autumn.

Flowering period, July and August.

## Jasminum Nudiflorum.

NUDE-FLOWERED JASMINE; *Nat. Ord.* JASMINACEÆ.

THIS was brought to this country from China a little less than forty years ago, and, as proof of its sterling worth, it is already in extensive use. The whole genus is a favourite one; but there

FIG. 55. JASMINUM NUDIFLORUM.
(One-third natural size.)

is a special and most attractive feature about this species that is sure to render it desirable to all—it flowers freely in midwinter, and it does so in the open garden. Like many of the genus, this species comes from a very warm climate, and for a time it was grown in glass-houses as a tender shrub, where it flowered during the winter months. It is now found to be a perfectly hardy subject, not only withstanding our most trying seasons without the least injury, but also proving true to the month of December as the period when it begins to produce its numerous golden flowers. It is a climbing deciduous shrub, though it has neither the habit of clinging nor twining.

The shrub produces bloom when only 18in. high, but it often grows to as many feet, and even taller. The flowers are borne singly at the joints from which the leaves have fallen, and as the latter were opposite, the blossom appears in pairs on the new twigs. In the bud state they are drooping, and are marked with a bright chestnut tint on the sunny side. The calyx is ample, almost leafy, but these parts are hidden when the flower opens and becomes erect. The form of the Jasmine blossom is well known; in size this one is rather larger than a full-blown violet, and quite as sweetly scented, which is saying very much, but the colour is yellow; the petals are of good substance and shining; the flowers last a long time, even during the roughest weather, they open most during sunshine, but do not wait for it, and they remain open until they fade. The leaves, which are produced in early spring, are very small and ternate; leaflets of unequal size, ovate, downy, and of dark green colour. The wood is very pithy, square, with sharp corners, and having the appearance almost as if winged; the younger branchlets are dark bronze green. The habit of the shrub is rampant, climbing, much branched, and very floriferous. The green leafless sprigs of bloom are very serviceable in a cut state for vase decoration, especially if mixed with dry grasses or well-foliaged flowers; the sweet odour, too, reminds one of spring time. Specimens growing against the house or other walls, either nailed or in a trellis, have a happy effect in winter, from the slender whip-like growths hanging down and being well bloomed. From the dark green colour and great number of branchlets, although leafless, a well-grown example has quite the effect of an evergreen.

It enjoys a sunny position, but I have it doing well in a northwest aspect; it may be used in bush form in almost any situation. Neither is it particular as to soil, but I should not think of planting a winter-blooming subject in stiff or retentive loam —that of a sandy nature is more likely to be productive of flowers. It is easily propagated from cuttings of the young wood; if they are taken in late summer, when the leaves are falling, they will root quickly. Before the strong west winds of autumn occur, it should be pruned, in order to prevent its being torn from the wall; if the prunings are laid in sandy loam, between shrubs, they will be sufficiently rooted for planting out by the following spring.

Flowering period, December to April.

## Kalmia Latifolia.

BROAD-LEAVED KALMIA; *Nat. Ord.* ERICACEÆ.

AN evergreen shrub, very hardy in our climate. It comes from North America, and from its dwarf character and free-blooming habit, it is not only one of the most useful shrubs, but may be freely planted in connection with herbaceous subjects, where it will help to redeem the deadness of beds and borders during winter (see Fig. 56). Like the rhododendron, it grows to various heights, according to the soil or situation in which it may be planted, but 18in. to 2ft. is the size at which it may often

FIG. 56. KALMIA LATIFOLIA.
(One-third natural size.)

—perhaps most often—be seen producing its wealth of flowers. There are many fine flowering shrubs, but they do not gain the esteem in which this is held. Its large clusters of delicate flowers, surmounting dark shining foliage, and which seem almost too pure and beautiful to withstand the vicissitudes of the open garden, are its winning points; moreover, the flowers last several weeks in perfection. The flowers are arranged in broad panicles; the pedicels and five-cleft calyx are a bright brown colour, and furnished with short stiff hairs. The salver-shaped corolla, which is white, pleasingly tinted with red, has a short tube and five divisions, curiously cornered; the flower is fully ¾in. across, and in its unopened state is hardly less pretty than when blown. The leaves are borne on stout woody branches, have short stalks, and a bent or contorted habit; they are thick, leathery, shining, smooth, and of a dark green colour on the upper side; underneath they are a yellowish-green. In form they are elliptical and entire, being 3in. to 4in. long. Healthy specimens are well furnished with foliage; otherwise it is spare, and when that is the case the flowering is rarely satisfactory.

As this subject requires to be grown in moist vegetable soil, such as leaf mould or peat, it is useless to plant it where these conditions do not exist; moreover, the rule with species of the order *Ericaceæ* is to require a pure, or approximately pure, atmosphere. Doubtless these conditions will debar many from growing this shrub successfully; but I may add, where its requirements can be afforded, not only should it be freely planted, but it will probably thrive without any further care.

As a cut flower it is exquisite, if taken with a good stem and a few leaves; to many it may appear odd when I say it is too good to cut, but there are others who will comprehend me. The flowers can nowhere show to more advantage than on the bush, and it seems a pity to take its strongest branches for the sake of transferring the blossom.

It is a slow-growing subject, but easily propagated by layering the lower branches; no matter how old or hard the wood has grown, if pegged well down they will soon become rooted.

Flowering period, June to August.

## Lactuca Sonchifolia.
### Sow Thistle-leaved Lettuce; *Nat. Ord.* Compositæ.

This is one of the few ornamental species of a somewhat numerous genus; it is, moreover, perennial and hardy in this climate—characteristics not common to the family. It came from Candia, in 1822, since which time it has been grown in English gardens, more or less, as a decorative plant; it is of unusual form, especially in the foliage. I think it would scarcely be called handsome; but the flowers, which are a fine pale blue, and of the form usual to the order, are too good to be overlooked, and their value is enhanced by the fact of their being produced so late in the year.

In speaking of the flower as a subject of the pleasure garden, it is unnecessary to describe it beyond saying that it is of a rich but pale blue colour, and over 1in. across, produced on stalks nearly 2ft. high, in lax panicles. The leaves are large—about 1ft. long and 9in. wide—have a stout midrib, are pinnate, and most curiously lobed. The leaflets, moreover, are fantastically shaped, being again lobed, also toothed and bent in various ways. The teeth have spine-like points, and the only uniform trait about their form seems to be that the edges are turned backwards. The upper surface is a pale green colour, the under side grey, almost white. It is of rather neat habit, and though I have not grown it in lines, it is only needful to see one good specimen in order to be certain of its effectiveness when so planted; it would be singularly distinct.

It enjoys sunny quarters and deep but light or sandy loam. With me it does well on a raised bed of light earth; its long tap roots will save it from drought during the driest summer, when its fleshy and fast-growing foliage would lead one to think that it could not endure a dry time. It is readily increased by division of the roots or seed.

Flowering period, September to strong frosts.

## Lathyrus Grandiflorus

LARGE-FLOWERED EVERLASTING PEA; *Nat. Ord.* LEGUMINOSÆ.

A HARDY, herbaceous climber, coming from the South of Europe. It was introduced to this country nearly seventy years ago; it is an attractive object when in bloom, growing 6ft. high and being very floriferous. The flowers are nearly 2in. across. Not only in good soil do specimens grow densely and become furnished from the ground to the extremities of the stalks with bloom, but the roots run under the surface so rapidly that a veritable thicket is formed in three or four years. It is as well to allow this fine pea a good broad space, in the midst of which several iron standards, 6ft. high, should be firmly fixed; to these, fresh twiggy branches might be secured every spring; if the old ones are left in, their rottenness will allow them to snap off during strong winds when the tendrils have laid hold of them; but fresh branches, used as suggested, will bend but not break, and will withstand the strongest winds. This is very important, as, if the mass of foliage heads over, it is spoilt for the season.

The flowers are dark rose colour, produced in twos and threes on longish stalks, which spring from the axils. The tendrils are three-cut, having a pair of oval leaflets; the stems are square, or four-angled, and slightly twisted and winged. This plant may be grown in any soil or situation. A specimen does well with me planted in rubble, where it covers a short rain-water pipe, the said pipe being feathered with twigs every spring; but to have flowers of extra size and luxuriant growth, plant in good loam, in a sunny site, and top dress with stable manure every spring. This large Pea-flower is most useful for cutting purposes, being not only handsome but very durable. The running roots may be transplanted in early spring, just before they make any stem.

Flowering period, June to August.

## Lathyrus Latifolius.

LARGE-LEAVED LATHYRUS, *or* EVERLASTING PEA; *Nat. Ord.*
LEGUMINOSÆ.

THIS deciduous climber is one of the handsomest plants of the British flora (see Fig. 57); in its wild state it is a charming object, and under cultivation, in full exposure to sunshine, with proper provision for its tendrils, and kept clear of weeds, it

FIG. 57. LATHYRUS LATIFOLIUS.
(One-sixth natural size.)

becomes in every way one of the finest objects in the garden, whether considered as a decorative climber, a floral specimen, or a source of cut flowers.

It grows fully 8ft. high, in deep and rich soil, and is furnished with large, many-flowered bunches of blossom from the leaf axils nearly all its length, each flower stalk being 6in. to 9in. long. The flowers are of a lively rose colour, about twelve in a cluster; tendrils five-cut, long, and two-leaved. The leaves are in pairs, elliptical, many ribbed, glaucous, and very large, whence the specific name; the internodes of the whole plant are winged, wings membranaceous; stipules large, broader than the stems. The habit is rampant; it enjoys sunshine, but will do in partial shade.

*L. l. albus* is a variety similar to the above in all its parts, but scarcely as large in the foliage, and the flowers are pure white, and produced a week or a fortnight later; for cutting purposes these are justly and highly esteemed.

Tall vases may be pleasingly dressed by the flowered stems, if cut about 3ft. long; these twined round or hanging down are very graceful, but they should not be used too freely—one, or two at most, on each large vase will be ample.

Both the above may be grown with good effect amongst other climbers, on a specially prepared trellis-work, ordinary pea-rods, or over defunct trees.

Propagated by seeds, or by division of very strong roots only. February is a good time for both methods.

Flowering period, June to August.

## Leucojum Æstivum.
SUMMER SNOWFLAKE; *Nat. Ord.* AMARYLLIDACEÆ.

As may be seen by the illustration (Fig. 58), this native bulbous plant is somewhat ungainly; blooming specimens are sometimes 2ft. high, and each one rarely produces more than three of its small flowers, but they are worth growing, because of their lasting properties, either cut or otherwise; the pretty snowdrop-shaped flowers are very effective when used in vases, their long stems rendering them more serviceable than they otherwise would be.

The white flower is without calyx, and has a corolla of six

FIG. 58. LEUCOJUM ÆSTIVUM. (One-third natural size).

petals, each one being delicately tipped with pale green; they are produced on long thick stems, each flower having a somewhat lengthened pedicel, by which they are suspended bell-fashion. The foliage is of the common daffodil form, but longer; bulb small.

There are, it is said, two varieties of this species, which have generally become mixed; the other variety is said to be more dwarf and later in flowering; if this is correct, possibly these mixed varieties may have something to do with the long time which they are known to continue flowering.

Not only for the sake of preventing the tall growths from heading over should it be grown in broad masses, but when so planted this flower is more effective. It will grow in any kind of soil, but it seems most at home amongst dwarf shrubs, where its flowers are always of a more delicate colour than when exposed. Propagated by division of the roots during autumn every third year.

Flowering period, May to July.

## Leucojum Vernum.

SPRING SNOWFLAKE; *Nat. Ord.* AMARYLLIDACEÆ.

A HARDY bulbous species from Germany. It is not necessary either to describe or praise this beautiful flower, beyond stating that in every way it closely resembles the snowdrop; it is larger, however, whence the appropriateness of its name, Snowflake, in relation to that of the snowdrop. It will thrive anywhere but in wet, sour situations; it most enjoys fine light soil and the partial shade of trees, where it rapidly increases by offsets of the bulbs; these may, with advantage, be divided every three or four years.

Flowering period, March and April.

## Lilium Auratum.

GOLDEN-RAYED or JAPANESE LILY; *Nat. Ord.* LILIACEÆ.

THIS is a hardy Lily, and though this particular species is comparatively new to our English gardens, it belongs to a noble genus which has had a place in our ancestors' gardens for ages. It was long thought that this bulb from Japan could not endure our winters, and though it is proved to be perfectly hardy, there are yet many who only cultivate it indoors, and seem surprised when they see it in beds and borders, where it is allowed to remain year after year.

The flowers vary very much in size, from 5in. to 8in. across; the divisions are richly tinted (golden-rayed), beautifully spotted and reflexed; the stems, at the height of 3ft. to 6ft., are furnished with flowers, mostly about five to eight in number.

Though the flowers appear delicate, it is surprising how well they stand out in the open garden. For beauty and effect this Lily is incomparable (see Fig. 59).

Much has been said about its culture, far more than need be put into practice. I have found the observance of three simple rules sufficient in order to have it in fine bloom year after year: First, begin with good sound bulbs, not over large. Second, plant them 9in. deep in sandy soil, and a moist situation,

FIG. 59. LILIUM AURATUM.
(One-half natural size).

surrounding each bulb with half-a-spadeful of fine charcoal, which protects them from rot, canker, and (what I believe to be the chief cause of failure) the wireworm. Third, grow them where they will be sheltered from high winds; otherwise their long and top-heavy stems become wrenched, and the upper roots, above the bulbs, so torn that the current season's bloom is more or less damaged and root development checked.

To put my simple method of growing this Lily in a plainer

way, I may state that my garden is naturally well drained, has light soil, and a south aspect. Under a west wall I planted small bulbs in the manner already stated, and though I have often seen this Lily nearly twice as tall as ever I grew it, I have not any cause to complain about the quantity of bloom. I never either water or put down stakes as supports. If the situation is moist no water is needed, and it is next to impossible to send down stakes without coming in contact with the large bulbs. Doubtless a few good waterings with liquid manure would be an advantage, but where *L. auratum* is esteemed as satisfactory with short stems, this need not be given.

When once a clump or batch of this Lily has become established, it should not be disturbed for several years, when, if the stems are becoming too rank to allow them to wave without damaging each other's flowers, or if there are many young unflowered stems, they may profitably be dug out in a careful manner when the bulbs have ripened, which will be the case when the tops have become thoroughly dry; there will then be found to be numbers of nice clean young bulbs, which, with a year's extra patience, will probably form a more vigorous batch than the parent one. Such bulbs are properly called "home grown."

Flowering period, September to November.

## Linum Flavum.

YELLOW FLAX; *Nat. Ord.* LINACEÆ.

THIS handsome shrub-like Flax comes from Austria, and is a comparatively new species in English gardens. It is not only a distinct form, but from the large quantities and more durable quality of its flowers, it proves itself a very useful subject for flower-beds and borders, where it should have the most select companions. It is classed as a hardy, herbaceous perennial; its woody character, and a few green leaves which it carries throughout the winter would, however, show that it is not strictly herbaceous. Its hardiness, too, will be questioned by many who have tried to winter it outside, more especially in the northern parts of Great Britain. It is only hardy under certain conditions, which, in effect, is saying that it is not perfectly hardy. It requires a light warm soil and a dry situation, besides which, if the winter is severe, it should be protected with a thick covering of ashes or cocoa fibre. This special treatment has been found needful in Yorkshire, but more south it has been proved hardy without such precautions. The neat habit and clusters of rich yellow flowers of this plant render it deserving of the little extra care above indicated; this, together with the fact that it is hardy in many parts, is a sufficient reason for naming it amongst hardy plants.

Its flowers are produced in branched heads, dense and numerous, on stems a foot or more high; each flower is 1in. or 1¼in. across, the five petals being of a transparent golden yellow, distinctly veined with orange; they are broad, and overlap each other; calyx small, and of a dark olive-green colour; segments finely pointed. The leaves are 2in. or more in length, lanced, but inclining to spoon shape; sessile, stout, smooth, entire, and glaucous. Through the summer new stems are quickly grown, which, in their turn, become topped with clusters of bloom, and so a succession of flowers is kept up until autumn. On rockwork it is effective, the situation, to some extent, meeting the requirements of its somewhat tender constitution; it may also be grown well in beds or borders, but they should be of a sandy character, and raised, unless it is intended to take up the plants for the winter; in such positions four or five specimens form a charming group, and nothing can be finer than the effect of other Flaxes, of a tall and spray-like character, grown near and amongst this golden yellow, such, for instance, as *L. Narbonnense* and *L. perenne*.

It is easily propagated by seeds, which should be sown in the autumn as soon as ripe; it may also be divided, but I have found the quickest and best results from cuttings taken in a half-ripened state. They should be put round the side of a rather large pot in sandy peat; the warmth, shade, and moisture of a cucumber-frame will cause them to root quickly, when they should be potted off singly, so as to make sturdy plants before the winter sets in, and such young stock ought to be wintered in a cold frame.

Flowering period, August and September.

## Lithospermum Prostratum.

PROSTRATE GROMWELL; *Nat. Ord.* BORAGINACEÆ.

SOMETIMES called the Gentian L., from its bright blue gentian-like flowers. By many this species is considered synonymous with *L. fruticosum*. They are, however, very dissimilar. Our subject is an evergreen and stunted trailer; *L. fruticosum* is a deciduous trailer and very vigorous; both, however, are perfectly hardy. The most striking characteristics of the Prostrate Gromwell are its fine dark blue flowers and procumbent habit. It is a native of France, and only within the last sixty years has it been introduced into this country. Its habit is most distinct as compared with the various long-stemmed species. It much resembles the well-known *Veronica prostrata* in its general appearance.

Its flowers are sparingly produced from the axils of the leaves, but, being large compared with the size of the foliage, they are very effective when they first open. The dark but bright blue corolla is tinged with red, but later on the colour becomes an unmixed blue, and the blooms increase in size until more than ½in. across. The complexion of the foliage is very dark (holly green), the leaves are about 1in. long, and are narrow and stalkless; they have much substance and are rather hard. The whole plant is thickly coated with hairs—a common feature of this order; but in this species the hairs are remarkably stiff, those of the edges of the leaves being almost thorny.

The form of growth assumed by this plant eminently fits it for rockwork. It should be so planted that its densely-branched stems can fall over the face of a light-coloured stone; in this respect it forms a good companion to the dwarf phloxes, but it is otherwise a superior rock plant, being more characteristic and prolonged in its flowering. It should be allowed to grow to a large size, which will require several years, or the object may be sooner gained by planting half-a-dozen specimens in a group; this should be done when the plants are young, as it is very impatient of being disturbed when once established. It would make a capital edging plant for small shrubs, to come next the grass, backed by a row of *Erica carnea*, which is also dwarf, a continued bloomer and contemporaneous. Its propagation can only be readily effected in this climate by cuttings, as it does not ripen seed well; it cannot be divided, because generally the little shrub has a short bole, therefore, cuttings must be struck from the previous year's growth; they should be dibbled into fine sand and peat, kept shaded and cool for several weeks; they root quicker during the warm season, when they are also less liable to be over-watered, which is a very common cause of failure in striking cuttings; they should be well rooted before the winter sets in.

Flowering period, May to July.

## Lobelia Cardinalis.

CARDINAL FLOWER; *Nat. Ord.* LOBELIACEÆ.

THIS is one of the finest herbaceous perennials that bloom in October; stately, brilliant and lasting. There are many varieties of it, and of late years some extra fine sorts have been raised and named, all of which are good. The varieties differ much in the foliage as well as the flowers, some being much larger, and of a dark brown or reddish colour. The illustration (Fig. 60) is drawn from the typical form, which has smooth foliage; it is not so large as some of the varieties, but it seemed desirable to figure the type, otherwise the varieties might have proved misleading. To a more than ordinary extent this plant is called by its common name, "the Cardinal Flower," and I have very frequently found that it has not been recognised by its proper name, even by amateurs who had long grown it. "Is that tall plant a Lobelia?" has often been asked; therefore, common as the plant is, I thought it might prove useful to give an illustration. One of its valuable qualities is that it flowers for a very long time, beginning about the latter end of August and continuing until stopped by frosts. In the early part of October it is simply grand, as then not only the main stems, but the lower ones, are all furnished with their brilliant colouring.

FIG. 60. LOBELIA CARDINALIS.
(One-twelfth natural size.)

This "old-fashioned" plant grows 2ft. or 3ft. high; the flowers are produced in terminal spikes on stout, round, and well-foliaged stems; each flower has a slender stalk, starting from the axil of a rudimentary leaf. The calyx is very finely formed, broadly cup-shaped and cornered; the five divisions are narrow, finely pointed, ¾in. long, and spreading; the corolla has a divided tube 1in. long, broadly set in the ample calyx, gradually narrowing to the divisions of the corolla. As may be seen by the engraving, the flowers much resemble some of our native orchids in form, the lip being most characteristic. The leaves are broadly lance-shaped, serrated, and sessile. The habit of the plant is erect, and almost rigid. The flowers are of the most attractive kind for borders, and, as cut bloom, can hardly be excelled.

The only drawback which attaches to it in this climate is that it is *not* perfectly hardy; in other words, it dies in winter when planted in certain soils and positions. But I can, from an experience extending over three trying winters, confidently state that, if it is planted in spring, in deep rich loam, fully exposed to the sun, it will both flower well and live through the winter. Only let the reader remember that it is a native of North America, and he may then judge that it can be no stranger to a cold climate. The advantages of the above method are, that the plant becomes well established during summer, its long cord-like roots get deep down to the moisture it loves so well, and from full exposure it withers seasonably and the crowns become fully ripened by the time the strongest frosts occur, so that they do it no harm. The reader may take it for what it is worth, that by leaving the dried stalks on, the plants are benefited; at any rate, I leave them on, for the following reasons: In a dry state they are very hollow, and when cut I have found them conductors of rain into the midst of the younger roots and dormant crowns, causing them to rot, and when the remaining part of the stalk has come away from rottenness too, it has been seen that a cavity of corruption had formed where it joined. When I have left the withered stalks untrimmed until the following growing season, no such decay has been seen. So that, after all, it is perhaps not less hardy than many other plants about which little doubt exists, but which may have been a little more fortunate as regards other conditions than cold.

To those who prefer to dig up their stock of *L. cardinalis* and winter it away from frost, I may say that it is only needful to pack the roots in sand, which should be kept moist, not wet. Propagation may be effected by division of the crowns in spring.

Flowering period, August to first frosts.

## Lychnis Chalcedonica.

CHALCEDONIAN LYCHNIS, *or* SCARLET LYCHNIS;
*Nat. Ord.* SILENACEÆ.

THIS hardy herbaceous perennial (see Fig. 61) came from Russia so long ago as 1596. It is a well-known and favourite flower, and, of course, a very "old-fashioned" one; it is commonly called the Scarlet Lychnis, but there are other forms of it with white flowers, both double and single, and there is also a double scarlet variety. The typical form comes into flower a fortnight earlier than the others, but all may be seen in bloom during July. The very brilliant flowers, which are produced for several weeks in large showy heads, must commend this plant, and its tall habit renders it all the more conspicuous. It ought to be grown in every collection of hardy perennial flowers, amongst which bright scarlets are not too plentiful. In sandy loam, enriched with well-rotted manure, it attains a height of 2ft. to 3ft. The flowers are ¾in. across, the five petals open flat, and each petal is divided into two rounded segments; the calyx is hairy, long, bellied, ribbed, five-cleft, and much narrowed at the divisions; the numerous flowers are arranged in flat clusters, interspersed with many small leaves or bracteoles; the stems are stout, round, and having hairs pointing downwards; the nodes or joints are distant and furnished with a pair of stem-clasping, lance-shaped leaves, whence issue short stems that flower later on. The leaves are 2in. to 4in. long, lance-shaped, hairy, waved at the edges, and somewhat recurved. The whole plant is of a clammy character, after the manner of other Catchflies.

As already hinted, this species, with its varieties, enjoys a sandy soil; a mulching of manure proves of great benefit; not only are the heads of bloom larger for it, but the side shoots are induced to flower freely. In borders of tall plants the scarlets are very showy; they cannot, however, endure shade; the position should be sunny and open. The propagation of the single forms may be carried out by seed, which ripens in large quantities; in fact, they sow themselves freely. The double kinds should be divided in early spring. In a cut state the flowers are both useful and effective, and if kept in a sunny window will continue in good form and open the buds.

Flowering period, June to August.

FIG. 61. LYCHNIS CHALCEDONICA.
(One-third natural size).

## Lychnis Viscaria Flore-pleno.

GERMAN CATCHFLY; *Nat. Ord.* SILENACEÆ.

THE double form of the red German Catchfly. The old Latin name for the type was *L. Angustifolia*, which is still used sometimes, being a good descriptive name. So much cannot be said of the common name; at any rate, it sounds odd that one of our native plants should be called the "German Catchfly," as name is evidently used in the geographical sense. There are several forms of this species having double flowers, which may be termed florists' or garden varieties; all are handsome and effective flowering plants, and last a long time in good form. A very short description will suffice for these, the flowers of which in many respects resemble pinks; they are, however, borne on stout stems in long heads, the petals being full, divided, and bent, each flower an inch across. The rose-coloured varieties are bright and attractive; the leaves are in tufts 3in. or 4in. long, narrow and reflexed. These double Catchflies are very showy in either borders or rockwork; they rank with our neatest subjects and brightest flowers, and certainly ought to be widely grown.

They enjoy a stiff soil, but are in no way particular; they should, however, have a sunny situation. They may be increased by root divisions in summer or early spring.

Flowering period, June to August.

## Lysimachia Clethroides.

CLETHRA-LIKE LOOSESTRIFE; *Nat. Ord.* PRIMULACEÆ.

THIS is a tall-growing and distinct species, newly imported from Japan; it is perfectly hardy and herbaceous, and differs very much indeed from its creeping and evergreen relation, the moneywort, or "creeping jenny," being more like a tall speedwell, having large leaves; it is so dissimilar, there can be no likelihood of confounding it with other species. As a decorative garden plant it is both attractive and interesting.

It attains a height of 3ft. in favourable quarters, and has both a wealth of rich foliage and showy one-sided spikes of white flowers; the latter are neatly formed and continue to develop along the spike for the length of a foot; the flowers are ½in. across, somewhat star-shaped, having five, and sometimes six, divisions of the corolla, which are oval and cupped; the short flower stalk is supported by a very narow bracteole of equal length —this helps not a little to enrich the yet unblossomed part of the spike, the buds of which are of the purest whiteness and pearl-shape, mounted in the claw-like setting of the pale green calyx; these pleasing spikes of flowers and buds have a peculiar habit of bending; the unbloomed part is at right angles with the erect stem, with the exception of the tip, which slightly erects itself; the angle is ever changing, being ruled by the change of flower to seed, the development causing the sharp bend to rise day by day. The leaves of the root are spoon-shaped, and those of the stems broadly lance-shaped, varying in length from 3in. to 5in., entire, veined, of good substance, and having attenuated stalks; the younger leaves have a changeable satiny hue; all the leaves at their junction with the stems are marked with a bright redness; the main stems are furnished with many side branches, which assist in maintaining floriferousness until late autumn. The habit of the plant is dense, and from the numerous spikes of flowers and bright green foliage strong specimens have a commendable appearance; with me, the growth has been remarkably vigorous, exceeding by nearly a foot the usual height; this I attribute to the enrichment of the soil. The bent spikes are scarcely suitable for cutting purposes, but that the plant is deserving of a place in the borders may fairly be inferred from the manner in which it wins admiration when in flower. It enjoys deep loam, which, as before hinted, should be rich; the situation should be such as will afford it protection from the winds—then, if its leaves remain untorn, they will afford a treat from their "autumnal tints." Propagated by root division during late autumn or early spring.

Flowering period, July to September.

## Margyricarpus Setosus.

BRISTLY PEARL-FRUIT; *Nat. Ord.* ROSACEÆ.

A CHARMING little evergreen shrub, and most aptly named, for not only does the name convey some idea of its beauty, but it is specific to the utmost degree; a glance at the illustration (Fig. 62) and the English name, which is a translation of the Latin one, will show this. It is the only species of the genus. It was introduced in the year 1829 from Peru, and for a time was considered too tender a subject for other than stove treatment, and even now it is treated as a shrub needing protection; but warm as is its native climate, it proves hardy in ours; it is not merely a safe subject to winter out under special conditions, but quite hardy in fully exposed parts. It stood out with me in the winters of 1879-80 and 1880-1, and in 1881-2, which, however, was specially mild, it held its berries until spring. Its evergreen character renders it all the more desirable, for though the foliage is small and somewhat spare, it is of a bright and pleasing colour. Quite young specimens are prolific, and only during the severe months are they without berries.

A full-grown example does not exceed the height of 6in. or 8in. in this climate. The flowers are green and insignificant—in fact, hardly visible, and must be closely looked for; they are produced singly on the riper parts of the soft wooded branches; they are chubby forms, all but stalkless, and supported by a brown stem-clasping sheath, which is long-pointed and bent backwards, resembling a spine; these sheaths are numerous, and probably suggested the specific name, *setosus*—rough or bristly. The flowers appear for many months, and there is a corresponding succession of berries; the latter form the main feature of this singular shrub, measuring ⅛in. to ¼in. in diameter, they are of a clear, shining white colour, and are well named "pearl

FIG. 62. MARGYRICARPUS SETOSUS.
(One-third natural size; fruit, natural size.)

fruit." Sooner or later in the season every joint of the main branches seems to be furnished with fruit, which lasts a long time in perfection. The leaves are ½in. to 1in. long, pinnate, leaflets awl-shaped, reflexed, and of a deep glistening green colour; they are arranged in minute tufts on stoutish branchlets, and, for the most part, have a single berry at the parent node. All these young shoots grow in the upward direction, leaving the procumbent branches to form an even line on the lower side. The habit of this shrub is spreading and prostrate, and, from the bright berries and foliage (the latter all turned upwards), it becomes a most pleasing object to look down upon, reminding one of a dwarf erica immediately after a hailstorm. For rockwork, this is a gem. Many amateurs will be glad to learn, if they do not already know the shrub, that it is one of those pretty, uncommon, and distinct forms ever desirable for choice collections.

It should be so planted that its branches can rest on a dark-coloured stone; this will show up its fruit to advantage. It enjoys a rich, light soil, thriving in a mixture of sand, loam, and rotten leaves. Beyond this there is nothing special about its culture; moreover, it is easily increased, either by cuttings taken in summer and pricked into moist peat under a bell glass, or by layering the branches. These only need to be pegged down and covered with soil, or to have a small boulder placed on the part where roots are desired.

Flowering period, all summer.

## Mazus Pumilio.
DWARF MAZUS; *Nat. Ord.* SCROPHULARIACEÆ.

THIS diminutive and pretty plant is a native of Australia, and was introduced into this country in 1823. It is hardy, herbaceous, and perennial; it is, however, sometimes said to be only annual, which may have been inferred from the fact of its perishing in winter in this climate when grown in cold, stiff soil, but that it is perennial is beyond doubt. Not only have I experienced that it dies every winter in clay soil, but also that the roots remain fresh and healthy year after year when in more suitable quarters, such as an open situation in light vegetable soil mixed with sand, where it quickly spreads by underground runners and asserts its perennial character.

Its flowers much resemble the small wild violet of the hedgerows, in size and colour more especially; the flower-stalks are, however, sometimes branched, carrying four or five flowers; and if I may be allowed to make another comparison in order to convey an idea of its form, I would mention *Pinguicula vulgaris*, the common butterwort. The flowers spring from the midst of flattened tufts of pale green foliage; the leaves are 1in. to 3in. long, spoon-shaped, slightly waved at the edges and occasionally notched, distinctly veined, of a light green colour, and flesh-tinted in the stalks; they are arranged in nearly rosette form up to the period of flowering, when they are not only longer, but become almost erect; but the younger tufts which do not produce flowers remain perfectly flat.

It is useful for rockwork or as a carpet plant where the soil is of a sandy nature. There should be few bare places in our gardens whilst we have such lovely creepers as this to fall back upon. The rooted stems, which run immediately under the surface, may be transplanted any time except during winter. If the roots are mutilated then, they will probably rot.

Flowering period, June to September.

## Melittis Melissophyllum.

*Syn.* M. GRANDIFLORUM; LARGE-FLOWERED BASTARD BALM;
*Nat. Ord.* LABIATÆ.

THIS is a somewhat uncommon but handsome native plant. The above names, together with the illustration (Fig. 63), will

FIG. 63. MELITTIS MELISSOPHYLLUM.
(One-sixth natural size.)

doubtless give the reader a fair idea of its appearance. It forms one of the best possible subjects for a border of "old-fashioned" plants, being of a distinct type and colour.

The flowers are a mixture of white, pink, and purple; and are nearly 2in. long, in general shape resembling the foxglove, but wider at the corolla and a little shorter in the broad tube. They are arranged in whorls springing from the axils of the leaves. The whorls are said to be of as many as eight flowers, but specimens are more commonly seen to have only two to four, being repeated the whole length of the stems, which are 18in. high. The leaves are two to three inches long, and half as broad, ovate, serrate, hairy, and short stalked. No one can be otherwise than pleased with the ancient style and soft colour of the large flowers, which last a long time in perfection. There is a trimness, too, about the plant which distinguishes it from the more weedy species to which it is related.

In a cut state the long stems are not only pretty of themselves when placed in old vases or crackle ware, but they have a remarkably good effect. They, however, should not be crowded or swamped by more showy foliage or flowers—in fact, they should be used alone.

It will grow anywhere and in any quality of soil, but slight shade and well-enriched loam will be found to make a vast difference in the size of the flowers, and their colour will be also improved. It may be divided or transplanted any time after it has done flowering.

Flowering period, June to August.

## Monarda Didyma.
*Syn.* M. KALMIANA; BEE BALM, *or* OSWEGO TEA; *Nat. Ord.* LABIATÆ.

ALL the Monardas are natives of North America, and, consequently, quite hardy in this country; they are also herbaceous and perennial. This species has been grown for 130 years in English gardens, and at the present time it is not only accounted an old flower but it is highly esteemed. The blooms are large and brilliant in colour, and their shaggy forms give them an effect which is decorative both in the garden and vase.

The flowers are not only numerous, but, for the most part, bright; moreover, they begin to flower at midsummer and continue until the frosts set in.

The species under notice has bright scarlet flowers, produced when the plant is about 18in. high; it, however, grows to nearly twice that size, flowering all the while. The whorls of bloom issue from half-globular arrangements of buds and persistent calyces; each flower is an inch long; corolla ringent, or gaping; helmet, or upper division, linear; the seed organs are longer; the calyx tubular, having five minute teeth, being striped and grooved; the whole head, or whorl, is supported by a leafy bract, the leaflets being of a pale green colour, tinted with red. The leaves are ovate-cordate, or broadly lance-shaped, taper-pointed, toothed, rough, and slightly wrinkled, and they have short stalks. The stems are square, grooved, and hard. The whole plant exhales a powerful but pleasant odour. The habit is branching, that of the root progressive, not only increasing rapidly, but such parts on the surface may be termed creeping or prostrate branches, forming a veritable mat of fibre.

The whole genus is made up of such species as may be used freely in most gardens, more especially in those having plenty of space.

For culture and flowering period, see *M. Russelliana.*

## Monarda Fistulosa.

WILD BERGAMOT; *Syns.* M. AFFINIS, M. ALTISSIMA, M. MEDIA, M. OBLONGATA, M. PURPUREA, *and* M. RUGOSA; *Nat. Ord.* LABIATÆ.

THE Wild Bergamot has a pleasant smell; it has, however, the objectionable property of attracting great numbers of bees and wasps.

Compared with the scarlet *M. didyma*, the more striking differences are the purple flowers, which are less, and mostly produced in single heads. The bracts are tinted with purple, and they are more bent down the stems; the latter, too, are only half as thick and of a dark brown colour.

For culture and flowering period, see *M. Russelliana*.

## Monarda Russelliana.

RUSSELL'S MONARDA; *Nat. Ord.* LABIATÆ.

ANOTHER distinct species. Its flowers are white, with pistil tinted purple, and less in size than either of the above. The bract is remarkably large, and further amplified by numerous small leaves amongst the flowers; all are deeply tinted or veined with purple; the leaves are larger than those of *M. didyma*, and those near the tops of the stems are also tinted with purple on their stalks, mid-ribs, and edges; the stems are green, rounded at the corners, channelled, and smooth.

There are other species than those I have named, but the above-mentioned are not only the more distinct, and well represent the genus, but as flowers they form a richly beautiful trio of colour, so that, when grown side by side, their effectiveness is much enhanced; as cut bloom they answer well for furnishing old vases. Either growing or cut, their flowers and leaves are pleasant, but if bruised the odour is too powerful; they, however, when used in moderation, form a valuable ingredient of *pot pourri*.

They may be grown in ordinary soil, and in any position but a too shady one. The propagation of these plants may be carried out any time, by cutting small squares of the matted roots from old specimens, but it will be found that if allowed to grow to bold examples their effect will be all the more telling.

Flowering period, July to September.

## Morina Longifolia.

*Syn.* M. ELEGANS; WHORL FLOWER; *Nat. Ord.* DIPSACEÆ.

UNTIL this plant comes into flower there is little about it for us, who are trained to dislike and almost despise thistles, to admire.

It is not a thistle certainly, but the resemblance is very close when not in flower, and the three or four specimens which I grow have often caused a laugh from visitors at my expense, but I pocket the laugh and ask them to come and see my thistles in June. When, too, weeding is being done, it is always needful, for the safety of the plants, to give some such hint as "Do not pull up those thistles;" but if this plant is no relation to that despised weed, it belongs to another race, the species of which are also formidably armed—viz., the Teasel. It comes from the Himalayas, and is comparatively new in English gardens.

It is hardy, herbaceous, and perennial, grows to a height of 2ft., and the flowers are produced in whorls or tiers interspersed with the thorny foliage near the top of the stems. At this stage of development the plant has a noble appearance, and the rings of flowers are very beautiful—though when I say flowers I here mean the combination of buds and blossoms in their different stages and colours. The buds are pure white and waxy, and when open, are of a delicate pink; as they get advanced, they turn to a lovely crimson; these are all the more pleasing, because the flowers last a long time. In form they are tubular and horn-shaped, having a spreading, uneven corolla, five-parted. Each flower is 1in. long and $\frac{3}{4}$in. across, six to fifteen in a whorl, the whorls being five to ten in number. The whorl-bracts are formed of three arrow-shaped leaves, deeply cupped, and overlapping at their junction with the stem or scape; they are spiny and downy underneath. Calyx, tubular and brown. Segments (two), pale green, notched, alternated with long spines, and surrounded with shorter ones. The leaves of the root are 9in. to 12in. long, and 2in. wide in the broadest parts; pinnate, waved, and spined, like the holly or thistle. The leaves of the stem are similar in shape, but very much smaller. The whole plant, and especially if there are several together, has a stately appearance, and attracts much attention; it is a good border plant, but it will be more at home, and show to equal advantage in openings in the front parts of the shrubbery, because it enjoys a little shade, and the shelter from high winds is a necessity, it being top heavy; if tied, it is robbed of its natural and beautiful form.

It thrives well in sandy loam. Slugs are fond of it, and eat into the collar or crown, and therefore they should be looked for, especially in winter, during open weather. To propagate it, the roots should be divided as soon as the plants have done flowering, they then become established before winter sets in. Plant in the permanent quarters, and shade with leafy branches for a fortnight.

Flowering period, June and July.

## Muhlenbeckia Complexa.
*Nat. Ord.* POLYGONACEÆ.

A HARDY climber, of great beauty; during November its nearly black stems are well furnished with its peculiar small dark green leaves, which, even when without flowers or fruit, render it an object of first-class merit as a decorative subject. The illustration (Fig. 64) is fairly representative of all its parts; still, it can

FIG. 64. MUHLENBECKIA COMPLEXA.
(One-fourth natural size; fruit, natural size.)

give no idea of the effect of a specimen climbing 4ft. to 6ft. high, diffuse and spreading withal. Although I have grown this handsome climber several years, my experience and information respecting it are very limited indeed; its hardiness and beauty are the inducements which have led me to recommend it for the pleasure garden. As a matter of fact, I have never bloomed it, and I am indebted to a lady for the wax-like and flower-shaped fruits illustrated; they were produced in a warm vinery, and

I have otherwise learned that in this climate the plant only flowers outside during very warm summers. I have also information from one of H.M. Botanic Gardens that this species "was introduced from South America, but when and by whom I am unable to say. It requires a warm, sheltered position. Before the severe winters came it used to be covered with starlike whitish flowers, which were succeeded by fruits."

The fruits given in the illustration (natural size) are a fine feature, but, considering the uncertainty of their production, they can hardly be claimed for outside decoration. They are of a transparent, wax-like substance, and the tooth-like divisions glisten like miniature icicles; they hang in small clusters on lateral shoots from the more ripened stems, and have a charming effect, contrasting finely with the black stems and dark green foliage. The leaves are small ($\frac{1}{4}$in. to $\frac{3}{4}$in. across) somewhat fiddle-shaped, of good substance, and having slender stalks; they are alternate and distantly arranged on the long trailing and climbing stems. The habit is dense and diffuse, and though it loses many leaves in winter, I have never seen it entirely bare; it is therefore entitled to be called evergreen with outdoor treatment. The distinct form and colour of its foliage, together with the graceful shape of the spray-like branches, render this subject of great value for cutting purposes. Seen in company, and used sparingly with white flowers for epergne work, the effect is unique; and I ask those who possess it to try it in that or a similar way.

It enjoys a sunny position and well drained or sandy soil. With me it grows entangled with a rose tree, the latter being nailed to the wall. I have also seen it very effective on the upper and drier parts of rockwork, where it can have nothing to cling to; there it forms a dense prostrate bush. It may be propagated by cuttings of the hardier shoots, which should be taken in early summer; by this method they become nicely rooted before winter.

Flowering periods, warm summers.

## Muscari Botryoides.
### GRAPE HYACINTH; *Nat. Ord.* LILIACEÆ.

THIS is a hardy species, somewhat finer than the more common *M. racemosum*, from the fact of its richer, bright sky blue flowers. The form of the Grape Hyacinth is well known (see Fig. 65), being a very old garden flower and a great favourite; when it is once planted, it keeps its place, despite all drawbacks common to a crowded border, with the exception of that wholesale destroyer, a careless digger; if left undisturbed for a year or two, it increases to very showy clumps.

The flowers, which are densely arranged on stout spikes 8in.

high, are very small, globular, and narrowed at the opening, where the tiny divisions are tipped with white. The foliage resembles that of the wood hyacinth, but it is more rigid, not so broad, and slightly glaucous.

It seems to do best in light earth, and the flowers are finer in colour when grown in shade, but not too much. Where quantities are available, they may be used as an edging, nothing looking better in a spring garden.

*M. b. alba* varies only in the colour of its flowers; the white is somewhat creamy for a time; it becomes much clearer after a few days, and remains in perfection for two weeks in ordinary weather. This is a charming variety; grown by the side of the different blues its beauty is enhanced. It is very effective as a cut flower, though rather stiff, but if sparingly used it is attractive for bouquets, whilst for a buttonhole one or two spikes answer admirably.

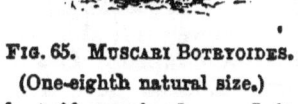

FIG. 65. MUSCARI BOTRYOIDES.
(One-eighth natural size.)

Flowering period, March to May.

## Muscari Racemosum.
### *Nat. Ord.* LILIACEÆ.

THIS is the commonest species, and although very pleasing, suffers by a comparison with the above blue kind, being more dwarf and the flowers less bright. The best time to transplant the bulbs is when the tops have died off, and the choicer sorts of these, as well as all other bulbs whose foliage dies off early in summer, should have something to mark their situation when in their dormant state.

Cultivation and flowering period, as for *M. botryoides*.

## Narcissus Minor.
### SMALLER DAFFODIL; *Nat. Ord.* AMARYLLIDACEÆ.

A VERY beautiful and effective spring flower. Though a native of Spain, it proves one of the hardiest denizens of our gardens; it is not often met with, but it has been cultivated in this country since 1629. It was well known in Parkinson's time. Not merely is it a species due to bloom early, but it does so, no matter how severe the weather may be, in March, and the flowers are freely produced. We could hardly have more severe weather than we had in March, 1883, when the snow was sometimes several inches deep and the frost as much as 17deg. to

23deg. Still this little Daffodil continued to push up its golden blossoms, so that in the latter half of the month, it formed one of the most pleasing of the hardy flowers of the spring garden. Its blue-green leaves are densely grown, and being only 4in. high and somewhat rigid, they not only form a rich setting for the bright blossom which scarcely tops them, but they support the flowers, which have a drooping habit. Later on, however, they lift their fair faces and look out sideways, but whether seen in profile or otherwise, they are alike charming.

I do not remember ever to have seen or heard this flower described as finely scented; as a matter of fact, it is deliciously so. The odour is aromatic and mace-like. If the bloom is cut when in its prime and quite dry, a few heads will scent a fair-sized room. Of course, all the species of the genus (as implied by the generic name) exhale an odour, and some kinds a very fragrant one, whilst others are said to be injurious; but the spicy smell of this can scarcely be otherwise than acceptable, and it must always be a desirable feature in a flower suitable for cutting, and more especially in a winter and spring flower. From its dwarfness this Daffodil is very liable to be soiled; either of three plans may be adopted to prevent this: Plant on grass; top-dress in January with longish litter, which by the blooming time will have a washed and not very objectionable appearance; or, lastly, let the patches grow broad and thick, when their own foliage will keep down the mud, excepting at the sides. I find the litter method to answer well for scores of things for a similar purpose.

Flowers are produced on slender scapes, 3in. to 4in. long, singly, from the long membranous spatha; they are 1¼in. across the expanded perianth, and about the same length; the six divisions are rather longer than the tube, and of a pale yellow or lemon colour; the crown or nectary is campanulate, longer than the petal-like divisions, lobed, fringed, and of a deep yellow colour. The leaves are strap-shaped, stout and glaucous, and about the same length as the scapes.

This plant is in no way particular as to soil, provided it is well drained. It enjoys, however, partial shade and liberal top-dressings of manure. It increases fast by offsets, and, if desirable, the bulbs may be lifted the third year for division, after the tops have died off in late summer.

Flowering period, March and April.

## Nierembergia Rivularis.
WATER NIEREMBERGIA, or WHITE CUP; *Nat. Ord.*
SOLANACEÆ.

THIS alpine plant comes from La Plata; when well grown (and it easily may be) it is a gem—hardy, herbaceous, and perennial.

It has a most pleasing habit; from its mass of root-like stems, which run very near the surface, it sends up a dense carpet of short-stalked leaves, which in July become studded over with large and chaste white flowers; though it rarely exceeds 4in. in height, it is very attractive.

The flowers are 1½in. across, of a variously tinted white, sometimes with pink and sometimes with purplish-grey inside the corolla. The outside is yellowish-green; the five lobes of the corolla are arranged cup-fashion, having four distinct ribs or nerves and wavy margins, the inner bases being richly tinted with lemon-yellow; what appears at first sight to be the flower-stalk, 2in. to 3in. long, is really a long round tube, very narrow for so large a flower; it is of even thickness all its length. The calyx nearly touches the earth; it is also tubular and five-cleft. The leaves are from less than an inch to 3in. long, somewhat spoon-shaped or sub-spathulate and entire, smooth, and very soft to the touch.

It thrives in a light soil, but it should not be dry. Moisture and a little shade are the chief conditions required by this lovely creeper, and where bare places exist, which are otherwise suitable, nothing more pleasing could well be planted; in dips or the more moist parts of rockwork, it may be grown with capital effect, but the patches should be broad. It also forms a good surfacing subject for leggy plants or shrubs. Lilies not only appear to more advantage when carpeted with the short dense foliage of this creeper, but their roots are kept more cool and moist by it, and there are many similar cases in which it will prove equally useful. It is easily propagated by division of the roots after the leaves have died off, but I have found spring much the better time, just as the new growth is pushing.

Flowering period, July and August.

## Œnothera Speciosa.

SHOWY EVENING PRIMROSE; *Nat. Ord.* ONAGRACEÆ.

A HARDY and beautiful perennial species from North America; it is aptly named, as the flowers are not only large but numerous (see Fig. 66). The plant has a gay appearance for many weeks. As a garden flower, it is one of those happy subjects which may be allowed to grow in any odd corner, no matter what quality the soil may be, and full exposure or a little shade is equally suitable. No matter where it grows in the garden, it is a showy and pleasing flower, which, if plucked, is found to have the delicate smell of the sweet pea. It grows 18in. high, is herb-like in the foliage, and very distinct from other species, more especially as regards its slender stems and somewhat large and irregular foliage.

The flowers are a satiny white, delicately nerved, and nearly

3in. across; the four petals are a pleasing yellowish-green at the bases; when fully expanded they form a cross, being clear of each other; they become tinted with rose when they begin to fade. The leaves are of various sizes, sometimes spotted, lance-shaped, toothed, and attenuated at the base. The general habit of the plant is erect, but it is often procumbent; it has, from its slender

FIG. 66. ŒNOTHERA SPECIOSA.
(One-sixth natural size.)

stems, a light appearance, and for one evening's use the sprays are very useful in a cut state.

It propagates itself freely by its root runners near the surface. These roots may be transplanted in early spring, and they will flower the same year.

Flowering period, June to August.

### Œnothera Taraxacifolia.
DANDELION-LEAVED EVENING PRIMROSE; *Nat. Ord.*
ONAGRACEÆ.

FROM the great beauty of the flowers of this plant, it has not only become widely distributed, but a great favourite, considering that it was so recently introduced into this country as 1825; it came from Peru. Fortunately this charming exotic proves perfectly hardy in our climate; it is also herbaceous and perennial. No garden ought to be without so easily grown a flower, and though its foliage much resembles that of the common dandelion, a fine mass of it proves no mean setting for the large white flowers which spring from the midst of it. Another pleasing feature in connection with the flowers is that for a day they are pure white, after which they partly close and turn to a scarcely less beautiful delicate flesh tint. This colour and the half closed form are retained for several days; it exhales a sweet odour, about which there is a peculiarity. When newly opened —the first night—while the flowers are white, they will be found to have a grateful scent like tea roses; but if the older and coloured blooms are tried, they will be found to have the refreshing smell of almonds.

There is yet another curious trait about this lovely flower— it has a long stalk-like tube, which may be called the flower stalk, as, so to speak, it has no other, and the lower part—it being 4in. to 6in. long—is inclined to squareness, but near the top it becomes round and widens into the divisions of the calyx, being, in fact, the tube or undivided part of the calyx. Let the reader carefully examine this interesting flower. First pluck it with all its length of stem or tube (it may be 6in. long); with a small knife or needle split it upwards, and there will be exposed the style of a corresponding length. The tube and segments of the calyx are of a pale green colour, segments an inch or more long, finely pointed; the four petals are large, nearly round, and overlapping each other, forming a corolla more than 3in. across; they are satiny in appearance, and transparent, beautifully veined or nerved, the nerves having delicate green basements, from which spring stamens of a like colour, but with anthers ½in. long, evenly balanced, and furnished with lemon-yellow pollen. The leaves are herb-like, and, as the common name implies, like the leaves of the dandelion, similar in size, but more cut or lobed. The plant, however, varies materially from the dandelion, in having stems which push out all round the crown, growing to a considerable length, and resting on the ground.

This plant cannot well be grown in too large quantities, where there is plenty of room; it produces flowers for a long time, and they are highly serviceable for cutting purposes, though lasting only a short time. It cannot well be planted wrong as regards position, as it will thrive anywhere, providing the soil is enriched, it being a gross feeder; it should not, however, be planted where it will be likely to overgrow smaller and less rampant subjects. On the whole, it is one of those plants which afford a maximum of pleasure for a minimum of care, and needs no special culture—in fact, takes care of itself. Its propagation is simple, and may be carried out either by division of the old roots or by transplanting the self-sown seedlings into their blooming quarters, during March or April.

Flowering period, June to August.

## Omphalodes Verna.
CREEPING FORGET-ME-NOT; *Syn.* CYNOGLOSSUM OMPHALODES; *Nat. Ord.* BORAGINACEÆ.

THE common name of this pretty, hardy, herbaceous creeper at once gives the keynote to its description; it is a very old plant in English gardens, and a native of South Europe. Parkinson gives a very neat description of it : "This small borage shooteth forth many leaves from the roote, every one upon a long stalke, of a darke greene colour; the stalkes are small and slender, not above halfe a foote high, with very few leaves thereon, and at the toppes come forth the flowers, made of five blew round pointed leaves, every one upon a long foote stalke." This, together with the well-known form and habit of the plant, leaves little more to be said by way of description; and it may be added that though the flowers are akin to forget-me-nots, but more brilliant, the foliage is very different indeed, being nearly heart-shaped, and over 2in. long. Its habit is such that though its flowers are small, they are somewhat conspicuous, from their brightness, abundance, and manner in which they are produced, *i.e.*, well above a bright green mass of leaves; only bold clumps, however, show to such advantage. When the plant is fairly established, it makes rapid growth, increasing itself somewhat strawberry fashion, by runners.

It is worthy of note here that this semi-woody creeper does well under trees not too densely grown. Many inquiries are made for such subjects, and this is one of the number (which is far from ample) that can be relied upon for not only covering the bare earth, but also for bespangling such position with its bright blossoms for two months in spring. I have also tried it in pots, grown and bloomed under the shade of a trellised peach tree, in a small house, without artificial heat, where it not only did well, but vied with the violets for effectiveness.

This otherwise robust plant I have found to die when divided in the autumn (a period when many—indeed, I may say most—perennials are best transplanted), but when its propagation is carried out in spring, it grows like a weed.

Flowering period, March to May.

## Ononis Rotundifolia.
ROUND-LEAVED RESTHARROW; *Nat. Ord.* LEGUMINOSÆ.

ONE of the most charming of the "old-fashioned" border flowers, having been grown in this country since 1570. It came from the Pyrenees, is hardy, evergreen, and shrubby. The common name of the genus, Restharrow, is in reference to the long, tough, and woody roots and branches. According to Gerarde, these properties "maketh the oxen, whilst they be in plowing, to rest or stand still." Although this species has tough roots and branches, it seems more likely that the name would be from the trouble caused by the weedy species of the genus of his time.

In its growing state there is seen an exquisiteness of form and colour rarely approached by any other subject; from the manner

FIG. 67. ONONIS ROTUNDIFOLIA.
(Plant, one-sixth natural size; blossom, natural size.)

in which the unopened scarlet buds blend with the thick and handsome-shaped foliage, the illustration (Fig. 67) can scarcely do justice to it. It should not be judged by other and better known species of the genus, some of which are of a weedy character, and from which this is as distinct as it well can be. Besides having the valuable property of flowering all summer, it is otherwise a suitable subject for the most select collections of hardy flowers.

It grows 18in. high, and is erect and branched in habit; the
flowers are produced on short side shoots; in form they are pea-
flower-shaped, as the reader will infer from the order to which
the shrub belongs. The raceme seldom has more than two or
three flowers fully open at one time, when they are of a shaded
pink colour, and nearly an inch in length; the leaves are 1in. to
2in., ternate, sometimes in fives, ovate, toothed, and covered with
glandular hairs.

The plant should be grown in bold specimens for the best effect.
Ordinary garden soil suits it; if deeply dug and enriched, all
the better. It is not so readily increased by division of the roots
as many border plants, though root slips may, with care, be
formed into nice plants the first season; the better plan is to sow
the seed as soon as well ripened, from which more vigorous plants
may be had, and they will sometimes flower the following
summer, though far short of their natural size.

Flowering period, June to September.

## Onosma Taurica.
GOLDEN DROP; *Nat. Ord.* BORAGINACEÆ.

A HARDY perennial, somewhat woody, and retaining much of its
foliage in a fresh state throughout the winter, though by some
described as herbaceous. The leaves which wither remain persistent, and sometimes this proves a source of danger to the
specimen, from holding moisture during our wet winters, causing
rot to set in. It is a comparatively new plant in English
gardens, having been introduced from the Caucasus in 1801, and
as yet is seldom met with. Not only is it distinct in the form of
its flowers—as may be seen by the illustration (Fig. 68)—from
other species of its order, but it has bloom of exceptional beauty,
and the plant as a garden subject is further enhanced in value
from the fact of its delicious perfume and perpetual blooming
habit—*i.e.*, it flowers until stopped by frosts; in short, it is one
of the very finest hardy flowers, and if I could only grow a small
collection of fifty, this should be one of such collection.

The flowers are bright yellow, 1½in. long, somewhat pear-
shaped, and tubular. The calyx is long and deeply divided; the
corolla is narrowed at the mouth; segments short, broad, and
rolled back, forming a sort of rim. The flowers are arranged
in branched heads, which are one-sided. The flower stalks are
short, and the flowers and buds closely grown. The stems are
about a foot long, having short alternate shoots, which flower
later on; they are weighed to the ground with the numerous
flowers and buds; the leaves are 3in. to 6in. long, narrow,
lance-shaped, reflexed, and covered with short stiff hairs, which
impart a grey appearance to the foliage.

It should be grown fully exposed, as it loves sunshine; if

188    HARDY PERENNIALS AND

planted in the frequented parts of the garden, its delicious perfume is the more likely to be enjoyed; on rockwork, somewhat elevated, will perhaps prove the best position for it, as then the pendent flowers can be better seen and studied. The whole habit of the plant renders it a suitable subject for the rock garden; it may be grown in either loam or vegetable soil if well drained, and when it once becomes established in genial quarters it makes rapid growth and is very floriferous. What a rich bed could be formed of this, judiciously mixed with hardy fuchsias

FIG. 68. ONOSMA TAURICA.
(Plant, one-quarter natural size; blossom, one-half natural size.)

and the various linums, having deep blue flowers and graceful slender stems! These all love a breezy situation and sunshine, they also all flower at the same time, and continuously. To increase this choice plant, cuttings should be taken during summer; they may be rooted quickly if placed in a cucumber frame and kept shaded for ten or twelve days; water should be given carefully, or the hairy leaves will begin to rot. Aim at having the young stock well rooted and hardened off before the cold weather sets in.

Flowering period, June to the frosts.

## Orchis Foliosa.
LEAFY ORCHIS; *Nat. Ord.* ORCHIDACEÆ.

THIS terrestrial Orchid is not generally known to be hardy, but that such is the fact is beyond doubt. It is not only hardy, though it comes from Madeira, but it thrives better in this climate when exposed to all the drawbacks belonging to the open garden, or hardy treatment, than when kept under glass. It only seems to require two things—a deep rich soil and leaving alone—being very impatient of disturbance at its roots. Many of the hardy Orchids, though interesting, are not showy enough as flowers for beds or borders. This, however, is an exception, and is not only, in common with other Orchids, an interesting species, but a handsome and durable flower.

It blooms at different heights, from 9in. to 2ft.; the spike, as implied by the name, is leafy up to and among the flowered portion, which is from 3in. to 9in. long; the flowers are a cheerful purple colour, each ¾in. in diameter; the sepals are erect, cupped, and paler in colour than the other parts of the flower; petals small; lip large, three lobed, the middle one somewhat pointed; leaves oblong and smooth, lessening and becoming more subulate near the top of the stem. When well grown, this plant has a noble appearance, and when closely viewed is seen to be a flower of a high order, as, in fact, all the Orchids are.

Fortunately, it is not so particular either as regards soil or atmosphere as most of its relations, and it may frequently be met with in cottage gardens in splendid form. Good sandy loam, in a moist situation, suits it well, and I have seen it with fine spikes of bloom both in partial shade and fully exposed. Its position should be correctly noted, otherwise, when the tops have died down, the roots may suffer damage; they should be well guarded against disturbance. When increase is desirable the roots may be divided, but if they can be left alone it will be much to the advantage of the specimens.

Flowering period, June and July.

## Orchis Fusca,
BROWN ORCHIS; *Nat. Ord.* ORCHIDACEÆ.

A RARE and noble British species, terrestrial, and having a tuberous root of moderate size; the specific name does not always apply, as this species varies considerably in the colour of its flowers—certainly all are not brown. According to Gray, the flowers are "large, greenish-brown, brownish-purple, or pale ash grey;" the specimen from which our illustration (Fig. 69) was drawn may be said to be "brownish-purple," from its great number of brown spots; it is also slightly tinged with green. According to Linnæus, it is synonymous with *O. Militaris*, the

190  HARDY PERENNIALS AND

Soldier, or Brown Man Orchis. Of the native kinds of Orchis, many of which are now getting very scarce, it is desirable to know what's what. But, as a garden flower, the one now under consideration has many points of merit. The plant is bold and portly, and the foliage ample compared with many of the genus. The head of flowers is large, numerous, and well lifted up, while, far from their least good quality, is that of their fine aromatic perfume.

The full size of a flower is shown in the drawing. The sepals are seen to be broad, converging, and pointed; the lip, which is

FIG. 69. ORCHIS FUSCA.
(One-fourth natural size; 1 and 2, natural size of flower.)

rough, is three-parted; lobes, unequal and ragged; the side ones are long and narrow, the middle lobe is twice notched in an irregular manner; the spur is straight with the stem; bracts, short; the flowers are densely produced, forming a compact bunch 3in. to 4in. long, on a spike rather over a foot tall; they continue in perfection three weeks or a month. The leaves are 9in. or more in length, lance-shaped, and fully an inch broad in the middle; they are of a pale, shining, green colour, the root leaves resting on the ground.

I find this Orchid capable of withstanding very rough treatment, but it requires some time (two years) to get fairly established. Silky loam and leaf soil are suitable for it; a moist situation, but in no way of a stagnant character, should be given, and the position should also be carefully selected, so as to secure the brittle and top-heavy flower spikes from strong winds, otherwise it will suffer the fate of hundreds of tulips after a gale. It is propagated by root division after the foliage has died off.

Flowering period, end of May to end of June.

## Origanum Pulchellum.
### BEAUTIFUL MARJORAM; *Nat. Ord.* LABIATÆ.

THIS is indeed a well-named species or variety, whichever it may be; little seems to be known of its origin, but that it is distinct and beautiful is beyond doubt. It shines most as a rock plant; its long and bending stems, which are somewhat procumbent, have as much rigidity about them as to prevent their having a weak appearance; the tips, moreover, are erect, showing off to advantage the handsome imbricate bracts, bespangled as they are with numerous rosy-purple blossoms. The long and elegant panicles of bracteæ, together with the pleasing arrangement thereof, are the main features of this subject.

The rosy flowers are very small, and have the appearance of being packed between the bracteoles; still, their gaping forms are distinctly traceable, but the pretty lipped calyxes are quite hidden; the bract leaves are roundly-oval, acute, cupped, and touched with a nutty-brown tint on the outer sides; the spikes have many minor ones, being as fine as a thread, covered with short soft hairs, and of a brown colour; the leaves are ¾in. long, oval, entire, and downy. The plant or shrub grows 18in. high. As already hinted, the habit is procumbent, the older flower stems being woody; not only is it a bright object for rockwork, but it is in its finest form when most other flowers are past. The branches are useful in a cut state; the slender spikelets, with their pale green and brown tinted bracts, are very pretty by gas light, and they keep well for a long time in water.

The Marjorams are fond of a dry situation, and this is no exception to that rule. Rockwork or raised beds of sandy loam suits it to perfection, provided the aspect is sunny. It will, therefore, be seen that there is nothing special about its culture, neither is there in its propagation; cuttings may be taken in summer, or the rooted shoots may be divided at almost any time.

It flowers from September to the time of severe frosts, and is in its greatest beauty in October.

## Orobus Vernus.

PEASELING, OR SPRING BITTER VETCH; *Nat. Ord.* LEGUMINOSÆ.

A HARDY herbaceous perennial; it flowers in very early spring, and sometimes sooner, but it is in full beauty in April, its blooming period being very prolonged. Not only is this bright and handsome pea flower worth attention being a very old subject of English gardens, but also because of its intrinsic merit as a decorative plant. I say plant designedly, as its form is both sprightly and elegant, which, I fear, the illustration (Fig. 70) can hardly do justice to—more especially its spring tints and colours.

FIG. 70. OROBUS VERNUS.
(One-fourth natural size.)

Pretty nearly as soon as the growths are out of the earth the flowers begin to appear. The greatest height the plants attain rarely exceeds a foot; this commends it as a suitable border plant. Individually the flowers are not showy, but collectively they are pleasing and effective. When they first open they are a mixture of green, red, blue, and purple, the latter predominating. As they become older they merge into blue, so that a plant shows many flowers in various shades, none of which are quite an inch long, and being borne on slender drooping stalks, which issue from the leafy stems, somewhat below the leading growths, the bloom is set off to great advantage. The foliage in form resembles the common vetch, but is rather larger in the leaflets, and instead of being downy like the vetch, the leaves are smooth and bright. In a cut state, sprays are very useful, giving lightness to the stiffer spring flowers, such as tulips, narcissi, and hyacinths. Rockwork suits it admirably; it also does well in borders; but in any position it pays for liberal treatment in the form of heavy manuring. It seeds freely, and may be propagated by the seed or division of strong roots in the autumn. Whether rabbits can scent it a considerable distance off, I cannot say, but, certain it is, they find mine every year, and in one part of the garden eat it off bare.

Flowering period, March to May.

## Ourisia Coccinea.
### Nat. Ord. SCROPHULARIACEÆ.

A HARDY herbaceous perennial from South America, as yet rarely seen in English gardens, and more seldom in good form. As may be judged by the illustration (Fig. 71), it is a charming plant, but it has beauties which cannot be there depicted; its deep green and shining leaves constitute wavy masses of foliage, most pleasing to see, and the short-stemmed, lax clusters of dazzling scarlet flowers are thereby set off to great advantage. I have no fear of overpraising this plant, as one cannot well do that. I will, however, add that it is a decorative subject of the highest order, without a single coarse feature about it; seldom is it seen without a few solitary sprays of flowers, and it is never met with in a seedy or flabby state of foliage, but it remains plump throughout the autumn, when it sometimes shows a disposition to indulge in "autumnal tints." Though seldom encountered, this lovely plant is well known, as it is pretty sure to be, from notes made of it and published with other garden news; but it has the reputation of being a fickle plant, difficult to grow, and a shy bloomer. I trust this statement will not deter a single reader from introducing it into his garden; if I had found it manageable only with an unreasonable amount of care, I would not have introduced it here. It certainly requires special treatment, but all the conditions are so simple and practicable, in even the smallest garden, that it cannot be fairly termed difficult, as we shall shortly see.

The flowers are 1½in. long, in form intermediate between the pentstemon and snapdragon, but in size smaller, and the colour an unmixed deep scarlet: they are produced on stems 9in. high, round, hairy, and furnished with a pair of very small stem-clasping leaves, and where the panicle of flowers begins there is

o

a small bract, and less perfectly developed ones are at every joint, whence spring the wiry flower stalks in fours, threes, and twos, of various lengths and a ruddy colour. The panicles are lax and bending; the flowers, too, are pendent; calyx, five-parted and sharply toothed; stamens, four, and long as petals; anthers, large and cream coloured, style long and protruding. The leaves are radical, and have long, hairy, bending stalks; the main ribs are also hairy; beneath, they are of a deep green colour, bald, shining,

FIG. 71. OURISIA COCCINEA.
(Plant, one-fourth natural size; 1, blossom, one-half natural size.)

veined and wrinkled; their form is somewhat heart-shaped, sometimes oval, lobed, but not deeply, and unevenly notched; they grow in dense masses to the height of 6in.

It is said to like a peaty soil, in which I have never tried it. In the management of this plant I have found position to be the main desideratum; the soil may be almost anything if it is kept moist and sweet by good drainage, but *Ourisia coccinea* will not endure exposure to hot sunshine; even if the soil is moist it will suffer. I have large patches of it, 3ft. in diameter, growing in a mixture of clay and ashes, formed into a bank 18in. high, sloping north and screened by a hedge nearly 6ft. high from the midday sun, and shaded by overhanging trees; and I may also add that during the three years my specimens have occupied this shady, moist, but well drained position they have grown and flowered freely, always best in the deepest shade. As before hinted, there is a sort of special treatment required by this plant, but it is, after all, very simple. It is a slow surface creeper, should be planted freely in frequented parts of the garden, if the needful conditions exist, and no more beautiful surfacing can be recommended; grown in such quantities it will be available for cutting purposes. As a cut flower it is remarkably distinct and fine; it so outshines most other flowers that it must either have well selected company or be used with only a few ferns or grasses.

It is readily increased by division of the creeping roots, which is best done in early spring. If such divisions are made in the autumn, according to my experience, the roots rot; they should therefore be taken off either in summer, when there is still time for the young stock to make roots, or be left in the parent clump until spring, when they will start into growth at once.

Flowering period, May to September.

## Papaver Orientale.
ORIENTAL POPPY; *Nat. Ord.* PAPAVERACEÆ.

THE Oriental Poppy is a bold and showy plant, very hardy and perennial. There are several colours, but the bright scarlet variety is the most effective. Specimens of it which have become well established have a brilliant appearance during June; they are 3ft. high and attract the eye from a distance. Among other large herbaceous plants, as lupines, pæonies, thalictrums, &c., or even mixed with dwarf shrubs, they are grandly effective; indeed, almost too much so, as by the size and deep colour of the flowers they dazzle the eye and throw into the shade the surrounding flowers of greater beauty. The kinds with brick-red and other shades are comparatively useless. Their flowers are not only smaller, but wind or a few drops of rain spot the petals. A night's dew has the same effect; the stems, too, are weak and bending, which makes them much wanting in boldness, and when the flowers are damaged and the stems down there is little left about the Oriental Poppies that is ornamental.

The flowers are 6in. to 8in. across when expanded, produced singly on stout round stems covered with stiff hairs flattened down, and also distantly furnished with small pinnate leaves. Only in some varieties is the leafy bract (Fig. 72) to be found. This variety is sometimes called *P. bracteatum*. The calyx is three-parted and very rough; the six petals (see engraving) are

Fig. 72. Papaver Orientale (var. Bracteatum).
(One-fourth natural size.)

large, having well defined dark spots, about the size of a penny piece. The leaves are a foot or more in length, stiff but bending; they are thickly furnished with short hairs, pinnate and serrated.

This large poppy can be grown to an enormous size, and otherwise vastly improved by generous treatment; in a newly trenched and well manured plot a specimen has grown 3ft. high, and produced flowers 9in. across, the colour being fine; it will, however, do well in less favoured quarters—in fact, it may be used to fill up any odd vacancies in the shrubbery or borders. It is readily increased by division of the roots, and this may be done any time from autumn to February; it also ripens seed freely.

Flowering period, May to June.

## Pentstemons.
### *Nat. Ord.* SCROPHULARIACEÆ.

THE hybrids, which constitute the numerous and beautiful class commonly grown as "florists' flowers," are the kinds now under notice. The plant, when a year old, has a half-shrubby appearance, and if I said that it was but half hardy I should probably be nearer the mark than if I pronounced it quite hardy. It may, therefore, appear odd that I should class it with hardy perennials; there are, however, good reasons for doing so, and as these extra fine border plants are great favourites and deserve all the care that flowers can be worth, I will indicate my mode of growing them; but first I will state why the hybrid Pentstemons are here classed as hardy. One reason is that some varieties really are so, but most are not, and more especially has that proved to be the case during recent severe winters—the old plants, which I never trouble to take in, are mostly killed. Another reason why I do not object to their being classed as hardy is that cuttings or shoots from the roots appear to winter outside, if taken in the summer or autumn and dibbled into sand or a raised bed (so that it be somewhat drier than beds of the ordinary level), where they will readily root. Such a bed of cuttings I have found to keep green all the winter, without any protection other than a little dry bracken. My plants are so propagated and wintered.

The Pentstemon has of late years been much improved by hybridising, so that now the flowers, which resemble foxgloves, are not only larger than those of the typical forms, but also brighter, and few subjects in our gardens can vie with them for effectiveness; moreover, they are produced for several months together on the same plants, and always have a remarkably fresh appearance.

The corolla, which can be well seen both inside and out, has the pleasing feature of clearly pronounced colour on the outside, and rich and harmonious shadings inside; such flowers, loosely arranged on stems about 2ft. high, more or less branched, and furnished with lance-shaped foliage of a bright glossy green, go to make this border plant one that is justly esteemed, and which certainly deserves the little extra care needful during winter.

It is grandly effective in rows, but if in a fully exposed position it flags during hot sunshine; it is, therefore, a suitable plant to put among shrubs, the cool shelter of which it seems to enjoy. The remarks I have already made respecting its hardiness sufficiently indicate the mode of propagation. Old plants should not be depended upon, for though they are thoroughly perennial, they are not so hardy as the younger and less woody stuff — besides, young plants are far more vigorous bloomers.

Flowering period, June to August.

FIG. 73. PENTSTEMON.
(One-fourth natural size).

## Petasites Vulgaris.

*Syns.* TUSSILAGO PETASITES *and* T. FRAGRANS; WIN'1.' HELIOTROPE *and* COM;" BUTTERBUR; *Nat. Ord.* COMPOSITÆ.

I MUST explain why this native weed, of rampant growth and perennial character, is here mentioned as a fit subject for the garden. It blooms in the depth of winter — in fact, all winter; the flowers are not showy at all, but they are deliciously scented, whence the specific name *fragrans* and the common one " Winter Heliotrope," as resembling the scent of heliotrope. In its wild state it does not flower so early as when under cultivation; the latter state is also more favourable to its holding some green foliage throughout the winter. It has been said that there are different forms—male and female, or minor and major.

Parkinson recognises two forms, and as his remarks are interesting and clearly point to the variety under notice, I will quote him from " The Theater of Plants," page 419 : " The Butter burre is of two sorts, the one greater and the other lesser, differing also in the flowers, as you shall heare; but because they are so like one another, one description shall serve for them both. Each of them riseth up very early in the yeare, that is, in *February*, with a thicke stalke about a foote high, whereon are set a few small leaves, or rather peeces, and at the toppes a long spiked head of flowers, in the one which is the lesse and the more rare to finde, wholly white and of a better sent than the other (yet some say it hath no sent), in the greater, which is more common with us, of a blush or deepe red colour, according to the soile wherein it groweth, the clay ground bringing a paler colour somewhat weake, and before the stalke with the flowers have abidden a moneth above ground will be withered and gon, blowen away with the winde, and the leaves will beginne to spring, which when they are full growne are very large and broad, that they may very well serve to cover the whole body, or at the least the head like an umbello from the sunne and raine."

The flowers are produced on bare, fleshy scapes, springing from amongst the old foliage; the new leaves not appearing until much later. The bloom is small, of a pinky white colour; they are miniature forms, resembling the coltsfoot flowers, being arranged, however, in clusters. The leaves are large, cordate, downy, and soft to the touch, having long stout stems; they vary much in size, from 3in. to more than a foot across, according to the nature of the soil.

The usefulness of this plant consists entirely in its flowers as cut bloom, the least bit of which fills a large room with its most agreeable perfume. The plant, therefore, need not be grown in the more ornamental parts of the garden, and it should have a space exclusively allotted to it. It runs widely underground, and soon fills a large space. It enjoys moisture, but I have proved it to be more productive of bloom with leaves of half their usual size when planted in a rather dry situation with light but good soil. Usually a root does not produce flowers until two years after it has been planted. Poor as the flowers otherwise are, they are of great value in winter, when finely-scented kinds are scarce. They may be mixed with more beautiful forms and colours so as not to be seen, when, like violets in the hedgerow, they will exhale their grateful odour from a position of modest concealment.

Flowering period, November to February.

## Phlox.

HYBRID TALL VARIETIES; SUB-SECTIONS, SUFFRUTICOSA *and* DECUSSATA (EARLY *and* LATE FLOWERING); *Nat. Ord.* POLEMONIACEÆ.

THESE noble flowers are not only beautiful as individuals, but the cheerful appearance of our gardens during the autumn is much indebted to them; the great variety in colour and shade is as remarkable as it is effective. The finer sorts are known as "florists' flowers," being named. Whence they came (from which species) is not so clear, but in other respects than form and habit they are much in the way of *P. paniculata*. The Phlox family is a numerous one, and the species are not only numerous but extremely dissimilar, consisting of the dwarf woody trailers, or *P. procumbens* section, the oval-leafed section (*P. ovata*), the creeping or stolon-rooted (*P. stolonifera*) section, and the one now under notice, which differs so widely that many have seemed puzzled that these bold tall plants are so closely related to the prostrate, Whin-like species. The sub-divisions of the section under notice, viz., early and late flowering varieties, in all other respects except flowering period are similar, and any remarks of a cultural nature are alike applicable. This favourite part of the Phlox family is honoured with a specific name, viz., *P. omniflora* (all varieties of flowers), but notwithstanding that it is a most appropriate name it is seldom applied.

As the flowers must be familiar to the reader, they need hardly be described, and it is only necessary to mention the general features. They are produced on tall leafy stems in panicles of different forms, as pyramidal, rounded, or flattish; the clusters of bloom are sometimes 8in. in diameter in rich soil; the corolla of five petals is mostly flat, the latter are of a velvety substance, and coloured at their base, which in most varieties forms the "eye;" the tube is fine and bent, so as to allow the corolla to face upwards; the calyx, too, is tubular, the segments being deep and sharply cut; the buds abound in small clusters, and although the flowers are of a somewhat fugacious character, their place is quickly supplied with new blossoms (the succession being long maintained) which, moreover, have always a fresh appearance from the absence of the faded parts. The leaves, as indicated by the name *suffruticosa*, are arranged on half wood stems, and, as implied by the name *decussata*, are arranged in pairs, the alternate pairs being at right angles; these names are more in reference to the habit and form of the plants than the period of flowering, which, however, they are sometimes used to indicate; the leaves of some early kinds are leathery and shining, but for the most part they are herb-like and hairy, acutely lance-shaped, entire, and 2in. to 5in long.

Under ordinary conditions these hybrid forms of Phlox grow into neat bushy specimens of a willow-like appearance, 2ft. to 4ft. high, but in well-prepared richly-manured quarters they will not only grow a foot taller, but proportionally stouter, and also produce much finer panicles of bloom; no flower better repays liberal culture, and few there are that more deserve it. In the semi-shade of trees, the more open parts of the shubbery, in borders, or when special plantings are made, it is always the same cheerful subject, sweet, fresh, and waving with the breeze; its scent is spicy, in the way of cinnamon. The whole genus enjoys loam, but these strong-growing hybrids have a mass of long hungry roots, and, as already hinted, if they are well fed with manure they pay back with interest.

As cut bloom, if taken in entire panicles, they are bouquets in themselves. All are effective, and many of the more delicate colours are exquisite, vieing with the much more cared-for bouvardias and tender primulas.

To grow these flowers well there is nothing special about their management, but a method of treatment may be mentioned which, from the improved form it imparts to the specimens, as well as the more prolonged period in which extra-sized blooms are produced, is well worthy of being adopted. When the stems are 12in. or 15in. grown, nip off the tops of all the outer ones, they will soon break into two or four shoots. These will not only serve to "feather" down the otherwise "leggy" specimens and render them more symmetrical, but they will produce a second crop of flowers, and, at the same time, allow the first to develope more strongly. When the taller stems have done flowering, or become shabby, the tops may be cut back to the height of the under part of the then-formed buds of the early pinched shoots, and the extra light will soon cause them to flower; they should then be tied to the old stems left in the middle; this will quite transform the specimen, not only making it more neat and dwarf, but otherwise benefiting it—the old worn stems will have gone, and a new set of beaming flowers will reward the operator. The tops pinched out in the early part of the season make the best possible plants for the following season's bloom. They root like willows in a shady place in sandy loam, and are ready for planting in the open by midsummer, so that they have ample time to become strong before winter. Another way to propagate these useful flower roots is to divide strong clumps in the autumn after they have ceased to bloom.

The very earliest kinds (some three or four) begin to flower early in August, and by the middle of the month many are in bloom; the late-flowering (*decussata*) section is a month later; all, however, are continued bloomers.

## Phlox Frondosa.
FRONDED P.; *Nat. Ord.* POLEMONIACEÆ.

A HARDY creeper; one of the dwarf section, having half-woody, wiry stems. For this and many other species of the Creeping Phlox we are indebted to North America. Of late years these beautiful flowers have received much attention, not only from the trade, but also from amateurs, some of whom have taken much pains in crossing the species by hybridising, notably the late Rev. J. G. Nelson. Perhaps the most distinct and beautiful of all the dwarf Phloxes is the one which bears his name—the white-flowered *P. Nelsoni*. I have selected the species *P. frondosa*, because the specific name is, perhaps, beyond that of any of the others, more generally descriptive of all the following kinds: *P. divaricata*, *P. glaberrima*, *P. Nelsoni* (white flowers), *P. reflexa*, *P. oculata*, *P. setacea*, *P. s. atropurpurea*, *P. s. violacœa*, *P. subulata*, *P. prostrata*. These differ but slightly from one another, so little, indeed, that many discard the distinctions; still, they do exist, and may be clearly seen when grown close together in collections. The flowers differ in depth of colour; the leaves of some are more recurved, crossed, twisted, shining, or pointed, also broader and longer; the stems likewise differ; herein the distinctions are seen, probably, more than in either flowers or leaves. Sometimes they are, in the different species, long or short, leafy, branched, dense, arched, and divaricate, but, although at any time when their fresh foliage is upon them, and when they are so close together that the eye can take them all in at a glance, their distinctions are fairly clear, autumn is the time to see them in their most definite and beautiful form. Like many other North American plants, they have lovely autumnal tints, then their forms have rich glistening colours, and they are seen to not only differ considerably, but, perhaps, to more advantage than when in flower; but let me add at once that I have only proved these plants to take such rich autumnal colours when they have been grown so as to rest on stones, which not only keep them from excess of moisture, from worm casts, &c., but secure for them a healthy circulation of air under their dense foliage. From the above, then, it will be seen that a general description of *P. frondosa* will apply to the other species and varieties mentioned.

The flowers are lilac-rose; calyx, tubular; corolla of five petals, narrow and notched; leaves, awl-shaped, short, bent, and opposite; stems, branched, dense and trailing.

The dwarf Phloxes are pre-eminently rock plants, as which they thrive well; when raised from the ground level, so as to be nearly in the line of sight, they are very effective. They should be so planted that they can fall over the stones, like the one from which the illustratiion (Fig. 74) was drawn. For at least a fortnight the plants are literally covered with flowers, and at all times they form neat rock plants, though in winter they have the appearance of short withered grass; even then the stems are full of health, and in early spring they become quickly furnished with leaves and flowers. These Phloxes make good edgings. Notwithstanding their dead appearance in winter, a capital suggestion occurred to me by an accidental mixture of croci with the Phlox. At the time when the latter is most unseasonable the crocuses, which should be planted in the same line, may be seen coming through the browned foliage. When in flower, the blooms will not only be supported by this means, but also be preserved from splashes; when the crocuses are past their prime, the Phlox will have begun to grow, and, to further its well doing, its stems should be lifted and the then lengthened foliage of the

FIG. 74. PHLOX FRONDOSA.
(Plant, one-sixth natural size; 1, natural size of flower.)

crocuses should be drawn back to the under side of the Phlox, where it might remain to die off. This would allow the Phlox to have the full light, and the arrangement would be suitable for the edge of a shrubbery or border of herbaceous plants, or even along the walks of a kitchen garden.

The Phloxes are easily propagated, either from rooted layers or cuttings. The latter should be put into a good loam and kept shaded for a week or two. Early spring is the best time.

Flowering period, March to May.

## Physalis Alkekengi.
WINTER CHERRY; *Nat. Ord.* SOLANACEÆ.

THIS plant begins to flower in summer; but as a garden subject its blossom is of no value; the fine large berries, however, which are suspended in orange-yellow husks of large size, are very ornamental indeed, and form a very pleasing object amongst other "autumnal tints." It is not till October that the fruit begins to show its richness of colour. The plant is quite hardy, though a native of southern Europe; it is also herbaceous and perennial, and it has been grown in this country for 330 years. Still, it is not to be seen in many gardens. An old common name for it was "Red Nightshade," and Gerarde gives a capital illustration of it in his Herbal, under the name *Solanum Halicacabum.*

*P. Alkekengi* grows to the height of about two feet. The stems of the plant are very curious, being somewhat zig-zag in shape, swollen at the nodes, with sharp ridges all along the stems; otherwise, they are round and smooth. The leaves are produced in twins, their long stalks issuing from the same part of the joint; they are of various forms and sizes, but mostly heart-shaped, somewhat acute, and 2in. to 4in. long. The little soft creamy white flowers spring from the junction of the twin leaf-stalks; their anthers are bulky for so small a flower. The calyx continues to grow after the flower has faded, and forms the Chinese-lantern-like covering of the scarlet berry; the latter will be over ½in. in diameter, and the orange-coloured calyx 1½in., when fully developed. In autumn the older stems cast their leaves early, when the finely-coloured fruit shows to advantage; the younger stems keep green longer, and continue to flower until stopped by the frost. To this short description I may add that of Gerarde, which is not only clear but pleasantly novel: "The red winter Cherrie bringeth foorth stalkes a cubite long, rounde, slender, smooth, and somewhat reddish, reeling this way and that way by reason of his weakness, not able to stande vpright without a support: whereupon do growe leaues not vnlike to those of common nightshade, but greater; among which leaues come foorth white flowers, consisting of five small leaues; in the middle of which leaues standeth out a berrie, greene at the first, and red when it is ripe, in colour of our common Cherrie and of the same bignesse, which is enclosed in a thinne huske or little bladder of a pale reddish colour, in which berrie is conteined many small flat seedes of a pale colour. The rootes be long, not vnlike to the rootes of Couch grasse, ramping and creeping within the vpper crust of the earth farre abroade, whereby it encreaseth greatly."

The stems, furnished with fruit of good colour, but otherwise bare, make capital decorations for indoors, when mixed with tall grasses, either fresh or dried, and for such purposes this plant is worth growing; any kind of soil will do, in an out-of-the-way part, but if in shade, the rich colour will be wanting.

**Flowering period, June to frosts.**

## Podophyllum Peltatum.

DUCK'S-FOOT, *sometimes called* MAY APPLE; *Nat. Ord.*
PODOPHYLLACEÆ.

A HARDY herbaceous perennial from North America, more or less grown in English gardens since 1664. As may be seen from the illustration (Fig. 75), it is an ornamental plant, and though

FIG. 75. PODOPHYLLUM PELTATUM.
(One-third natural size.)

its flowers are interesting, they are neither showy nor conspicuous, as, from the peculiar manner in which they are produced, they are all but invisible until sought out. Its leaves and berries constitute the more ornamental parts of the plant.

The flowers are white, not unlike the small white dog-rose in both size and form; the calyx is of three leaves, which fall off; the corolla, of six to nine petals; peduncle nearly an inch long, which joins the stem at the junction of the two leaf stalks, only one flower being produced on a stem or plant. The leaves join the rather tall and naked stem by stalks, 2in. to 3in. long; they are handsome in both form and habit. As the specific name implies, the leaves are peltate or umbrella-shaped, deeply lobed, each lobe being deeply cut, and all unevenly toothed and hairy at the edges, with a fine down covering the under sides; the upper surface is of a lively, shining green colour, and finely veined. The flower is succeeded by a large one-celled ovate berry, in size and form something like a damson, but the colour is yellow when ripe, at which stage the berry becomes more conspicuous than the flower could be, from the manner in which the young leaves were held.

We want cheerful-looking plants for the bare parts under trees, and this is a suitable one, provided the surface soil has a good proportion of vegetable matter amongst it, and is rather moist. The thick horizontal roots creep near the surface, so it will be seen how important it is to secure them against drought otherwise than by depth of covering; a moist and shady position, then, is indispensable. In company with trilliums, hellebores, anemones, and ferns, this graceful plant would beautifully associate. Another way to grow it is in pots, when exactly the required kind of compost can easily be given, viz., peat and chopped sphagnum. Thus potted, plunged in wet sand, and placed in a northern aspect, it will be found not only to thrive well, as several specimens have done with me, but also to be worth all the trouble. To propagate it, the long creeping roots should be cut in lengths of several inches, and to a good bud or crown. When so cut in the autumn, I have proved them to rot when planted, but others buried in sand until February, and then planted, have done well.

Flowering period, May and June.

## Polyanthus.
### *Nat. Ord.* PRIMULACEÆ.

THIS, with its numerous varieties, comes under *Primula veris*, or the common Cowslip. The improved varieties which have sprung from this native beauty of our meadows and hedgerows are innumerable, and include the rich "gold-laced" kinds—which are cared for like children and are annually placed on the exhibition tables—as well as the homely kinds, which grow in the open borders by the hundred. The Polyanthus is eminently a flower for English gardens; and this country is noted for the fine sorts here raised, our humid climate suiting the plant in every way;

its flowers offer a variety of colour, an odour of the sweetest kind, full and rich, reminding us not only of spring time, but of youthful rambles and holidays.

As an "old-fashioned" flower for garden decoration it is effective and useful, from the great quantity of bloom it sends forth and the length of its flowering season; from its love of partial shade it may be planted almost anywhere. Its neat habit, too, fits it for scores of positions in which we should scarcely think of introducing less modest kinds; such nooks and corners of our gardens should be made to beam with these and kindred flowers, of which we never have too many. Plant them amongst bulbs, whose leaves die off early, and whose flowers will look all the happier for their company in spring; plant them under all sorts of trees, amongst the fruit bushes, and where only weeds have appeared, perhaps, for years; dig and plant the Polyanthus, and make the wilderness like Eden.

Flowering period, February to June.

## Polygonum Brunonis.
### KNOTWEED; *Nat. Ord.* POLYGONACEÆ.

THIS is a dwarf species from India, but quite hardy. It is pretty, interesting, and useful. The flowers are produced on erect stems a foot high, and formed in spikes 3in. to 5in. long, which are as soft as down and smell like heather. The colour is a soft rose. These flowers spring from a dense mass of rich foliage; the leaves in summer and early autumn are of a pleasing apple-green colour, smooth, oblong, and nearly spoon-shaped from the narrowing of the lower part; the midrib is prominent and nearly white; the leaf has rolled edges, and is somewhat reflexed at the point. Let the reader closely examine the leaves of this species while in their green state, holding them up to a strong light, and he will then behold the beauty and finish of Nature to a more than ordinary degree. This subject is one having the finest and most lasting of "autumnal tints," the dense bed of leaves turn to a rich brick-red, and, being persistent, they form a winter ornament in the border or on rockwork. The habit of the plant is creeping, rooting as it goes. It is a rampant grower, and sure to kill any dwarf subject that may be in its way.

It may be grown in any kind of soil, and almost in any position, but it loves sunshine. If its fine lambtail-shaped flowers are desired, it should be grown on the flat, but, for its grand red autumnal leaf tints, it should be on the upper parts of rockwork. It is self-propagating, as already hinted.

The flowers prove capital for dressing epergnes. I had not seen them so used, until the other day a lady visitor fancied a few spikes, and when I called at her house a day or two later saw them mixed with white flowers and late flowering forget-me-nots—they were charming.

Flowering period, August to the time of frosts.

## Polygonum Cuspidatum.
CUSPID KNOTWEED; *Nat. Ord.* POLYGONACEÆ.

A RECENT introduction from China, perfectly hardy, shrub-like but herbaceous; a rampant grower, attaining the height of 6ft. or 7ft., and spreading fast by means of root suckers. During the early spring it pushes its fleshy shoots, and the coloured leaves, which are nearly red, are very pleasing; as they unfold they are seen to be richly veined, and are as handsome as the beautiful Fittonias, so much admired as hothouse plants.

The long slender stems grow apace, and when the growth has been completed the flowers issue from the axils of the leaves; they are in the form of drooping feathery panicles, 4in. to 5in. long, creamy white, and produced in clusters, lasting for three weeks or more in good condition. The leaves are 3in. to 4in. long, nearly heart-shaped but pointed, entire, and stalked, of good substance, and a pale green colour; they are alternately and beautifully arranged along the gracefully-arching stems. The specimens are attractive even when not in bloom. If the roots are allowed to run in their own way for two or three years they form a charming thicket, which must prove a pleasant feature in any large garden.

All through the summer its branches are used as dressings for large vases, and, either alone or with bold flowers, they prove most useful. In the shrubbery, where it can bend over the grass, from its distinct colour and graceful habit, it proves not only an effective but a convenient subject, as it allows the mowing machine to work without hindrance or damage. It is a capital plant for the small town garden. After sending to a friend several hampers of plants season after season, all without satisfactory results, owing to the exceptionally bad atmosphere of the neighbourhood, I sent him some of this, and it has proved suitable in every way.

Flowering period, July and August.

*P. c. compactum* is a variety of the above. It is, however, very distinct in the way implied by its name, being more compact and rigid, and not more than half as tall. The leaves, too, are somewhat crimped, and of a much darker colour, the stems are nearly straight and ruddy, and the flowers are in more erect racemes, the colour yellowish-white. It forms a handsome bush, but is without the graceful habit of the type. Like the other knotweeds described, it enjoys a sandy loam, and requires nothing in the way of special culture. The roots may be transplanted or divided when the tops have withered.

## Polygonum Filiformis Variegatum.

KNOTWEED; *Nat. Ord.* POLYGONACEÆ.

VERY hardy and effective. I simply mention this as a foliage plant. The leaves are large, drooping, and finely splashed or marbled with pale green and yellow, in shape oval-oblong, being crimped between the veins. It is a scarce variety. Fine for the sub-tropical garden. Culture, the same as for all the Knotweeds. Flowering period, late summer.

## Polygonum Vaccinifolium.

VACCINIUM-LEAVED KNOTWEED; *Nat. Ord.* POLYGONACEÆ.

IT may seem odd that we should go into the Dock family for plants and flowers for our gardens; still we may, and find some truly beautiful species. The above-named is a charming alpine, coming from the Himalayas, and proves perfectly hardy in our climate; it is seldom met with and cannot be generally known, otherwise it would be more patronised; it forms a pretty dwarf shrub, with woody slender stems, clothed with small shining foliage.

The flowers are very small, resembling those of the smaller ericas, and of a fine rosy colour; the unopened ones are even more pretty, having a coral-like effect; they are arranged in neat spikes, about 2in. long, and tapering to a fine point; they are numerously produced all along the procumbent branches, becoming erect therefrom. As the specific name denotes, the leaves are Vaccinium-like—*i.e.*, small and oval, like box, but not so stout; they are closely set on the stems, are of a pale shining green, and somewhat bent or rolled. The habit is exceedingly neat, and, when in flower, a good specimen is a pleasing object; it is only a few inches high, but spreads quickly.

On rockwork it seems quite at home. My example has shade from the mid-day sun, and, without saying that it should have shade, I may safely say that it does well with it. The plant will thrive in sandy loam and is readily increased by putting small stones on the trailing stems, which soon root.

The leafy stems, with their coral-like, miniature spires, are useful in a cut state, so pretty, in fact, that it does not require any skill to "bring them in."

Flowering period, August to the frosts.

## Potentilla Fruticosa.

SHRUBBY CINQUEFOIL; *Nat. Ord.* ROSACEÆ.

IN mountainous woods this native deciduous shrub is found wild, and it is much grown in gardens, where it not only proves very attractive, but from its dwarf habit and flowering throughout the summer and autumn months, it helps to keep the borders or rock garden cheerful.

The flowers, which are lemon yellow, are in form like those of its relative, the strawberry, but smaller; they are produced in terminal small bunches, but seldom are more than two or three open at the same time, and more often only one; but from the numerous branchlets, all of which produce bloom, there seems to be no lack of colour. In gardens it grows somewhat taller than in its wild state, and if well exposed to the sun it is more floriferous, and the individual flowers larger.

It attains the height of 2ft. 6in.; the flowers are 1in. across; the petals apart; calyx and bracteæ united; ten parted; each flower has a short and slender stalk. The leaves are 2in. or more in length, pinnate, five but oftener seven parted, the leaflets being oblong, pointed, entire and downy; the leaf stalks are very slender, and hardly an inch long; they spring from the woody stems or branches, which are of a ruddy colour, and also downy. The habit of the shrub is densely bushy, and the foliage has a greyish green colour from its downiness.

This subject may be planted in any part of the garden where a constant blooming and cheerful yellow flower is required; it is pretty but not showy; its best quality, perhaps, is its neatness. It enjoys a vegetable soil well drained, and propagates itself by its creeping roots, which push up shoots or suckers at short spaces from the parent stock.

Flowering period, summer to early frosts.

## Pratia Repens.

*Syn.* LOBELIA PRATIANA; CREEPING PRATIA; *sometimes called* LOBELIA REPENS; *Nat. Ord.* LOBELIACEÆ.

IN October this small creeper is a very pretty object on rockwork, when the earlier bloom has become changed into oval fruit-pods. These berry-like capsules are large for so small a plant, and of a bright and pleasing colour. These, together with the few flowers that linger, backed up, as they are, with a dense bed of foliage, interlaced with its numerous filiform stems, present this subject in its most interesting and, perhaps, its prettiest form.

The flowers may be called white, but they have a violet tint, and are over half-an-inch in length. The calyx is adnate in relation to the ovarium, limb very short, but free and five-toothed; the corolla is funnel-shaped, but split at the back, causing it to appear one-sided. The solitary flowers are produced on rather long stems from the axils of the leaves. As they fade the calyces become fleshy and much enlarged, and resemble the fruit of the hawthorn when ripe. The leaves are distantly arranged on the creeping stems, $\frac{1}{2}$in. long, oval, roundly toothed and undulated, fleshy, somewhat glaucous and petiolate. The habit of the plant is to root as it creeps, and the thread-like stems intersect each other in a pleasing way. They are to be seen distinctly, as the leaves are not only small, but distant, and seem to rest on a lattice-work of stems. This species comes from the Falkland Islands, and is of recent introduction.

It is herbaceous and perennial, and proves hardy in this climate if planted on a well-drained soil of a vegetable character. It not only enjoys such a position as the slope of rockwork, but, when so placed, it may be seen to advantage. It should be free from shade, or the fruit will not colour well. It will therefore be seen that this is a rock plant, so far as its decorative qualities are concerned. It may, however, be grown well on flat beds of peat soil, where its fruit will mature finely, but it cannot be so well seen. It is self-propagating. Transplantings should be made in spring, or tufts may be placed in pots, during the autumn, and put in cold frames, as then they would not suffer displacement by frosts.

Flowering period, June to frosts.

## Primula Acaulis.
*Syn.* P. VULGARIS, COMMON PRIMROSE; *Nat. Ord.*
PRIMULACEÆ.

THIS common native flower needs no description, growing everywhere, yet we all seem to enjoy its company in our gardens, though it may, perhaps, be seen wild close by. It is a flower of more interest than ordinary, and to the florist of some importance. The great variety of double and single primroses have all sprung from this, the modest form found in our woods and damp hedgerows, and the number is being added to year by year. The generic name is in allusion to a quality—that of early or first flowering. The specific name, *acaulis*, is in reference to its stemlessness, which is its main distinguishing feature from the Polyanthus and Oxlip (*P. veris*). I may add, that from the great variety of *P. acaulis* and *P. veris*, and their mutual resemblance in many instances, the casual observer may often find in this feature a ready means by which to identify a specimen. Of course, there are other points by which the different species can be recognised, even when the scape is out of sight, but I am now speaking of their general likeness to each other in early spring.

Common Cowslips or Paigles (*P. veris*), great Cowslips or Oxlips (*P. elatior*), field primrose or large-flowered primrose (*P. acaulis*), were all in olden times called by the general name of primrose, the literal meaning of which is first-rose Old authorities give us many synonymous names for this plant, as *P. grandiflora, P. vulgaris, P. sylvestris,* and *P. veris*. The last is given by three authorities, including Linnæus. As this seems to clash hard with the name as applied to the Cowslip species, I may at once state that Linnæus has only that one name for the three species, viz: *P. acaulis, P. elatior, P. veris;* the name *P. vulgaris,* by another authority, is explained by the same rule; Curtis (*Flora Londinensis*) is the authority for the name *P. acaulis.*

I need not here go into any of the varieties, beyond giving a cursory glance at them as a whole. The double kinds are all beautiful, some superb and rare, as the ruby and crimson; the white, sulphur, mauve, magenta, and other less distinct double forms are more easily grown, and in some parts are very plentiful. The single kinds have even a more extensive range in colour. We have now fine reds and what are called blue primrose; the latter variety is not a blue, but certainly a near appoach to it. It is an interesting occupation to raise the coloured primroses from seed, not only because of the pleasing kinds which may be so obtained, but under cultivation, as in a wild state, seedlings are always seen to be the more vigorous plants; self-sown seed springs up freely on short grass, sandy walks, and in half-shaded borders; but when it is sought to improve the strain, not only should seedlings be regularly raised, but it should be done systematically, when it will be necessary, during the blooming season, to look over the flowers daily and remove inferior kinds as soon as proved, so that neither their seed nor pollen can escape and be disseminated. This part of the operation alone will, in a few years, where strictly carried out, cause a garden to become famous for its primroses. Seasonable sowing, protection from slugs, and liberal treatment are also of the utmost importance.

Briefly stated, the *modus operandi* should be as follows: Sow the seed at the natural season, soon as ripe, on moist vegetable soil; do not cover it with more than a mere dash of sand; the aspect should be north, but with a little shade any other will do; the seedlings will be pretty strong by the time of the early frosts; about that time they should, on dry days, have three or four slight dressings of soot and quicklime; it should be dusted over them with a "dredge" or sieve; this may be expected to clear them of the slug pest, after which a dressing of sand and half-rotten leaves may be scattered over them; this will not only keep them fresh and plump during winter, but also protect them from the effects of wet succeeded by frost, which often lifts such things entirely out of the earth. In March, plant out in well enriched loam, in shady quarters; many will flower in late spring. Another plan would be to leave them in the seed bed if not too rank, where most would flower; in either case, the seed bed might be left furnished with undisturbed seedlings. The main crop of bloom should not be looked for until the second spring after the summer sowing.

The double forms are not only less vigorous, but the means of propagation are limited; offsets of only healthy stock should be taken in early summer. A rich retentive loam suits them, or moist vegetable soil would do: shade, however, is the great desideratum; exposure to full sunshine harms them, even if well moistened at the roots; besides, in such positions red spider is sure to atta:k them. This mode of propagation is applicable to desirable single varieties, as they cannot be relied upon to produce stock true to themselves from seed. In planting offsets it is a good practice to put them in rather deeply; not only are the new roots emitted from above the old ones, but the heart of the offset seems to be sustained during the warm and, perhaps, dry weather, by being set a trifle below the surface. This I have ever proved to be a sure and quick method in the open garden. Flowering period, February to June.

## Primula Capitata.
ROUND-HEADED PRIMULA; *Nat. Ord.* PRIMULACEÆ.

HARDY, herbaceous, and perennial. Before referring to this Primula in particular, I would say a word or two respecting hardy and alpine Primulæ in general. It may appear strange and, on my part, somewhat presumptuous, when I state that this section of the Primula family is little known. Gardeners, both old and young, who have seen them in collections, have asked what they were as they stood over them admiring their lovely flowers. They are, however, very distinct on the one hand from the primrose (*Primula vulgaris* or *acaulis*) and polyanthus (*Primula elatior*) sections; and also from the *P. sinensis* section—the species with so many fine double and single varieties, much grown in our greenhouses, and which, of course, are not hardy. The hardy and distinct species to which I now allude are mostly from alpine habitats, of stunted but neat forms, widely distinct, and very beautiful.

The British representatives of this class are *Primula farinosa* and *P. Scotica*, but from nearly all parts of the temperate zone these lovely subjects have been imported. It may not be out of place to name some of them: *P. Allioni*, France; *P. amœna*, Caucasus; *P. auricula*, Switzerland; *P. Carniolica*, Carniola; *P. decora*, South Europe; *P. glaucescens* and *P. grandis*, Switzerland; *P. glutinosa*, South Europe; *P. latifolia*, Pyrenees; *P. longifolia*, Levant; *P. marginata*, Switzerland; *P. minima*, South Europe; *P. nivalis*, Dahuria; *P. villosa*, Switzerland; *P. viscosa*, Piedmont; *P. Wulfeniana*, *P. spectabilis*, *P. denticulata*, *P. luteola*, *P. Tirolensis*, and others, from the Himalayas and North America, all of which I have proved to be of easy culture, either on rockwork, or in pots and cold frames, where, though they may be frozen as hard as the stones amongst which their roots delight to run, they are perfectly safe. The treatment they will not endure is a confined atmosphere.

*P. capitata*, which is a native of Sikkim, is still considered to be new in this country, though it was flowered at Kew about thirty years ago, but it has only become general in its distribution during the past three or four years.

The flowers are borne on stems which are very mealy, and 6in. to 9in. high; the head of bloom is round and dense, 1½in. across. The outer pips are first developed, and as they fade the succeeding rings or tiers extend and hide them. The very smallest in the centre of the head remain covered with the farina-like substance, and form a beautiful contrast to the deep violet-blue of the opened, and the lavender-blue of the unopened pips. One head of bloom will last fully four weeks. The denseness and form of the head, combined with the fine colour of the bloom, are the chief points which go to make this Primula very distinct. The leaves, which are arranged in rosette form, are otherwise very pretty, having a mealy covering on the under side, sometimes of a golden hue; they are also finely wrinkled and toothed, giving the appearance, in small plants, of a rosette of green feathers. Sometimes the leaves are as large as a full-grown polyanthus leaf, whilst other plants, which have flowered equally well, have not produced foliage larger than that of primroses, when having their earliest flowers.

It makes a fine pot subject, but will not endure a heated greenhouse. It should be kept in a cold frame, with plenty of air. It may be planted on rockwork where it will not get the midday sun. I hear that it grows like grass with a correspondent whose garden soil is stiff loam; there it seeds and increases rapidly. My first experience with it was troublesome; when dying down in the winter, the leaves, which are persistent, seemed to collect moisture at the collar and cause it to rot. I tried planting not quite so deeply, and I imagine that it has proved a remedy. So choice a garden subject should not be passed by because it cannot be dibbled in and grown as easily as a cabbage. Old plants produce offsets which, as soon as the April showers come, may be transplanted in loamy soil and a shady situation. Propagation may also be carried on by seed when well ripened, but that has not been my experience of it hitherto.

Flowering period, April to June.

## Primula Cashmerianum.

CASHMERE PRIMROSE; *Nat. Ord.* PRIMULACEÆ.

THIS belongs to the large-leaved and herbaceous section, and though it comes (as its name specifies) from a much warmer climate than ours, its habitat was found at a great altitude, and

OLD-FASHIONED GARDEN FLOWERS. 215

it has been proved to be perfectly hardy in North Britain. This species is comparatively new to English gardens, but it has already obtained great favour and is much grown (see Fig. 76).

FIG. 76. PRIMULA CASHMERIANUM.
(One-fourth natural size.)

No collection of *Primulæ* can well be without it; its boldness, even in its young state, is the first characteristic to draw attention, for with the leaf development there goes on that of the scape. For a time the foliage has the form of young cos lettuce, but the under sides are beautifully covered with a meal resembling gold dust. This feature of the plant is best seen at the early stage of its growth, as later on the leaves bend or flatten to the ground in rosette form, the rosettes being often more than 12in. across. The golden farina varies in both quantity and depth of colour on different plants.

The flower scape is from 9in. to 12in. high, nearly as stout as a clay pipe stem, and very mealy, thickening near the top. The flowers, which are small, of a light purple colour, and having a yellow eye, are densely arranged in globular trusses, each lasting more than a fortnight in beauty. The leaves when resting on the ground show their finely serrated edges and pleasing pale green, which contrasts oddly with the under sides of those still erect, the latter being not only of a golden colour, as already mentioned, but their edges are turned, almost rolled under.

This plant loves moisture, and it will adorn any position where it can be well grown; it will also endure any amount of sunshine if it has plenty of moisture at the roots, and almost any kind of soil will do except clay, but peat and sand are best for it, according to my experience. During winter the crown is liable to rot, from the amount of moisture which lodges therein somewhat below the ground level; latterly I have placed a piece of glass over them, and I do not remember to have lost one so treated. Offsets are but sparingly produced by this species; propagation is more easily carried out by seed, from which plants will sometimes flower the first year.

Flowering period, March to May.

## Primula Denticulata.
TOOTHED PRIMULA; *Nat. Ord.* PRIMULACEÆ.

THIS is one of that section of the Primrose family having stout scapes and compact heads of bloom. It is a comparatively recent introduction from the Himalayas, a true alpine, and perfectly hardy in this climate. As a garden flower, it has much merit, blooming early and profusely. It cannot be too highly commended for its fine form as a plant and beauty as a flower, more especially as seen on rockwork. The flower buds begin in very early spring to rise on their straight round stems, new foliage being developed at the same time.

The flowers are arranged in dense round clusters, and are often in their finest form when nearly a foot high. They are of a light purple colour, each flower $\frac{1}{2}$in. across, corolla prettily cupped, segments two-lobed, greenish white at bases, tube long and cylindrical, calyx about half length of tube, teeth rather long and of a dark brown colour. The scape is somewhat dark-coloured, especially near the apex. The leaves are arranged in rosette form, are lance-shaped, rolled back at the edges and toothed, also wrinkled and downy; they continue to grow long after the flowers have faded.

Delicate as the flowers seem, they stand the roughest storms without much hurt.

*P. d. major* is a larger form in all its parts.
*P. d. nana* is more dwarfed than the type.
*P. d. amabilis* is a truly lovely form, having darker foliage and rosy buds; its habit, too, is even more neat and upright, and the blooming period earlier by about two weeks.

A moist position and vegetable mould suit it best, according to my experience, and the dips of rockwork are just the places for it, not exactly in the bottom, for the following reason: The large crowns are liable to rot from wet standing in them, and if the plants are set in a slope it greatly helps to clear the crowns of stagnant moisture. Propagation is by means of offsets, which should be taken during the growing season, so that they may form good roots and become established before winter.

Flowering period, March to May.

## Primula Farinosa.
MEALY PRIMROSE, or BIRD'S-EYE; *Nat. Ord.* PRIMULACEÆ.

THE pretty native species, very common in a wild state in some parts, near which, of course, it need not be grown in gardens; but as its beauty is unquestionable, and as there are many who do not know it, and evidently have never seen it, it ought to have a place in the garden. It is herbaceous and perennial. All its names are strictly descriptive. The little centre has a resemblance to a bird's eye, and the whole plant is thickly covered with a meal-like substance. Small as this plant is, when properly grown it produces a large quantity of bloom for cutting purposes.

It is 3in. to 8in. high, according to the situation in which it is grown. The flowers are light purple, only ½in. across, arranged in neat umbels; the corolla is flat, having a bright yellow centre; leaves small, ovate-oblong, roundly toothed, bald, and powdery beneath; the flower scapes are round and quite white, with a meal-like covering.

In stiff soil and a damp situation this little gem does well, or it will be equally at home in a vegetable soil, such as leaf mould or peat, but there must be no lack of moisture, and it is all the better for being screened from the mid-day sun, as it would be behind a hedge or low wall. So freely does it bloom, that it is not only worth a place in the garden, but repays all the trouble required to establish it in proper quarters, after which it will take care of itself, by producing offsets and seedlings in abundance.

Flowering period, April to June.

## Primula Marginata.
*Syn.* P. CRENATA; MARGINED PRIMROSE; *Nat. Ord.* PRIMULACEÆ.

A NATIVE of Switzerland, so rich in alpine flowers; this is but a small species, yet very distinct and conspicuous (see Fig. 77).

As its specific name denotes, its foliage has a bold margin, as if stitched with white silken thread, and the whole plant is thickly covered with a mealy substance. So distinct in these respects is this lovely species that, with, perhaps, one exception, it may easily be identified from all others, *P. auricula marginata* being the one that most resembles it, that species also being edged and densely covered with farina, but its foliage is larger, not toothed, and its flowers yellow.

*P. marginata* has bright but light violet flowers on very short scapes, seldom more than 3in. high; these and the calyx also

FIG. 77. PRIMULA MARGINATA.
(Two-thirds natural size.)

are very mealy. The little leaves are of various shapes, and distinctly toothed, being about the size of the bowl of a dessert spoon. They are neatly arranged in tufts on a short footstalk, which becomes surrounded with young growths, all as clear in their markings as the parent plant, so that a well grown specimen of three years or even less becomes a beautiful object, whether it is on rockwork or in a cold frame.

The flowers are produced and remain in good form for two or three weeks on strong plants, and for nearly the whole year the plant is otherwise attractive.

I scarcely need mention that such plants with mealy and downy foliage are all the better for being sheltered from wind and rain. In a crevice, overhung by a big stone, but where the rockwork is so constructed that plenty of moisture is naturally received, a specimen has done very well indeed, besides keeping its foliage dry and perfect. When such positions can either be found or made, they appear to answer even better than frames, as alpine species cannot endure a stagnant atmosphere, which is the too common lot of frame subjects. It is not very particular as to soil or situation. I grow it both in shade and fully exposed to the midday sun of summer, and, though a healthy specimen is grown in loam, I find others to do better in leaf mould mixed with grit and pebbles. It enjoys a rare immunity—the slugs let it alone, or at least my slugs do, for it is said that different tribes or colonies have different tastes. To propagate it, the little offsets about the footstalk should be cut off with a sharp knife when the parent plant has finished flowering; they will mostly be found to have nice long roots. Plant in leaf soil and grit, and keep them shaded for a month.

Flowering period, March to May.

## Primula Purpurea.

PURPLE-FLOWERED PRIMULA; *Nat. Ord.* PRIMULACEÆ.

A TRULY grand primrose of the same section as *P. denticulata*, coming also from an alpine habitat, viz., the higher elevations of the Himalayas. It has not long been in cultivation in this country compared with our knowledge of the Himalayan flora. It is perfectly hardy, but seems to require rather drier situations than most of the large-leaved kinds. I never saw it so fine as when grown on a hillock of rockwork in sand and leaf mould; the specimen had there stood two severe winters, and in the spring of 1881 we were gladdened by its pushing in all directions fifteen scapes, all well topped by its nearly globular heads of fine purple flowers. It begins to flower in March, and keeps on for quite a month.

The flower stems are 9in. high, stout, and covered with a mealy dust, thickest near the top and amongst the small bracts. The umbels of blossom are 2in. to 3in. across, each flower nearly ¾in. in diameter, the corolla being salver shaped and having its lobed segments pretty well apart; the tube is long and somewhat bellied where touched by the teeth of the calyx; the latter is more than half the length of tube, of a pale green colour, and the teeth, which are long, awl shaped, and clasping, impart to the tubes of the younger flowers a fluted appearance; later on they become relaxed and leafy. The leaves have a strong, broad, pale green, shining midrib, are lance-shaped, nearly smooth, wavy, and serrulated; the upper surface is of a lively green colour, and the under side has a similar mealy covering to that of the scape. Flowers and leaves develope at the same time, the latter being 8in. long and of irregular arrangement.

The exceedingly floriferous character of this otherwise handsome primula renders it one of the very best subjects for the spring garden; it should have a place in the most select collections, as well as in more general assemblages of plants, for not only does it take care of itself when once properly planted, but it increases fast, forming noble tufts a foot in diameter, than which few things give a finer effect or an equal quantity of flowers at a time when they are not too plentiful. As already hinted, it should have a somewat drier position than *P. denticulata*, but by no means should it suffer from drought, and a little shade will be beneficial. Propagated by division during the growing season, immediately after flowering being the best time.

Flowering period, March and April.

## Primula Scotica.
SCOTTISH PRIMROSE; *Nat. Ord.* PRIMULACEÆ.

THIS charming little member of the British flora very much resembles the native Bird's-eye Primrose (*P. farinosa*), which is very common in some parts. It is not uniformly conceded to be a distinct species, but many botanists believe it to be such. As a matter of fact, it is different from *P. farinosa* in several important points, though they are not seen at a mere glance. That it has darker flowers and a more dwarf and sturdy habit may, indeed, be readily seen when the two are side by side. Size and colour, however, would not in this case appear to be the most distinctive features. The seed organs differ considerably. "In *P. farinosa* the germen is broadly obovate and the stigma capitate; here the germen is globose and the stigma has five points." But there is another dissimilarity which may or may not prove much to the botanist, but to the lover of flowers who tries to cultivate them it is all-important. Whilst *P. farinosa* can be easily grown in various soils and positions, in the same garden *P. Scotica* refuses to live; so fickle, indeed, is it, that were it not a very lovely flower that can be grown and its fastidious requirements easily afforded, it would not have been classed in this list of garden subjects. Here it begins to blossom in the middle of March at the height of 3in. In its habitats in Caithness and the north coast of Sutherland it is considerably later—April and May.

The flowers are arranged in a crowded umbel on a short stoutish scape; they are of a deep-bluish purple, with a yellow eye; the divisions of the corolla are flat and lobed; calyx nearly as long as tube, and ventricose or unevenly swollen. The whole flower is much less than *P. farinosa*. The leaves are also smaller than those of that species; obovate, lanceolate, denticulate, and very mealy underneath.

To grow it requires not only a light but somewhat spongy soil, as peat and sand, but it should never be allowed to get dry at the roots; a top dressing during summer of sand and half decayed leaves is a great help to it, for the roots are not only then very active, going deep and issuing from the base of the leaves, but they require something they can immediately grow into when just forming, and to be protected from drought. It will be well to remember that its principal habitats are on the sandy shores, as that gives a proper idea of the bottom moisture, and, from the looseness of the sand, the drier condition of the immediate surface. My specimens have always dwindled during summer and failed to appear the following spring, excepting where such treatment as the above has been adopted. I am much indebted for these hints to several amateurs, who grow it well. That many fail with it is evidenced by the facts that it is in great demand every spring and that there are few sources of supply other than its wild home. Never was it more sought for, perhaps, than at the present time, not only by amateurs at home, but by both private and trade growers abroad. The exquisite beauty of this primrose when well grown and the technical care required to have it in that condition are both things of which any plant lover may be proud.

If once established, its propagation is scarcely an affair of the cultivator's; the self-sown seed appears to germinate with far more certainty when left alone, and, as the plants are always very small, they hardly need to be transplanted. If left alone, though they are often much less than an inch across, many will flower the first season. Some have taken it as something of a biennial character. The treatment is at fault when it gives cause for such impressions; its perennial quality is both authorised and proved under cultivation.

Flowering period, March to May.

## Primula Sikkimensis.
### *Nat. Ord.* PRIMULACEÆ.

THE specific name of this noble and lovely plant has reference to its habitat, Sikkim, in the Himalayas, where it was found not many years ago. It is not largely cultivated yet—probably not well known. It may, however, be frequently met with in choice collections, where no plant is more worthy of a place. Its general character may be said to be very distinct, especially when in flower. It is herbaceous, hardy, and perennial. Its hardiness has been questioned for several years, but the winters of 1880 and 1881 settled that beyond the region of doubt. I had then many plants of it fully exposed, without even a top-dressing, which is sometimes given to plants of unquestionable hardiness, and they stood the winters as well as their kindred species—our common Cowslip. It was also said to be not more than biennial, as if it were a plant too good to be without some fatal fault for our climate. However, I can say emphatically that it is more than biennial, as the specimens from which the drawing (Fig. 78) is taken are three years old. Several correspondents have written me stating that their plants are dead. That has been during

Fig. 78. Primula Sikkimensis.
(Plant, one-sixth natural size; *a*, blossom, two-thirds natural size.)

their season of dormancy, but in every case they have pushed at the proper time. I may as well here explain, though somewhat out of order, a peculiarity in reference to the roots of this species: it dies down in early autumn, and the crown seems to retire within the ball of its roots, which are a matted mass of fibres, and not only does it seem to retire, but also to dwindle, so that anyone, with a suspicion, who might be seeking for the vital part, might easily be misled by such appearances, which are further added to by the fact that the species does not start into growth until a late date compared with others of the genus. So peculiar are the roots and crown of this plant, that if a root were dug up in mid-winter, and the soil partly shaken from it, a two-year-old specimen would be found to be the size and shape of a cricket ball, and the position of the crown so difficult to find that, on planting the root again, considerable discrimination would have to be exercised, or the crown might be pointed the wrong way.

*P. Sikkimensis* is a Cowslip. The flowers are a pale primrose yellow, rendered more pale still by a mealiness which covers the whole stem, being most abundant near the top, but whether it is produced on the petals, or, owing to their bell-shape and pendent form they recieve it from the scape and pedicels by the action of the wind, I cannot say. The flowers are considerably over 1in. long; they are numerously produced on long drooping pedicels, of irregular lengths; the tallest scape of the specimen illustrated is 18in. high, but under more favourable conditions this Cowslip has been said to reach a height of 3ft. The leaves are 6in. to 12in. long, wrinkled, unevenly dentate, oblong and blunt; during the time of seeding the leaves increase in length, some becoming spathulate, or broadly stalked; it ripens seed plentifully, from which seedlings come true.

Although I have never grown this noble plant otherwise than in ordinary garden loam well enriched and in shady borders, it is said to be more at home in peaty soil always in a moist state. However that may be, I have proved it to do well under ordinary treatment; it should be well watered during hot dry weather; amongst dwarf trees, in the more damp parts of rockwork, or at the foot of a north wall covered with any kind of foliage, it will be grown and seen to advantage.

Besides by seed, which should be sown as soon as ripened, it may be propagated by root divisions at the time the crowns are pushing in spring.

Flowering period, June and July.

## Primula Vulgaris Flore-pleno.

DOUBLE-FLOWERED PRIMROSE; *Nat. Ord.* PRIMULACEÆ.

IT is not intended to descant upon, or even attempt to name, the many forms of Double Primrose; the object is more to direct the attention of the reader to one which is a truly valuable flower and ought to be in every garden. Let me at once state its chief points. Colour, yellow; flowers, large, full, clear, and sweetly scented, produced regularly twice a year; foliage, short, rigid, evergreen, handsome, and supporting the flowers from earth splashes. Having grown this variety for five years, I have proved it to be as stated during both mild and severe seasons. It seems as if it wanted to commence its blooming period about October, from which time to the severest part of winter it affords a goodly amount of flowers; it is then stopped for a while, though its buds can be seen during the whole winter, and when the longer days and vernal sunshine return, it soon becomes thickly covered with blossoms, which are of the most desirable kind for spring gathering.

Its flowers need no further description beyond that already given; but I may add that the stalks are somewhat short, which is an advantage, as the bloom is kept more amongst the leaves and away from the mud. The foliage is truly handsome, short, finely toothed, rolled back, pleasingly wrinkled, and of a pale green colour. It is very hardy, standing all kinds of weather, and I never saw it rot at the older crowns, like so many of the fine varieties, but it goes on growing, forming itself into large tufts a foot and more across.

It has been tried in stiff loam and light vegetable soil; in shade, and fully exposed; it has proved to do equally well in both kinds of soil, but where it received the full force of the summer sun the plants were weak, infested with red spider, and had a poorer crop of flowers. It would, therefore, appear that soil is of little or no importance, but that partial shade is needful. It is not only a variety worth the having, but one which deserves to have the best possible treatment, for flowers in winter—and such flowers—are worth all care.

Flowering periods, late autumn and early spring to June.

## Pulmonarias.
### LUNGWORTS; *Nat. Ord.* BORAGINACEÆ.

IN speaking of these hardy herbaceous perennials, I should wish to be understood that the section, often and more properly called *Mertensia*, is not included because they are so very distinct in habit and colour of both flowers and foliage. Most of the Pulmonarias begin to flower early in March, and continue to do so for a very long time, quite two months.

For the most part, the flowers (which are borne on stems about 8in. high. in straggling clusters) are of changing colours, as from pink to blue; they are small but pretty, and also have a quaint appearance. The foliage during the blooming period is not nearly developed, the plants being then somewhat small in all their parts, but later the leaf growth goes on rapidly, and some kinds are truly handsome from their fine spreading habit and clear markings of large white spots on the leaves, which are often 9in. or 10in. long and 3in. broad, oblong, lanceolate, taper-pointed, and rough, with stiff hairs. At this stage they would seem to be in their most decorative form, though their flowers, in a cut state, formed into "posies," are very beautiful and really charming when massed for table decoration; on the plant they have a faded appearance.

Many of the species or varieties have but slight distinctions, though all are beautiful. A few may be briefly noticed otherwise than as above:

*P. officinalis* is British, and typical of several others. Flowers pink, turning to blue; leaves blotted.

*P. off. alba* differs only in the flowers being an unchanging white.

*P. angustifolia*, also British, having, as its specific name implies, narrow leaves; flowers bright blue or violet.

*P. mollis*, in several varieties, comes from North America; is distinct from its leaves being smaller, the markings or spots less distinct, and more thickly covered with *soft* hairs, whence its name.

*P. azurea* has not only a well-marked leaf, but also a very bright and beautiful azure flower; it comes from Poland.

*P. maculata* has the most clearly and richly marked leaf, and perhaps the largest, that being the chief distinction.

*P. saccharata* is later; its flowers are pink, and not otherwise very distinct from some of the above kinds.

It is not necessary to enumerate others, as the main points of difference are to be found in the above-mentioned kinds.

All are very easily cultivated; any kind of soil will do for them, but they repay liberal treatment by the extra quality of their foliage. Their long and thick fleshy roots allow of their being transplanted at any time of the year. Large clumps, however, are better divided in early spring, even though they are then in flower.

Flowering period, March to May.

## Puschkinia Scilloides.

SCILLA-LIKE PUSCHKINIA, *or* STRIPED SQUILL; *Syns.* P. LIBANOTICA, ADAMSIA SCILLOIDES; *Nat. Ord.* LILIACEÆ.

As all its names, common and botanical, denote, this charming bulbous plant is like the scillas; it may, therefore, be useful to point out the distinctions which divide them. They are (in the flowers) to be seen at a glance; within the spreading perianth there is a tubular crown or corona, having six lobes and a membranous fringe. This crown is connected at the base of the divisions of the perianth, which divisions do not go to the base of the flower, but form what may be called an outer tube. In the scilla there is no corona, neither a tube, but the petal-like sepals or divisions of the perianth are entire, going to the base of the flower. There are other but less visible differences which need not be further gone into. Although there are but two or three known species of the genus, we have not only a confusion of names, but plants of another genus have been mistaken as belonging to this. Mr. Baker, of Kew, however, has put both

Q

the plants and names to their proper belongings, and we are no longer puzzled with a chionodoxa under the name of *Puschkinia*. This Lilywort came from Siberia in 1819, and was long considered a tender bulb in this climate, and even yet by many it is treated as such. With ordinary care—judicious planting—it not only proves hardy, but increases fast. Still, it is a rare plant, and very seldom seen, notwithstanding its great beauty. It was named by Adams, in honour of the Russian botanist, Count Puschkin, whence the two synonymous names *Puschkinia* and *Adamsia*; there is also another name, specific, which, though still used, has become discarded by authorities, viz., *P. Libanotica*—this was supposed to be in reference to one of its habitats being on Mount Lebanon. During mild winters it flowers in March, and so delicately marked are its blossoms that one must always feel that its beauties are mainly lost from the proverbial harshness of the season.

At the height of 4in. to 8in. the flowers are produced on slender bending scapes, the spikes of blossom are arranged one-sided; each flower is ½in. to nearly 1in. across, white, richly striped with pale blue down the centre, and on both sides of the petal-like divisions. The latter are of equal length, lance-shaped, and finely reflexed; there is a short tube, on the mouth of which is joined the smaller one of the corona. The latter is conspicuous from the reflexed condition of the limb of the perianth, and also from its lobes and membranous fringe being a soft lemon-yellow colour. The pedicels are slender and distant, causing the flower spikes, which are composed of four to eight flowers, to have a lax appearance. The leaves are few, 4in. to 6in. long, lance-shaped, concave, but flatter near the apex, of good substance and a dark green colour; bulb small.

As already stated, a little care is needed in planting this choice bulbous subject. It enjoys a rich, but light soil. It does not so much matter whether it is loamy or of a vegetable nature if it is light and well drained; and, provided it is planted under such conditions and in full sunshine, it will both bloom well and increase. It may be propagated by division of the roots during late summer, when the tops have died off; but only tufts having a crowded appearance should be disturbed for an increase of stock.

Flowering period, March to May.

*P. s. compacta* is a variety of the above, having a stronger habit and bolder flowers. The latter are more numerous, have shorter pedicels, and are compactly arranged in the spike—whence the name  Culture, propagation, and flowering time, same as last.

## Pyrethrum Uliginosum.

MARSH FEVERFEW; *Nat. Ord.* COMPOSITÆ.

A VERY bold and strong growing species, belonging to a numerous genus; it comes to us from Hungary, and has been grown more or less in English gardens a little over sixty years. It is a distinct species, its large flowers, the height to which it grows, and the strength of its willow-like stalks being its chief characteristics. Still, to anyone with but a slight knowledge of hardy plants, it asserts itself at once as a Pyrethrum. It is hardy, herbaceous, and perennial, and worth growing in every garden where there is room for large growing subjects. There is something about this plant when in flower which a bare description fails to explain; to do it justice it should be seen when in full bloom.

Its flowers are large and ox-eye-daisy-like, having a white ray, with yellow centre, but the florets are larger in proportion to the disk; plain and quiet as the individual flowers appear, when seen in numbers (as they always may be seen on well-established specimens), they are strikingly beautiful, the blooms are more than 2in. across, and the mass comes level with the eye, for the stems are over 5ft. high, and though very stout, the branched stems which carry the flowers are slender and gracefully bending. The leaves are smooth, lance-shaped, and sharply toothed, fully 4in. long, and stalkless; they are irregularly but numerously disposed on the stout round stems, and of nearly uniform size and shape until the corymbose branches are reached, *i.e.*, for 4ft. or 5ft. of their length; when the leaves are fully grown they reflex or hang down, and totally hide the stems. This habit, coupled with the graceful and nodding appearance of the large white flowers, renders this a pleasing subject, especially for situations where tall plants are required, such as near and in shrubberies. I grow but one strong specimen, and it looks well between two apple trees, but not over-shaded. The idea in planting it there was to obtain some protection from strong winds, and to avoid the labour and eyesore which staking would create.

It likes a stiff loam, but is not particular as to soil if only it is somewhat damp. The flowers last three weeks; and in a cut state are also very effective; and, whether so appropriated or left on the plant, they will be found to be very enduring. When cutting these flowers, the whole corymb should be taken, as in this particular case we could not wish for a finer arrangement, and being contemporaneous with the Michaelmas daisy, the bloom branches of the two subjects form elegant and fashionable decorations for table or vase use. To propagate this plant, it is only needed to divide the roots in November, and plant in deeply-dug but damp soil.

Flowering period, August to September.

## Ramondia Pyrenaica.

*Syns.* CHAIXIA MYCONI *and* VERBASCUM MYCONI; *Nat. Ord.* SOLANACEÆ.

THIS is a very dwarf and beautiful alpine plant, from the Pyrenees, the one and only species of the genus. Although it is sometimes called a Verbascum or Mullien, it is widely distinct from all the plants of that family. To lovers of dwarf subjects this must be one of the most desirable; small as it is, it is full of character.

The flowers, when held up to a good light, are seen to be downy and of ice-like transparency; they are of a delicate, pale, violet colour, and a little more than an inch in diameter, produced on stems 3in. to 4in. high, which are nearly red, and furnished with numerous hairs; otherwise the flower stems are nude, seldom more than two flowers, and oftener only one bloom is seen on a stem. The pedicels, which are about half-an-inch long, bend downwards, but the flowers, when fully expanded, rise a little; the calyx is green, downy, five-parted, the divisions being short and reflexed at their points; the corolla is rotate, flat, and, in the case of flowers several days old, thrown back; the petals are nearly round, slightly uneven, and waved at the edges, having minute protuberances at their base tipped with bright orange, shading to white; the seed organs are very prominent; stamens arrow-shaped; pistil more than twice the length of filaments and anthers combined, white, tipped with green. The leaves are arranged in very flat rosettes, the latter being from four to eight inches across. The foliage is entirely stemless, the nude flower stalks issuing from between the leaves, which are roundly toothed, evenly and deeply wrinkled, and elliptical in outline. Underneath, the ribs are very prominent, and the covering of hairs rather long, as are also those of the edges. On the upper surface the hairs are short and stiff.

In the more moist interstices of rockwork, where, against and between large stones, its roots will be safe from drought, it will not only be a pleasing ornament, but will be likely to thrive and flower well. It is perfectly hardy, but there is one condition of our climate which tries it very much—the wet, and alternate frosts and thaws of winter. From its hairy character and flat form, the plant is scarcely ever dry, and rot sets in. This is more especially the case with specimens planted flat; it is therefore a great help against such climatic conditions to place the plants in rockwork, so that the rosettes are as nearly as possible at right angles with the ground level. Another interesting way to grow this lovely and valuable species is in pans or large pots, but this system requires some shelter in winter, as the plants will be flat. The advantages of this mode are that five or six specimens so grown are very effective. They can, from higher cultivation (by giving them richer soil, liquid manure, and by judicious confinement of their roots), be brought into a more floriferous condition, and when the flowers appear, they can be removed into some cool light situation, under cover, so that their beauties can be more enjoyed, and not be liable to damage by splashing, &c. Plants so grown should be potted in sandy peat, and a few pieces of sandstone placed over the roots, slightly cropping out of the surface; these will not only help to keep the roots from being droughted, but also bear up the rosetted leaves, and so allow a better circulation of air about the collars, that being the place where rot usually sets in. In the case of specimens which do not get proper treatment, or which have undergone a transplanting to their disadvantage, they will often remain perfectly dormant to all appearance for a year or more. Such plants should be moved into a moist fissure in rockwork, east aspect, and the soil should be of a peaty character. This may seem like coddling, and a slur on hardy plants. Here, however, we have a valuable subject, which does not find a home in this climate exactly so happy as its native habitat, but which, with a little care, can have things so adapted to its requirements as to be grown year after year in its finest form; such care is not likely to be withheld by the true lover of choice alpines.

This somewhat slow-growing species may be propagated by division, but only perfectly healthy specimens should be selected for the purpose, early spring being the best time; by seed also it may be increased; the process, however, is slow, and the seedlings will be two years at least before they flower.

Flowering period, May to July.

### Ranunculus Aconitifolius.
ACONITE-LEAVED CROWFOOT, *or* BACHELORS' BUTTONS;
*Nat. Ord.* RANUNCULACEÆ.

AN herbaceous perennial, of the alpine parts of Europe, and for a long time cultivated in this country. It grows 1ft. high, is much branched in zigzag form, and produces numerous flowers, resembling those of the strawberry, but only about half the size; the leaves are finely cut and of a dark green colour; it is not a plant worth growing for its flowers, but the reason why I briefly speak of it here is that I may more properly introduce that grand old flower of which it is the parent, *R. a. fl.-pl.* (see Fig. 79), the true "English double white Crowfoote," or Bachelor's Buttons; these are the common names which Gerarde gives as borne by this plant nearly 300 years ago, and there can be no mistaking the plant, as he figures it in his "Historie of Plantes," p. 812; true, he gives it a different Latin name to the one it bears at the present time; still, it is the same plant, and his name for it (*R. albus multiflorus*) is strictly and correctly specific. Numerous flowers are called Bachelor's Buttons, including daisies, globe flowers, pyrethrums, and different kinds of ranunculi, but here we have the "original and true;" probably it originated in some ancient English garden, as Gerarde says, "It groweth in the gardens of herbarists & louers of strange plants, whereof we have good plentie, but it groweth not wild anywhere."

Its round smooth stems are stout, zigzag, and much branched, forming the plant into a neat compact bush, in size (of plants

FIG. 79. RANUNCULUS ACONIT FOLIUS FLORE-PLENO.
(One-fourth natural size; a, natural size of flower.)

two or more years old) 2ft. high and 2ft. through. The flowers are white, and very double or full of petals, evenly and beautifully arranged, salver shape, forming a flower sometimes nearly an inch across; the purity of their whiteness is not marred by even an eye, and they are abundantly produced and for a long time in succession. The leaves are of a dark shining green colour, richly cut—as the specific name implies—after the style of the Aconites; the roots are fasciculate, long, and fleshy

This "old-fashioned" plant is now in great favour and much

sought after; and no wonder, for its flowers are perfection, and
the plant one of the most decorative and suitable for any position
in the garden. In a cut state the flowers do excellent service.
This subject is easily cultivated, but to have large specimens,
with plenty of flowers, a deep, well enriched soil is indispensable;
stagnant moisture should be avoided. Autumn is the best time
to divide the roots.

Flowering period, May to July.

## Ranunculus Acris Flore-pleno.
DOUBLE ACRID CROWFOOT, YELLOW BACHELOR'S BUTTONS;
*Nat. Ord.* RANUNCULACEÆ.

THE type of this is a common British plant, most nearly related
to the field buttercup. I am not going to describe it, but mention
it as I wish to introduce *R. acris fl.-pl.*, sometimes called "yellow
Bachelor's Buttons"—indeed, that is the correct common name
for it, as used fully 300 years ago. In every way, with the
exception of its fine double flowers, it resembles very much the
tall meadow buttercup, so that it needs no further description;
but, common as is its parentage, it is both a showy and useful
border flower, and forms a capital companion to the double white
Bachelor's Buttons (*R. aconitifolius fl.-pl.*).

Flowering period, April to June.

## Ranunculus Amplexicaulis.
STEM-CLASPING RANUNCULUS; *Nat. Ord.* RANUNCULACEÆ.

A VERY hardy subject; effective and beautiful. The form of
this plant is exceedingly neat, and its attractiveness is further
added to by its smooth and pale glaucous foliage. It was introduced into this country more than 200 years ago, from the
Pyrenees. Still it is not generally grown, though at a first
glance it asserts itself a plant of first-class merit (see Fig. 80).

The shortest and, perhaps, best description of its flowers will
be given when I say they are white *Buttercups*, produced on stout
stems nearly a foot high, which are also furnished by entire
stem-clasping leaves, whence its name; other leaves are of
varying forms, mostly broadly lance-shaped, and some once-
notched; those of the root are nearly spoon-shaped. The whole
plant is very smooth and glaucous, also covered with a fine meal.
As a plant, it is effective; but grown by the side of *R. montanus*
and the geums, which have flowers of similar shape, it is seen to
more advantage.

On rockwork, in leaf soil, it does remarkably well; in loam it
seems somewhat stunted. Its flowers are very serviceable in a
cut state, and they are produced in succession for three or four

weeks on the same plant. It has large, fleshy, semi-tuberous roots, and many of them; so that at any time it may be trans-

Fig. 80. RANUNCULUS AMPLEXICAULIS
(One-fourth natural size.)

planted. I have pulled even flowering plants to pieces, and the different parts, which, of course, had plenty of roots to them, still continued to bloom.

Flowering period, April and May.

## Ranunculus Speciosum.
SHOWY CROWFOOT; *Nat. Ord.* RANUNCULACEÆ.

THIS is another double yellow form of the Buttercup. It has only recently come into my possession. The blooms are very large and beautiful, double the size of *R. acris fl.-pl.*, and a deeper yellow; the habit, too, is much more dwarf, the leaves larger, but similar in shape.

Flowering period, April to June.

All the foregoing Crowfoots are of the easiest culture, needing no particular treatment; but they like rich and deep soil. They may be increased by division at almost any time, the exceptions being when flowering or at a droughty season.

## Rudbeckia Californica.

CALIFORNIAN CONE-FLOWER; *Nat. Ord.* COMPOSITÆ.

THIS, in all its parts, is a very large and showy subject; the flowers are 3in. to 6in. across, in the style of the sunflower. It has not long been grown in English gardens, and came, as its name implies, from California: it is very suitable for association with old-fashioned flowers, being nearly related to the genus *Helianthus*, or sunflower. It is not only perfectly hardy in this climate, which is more than can be said of very many of the Californian species, but it grows rampantly and flowers well. It is all the more valuable as a flower from the fact that it comes into bloom several weeks earlier than most of the large yellow Composites. Having stated already the size of its flower, I need scarcely add that it is one of the showiest subjects in the garden; it is, however, as well to keep it in the background, not only on account of its tallness, but also because of its coarse abundant foliage.

It grows 4ft. to 6ft. high, the stems being many-branched. The flowers have erect stout stalks, and vary in size from 3in. to 6in. across, being of a light but glistening yellow colour; the ray is somewhat unevenly formed, owing to the florets being of various sizes, sometimes slit at the points, lobed, notched, and bent; the disk is very bold, being nearly 2in. high, in the form of a cone, whence the name "cone flower." The fertile florets of the disk or cone are green, and produce an abundance of yellow pollen, but it is gradually developed, and forms a yellow ring round the dark green cone, which rises slowly to the top when the florets of the ray fall; from this it will be seen that the flowers last a long time. The leaves of the root are sometimes a foot in length and half as broad, being oval, pointed, and sometimes notched or lobed; also rough, from a covering of short stiff hairs, and having once-grooved stout stalks 9in. or more long; the leaves of the stems are much smaller, generally oval, but of very uneven form, bluntly pointed, distinctly toothed, and some of the teeth so large as to be more appropriately described as segments; the base abruptly narrows into a very short stalk. The flowers of this plant are sure to meet with much favour, especially while the present fashion continues; but apart from fashion, merely considered as a decorative subject for the garden, it is well worth a place. There are larger yellow Composites, but either they are much later, or they are not perennial species, and otherwise this one differs materially from them.

I need not say anything respecting this form of flower in a cut state—its effectiveness is well known. If planted in ordinary garden loam it will hold its place and bloom freely year after year without further care. Smaller subjects should not be set too near it; it may be unadvisable to plant too many clumps in the same garden, but it can be allowed to spread into one bold patch. The best time to divide or transplant is in early spring, when growth is just pushing, for vigorous as this and many other perennials are, I have often found them to rot, when the dormant roots, after being cut into pieces, have had to face the winter.

Flowering period, July to September.

## Rudbeckia Serotina.
### *Late* CONE-FLOWER; *Nat. Ord.* COMPOSITÆ.

THIS hardy American species, though not an old plant in English gardens, is nevertheless classed with "old-fashioned" plants and flowers; and certainly its sombre but pleasing dark golden ray flowers, together with its likeness to many of the old sunflowers, favours such classification. It is the latest of a late-flowering genus.

It attains the height of 2ft.; the root leaves are of irregular shape, some oval and pointed, others, on the same plant, being lance-shaped, with two or three large teeth or acute lobes; in size the leaves also vary from 3in. to 8in. long, and being covered with short bristly hairs, they are very rough, also of a dull green colour; the flower stems have but few leaves, so it will be judged that the plant has but a weedy appearance, but this is compensated for by the rich and numerous large dark orange flowers, 3in. across; the ray is single, and the centre, which is large and prominent, is a rich chocolate brown.

This subject, to be effective, should be grown in large specimens; mine is about 3ft. in diameter, and the level mass of flowers, as I have often noticed them in twilight, were grandly beautiful. I can well understand that many have not cared for this cone flower when they have judged it from a small plant which has sent up its first, and perhaps abnormal, bloom. It is especially a subject that should be seen in bold clumps, and in moderately rich soil it will soon become such. Moreover, the flowers are very effective in a cut state, when loosely arranged in vases, only needing something in the way of tall grasses to blend with in order to form an antique "posy."

Autumn is the best time to plant it; its long roots denote that it enjoys deep soil, and, when planted, the roots of this, as well as all others then being transplanted, should be made firm, otherwise the frost will lift them out and the droughts will finish them off. Many plants are lost in this manner, and, indeed, many short-rooted kinds are scarcely saved by the greatest care. The stem-rooting character of this plant affords ready means of propagation by root divisions.

Flowering period, from September till strong frosts.

## Salix Reticulata.

WRINKLED *or* NETTED WILLOW; *Nat. Ord.* SALICACEÆ.

A NATIVE deciduous shrub, of creeping or prostrate habit, not growing higher than 2in. As the flowers are inconspicuous and only interesting to the botanist or when under the microscope, let me at once say I mention this subject because of its beautiful habit and distinct quality of foliage. When grown on rockwork, no other plant can compare with it, and where choice spring bulbs are planted, this handsome creeper may be allowed, without injury to such roots, to broadly establish itself; so grown, its little stout leaves, thickly produced, flatly on the surface, are much admired.

The flowers or catkins stand well above the foliage, but are unattractive, being of a dusky brown colour; the leaves are dark green, downy, of much substance, 1½in. long, and nearly 1in. broad, but the size of foliage varies according to the conditions under which the specimens are grown; the sizes now referred to are of plants grown on rather dry rockwork and fully exposed; the form of the leaves is orbicular, obtuse, not in the least notched, bald, reticulately veined, and glaucous beneath; the stems are short and diffuse, and tinged with red on the younger parts.

During winter, when bare of foliage, its thick creeping stems, covered with fat buds and interlaced in a pleasing manner, render it interesting in almost any situation not shaded. It forms a capital carpet plant from early spring to the end of summer.

It is in no way particular as regards soil, and though it loves moisture, like most other willows, it proves thriving in dry places. It is, moreover, a good grower in large towns. Its propagation may be carried out before the leaves unfold in spring. Little branches with roots to them may be cut from the parent plant, and should be set in sandy loam and watered well to settle it about the roots.

Flowering period, September to strong frosts.

## Sanguinaria Canadensis.

BLOODROOT; *Nat. Ord.* PAPAVERACEÆ.

THIS is a native of North America, and is, therefore, hardy in this climate; tuberous rooted. It is a curious plant, not only from its great fulness of sap or juice, which is red (that of the root being darker, whence its name Bloodroot), but also because of the shape of its leaves, their colour, and method of development (see Fig. 81). Though very dwarf, it is handsome and distinct.

The flowers are pure white and nearly 2in. across; the petals have good substance, but they fall in five or six sunny days; the

236   HARDY PERENNIALS AND

stamens are numerous and bright yellow. Though belonging to
the order of the Poppy, it is in many respects unlike it; each
flower stem, which is 6in. high, springs directly from the root,
and only one flower is produced on a stem; the leaves are also
radical, so that the plant is branchless and stemless; the leaf
stalks are rather shorter than those of the flowers. The foliage
is of a slate-grey colour, prominently veined on the under side,
the upper surface being somewhat wrinkled; the leaves are 3in.

FIG. 81. SANGUINARIA CANADENSIS.
(One-half natural size.)

across when fully developed, vine-leaf shaped, deeply and beautifully lobed; their development is slow, not being completed
until the bloom is past. Both leaves and flowers are produced
in a curious fashion; for a time the flower-bud is compactly
enfolded by a leaf, and so both grow up to the height of 2in. or
3in., when the former pushes through, and soon swells its olive-
shaped buds. At this stage a good specimen clump is very
attractive, and is only more so when the fine blooms first open.

It should be grown amongst some such carpeting plants as *Sibthorpia Europœa* or *Linaria pilosa*, so as to protect it; moreover, these creepers are suited for a similar soil and position. The soil should be light, either of sandy or vegetable character, but one that cannot bake; shade from the midday sun is essential, as also is plenty of moisture. When the growths have become crowded, as they do in about three years, it is as well to lift, divide, and replant at a distance of 3in.; this is best done after the tops have died off in summer; plant 4in. or 5in. deep.

Flowering period, April and May.

## Saponaria Ocymoides.

ROCK SOAPWORT, *or* BASIL-LEAVED SOAPWORT: *Nat. Ord.* SILENACEÆ.

A VERY hardy alpine from France, and one of the most floriferous subjects that can be placed on rockwork, where should be its position. During a single season it is no uncommon thing to see a small plant grow into a large cushion 2ft. in diameter, and only 6in. or 9in. high. In planting it this fact should not be overlooked, not only for the sake of giving it plenty of room, but also in order that less vigorous subjects near it may not become overgrown; it blooms all summer, and though the flowers are small and not at all bright, their numbers render it attractive.

The flowers, which are about ½in. across, are of a pink colour, and produced on many-branched prostrate stems; the calyx is five-toothed; the corolla is formed of five flat petals; the leaves are small, basil-like, oval-lance shaped, entire and smooth; the general appearance of the plant when in bloom is that of a compact mass of small leaves and flowers, the latter predominating.

It will grow in any kind of soil, but prefers that of a vegetable character, with its roots amongst large stones; but, strictly speaking, it needs nothing but an open situation and plenty of room to spread. It ripens an abundance of seed, and there is not a better mode of propagation than its own; hundreds of stout seedlings appear the following spring around the parent plant, and these may then be transplanted, and they will flower the same season.

*S. o. splendens* is a variety of the above very much improved indeed; and though one cannot discard the good old plant for its very recent offspring, the former is certainly very much eclipsed. *Splendens* has foliage slightly different, but its flowers are much larger and brighter; and though it may not be quite so vigorous, in this case that may be considered an improvement. It is said to come true from seed.

Flowering period, May to August.

## Saxifraga Burseriana.

BURSER'S SAXIFRAGE; *Nat. Ord.* SAXIFRAGACEÆ.

A HARDY evergreen alpine. A native of Carniola, not long discovered, and quite new to English gardens. Though it belongs to a very extensive genus, it is a distinct species; many of the Saxifrages are not so, neither are they sufficiently decorative to merit a place in any but large or scientific gardens. This one, however, is a truly handsome kind, and its flowers are produced amid the snow and during the bleak and dull weather of mid-winter.

The plant in form is a dense cushion of little spiked rosettes, of a dark green colour, slightly silvered. The flowers are produced on bright ruddy stems 3in. high, and are creamy white, nearly the size of a sixpence. Small as the plant is, a moderate sized specimen is very attractive, especially before the flowers open, when they are in their prettiest form. They open slowly and endure nearly two months.

It enjoys light soil and a well drained situation, such as the edge of a border, where strong growing kinds cannot damage it, or on rockwork, where it will be fully exposed to the sun. To be effective, it should be grown into strong clumps, which may easily be done by annually giving a top-dressing of leaf-mould; the older parts of the plant will remain perfectly sound and healthy for years. When it is desirable to propagate it, it may best be done in April, when the tufts should be carefully divided, and its short roots made firm in the soil by one or two stones being placed near.

Flowering period, January to April.

## Saxifraga Cæsia.

SILVER MOSS, *or* GREY SAXIFRAGE; *Nat. Ord.* SAXIFRAGACEÆ.

ONE of the alpine gems. This has been grown in English gardens since 1752, yet good specimens are rarely met with, though its culture is simple and easy. It is found wild on the Alps of Switzerland, Austria, and the Pyrenees. To the lover of the minute forms of genuine alpine plants, this will be a treasure; it is very distinct in form, habit, and colour. Its tiny rosettes of encrusted leaves can scarcely be said to rise from the ground, and the common name, "silver moss," which it is often called by, most fittingly applies; but perhaps its colour is the main feature of notice. The meaning of its specific name is grey, to which it certainly answers; but so peculiar is the greyness that a more definite description may be useful, in giving which I will quote that of Decandolle and Sprengle: "The *lavender*-blue is a pale blue (cæsius); it is mixed with a little grey." This exactly answers to the colour of the pretty Saxifrage under notice, and it is far from a common one in foliage.

The flowers differ but slightly from those of other encrusted forms of the genus, but they are a creamy white, arranged in small panicles on short and slender stems. They are sparingly produced in May and June. The leaves are ¼in. long, aggregate or in miniature rosettes; in shape, linear-oblong, recurved, and keeled. The upper surface is concave, having marginal dots, evenly disposed; the dots are bright and excavated, and some of the leaves (those of the stems) are scale formed. The glaucous

Fig. 82. Saxifraga Cæsia Major.
(1, single rosette, natural size.)

or lavender-blue colour is beautifully enlivened with the crystal dots. Its habit reminds one of the more distinct forms of lichens, and, when it is grown with suitable companions on rockwork, it has a happy way of showing and adapting itself in such situation; besides, its colour then shows with more effect.

There is a variety of this species not yet in general cultivation, and it cannot be too strongly recommended to lovers of the finest forms of rock or alpine plants. It is called *S. c. major* (see Fig. 82). The name at once suggests the main difference from the type, but there are other features quite as marked as that of its extra size in all its parts; the foliage is more crowded, which seems to cause the largest leaves to become more erect, and the habit, too, perhaps from the same cause, is ball shaped; the small rosettes of thick encrusted leaves, from the manner in which they are packed together, form a rigid mass, which differs widely both in detail and effect from any other Saxifrage I know.

These dwarf subjects are best suited for rockwork; but another plan, now much practised, is to grow them in pots. This in no way implies that protection is given or needed—these sturdy subjects are far better fully exposed—but the pot system has advantages; when so planted, the roots are more likely to be placed in a better selected compost, and the specimens can be raised in order to examine their miniature beauties. The above kinds enjoy a gritty vegetable soil; perfect drainage is indispensable. These are not among the Saxifrages that are readily propagated; a few crowns or rosettes with short pieces of stem are not sure to root, and if more careful division is not carried out, perhaps but two or three growing bits from a large specimen may be the result, so lessening instead of increasing the stock. Before cutting let the roots be washed clear of soil, trace the long roots, and so cut up the plant that each division will have a share of them. Sometimes a rather large specimen will have but few of such roots, in which case it will prove the better and safer plan to make only a corresponding number of divisions, so making sure of each. A further help to such newly planted stock is gained by placing small stones about the collars; this keeps the plants moist and cool during the dry season, when (after flowering) the divisions should be made.

Flowering period, May and June.

## Saxifraga Ceratophylla.

HORN-LEAVED SAXIFRAGE; *Nat. Ord.* SAXIFRAGACEÆ.

FOR the most part, this numerous genus flowers in spring and early summer, the species now under notice being one of the late bloomers; its flowers however, like most of the Saxifrages, are small and insignificant; on the other hand, its foliage, as may be seen by the illustration (Fig. 83) is highly ornamental. In November, the grand half-globular tufts of rigid dark green foliage are delicately furnished with a whitish exudation, which, seen through a magnifying glass, resembles scales, but seen by the naked eye—and it can be clearly seen without stooping—it gives the idea of hoar frost. We have here, then, an interesting and ornamental subject, which, when grown in collections of considerable variety, proves attractive; and as even after many degrees of frost, it retains its beauty, and, I may add, its finest form, it may be confidently recommended as a suitable winter garden subject. This species proves evergreen in our climate, though a native of Spain, from which country it was imported about eighty years ago. It is sometimes called *S. cornutum*, a name quite applicable, and it is frequently confounded with *S. pentadactylis* (the Five-fingered-leaved Saxifrage), which it much resembles, from which, however, it is distinct in several respects.

Its flowers are small, white, and numerous, produced on slender stalks in summer; they are of the general type of the flowers of the mossy section, and need not be further described. The foliage forms rigid cushions, dense, rounded, and of a dark

Fig. 83. SAXIFRAGA CERATOPHYLLA.
(Leaf, one-half natural size.)

green colour in the early season; later it becomes grey, with an exudation; the leaves are arranged in rosette form, having stout stalks, channelled or folded on the upper surface; there are three deep divisions, and others less cut; the segments are subulate, bent back and tipped with horny mucrones, whence its specific name; these horn-like points are bent under, which, together with their transparency, renders them all but invisible; they can, however, be clearly seen if brought near the eye and looked for on the under side of the foliage. The leaves are of good substance, 1in. to 2in. long, having broad stipules; the stems are exceedingly slender in the older parts, and somewhat woody, having the appearance of being dried up and dead.

R

On rockwork it is seen in its best form, as the slope not only shows it off better, but is conducive to a finer growth. In flat places, the dense cushions, which are 6in. or 8in. high, often rot from too much moisture. I have never seen this occur in the drier positions afforded by the slopes of a rockery. If planted between large stones it has a happy way of adapting itself to them, and few plants are more effective. It thrives equally well in soil of a loamy or vegetable character, but it seems to enjoy a little limestone, small pieces of which I place round the specimens; they also serve to hold up the lower foliage and favour the admission of air. Where alpines are grown in pots this should form one, as it makes a charming specimen; the drainage should be perfect. It also makes a capital edging plant, especially for raised beds, as then it is accommodated in the same way as on rockwork.

It may be propagated by taking the slips nearest the earth, which will often be found to have a few rootlets, but if not they will still prove the more suitable; if taken in summer and dibbled into sand, they will make good roots in a week or two, when they may be transplanted to their permanent quarters, so as to become established before winter.

## Saxifraga Ciliata.

HAIRY-MARGINED SAXIFRAGE; *Syn.* MEGASEA CILIATA;
*Nat. Ord.* SAXIFRAGACEÆ.

THIS is a peculiar, distinct, and beautiful form of Saxifrage; there seems, however, to be some confusion in reference to its nomenclature. That it belongs to the *Megasea* section there can be little doubt, so that its synonym (*M. ciliata*) is fairly descriptive; but when it is said to be *identical* with *S. ligulata*, also of the *Megasea* section, the difficulty of recognising the form illustrated as such is very great indeed. It is also supposed to be a *variety* of *S. ligulata*, and though it has many important dissimilarities, it has also many affinities. So much does it differ from *S. ligulata* that it seems to be fully entitled to the specific honours which some authorities have given to it. It differs from *S. ligulata*, described by Don, in being rough and hairy on both sides of the leaves; in other respects it agrees, more especially in the colour of the flowers, which is uncommon. It may be the *Megasea ciliata* of Haworth, which Don refers to under *S. ligulata*, or it may be a distinct form of the latter, as, on the authority of Dr. Wallich, of the Botanical Gardens of Calcutta, the species has varieties. Wherever its proper place may be in its numerous genus, the name at the head hereof is a good descriptive one. It is an Indian contribution, hailing from the mountains east of Bengal. In this climate it endures our winters, though it is not one of the hardiest of its tribe. It has not long been cultivated in this country, and is rarely met with. Its distinct habit and fine flowers render it desirable, and it will with many be more so on the score of its peculiarities. A few of the latter may be mentioned here. Anthers very large, and brick-red before becoming pollenized; scapes and scape-sheaths nearly smooth, though all other foliar parts are hairy; stipules very large and fully developed whilst the leaves are in their rudimentary stage. When not in flower the plant has a strong resemblance to *S. sarmentosa*, which belongs to another section, but *S. ciliata* has features belonging to both sections. The habit, however, is more flat, and leaves more oval, and if, as has

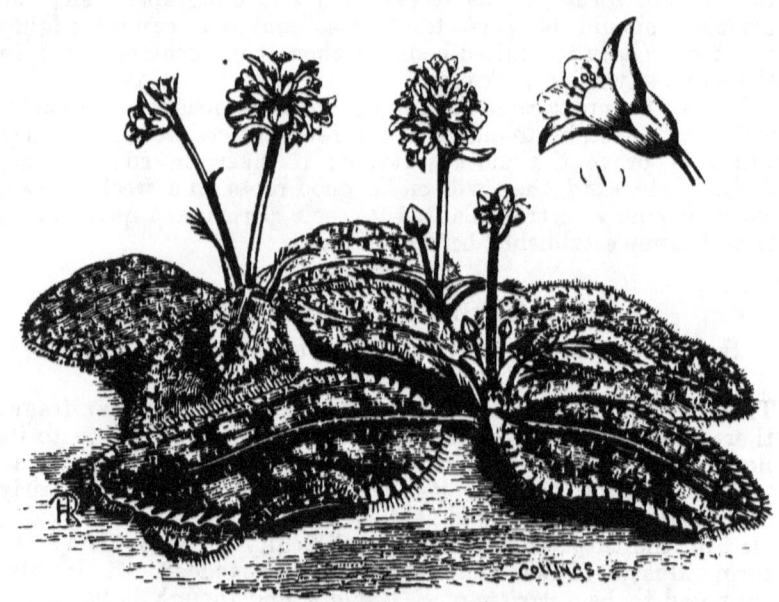

FIG. 84. SAXIFRAGA CILIATA.
(One-fourth natural size; (1) two-thirds natural size.)

been hinted, this is a hybrid, it may not be without some relationship to that species, which is also of Asian origin. Further, on the authority of Murray, *Sax. sarmentosa* is identical with *S. ligulata*; so that, if we may suppose *S. ciliata* to be a distinct variety of *S. ligulata*, and the latter to have such affinity to *S. sarmentosa* that Murray puts it as identical, the chief difference between our subject and the form generally accepted as *S. ligulata* is accounted for, viz., the hairy and rougher surfaces of the leaves, which are traits of the well-known *S. sarmentosa*. If these remarks prove nothing, they may serve to show the difficulty of recognising the various forms and species of so popular a genus from reading alone, it having been so extensively treated of, and the classifications being so varied. Its study, when the species are being cultivated, is simply delightful, compared with the confusion of book study alone; and yet it is no uncommon thing, when forming a collection of Saxifrages, to receive three or four different forms from different sources under the same name, and each perhaps more or less authorised. The student by growing this genus of plants will reap other pleasures than that of identification, and in a few years time will find in his own garden (as the outcome of growing allied species) new forms springing from seed, and scattered about the beds and walks in a pleasing and suggestive manner. (See Fig. 84.)

The present subject has bell-shaped flowers, arranged in short-branched panicles, each flower ¾in. across, and sometimes, when well expanded, quite an inch; the colour is a delicate pink-tinted white; petals obovate and concave, inserted in the calyx, clawed, sometimes notched and even lobed; stamens long as petals, inserted in throat of calyx, stout, green changing to pink; anthers large and brick red when young; styles massive, joining close together, turgid, nearly long as stamens, and pale green; stigmas, simple, beardless, turning to a red colour; calyx bell-shaped, five-parted, wrinkled; segments slightly reflexed and conniving or joining; scapes 4in. to 6in. high, stout and smooth, excepting solitary hairs; bracts, leaf-like; leaves oval or cordate, 2in. to 4in. long, wrinkled, slightly waved, and toothed, conspicuously ciliated or haired on the margin, whence the specific name "*ciliata.*" Both surfaces are also furnished with short stiff hairs, the whole leaf being stout and flatly arranged; leaf stalks short, thick, and furnished with numerous long hairs, and ample stipules, which are glabrous, but beautifully ciliated. Roots, woody, and slightly creeping on the surface. Habit of foliage reflexing, forming flat masses; smaller or supplementary scapes are sent up later than the main scape, from the midst of the stipules, bearing flowers in ones and twos. The blossom, which is effective and very beautiful, is also sweetly scented, like the hawthorn.

As already hinted, this is not one of the most hardy Saxifrages, but I have twice wintered it out on gritty beds, well raised, also on rockwork, under a warm south wall; and, as such positions can be found or made in most gardens, it would be advisable to try and establish this distinct and lovely spring bloomer. Lime and sandstone grit mixed with loam and leaf soil I find to be the best compost I have yet tried for it; in fact, until a dry situation and a little lime were given, it proved a shy bloomer. It is now quite the reverse, notwithstanding that the roots were divided during the previous autumn. Fogs and rain are its greatest plagues, owing to its hairy nature; the glass and wire shelters should be used for this most deserving subject. Propagated by division of the woody semi-creeping roots during early autumn; each division should have a crown and some roots, when they may be planted in their permanent quarters.

Flowering period, March to May.

## Saxifraga (Megasea) Cordifolia.
### *Nat. Ord.* SAXIFRAGACEÆ.

A FIRST-CLASS herbaceous perennial, grown for over a hundred years in English gardens; it comes from Siberia, and consequently, it is very hardy in this climate. The *Megasea* section of the Saxifraga is a very distinct genus; there are several forms with but slight distinctions in the section, but the species now under notice may be readily distinguished from its nearest known relatives, first by its extra size in all its parts, next by its wrinkled heart-shaped leaves.

The flowers are produced on stout stems nearly a foot high, a section of which will cut the size of a sixpenny piece; the rose-coloured flowers are perfectly developed before they push through the many-times over-lapped foliage; they are neatly arranged, the branching stems sometimes giving the panicle, of blossom the form and also the size of a moderate bunch of grapes. Just at this stage the flowers, to be most enjoyed, should be cut before the weather spoils their delicate colour. The fine pale green calyx, which is also conspicuous by its handsome form and extra length, is far from the least important feature of this flower, especially at the above-mentioned stage. The leaves are 6in. to 10in. across.

Of the use of its flowers in a cut state, a few words may be said The weather soon destroys their beauty, but when cut they may be preserved for fully a fortnight. On one occasion I took a blossom and placed it in a flower stand for single specimen blooms; in this instance all the other glasses held such fine roses as Baroness Rothschild, Madame Lacharme, and Edouard Morren, but so richly did it compare with these roses that it was given the place of honour—the top centre glass; this flower I should say had never seen the full light in the open. After that others pushed out of the leaves and were speedily damaged, and not fit to cut.

Flowering period, March to May.

## Saxifraga Coriophylla.
### *Nat. Ord.* SAXIFRAGACEÆ.

THIS is a rather recently discovered alpine species, very dwarf, but beautiful. The specific name would appear to be in allusion to its flowers as pink-shaped; they are very small, but the reader, by referring to the cut (Fig. 85), may form his own opinion of such likeness; however well founded or otherwise the name may be, we have in this subject a gem for the rock garden. It is a native of Albania, and belongs to that section of its extensive genus having triquetrous and obtuse leaves, or blunt three-sided foliage, as formed by a well developed keel. It is in flower in the middle of March, at the height of 2in. All its parts are of miniature dimensions, and yet when grown in a suitable position it is effective.

The flowers are pure white, produced on leafy stems an inch or

FIG. 85. SAXIFRAGA CORIOPHYLLA.
(One half natural size.)

more high; they are few, and open in succession; petals round and overlapping; calyx large for the size of flower, and covered with down; sepals obtuse and tipped with a brown, almost red-tint; stamens short, having rather large yellow anthers, which fill the throat of the corolla. The leaves are evergreen or silvery grey, arranged in small rosettes, and ¼in. long, of good substance, rigid and smooth; their shape is obtuse, concave, and keeled; they are furnished with marginal excavations, which present themselves as dots; the habit is compact, the rosettes being crowded and forming cushioned-shaped specimens; the flowers last for a fortnight in average weather.

Between large stones in vegetable mould and grit, it both thrives and shows to advantage; it is also a charming subject for the pot culture of alpines. In company with the red-stalked and white-flowered *S. Burseriana*, the purple *S. oppositifolia*, and the many other forms of the mossy section, all, or nearly all in bloom about the same time, it offers a pleasing variety, as being distinct in every way from its contemporaries, more especially in the foliage. It is rather a slow grower, and not so readily increased as most Saxifrages; it is greatly benefited by having pebbles or small stones about the collar. These keep it moist at the roots during the growing season. If a little dry cow manure or guano is dusted amongst the stones during early summer, the results will soon be seen; such growth, however, should not be stimulated during the latter half of the year, or from its want of ripeness it will be liable to damage during winter. This practice of top dressing greatly assists the parts touching the earth to root, and so either an increased stock or larger specimens may sooner be obtained.

Flowering period, March.

## Saxifraga Fortunei.

FORTUNE'S SAXIFRAGE; *Nat. Ord.* SAXIFRAGACEÆ.

THIS, as may at once be seen by a glance at Fig. 86, belongs to the lobed-leafed section. It is as yet new in English gardens, and is often grown in pots in warm glasshouses. It is, however, perfectly hardy, having stood out with me in the open for the past three years. It is nearly related to *S. japonica* and its varieties, but is without the stolons or runners. In this climate, with outdoor treatment, it flowers in October until cut down by frost, which sometimes happens before the flowers get well out. It has been stated not only that it is not hardy, but that its flowering period is May. With me it has proved otherwise, and others have proved it to flower naturally in October. I also observed it in bloom in the Hull Botanic Gardens on the open rockwork in November, 1882. I have no doubt that autumn is the natural season for well-established plants to flower; weaker specimens may fail to push forth ere the frost cuts down their leaves, when the dormant buds must remain sealed for the winter, but ready to develope with the return of longer and warmer days.

The flowers are arranged in panicles on scapes nearly a foot high, the panicles being 6in. long and 3in. in diameter. The petals are long and narrow, of uneven length, and notched; colour pure white. The calyx is well developed; segments oval, notched at the ends; colour, pale apple green. Stamens, long and tipped with beautifully orange-coloured anthers. The ovary is prominent, and of a pale yellow. Besides the above features, the flowers, which mostly look sideways and are quite an inch across their broadest parts, have one very long petal at the low side, and the two next are at right angles with it, less than half its size, the two upper ones being still less; the effect is both unusual and pleasing. The leaf stalks are long, stout, and of a succulent nature, semi-transparent, and slightly furnished with longish hairs; the stipules are ample, and of a bright red, which colour extends for a short length up the stalk. The leaves are kidney-shaped, 2in. to 5in. across, eight or ten lobed, toothed and reflexed; they are furnished with solitary stiff hairs, are of good substance, and a very dark green colour, but herbaceous. The habit of this species is neat and very floriferous; therefore it is a valuable plant for in or outdoor gardening; but owing to its late season of flowering outside, the blossom is liable to injury. A bell glass, however, will meet the case; it should be placed over the plant, but tilted slightly, when there are signs of frost—the flowers will amply reward such care. If the bloom can be cut

FIG. 86. SAXIFRAGA FORTUNEI.
(One-fifth natural size; 1 and 2, full size.)

clean, a good cluster will vie with many orchids for delicacy and effect.

I find it to do well in fat loam, and with the same kind of soil in pots, which comes in for placing in cold frames when frost threatens. I find it one of the easiest plants possible to manage—in fact, it needs no care to grow it; still, many amateurs fail to keep it, I suppose from taking it into a warm greenhouse, where it is sure to dwindle. It is readily propagated by division of the crowns, which should be done in spring.

Flowering period, October until strong frosts.

## Saxifraga (Megasea) Ligulata.
*Nat. Ord.* SAXIFRAGACEÆ.

ONE of the large-leaved species (see Fig. 87) compared with others of the *Megasea* section, its leaves are strap-like, as implied by the specific name. It is sometimes called *Megasea ciliata*, but there is a large-leaved species, commonly called *S. ciliata*, which is very distinct from this one, and it is all the more important that they should not be confounded with each other, as *S. ciliata* is not very hardy, whilst this is perfectly so, being also one of

FIG. 87. SAXIFRAGA (MEGASEA) LIGULATA.

our finest herbaceous perennials. It comes to us from Nepaul, and has not long been cultivated in this country.

Its flowers are produced numerously on bold stout stems 10in. high. Sometimes the flower-stem is branched. The pale but clear rosy flowers are not only showy, but very enduring, lasting several weeks. The leaves are six to ten inches long, of irregular form, but handsomely ribbed and wavy; the new growths are bright yellowish-green, and tinted from the edges with a reddish bronze, so that, during spring, besides being finely in flower, it is otherwise a pleasing plant to look upon. Moreover, it is one of the few bold kinds of plants which flower so early and therefore a most valuable subject for the spring flower-beds.

It looks well in any position, either near or back from the walks, in shrubs, or as a centre specimen for beds; it is also a plant that may be moved easily, as it carries plenty of root and earth, consequently it may be used in such designs as necessitate frequent transplantings. It is not particular as to soil or position, but in light earth, well enriched with stable manure, I have found it to thrive, so as to be equal to many of the so-called "fine foliage" plants during summer; therefore, I should say, give it rich food. To propagate it, a strong specimen with branched crowns should be selected. These branches or stems are ½in. to 1in. thick. They should be cut off with as much length as possible; if they have a bit of root, all the better; if not, it does not much matter. Let the cut end dry for a little time, take off half, or even the whole, of the largest leaves, or the action of the wind will prevent their remaining firm. When so prepared, the cuttings may be deeply planted in sandy loam, which has previously been deeply stirred. This may be done as soon as the flowers are past, and by the end of the year the cuttings should be well rooted and suitable for moving into the ornamental part of the garden.

Flowering period, March to May.

## Saxifraga Longifolia.

LONG-LEAVED SAXIFRAGE; QUEEN OF SAXIFRAGES; *Nat. Ord.* SAXIFRAGACEÆ.

NUMEROUS and beautiful as are the species and varieties of this genus, this is the most admired of them all, from which fact it derives its proud name of "Queen." It is of recent introduction; habitat, the Pyrenees; but though of alpine origin, it thrives in lower, I may say the lowest, situations even in our wet climate. As will be seen by the illustration (Fig. 88), it belongs to the rosette section, and may indeed be said, for size and symmetry, to head the list. There are many forms of it, differing more or less in shape of leaves, colour, habit, and size of rosette. The original or reputed type is but an indifferent form compared with the one now generally accepted as the representative of the species. So readily do the various Saxifrages become crossed, that it is hard to distinguish them; and when a distinct form is evolved the question occurs, What constitutes or entitles it to specific honours? Surely the form of which we are speaking must be fully entitled to a name all its own, as it is not possible

OLD-FASHIONED GARDEN FLOWERS. 251

to find another Saxifrage that can so widely contrast with the whole genus.

It may be as well, in a few words, to refer to one or two varieties; and it shall only be from an amateur's point of view, whose estimate of their worth or importance is based entirely on their ornamental qualities under cultivation. Such varieties, as far as I know, have not had any name given them, descriptive or otherwise, and I for one have no desire to see any, as the genus is already overloaded with names.

Fig. 88. Saxifraga Longifolia.
(One-fourth natural size.)

There is, first, a form whose main distinction is its dark olive-green leaves; the ends are rather inclined to be spathulate, they are long, narrow, and arch well, rather nearer the centre of the rosette; this causes the end of the outer circle of leaves to come flat on the ground. The whole specimen has a sombre appearance compared with the more silvery kinds. The second form has broader leaves, is more distinctly toothed and spotted; as a consequence of their width, the leaves are fewer, and though all the varieties are very formal, this is the most so. When by the side of what we may term the true form, which has sometimes *vera* added to its name, this one has a plain and somewhat "dumpy" appearance, and frequently the tips of the leaves curl back, which further detracts from its ornamental quality. A third form has small rosettes, pale green foliage, indistinct silvery dots, and, worse than all, the habit of throwing out a progeny of young growths all round the collar, furnishing itself as with a ruff, when the parent rosette turns to a yellowish-green. Of all the forms this is the most constant bloomer. The favourite variety, to which an engraving can do but scant justice, is superior to the above kinds in all its parts. Its blooming period is in early summer, but specimens often grow in size and beauty for three or five years without producing flowers. The foliage is the more admired feature, and is at its greatest beauty in December.

The flowers are borne in handsome panicles, in the style of those of *S. pyramidalis*, which are about 18in. high. The blossom is of the kind common to this section. The leaves are long, narrow, toothed bluntly, and spotted with silvery dots; the whole leaf is greyish; the habit is rigid and of even arrangement; the rosettes are of all sizes, from 2in. to 10in. in diameter. At 3in. to 6in. they are attractive, and as they grow larger, they become conspicuous in their beauty. It is not desirable to have them flower, inasmuch as the rosettes are then destroyed, though the plants do not die. Of course, if a specimen "shows bloom" it cannot be helped, but rather than lose a season's produce of young stock I would nip out the "lead," and so cause offsets to be produced instead of flowers.

In the rock garden this is one of the most telling subjects that can be introduced; not only does it love to have its roots amongst the stones, but it is a form which harmonises and yet contrasts finely with such shapeless material, and, further, relieves the sameness of verdure of other plants in a more than ordinary degree. It will grow in borders or beds, but looks nowhere so well as on rockwork. True, its uses are limited, but then they are exceedingly effective. I have grown this subject in almost every kind of soil and compost, and it has done well in most; stiff clay-like loam appears too cold or wet for it; on the other hand, a sandy loam, mixed with leaf soil, grows it finely; perfect drainage is the desideratum, in no matter what position it is planted. It may be increased in various ways—1st, By seeds, which may be bought, as it is carefully harvested abroad; 2nd, from offsets, as already stated; and, 3rd, from offsets produced by cutting out the leaves in two or more parts, so as to let the light in at the collar. This method may seem heartless, and it certainly spoils the specimen; it is a mode to be followed only where there are spare old plants and young stock is needed.

Flowering period, June and July.

## Saxifraga Macnabiana.

MACNAB'S SAXIFRAGA; *Nat. Ord.* SAXIFRAGACEÆ.

THIS is a new and very beautiful variety, called after Mr. Mac Nab, who raised it in 1877. Of the several hundreds of species and varieties of this genus, it is doubtless one of the best and most distinct as regards its habit and rich flowers. So pronounced are its merit that, although I have not grown it for more than four years or so, I can have no hesitation in sounding its praise. It is possible that when it has become better established in the collections of amateurs and others, and when it has regained what may be termed its natural vigour, lost by the too rapid propagation common to new plants, it may prove to be even better than I have yet proved it. However that may be, there can at present be only one opinion respecting it.

The rosette foliage is in the style of *S. longifolia* and *S. pyramidalis*, intermediate; the flowers are quite distinct, but they remind one of the charming *S. mutata*, which is also a rosette form, having a fine panicle of blossom. It is said to be a seedling from *S. Nepalensis* crossed by *S. cotyledon* or *S. pyramidalis*, but, as the cross was accidental, there must be some uncertainty; both parents are evidently incrusted forms.

The flowers are ½in. across, corolla flat, petals richly spotted with numerous bright red spots; they are much shorter than the petals of most of the other incrusted varieties; they are also slightly reflexed in the more matured flowers; the calyx, too, is less hairy and the segments shorter than those of its reputed parents. The stem of my tallest specimen is not more than 15in. high; the panicle is large, beginning about four inches above the rosette, It is well branched, the flowers being clustered at the ends of the branchlets. The whole panicle will be about 10in. long and 6in. or 8in. through. As regards the foliage, I only need add to what has already been stated, that the leaves are arranged in somewhat lax rosettes, are strap, or tongue-shaped, evenly serrated, and, in the winter bright at the edges, with frosted or silvery markings; the flowers are so very attractive that casual observers readily recognise their beauties amongst hundreds of other Saxifrages, and they have not inaptly been compared with fine old china.

I ought not to omit mention of that rare quality possessed by this Saxifrage, viz., a rich perfume.

Though it is perfectly hardy, it may be grown in pots with great advantage, as then it can be the more closely examined; but if it is not convenient to grow it in that manner, it may be planted either on rockwork or in borders amongst choice things, where its flowers will not fail to command admiring notice. As to the kind of soil, it seems in no way particular. Sandy loam, mixed with peat, however, suits it well. It is propagated by offsets, but these are rarely produced in numbers, as is common with most of the incrusted Saxifrages. I may say that I have only met with one specimen which has thus proved useful in any degree worth notice, and it produced nearly a score of off-sets during one season; it ripens much seed, which may, or may not come true.

Flowering period, June and July.

## Saxifraga Mutata.
### Nat. Ord. SAXIFRAGACEÆ.

A SOMEWHAT rare alpine species, evergreen, hardy, very distinct and beautiful. It is one of the rosette forms, after the style of *S. pyramidalis*, but there are several important variations about the plant, other than in the flowers, which are totally different. There are many peculiarities about this species, but they would hardly require to be noticed here were not the plant otherwise of great merit. When in bloom it is highly decorative, and the flowers in a cut state are unique.

The flower stem is 12in. to 18in. high, furnished with supplementary ones all its length; the lower ones are 8in. long, and spreading; they become shorter as they near the top, the whole forming a fine symmetrical panicle. The flowers are over $\frac{1}{2}$in. across, petals awl-shaped, and, when first open, are nearly red; they change to dark orange and again to pale yellow; the calyx is very large, the sepals four times as broad as the petals and bluntly pointed; the stamens and anthers are coloured, and change like the petals; the ovary, which is very conspicuous, is a fine purple, but later, it, too, changes to a pink colour; the outer parts of the calyx and all the shorter flower-stalks, which are clustered at the ends of the supplementary stems, are greenish-yellow, and this feature of the plant adds much to its beauty. Calyx, stems, and stem-leaves are densely furnished with stiff gland-tipped hairs, rendering them clammy to the touch. The leaves of the rosettes are tongue-shaped, rough at the edges, fleshy, covered with glandular hairs, of a shining green colour, and slightly reflexed. The changeable nature of the flowers doubtless gives rise to the specific name. A well-flowered specimen is very effective on rockwork, but the panicles have a fault of heading over, from their weight, and also because, unlike *S. longifolia* and *S. cotyledon*, which have large and firm rosettes close to the ground to stay them, this species has a somewhat "leggy" rosette or a foot stalk, which is more or less furnished with browned and very persistent foliage. The flowers last a long time in good form, and, if grown clean, their yellow—nearly golden—stalks render them very useful in a cut state.

The propagation of this Saxifraga is more difficult than any other according to my experience, and I have heard of many who have found it the same. The offsets are not produced close to the ground, consequently have no rootlets; neither, from their hairy character, can they resist rot from moisture so well when planted as if they were bald, like the stolons of other species. I have found the best plan to be as follows: Take offsets before the plants flower; if there are none, which will often be the case, the bloom must be sacrificed by pinching out the stem. As soon as there are nice sized shoots ready, cut them off with all possible length of stalk; prepare a sandy patch of soil in a warm situation, lay them in a row on the surface, heads to the north, and then place a brick on them so as to hold all the cuttings in position; gently press on the brick, to cause the cuttings to assume a more natural position, and they will need no other attention until they become rooted; the brick will act as a screen from the hot sunshine, absorbing the heat to the benefit of the cuttings, as it will also absorb superfluous moisture. During the summer I have rooted many offsets in this way. That contact with the brick is favourable to the roots is evidenced by their clinging to it; no water should be given, however droughty the season may be—excessive moisture is the main thing to guard against.

Flowering period, June to August.

## Saxifraga Oppositifolia (*Lin.*)

PURPLE MOUNTAIN SAXIFRAGE, PURPLE SAXIFRAGE, BLUE SAXIFRAGE, OPPOSITE-LEAVED SAXIFRAGE; *Nat. Ord.* SAXIFRAGACEÆ.

DURING the month of March this is one of the most effective flowers in our gardens. The mossy appearance of its foliage, when dotted with its large blossoms, is hardly less beautiful than when the whole broad spreading tufts are literally packed with them. This must be a dear flower to all lovers of our native flora, for it not only comes very early, and in its wild homes on the Ingleborough, Welsh, and Scottish hills, greets and gladdens the rambler, who is, perhaps, making his first excursion of the year, but it is one of our most striking and beautiful flowers, even though they are produced on a plant of such humble size and habit. The pleasing and descriptive names of this gem of our hills would form a chapter in themselves. Even the old Latin names by which it was known, before the time when Linnæus arranged and re-named most of our native plants, bespeak a desire to do justice to a flower of more than ordinary beauty; and, as they were so strictly descriptive, at least one, I think, may be given without trying the reader's patience: *Saxifraga alpina ericoides flore cœruleo*, or the Blue-flowered Erica-like Mountain Saxifrage. Doubtless, shorter names are more convenient, but such specific names as the one just given are not entirely useless. Its present botanical name is in reference to the foliage only, but otherwise so distinct is this plant either in or out of bloom that no one could well mistake it.

The flowers are ½in. to ¾in. across, produced terminally and singly on short procumbent stems. They are of a bright purple colour; petals ovate; the longish stamens carry bold anthers furnished with dark orange-coloured pollen, which forms a pretty feature. The leaves are small, crowded, opposite, ovate, entire, leathery, fringed or ciliated, and retuse. A peculiar feature about this species is the pore at the blunt apex of each leaf. The habit is prostrate; the stems being long, tufted, or pendulous, according to the situation; the flower shoots are upright, on which the leaves are more remote. Under cultivation newly planted roots will be found not only to flower sparingly, but the blooms will be rather small until the plant grows large and strong.

On rockwork, with its roots near or between large stones, is in every way the best place for it; it however, thrives in the borders. The soil is not of much importance, but without doubt it does best in a compost of the nature of that of its wild homes. The humus and grit may be represented by sand and small stones, and peat or leaf soil, all mixed with loam. This, let me here state, will be found generally the right stuff for alpines and rockery plants. This plant is useful as a spring bedder, or for carpeting bare places; and any conspicuous part of the garden needing bright objects during March and April should give room largely for this cheerful subject. The bloom is very lasting; no storm seems to do it any hurt, and in every way it is reliable. It may be readily propagated by divisions. The procumbent stems will, in strong patches, be found to supply rootlets in abundance. These may be transplanted at almost any time of the year.

Flowering period, March and April.

*S. opp. alba* is a white flowered variety of the above. It is not found wild. Other dissimilarities are the smaller parts throughout the whole plant, and the less straggling habit. The white petals show up the dark orange anthers finely. There are other varieties of the above type, but their points of difference are so slight as not to need description for garden uses. It may, however, be useful to give their names: *S. opp. major*, *S. opp. pyrenaica*, *S. opp. retusa*, *S. opp. pallida*. All the above varieties may be grown like the common form; their uses, propagation, and blooming period are the same, with the exception of *pyrenaica*, which not only flowers a little later, but is less rampant, and not nearly so easy to propagate. I have imagined that a little limestone has helped it, bits of which are placed over its roots.

## Saxifraga Paradoxa.

PARADOXICAL SAXIFRAGE; *Nat. Ord.* SAXIFRAGACEÆ.

ONE of the less known and, perhaps, somewhat rare saxifrages; it is a curious, distinct, and beautiful form, being of that class which the lover of the ornamental kinds most admires, for not only is it attractive all the year round, but additionally so when there cannot be seen any part of a growing or decaying flower stem upon it, and when its silvery, but lax rosettes, with their encrustments and glistening leaf dots, are perfectly matured, which is the case during mid-winter. I fear the illustration (Fig. 89), can give but a poor idea of the pleasing silvery-grey

Fig. 89. SAXIFRAGA PARADOXA.
(Two-thirds natural size.)

colour, which, when the specimen is dry, overlays foliage of a dark and glossy green, to say nothing of the numerous and regular spots which so charmingly enliven the specimens. I am unable to learn to what species it is most nearly related; its name, which doubtless has reference to its peculiar form and habit, would seem to isolate it even from its parents, if such are known; it, however, belongs to that section having thick leathery leaves, ligulate, encrusted, arranged in rosette form, and having excavated dots. *Saxifraga lingulata, S. crustata, S. Australis, S. longifolia,* and *S. carinthiaca* belong to the same section; but *S. paradoxa* differs much in general appearance from them all, and remarkably so in one or two respects, as, indeed, it does from the whole genus, thus justifying its name. The uneven length and arrangement of leaves, the casting off of

s

the encrustments as a skin or in flakes, exposing to view a finely-polished surface, and the general web-like appearance of the tufts, are all peculiar to it. Of all the varieties of its section it most resembles S. *carinthiaca* and S. *Australis*; these forms, however, grow in compact rosette form, having leaves of more even size and shape. Our subject is irregular in every way, many of the leaves pushing out to double the length of others, and becoming attenuated at their junction, or club-shaped.

Its flowers are insignificant and similar to those of S. *Aizoon*, but more dwarf in the stem. The leaves are ½in. to 3in. long, very narrow and tongue-shaped, sometimes obtuse and club-shaped; stout, dark green, with a greyish crust-like covering, and deeply dotted with bright spots. The leaves are arranged in lax rosettes and are reflexed or pressed flat to the earth nearly all their length. The habit is very pretty in established and fair-sized specimens, which accommodate themselves to the form of surface, and the longer or erratic leaves become so interlaced with the other parts as to appear woven; this habit and the bright bead-like dots go to make the plant more than ordinarily attractive. It should be in every collection of choice Saxifrages; it is charming as a pot specimen, plunged and grown out of doors the year round.

On rockwork it should have a place, too, among the gems, being a neat and slow grower; its position should be near dark-coloured stones, where it will prove most telling. In damp weather its silvery parts are obliterated, but a breeze of half-an-hour or a beam of sunshine soon brings it into full beauty again. Gritty peat and a little loam suits it well; I have it doing nicely in ordinary garden soil; but if the more carefully prepared composts are employed, the results well repay the pains so taken. Its propagation is easily carried out by root divisions; early spring is a good time for the operation.

Flowering period, May and June.

## Saxifraga Pectinata.
### *Nat. Ord.* SAXIFRAGACEÆ.

THIS belongs to the encrusted section, being most distinctly toothed; from this it takes its name; the teeth are large for such small leaves. Specimens of this Saxifrage, though small, are exceedingly pretty. Excepting when there is fog or rain, it is nearly white; and the rosettes, of various sizes, from ¼in. to 1in. across, are not only neat in themselves, but are densely and pleasingly arranged in a hard flat mass. It is never more beautiful, not even in May and June, when it flowers, than in November, when the growth is both complete and ripened, and the scaly substance which is spread over the leaves and the silvery teeth combine to render it attractive.

The flowers are of the usual form, and are produced on stems 4in. to 6in. high; they are white. The leaves seldom exceed ½in. in length and ¼in. in width; they are spathulate in form, stout, and rigid. The rosettes are somewhat flattened and numerous, and give the idea of greenish-white flowers.

*S. p. hybrida* is a variety of the foregoing species, and without pretending to say what the type has been crossed with to produce this handsome form, I may, for the purpose of conveying an idea of what it is like, say that it approaches *S. aizoon*, which also flowers in May and June. In all its parts it is larger than the type; the leaves are greener and more strap-shaped, and are more erect, but not so rigid; the habit, too, differs—it forms more rounded tufts. In all these respects it will be seen to resemble *S. aizoon*. It is a lovely form; the sparkling teeth are relieved by the fine dark green ground of the foliage.

These comb-leaved Saxifrages belong to the more neat and effective rock plants; the type, at least, is of alpine origin, and under cultivation it seems most happy amongst the stones. I have grown these kinds as pot specimens, on nearly flat beds, and as edging plants; and in every position they prove attractive. It is very strange that such pretty forms are not more generally seen in gardens; they will grow well on walls and the tops of outhouses, and are good subjects for town gardens. Any kind of sandy soil will do for them; that of a vegetable character is, however, the best; they may be planted with choicer things, for, unlike many of the genus, they are not rampant growers. Practically, they need no propagating; for as the specimens spread they make new roots, and at any time one or half a dozen rosettes may be slipped off for planting elsewhere. It is better, though, to avoid this with small plants, as their full beauty is not realised until they become of considerable size.

Flowering period, May and June.

## Saxifraga Peltata.
### *Nat. Ord.* SAXIFRAGACEÆ.

A NEW species to English gardens, hardy, herbaceous, and perennial, imported from North America; it is a truly noble plant. The illustration (Fig. 90) will convey some idea of its fine form, but the reader must rely on the description for its size when fully developed. When the flowers of this Saxifrage are in their best form, the noble foliage is scarcely half developed; a drawing, therefore (though it could hardly be made at a stage when the plant is more interesting), must necessarily fail, in this case, to give any more than an approximate idea of the parts undeveloped. Not only is this the largest species of the extensive genus at present grown in this country, but its form is both distinct and noble.

The flowers are produced on stems 18in. high and ¾in. thick at the base, being covered with long stiff white hairs, which are very conspicuous on the reddish stems. The flowers are similar to those of most of the genus, as may be seen by the one given in the drawing; they are arranged in massive heads, 3in. to 6in. in diameter, and rose-coloured. The leaves at the flowering time are 6in. or 9in. across, having stout, round, ruddy stems, 8in. long, covered with stiff hairs; they form a junction with the leaves in an unusual way, viz., near the centre, whence the specific name *peltata*, or umbrella shape; but the form of the leaves at

FIG. 90. SAXIFRAGA PELTATA.
(1, Single blossom, natural size.)

the flowering period, which is funnel-shape. is, a little later on, reversed, the edges bending downwards. The younger leaves are folded and hooked downward, having the appearance of stout fern fronds just out of the ground, and their stalks are much contorted. The more advanced leaves are seen to be seven-cut, each lobe divided and sub-divided by cuts less deep, the whole leaf being richly toothed and veined. The under side is covered with hairs, the upper surface being smooth, shining, and of a pleasing bronze-green colour. Later, the foliage in every way increases very much in size, reaching a height of 2ft., and each leaf measuring nearly a foot across. The root or rhizoma is horizontal, progressive, jointed, and fibrous at the joints, and nearly 2in. in diameter; it may be clearly traced on the surface, but the fibrous parts go very deep.

It is said to be a bog subject; fortunately, however, this fine plant may be grown otherwise than in a bog, but it should not want for depth of rich soil. This I believe to be a more important condition than a boggy situation, inasmuch as I have grown my specimen for three years on the top of a dry mound; but the soil is good rich loam, and fully 5ft. deep; and to show that this strong-growing subject needs a good depth of soil, I may mention that I had occasion to dig up a piece, when it was found, for the operation, to require both the strength and tools that trees demand, the fibrous parts being deep and tough. When fairly established it makes rapid growth, and when in full leaf it proves very effective. Its propagation is easy with healthy plants; a length of the creeping root, with a crown to it, should be cut from the parent stock just before growth commences in early March. If planted as indicated in the foregoing remarks, and kept shaded with a leafy branch for a month or two, there need not be any fear about young plants becoming established the first season.

Flowering period, June.

## Saxifraga Purpurascens.

LARGE-LEAVED PURPLE SAXIFRAGA, MEGASEA *section*; *Nat. Ord.* SAXIFRAGACEÆ.

A RARE plant of great beauty. It is figured here without flowers, as I consider it in finer form then than when in bloom. Fine as its flowers are, much resembling those of *S. cordifolia* and *S. crassifolia* (also of the *Megasea* section); the brightness and colouring of its leaves in autumn are such as to render it distinct from all the other species. I need only ask the reader to note the fine foliage indicated in the cut (Fig. 91), and inform him that in the autumn it turns to a glossy vermilion colour, and I think he will admit that it will not come far short in beauty of any flower. The species is a recent introduction from the Himalayas, and in this climate proves all but evergreen (if tinted foliage can be so called) and hardy. The latter quality has been doubted by some, but by others re-asserted. My present specimen was planted in the open garden in the spring of 1880, since which time it has withstood 22deg. of frost.

The flowers are produced on stout stems, 8in. high, arranged in branched heads, of a rose or rosy-purple colour, and bell-shaped. They are, however, soon damaged by unfavourable weather, and there is little about the plant at that period to render it more attractive than its fellows; its finer qualities are developed as more genial weather prevails. When the stout foliage grows glossy, waved, and of a deep clear green colour, the edges of the leaves become lined with red as if hemmed with red silk; the leaves also have the edges irregular in form, the outline broadly oval, 4in. to 6in. long, and they are veined and slightly wrinkled; during the autumn a yellow tint starts from the edge, and in time becomes a vermilion, which is all the more effective from the leaf being of leather-like substance.

It enjoys a deep rich loam; and, evidently, to place its roots in contact with pieces of limestone is beneficial. Rare as the

FIG. 91. SAXIFRAGA PURPURASCENS.
(One-third natural size.)

plant is, this is all that I do for it, and not only does it remain healthy, but it has increased greatly in size during the last year. I have not as yet tried to propagate it, but so far as I can judge there will be no difficulty in forming young stock by root division. It has hitherto enjoyed a happy immunity from all garden pests, not excepting slugs.

Flowering period, April to June.

## Saxifraga Pyramidalis.

PYRAMIDAL SAXIFRAGA; *Nat. Ord.* SAXIFRAGACEÆ.

THIS is a very handsome form or variety of *S. Cotyledon*, and belongs to the alpine regions of Europe. As a decorative

OLD-FASHIONED GARDEN FLOWERS. 263

subject for our gardens, it is highly and deservedly esteemed; its attractiveness consists more in the numbers and arrangement of the flowers than in any beauty which belongs to them individually, though they are not devoid of that quality.

Of the many hundreds of species and varieties of Saxifrages which bloom during the month of June, this is one of the most distinct and useful as a decorative flower, and where the Saxifrages are grown in large collections, as they often are, giving more than an ordinary amount of pleasure compared

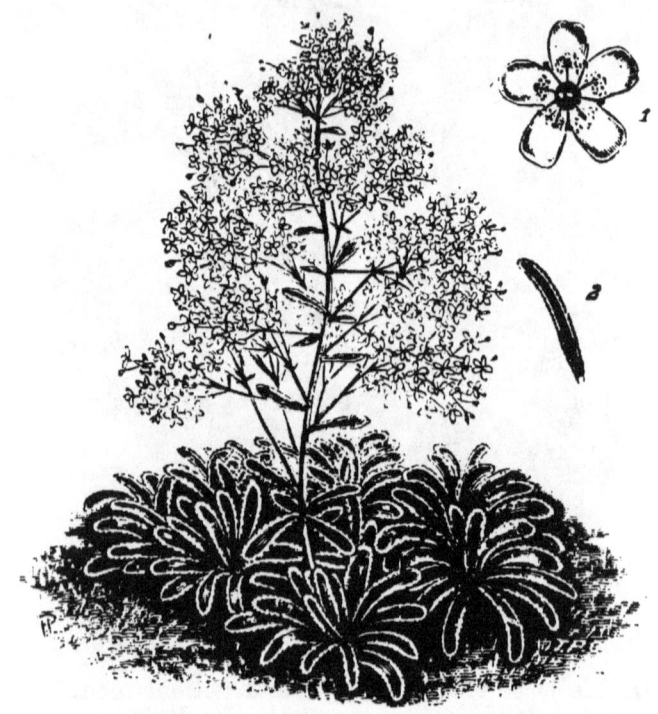

FIG. 92. SAXIFRAGA PYRAMIDALIS.
(One-eighth natural size; 1, single blossom, natural size; 2, leaf, one-eighth natural size).

with collections of other genera, the kind now under consideration always asserts itself as one of the first order of merit. Not only in its blooming state, but all the year round, it is very effective and striking; it is a free grower, having handsome, large rosetted foliage.

The flowers, as will be seen by the one given, natural size, in the illustration (Fig. 92), are of the common Saxifrage form, but rather more highly coloured in the central markings than the general run. They are produced on stout stems, 2ft. high, well and evenly branched in the form of a pyramid, whence the specific name. Each flower will be ½in. or more across; they are very numerous, and, partly from the fact that they remain perfect for a very long while, and partly because of the habit of the plant being to open all its flowers about or near the same time, the large panicle of bloom is very fine. The leaves, as already hinted, are formed into lax rosettes, which are 5in. to 7in. across; they are strap-shaped, narrowing slightly at the connection, half an inch wide, the outer ones being reflexed; the edges are finely serrated, and irregularly lined with a silver colouring.

This is a capital plant for rockwork, where it shows itself to much advantage; but specimens are much finer grown in beds or borders, where the moisture and temperature at the roots are likely to be more equable; besides, I find that, owing to its small quantity of roots, all of which are very near the surface, when grown on rockwork they may often be seen bare on inclined surfaces, and the weight of the flowers drags them entirely out of the soil on one side. They may be planted as an edging to a shrubbery, in bold groups, or as ordinary border flowers. So useful has this variety been found by professional gardeners that it is now largely grown in pots in single rosettes, which, after becoming well established, send up their rich plumes of blossom, all the finer for having been kept clean under glass. So grown, nothing can better repay the small amount of trouble which they give in order to place them in the conservatory as showy specimens; all they require being a 4in. pot, well drained, a compost of half-rotted leaves, and fat loam and sand. Put in one rooted offset any time from June to the end of July, the earlier the better; plunge the pot to its rim in sand or ashes until next spring, when it may be taken under glass if desired. To have fine flowers, the offsets should be pinched off as they appear. I may also mention that a somewhat shady situation has proved conducive to large and better coloured flowers; between irises 4ft. high and shrubs 6ft. high, the opening being not more than 3ft., running north and south. The specimen from which the drawing is taken was grown along with many others. A baking or dry treatment is often not only given to plants of this genus, but believed to be of advantage to them; it may be to some, but there are exceptions, and this is one without doubt. All the sections of Saxifraga to which it belongs are fond of good loam, well enriched. It is propagated from offsets taken as soon as they are from an inch to two inches across; they may either be put into nursery beds or be planted in their blooming quarters.

Flowering period, June and July.

## Saxifraga Rocheliana.
ROCHEL'S SAXIFRAGE; *Nat. Ord.* SAXIFRAGACEÆ.

ANOTHER hardy evergreen species, distinct in form, foliage and flowers, and a native of the alpine regions of central Europe; it nevertheless thrives well in our climate with ordinary care. Its foliage takes the form of miniature rosettes, which are closely packed; the tiny leaves are distinctly and regularly dotted; and present a frosted appearance.

The flowers are unimportant, though they form an interesting feature of such a choice and somewhat rare plant; they are small, white, and produced on stems 3in. to 4in. high, which are thick and curiously furnished with leaves. During summer this species has a very bright silvery appearance, as if laid on in patches.

Similar treatment is required for this as for *S. Burseriana*, but it will be found much more difficult to propagate, as its roots are of the tap kind, and are more sparingly produced, while its seed seldom ripens, I believe, in this climate. To increase it, the better plan is to prepare the old plant by keeping it well earthed up, and so encouraging new roots; after a year's patience it may be divided in April. The small pieces should be secured by stones or verbena pins, and a supply of pebbles placed around them will keep them cool and moist during summer.

Flowering period, March and April.

## Saxifraga Umbrosa.
LONDON PRIDE; *Nat. Ord.* SAXIFRAGACEÆ.

THIS common flower is well known, and is only mentioned here as the typical form, and by way of introducing a beautiful variety called *S. u. variegata*, broad cushions of which, from their verdant condition, good habit, and pleasing variations of leaf colour, are amongst the more attractive objects of the garden in January. It hardly need be said that the plant is not valued for its flowers, which are similar to those of the parent form and borne at a corresponding date. The leaves, however, are much less in size and more flatly arranged in rosette form, they are also recurved at the edges. The markings are of two colours, creamy-white and pink, and there are many shades of green. The forms of the markings are most irregular, as striped, flecked, marbled, dotted, and edged; the various shades of green blended with pink and white, although figured on one of the commonest plants we know, render such plant worthy of a place in every garden, and more especially on rockwork.

It has this drawback—it is not constant. In some gardens the markings die out. This, however, need not be, for a rather dry situation and rich soil will produce rosettes of large size and good figuring. Still, there will be fully half of the rosettes entirely green in a large patch; this is more desirable than otherwise. The marked ones have a more starry effect in such a green setting; it is only when all become green that disappointment is felt. Sometimes I have noticed rosettes, about the size of a penny-piece, all one colour—creamy-white—which, when cut from the plant, very much resembled a carnation. Such abnormal forms are of no moment to the botanist, but if nine out of every ten persons who see this plant are interested, not to say pleased with it, it ought not to be entirely neglected. It is most effective in patches 1ft. to 2ft. broad. In propagating it the more finely marked pieces only should be taken.

Flowering period, May to July.

## Saxifraga Wallacei.
### *Nat. Ord.* SAXIFRAGACEÆ.

A HARDY perennial hybrid variety, of first-class merit. Its loose and spreading panicles of large pure white flowers are something better than the ordinary run of bloom belonging to this extensive genus; it is said to be the offspring of species of the mossy section; but there is certainly a great likeness about its foliage to some of the horny section, such as *S. cornutum* or *S. pentadactylis*, or even the handsome *S. geranioides*. It would, however, be hard to say what it is from; but in it we have not only a showy but most useful variety (see Fig. 93). It has deservedly grown into great favour, though known to amateurs but for three years. It begins to flower in April, but in May it is in its best form, being covered with a rich mass of bloom from the foliage to the height of a foot.

The flowers, as before stated, are of a pure white—an unusual colour amongst the genus; they are bell-shaped but erect, the ovate petals reverse. Well-grown specimens with me have flowers quite an inch across. The individual blooms last more than a week, and the succession is well maintained during summer. The panicles are leafy, having small entire leaves, and others once and twice-cut. The stems of the present season's growth are stout, semi-transparent, and ruddy; the leaves are palmate, slender at the bottom, mostly five-fingered, fleshy, and covered with long silky hairs which stand well off; the fine apple-green foliage is shown to great advantage by the ruddy stems.

This plant may be grown in pots or borders, as edging, or on rockwork, and in any kind of soil; but to have fine specimens and large flowers it should be planted in calcareous loam, and be top dressed in early spring with well rotted manure. I have it as an edging to a small bed of roses; the position is bleak, but the soil is good; it furnishes large quantities of cut bloom, and otherwise, from its rich hawthorn-like scent, it proves a great treat. So freely is its handsome foliage produced that it, too, may be cut in quantities for table decoration. If the flowers, or

FIG. 93. SAXIFRAGA WALLACEI.
(One-half natural size.)

some of them, be left on, the tufts will form a pretty setting for a few other small flowers of decided colours.

To increase this Saxifrage is a simple matter during the warm season: The twiggy tufts should be pulled asunder, no matter whether they have roots or no roots; if dibbled into fine soil, deeply dug, and shaded for a week or two, they will form strong plants before the winter sets in.

Flowering period, April to August.

## Scilla Campanulata.

BELL-FLOWERED SCILLA or BLUEBELL; *Nat. Ord.* LILIACEÆ.
A HARDY bulbous perennial, introduced from Spain 200 years ago. It very much resembles the English hyacinth—*H. nutans*,

or *Scilla non-scripta*—better known as the wood hyacinth. Handsome as this simple flower is, it might have been omitted from these notes as a plant too well known, but for the fact that there are several varieties of the species which are less known, very beautiful, and deliciously fragrant, entitling them to a place amongst other choice flowers, both in books and gardens.

Of the typical form little need be said by way of description. The flowers are bell-shaped, pendent, blue, and produced in

FIG. 94. SCILLA CAMPANULATA ALBA.
(One-fourth natural size; single flower, one-half natural size.)

racemes of many flowers. The leaves are lance-shaped, prostrate, and of a dark shining green colour.

*S. c. alba* differs from the type in having its white flowers arranged more evenly round the scape, being shorter in the divisions of petals and wider at the corolla; the habit of the plant, too, as may be seen by the illustration (Fig. 94), is more rigid and neat. In a cut state the flowers are not only very lasting, but if gathered clean, they are suitable for the most delicate wreath or bouquet.

*S. c. carnea* has pink flowers.

All the forms of *S. campanulata* are cheerful and effective spring flowers. They should be grown in bold clumps, and if under slight shade, where many other things cannot be well grown, all the better; still, they are in no way particular—any aspect, position, or soil will answer for these robust flowers. Such being the case, few gardens should be without at least the finer forms of the large Bluebell. So fast do these varieties increase by seed and otherwise, that any remarks on their propagation are unnecessary.

Flowering period, April to June.

## Sedum Sieboldi.
SIEBOLD'S STONECROP; *Nat. Ord.* CRASSULACEÆ.

THIS is a capital species. It is perfectly hardy, though not generally known to be so. It is more often seen under glass, and is certainly a pretty pot plant.

Its stems are 12in. or less in length, slender and procumbent. The leaves, which are rather larger than a shilling, fleshy, cupped, and glaucous, are curiously arranged on the stems, somewhat reflexed, and otherwise twisted at their axils, presenting a flattened but pleasing appearance. The small flowers, which are bright rose, are borne in clusters, and remain two or three weeks in perfection.

It is a fine subject for rockwork, and, moreover, likes such dry situations as only rockwork affords. It should be so planted that its graceful stems can fall over the stones. There is a variety of this species, with creamy foliage, but it is less vigorous; neither are the flowers so fine in colour. Slugs are fond of these, and sometimes they will eat off nearly every leaf. A sprinkling of sharp sand once a week keeps them off, but trapping them with hollowed turnips is a more effective remedy. Propagated by cuttings pricked into sand in summer, or division of roots when the tops have died down.

Flowering period, August and September.

## Sedum Spectabile.
SHOWY STONECROP; *Nat. Ord.* CRASSULACEÆ.

HARDY and herbaceous. This is one of our finest autumn bloomers. During September, the broad massive heads of small rosy flowers, which are arranged in cymes 6in. across, are very attractive, and will, with average weather, keep in good form for a month. This species is somewhat mixed up with another called *S. Fabarium*; by many they are said to be identical, but such is not the case. I grow them side by side, and I may say that they are as "like as two peas" up to midsummer, when they begin to diverge. *S. Fabarium* continues to grow to the height, or rather length, of 2ft., and tumbles over;

the foliage has a lax appearance, and the flowers are very pale. Concurrently S. *spectabile* has grown its stems and glaucous leaves to stouter proportions, and crowned them with more massive heads of bright rose-coloured flowers, at the height of 15in. It is larger in all its parts, with the exception of length of stem, and by September it is nearly twice the size of S. *Fabarium*; it also stands erect, so that then the two species suggest a contrast rather than a comparison, S. *spectabile* being by far the more desirable.

I find, however, that it is much slower in increasing itself; the best way to propagate it is by cuttings dibbled into sand in early summer. The commoner one increases rapidly and often bears the wrong name; care should therefore be taken to obtain the true species, after which it will not give much further trouble, thriving in any kind of soil, but it should be planted in the full sunshine, when its habit and flowers will be greatly improved. It will bear any amount of drought—indeed, it seems to enjoy it. My finest clump is on a very dry part of rockwork, where it has always flowered well. These two Stonecrops and a variegated variety are some of the very few hardy plants which slugs do not graze; at any rate, it is so with me; neither do other pests attack them, but the humble bees literally cover their flowers the whole day long at times.

Flowering period, August to October.

## Sempervivum Laggeri.
LAGGER'S HOUSELEEK; *Nat. Ord.* CRASSULACEÆ.

OF the numerous species and varieties of Houseleek, this is at once the most curious, interesting, and beautiful. It is by far the finest of the webbed forms. It has, however, the reputation of not being quite hardy, but that it will endure our severest winters is without doubt, and if we recall its habitats, which are in alpine regions, its hardiness in a low temperature need not be further questioned. Still, partly from its downy nature, and partly from the dampness of our winters, this climate causes it to rot. There are, however, simple and most efficient remedies, which shall be mentioned shortly.

The illustration (Fig. 95) gives some idea of its form and habit. The flowering rosettes send up stems 6in. high; they are well furnished with leaves—in fact, they are the rosettes elongated; they terminate with a cluster of buds and flowers, which remain several weeks in perfection, however unfavourable the weather may be.

The flowers are more than an inch across, of a bright rose colour, and very beautiful; the central flower is invariably the largest, and the number of petals varies from six to twelve. The leaves are in rosette form, the rosettes being sometimes 2in.

across, nearly flat, and slightly dipped in the centre; a downy web, as fine as a cobweb, covers the rosette, it being attached to the tips of the leaves, and in the middle it is so dense that it has a matted appearance. The leaves are very fleshy, glandular, and of a pale green colour. Slow in growth, habit very compact; it has a tender appearance, but I never saw its web damaged by rain or hail.

Many grow it in pots for indoor use; it finds a happy home

FIG. 95. SEMPERVIVUM LAGGERI.
(Two-thirds natural size.)

on rockwork or old walls; it should have a dry and sunny situation, and, with these conditions, it will prove attractive all the year round. It thrives well in gritty loam; a little peat rubbed in with the grit will be an improvement and also more resemble its native soil. To preserve it from the bad effects of our damp winters, it need not be taken indoors, but sheets of glass should be tilted over the specimens during the short days, when they are dormant; the glass should not touch the plant. This seems to be the nearest condition we can afford it as a substitute for the snows of its mountain home, and I may add, for years it has proved effective; in fact, for several years I have left specimens in the open without any shelter whatever, and the percentage of loss has been very low, though the seasons were trying. It propagates itself freely by off-sets; if it is intended to remove them from the parent plant, it should be done early in summer, so that they may become established before winter, otherwise the frosts will lift them out of position.

Flowering period, June to August.

## Senecio Pulcher.
NOBLE GROUNDSEL; *Nat. Ord.* COMPOSITÆ.

AUTUMN is the heyday of Composite flowers. The one now under notice has the merit of being of an unusual and beautiful colour,

FIG. 96. SENECIO PULCHER.
(One-tenth natural size.)

viz., purplish crimson. It is, in fact, a new plant in English gardens, and has been justly described as one of the finest imports of recent years; it has only to be seen in order to commend itself to all lovers of hardy flowers (see Fig. 96). It is a robust grower, ranking with the more noble subjects suitable for the borders. Its hardiness is doubted by many, and a few have suspected its perennial quality; but notwithstanding the warm climate of South America (whence it hails), it has proved both hardy and perennial in this country. Excessive moisture is its greatest enemy.

Its bright purplish-crimson flowers are daisy-shaped and large, the centre being a fine golden yellow—on strong young plants the flowers will be 3in. across. Moreover, they are numerously produced on stems 3ft. high, in branching cymes, and last a long time in perfection; with favourable weather an individual bloom will stand above a week, and the plant provides itself with abundance of buds for succession. I never yet saw a specimen that developed half its buds, but this brings me to notice one of its faults (for it has more than one), viz., it is too late in blooming; at any rate, in Yorkshire we rarely get more than three weeks' enjoyment of its flowers, when, but for severe frosts, it appears capable of blooming for two months. To some extent this may be remedied, as will be shown when I refer to its culture. The radical leaves are over a foot long, stem leaves much smaller, very dark holly green of leather-like substance, the edges very unevenly shaped, the general form of the leaf being something like the cos lettuce.

The cut blooms are indeed fine and cannot well be inappropriately used. This brings me to fault No. 2. The flower stems are very hollow and dry, nearly as much so as the hemlock or kex, and I have found that when flowers have been cut, either from the moisture collecting in the stem, or some such cause, rot sets in lower down, and soon the branches of bloom head over. I tried cutting to a joint where the cavity was stopped, but the pith when so exposed soon gave way, so that latterly I have ceased to cut the flowers, unless the occasion was worth the risk. A specimen not cut from did not suffer from stem rot. I, therefore, blamed the cutting. There may, however, be other causes; at any rate, there is the fact of fine flowers in their prime falling over, and it is worth one's while to try to find out from what cause it happens, and if my theory is not the true one, it may prove useful as a hint.

It likes a deep and rich soil, and well deserves to have it; if left out all the winter, a piece of glass should be put over the crown, because it has the fault (No. 3) of rotting in the centre, as I believe from water being conducted down its spout-like stems; but even under the most neglected conditions it stands our winters, and the rootlets send up a number of small growths in spring. These may make plants, but will not be reliable for bloom the following autumn; the damage should be prevented if possible. Another plan, by which two points are gained, is to grow young plants in good-sized pots and winter them, plunged in cold frames, not failing to give plenty of air. In April these, if compared with others in the open garden, will be found to be much more forward, and the first gain will be that, if planted out then, they will flower much more vigorously, and, secondly, they will start earlier by two weeks at least. To propagate this fine border plant, the very long and fleshy roots may be cut into pieces 6in. long and dibbled into fine soil; they are somewhat slow, but pretty sure to "go"; they should be protected from slugs, which are very fond of the young leaves. On young stuff, grown apart from the flower beds and borders, quicklime may be used, which would otherwise be unsightly.

Flowering period, August to October.

## Sisyrinchium Grandiflorum.

SATIN-FLOWER, *or* RUSH LILY; *Nat. Ord.* IRIDACEÆ.

THE generic name of this flower is in reference to the grubbing of swine for its roots, and means "pig-snout." The common

FIG. 97. SISYRINCHIUM GRANDIFLORUM.
(One-third natural size.)

names may be seen, by a glance at the cut (Fig. 97), to be most appropriate; that of Satin-flower is of American origin the plant being a native of Oregon, and is in reference to its rich satiny blossom; that of Rush-lily, which is, perhaps, an even more suitable name, has been recently applied to it, I believe, in this country. It is applicable alike to the rush-like form and habit of foliage, and the lily-like purity and style of flowers. It was sent to this country in 1826, and yet it is rarely met with in English gardens. Some think it scarcely hardy in our climate in certain soils. I happen to have grown it for six years, which period includes the recent severe winters, and it has not only survived but increased in a moderate degree. This took place on rockwork facing south; in the autumn of 1881 I divided the specimen, and planted a part of it in the coldest part of my garden, which is not without clay, though far from all clay; that division is now a strong plant, and has made an extra crown; it forms the subject of the present illustration. Let me state, in passing, that it is naturally a slow grower. The very severe weather of the week previous to my writing this note, in March, 1883, when 23deg. of frost was registered, which cut down the bloom stems of Hellebores and many other well-known hardy things, did not hurt this subject very much; I am, therefore, confident of its hardiness from six years of such experience.

The flowers are 1in. to ·1½in. long, and about as much across when open, of a fine purple colour, with a shining satiny appearance; the six transparent petal-like divisions are of uneven form, having short bluntish points; from the openness of the corolla the stamens and style are well exposed, and they are very beautiful. The flowers are produced when the plant is about 6in. or 9in. high, the buds being developed on a rush-like stem, and enfolded in an almost invisible sheath 2in. or 3in. from the apex. Gradually the sheath, from becoming swollen, attracts notice, and during sunshine it will suddenly burst and let fall its precious contents—a pair of beautiful flowers—which dangle on slender arching pedicels, springing from the sheath-socket. They seem to enjoy their new-born freedom, and flutter in the March wind like tethered butterflies. Their happy day, however, is soon over; their fugacious petals shrivel in three or four days. The leaves are rush-like, ribbed, and sheathed.

I have found it to thrive in loam, both light and moderately stiff, also in vegetable soil and sand; it likes moisture, but not of a stagnant character; between large stones, at the base of rockwork, suits it in every way; it may also be grown by the side of the larger kinds of snowdrops for contrast and effect. Impatient of being disturbed, it is not wisdom to lift it for any purpose, provided it is making progress, or until it has formed strong tufts; when, if it is desirable to increase it, and during early autumn, the long roots should be got well under, and taken out of the ground as entire as possible; from their wiry nature they are then both easily cleared of earth and divided into single crowns; these should be replanted in positions deeply dug, and where they are intended to remain, being carefully arranged without any doubling up. After such pains have been taken with so well-deserving a plant, there will be little to fear for its future, no matter how severe the winter may prove.

*S. g. album* is a white-flowered variety, of which, however, I have had no experience. Since these lines appeared in serial form, a lady, cultivating a good collection of choice hardy flowers, has informed me that this variety is very fine, and in every way commendable.

Flowering period, March to May, according to positions or climatic conditions.

## Soldanellas.
### *Nat. Ord.* PRIMULACEÆ.

DIMINUTIVE herbaceous alpine perennials. This genus is small in number of known species as in size of specimens. They are found in very high altitudes in the Tyrol, Switzerland, and Germany; but they are easily managed even in our foggy climate, as is shown by the fact of the various species being grown in all collections of alpines; and, indeed, no collection can be said to be complete without such gems—they are great favourites, as they well deserve to be. They flower in early spring, some with one, and others more than one flower on a stem.

The flowers are very small, broadly bell-shaped, and of a feathery appearance, from the fact of their petals being finely divided. The foliage is also small, nearly round, of good substance, and in all the following species very bright green; the leaf stalks are long and wiry, and form neat and handsome little tufts, independent of the flowers, which, I may add, do not last more than five or six days.

*S. alpina*, smaller in all its parts, but otherwise much resembling *S. montana*—has leaves the size of a shilling piece, flowers bright blue, mostly two on a stem.

*S. Clusii*, from Germany, is smaller than *S. alpina*; in other respects similar, with the exception of flowers, which are purple.

*S. minima* (smallest). Very tiny in all its parts, many of its little thick leaves being only ¼in. across; flowers purple, single on the stem, which is only ½in. to 1in. long.

*S. montana* (Fig. 98) is the largest species of all—leaves the size of a half-crown piece, flowers bright blue, four or five on a stem, 5in. high. It has other distinctions, of a minute character, from the smaller species, but by difference of size alone it may be readily identified.

All the Soldanellas love a vegetable soil, as peat or leaf mould, to which, when under cultivation, a liberal quantity of sand should be added. If grown in pots, they make lovely specimens, and should be plunged in sand and kept moist; but I find my specimens to grow much more vigorously when planted out, as they are at the base of a small rockery, rather below the level of the neighbouring walk, which forms a miniature watershed for the supply of moisture. I also fancy the liverwort, which

Fig. 98. Soldanella Montana.
(One-half natural size.)

surrounds them, rather helps them than otherwise. Certain I am, however, that moisture is the great desideratum in the culture of this genus. My difficulty with the planted-out specimens is to keep them from being grazed off by the slugs; a dash of silver sand every day or two has sometimes proved of use. When the Soldanellas once get into proper quarters they make rapid growth; I have divided them most successfully in April and May.

Flowering period, March to May.

## Spiræa Palmata.

PALM-LIKE SPIRÆA; *Nat. Ord.* ROSACEÆ.

A BOLD and handsome species from China, imported about sixty years ago. It is perfectly hardy, though generally grown in pots and under glass. It belongs to the herbaceous section, and I may as well state at once that the Spiræas—more especially the herbaceous kinds—are only decorative when in flower, by which I wish to convey the idea that after they have done

FIG. 99. SPIRÆA PALMATA.
(One-eighth natural size.)

flowering, from their abundant foliage, which then begins to turn sere and ragged, they become unsightly if planted in conspicuous parts. Still, their flowers and general habit are both rich and handsome when in their prime, and they are certainly worth growing, especially by those who have large gardens, where they can be planted in large patches in some of the less frequented parts.

*S. palmata* (Fig. 99) has remarkably bright rosy-crimson flowers; they are of indistinct form unless closely examined. It is, however, a well-known form of flower, or arrangement of flowers, and need not be further described, beyond saying they are in panicles and have a feathery appearance. The leaves, which are 6in. or more across, have long smooth stems, are mostly seven-lobed, the lobes being long, pointed, and unevenly serrated. The size of foliage and height of plants vary very much; if grown in a bog or by the side of a stream, it attains the height of 3ft. to 4ft.; in drier situations I have seen it flower when only 10in. high. The specimen illustrated is about 15in. high.

A light spongy vegetable soil, with plenty of moisture, is the main requirement of most of the Spiræas, and to grow them to perfection little less will do; but a creditable display of bloom may be enjoyed from plants grown in ordinary garden loam, provided the situation is moist. By way of experiment, I planted a dozen roots of this species in an exposed border, drained, and in all respects the same as for the ordinary run of border flowers. They none of them flowered, and scarcely grew; at no time would they be higher than 6in. I wish to make it clear that the Spiræas, and especially *S. palmata*, cannot be grown and bloomed well without an abundance of moisture at the roots, as I am aware that many have tried and failed with this desirable kind. It should be treated as a bog plant, then it can scarcely fail to do well. In sunk parts of rockwork, by the walk gutters, by the side of a pond or stream, or (if there is one) in the hedge dyke, are all suitable places for this bright flower, and if only for the fine spikes which it produces for cutting purposes, it should be grown largely; and as most of the positions indicated are somewhat out of the way, they may perhaps be the more readily thus appropriated. Propagated by division of strong roots during autumn.

Flowering period, July and August.

## Spiræa Ulmaria Variegata.

*Syn.* S. ODORATA FOL. VAR.; *Nat. Ord.* ROSACEÆ.

THE beautiful variegated form of the well-known "Meadow-sweet," other old names being "Mead-sweet," and "Queen of the Meadows." The typical form, at least, needs no description, it being one of the commonest and most appreciated plants of the British flora. This variety, however, is less known; it differs only as regards the markings of the foliage. When the crimped leaves are young, the broad golden patches are very effective, and when the plants are fully grown, the markings of the older foliage become lighter coloured, but not less rich. Of the value of this as a "fine foliage" plant there can be no doubt; it is very telling, and always admired. As regards its flowers, they ought not to be allowed to develope. I only mention this subject for the sake of its beautifully coloured leaves.

Requirements: Ordinary garden loam, in a moist situation; propagated by root divisions during autumn.

Flowering period, May to August.

## Spiræa Venusta.
QUEEN OF THE PRAIRIE; *Nat. Ord.* ROSACEÆ.

A COMPARATIVELY new species of the herbaceous section, from North America. In good deep loam it grows to the height of 3ft. or more.

The flowers are of a soft red, after the manner of those of *S. palmata*, but rather differently arranged, viz., in clustered sprays or cymes, which bend outwards; they are durable and very effective, even when seen at some distance in the garden, whilst for cutting they are flowers of first-class merit; the leaves are large, somewhat coarse, pinnate, segments sharply lobed and irregularly serrated.

I find this plant to flower indifferently under the shade of trees, but in a fully exposed situation, planted in a deep retentive loam, it thrives and flowers well. It is perfectly hardy, and easily propagated by division during autumn.

Flowering period, June to August.

## Statice Latifolia.
BROAD-LEAVED SEA-LAVENDER; *Nat. Ord.* PLUMBAGINACEÆ.

THIS hardy perennial is all but evergreen in this climate. Probably there are two varieties of it, as although the plants in growth and form correspond, there is a notable difference in the habit of some specimens, as regards the greenness of the foliage in winter; whilst one shrivels and blackens the other will remain more or less green. It is possible that the native countries from which they come may have something to do with this fact. The species was introduced from Portugal in 1740, and again from Siberia in 1791. It need not be wondered at if the variety from the northern habitat proved the more verdant, notwithstanding its becoming acclimatised. Its lofty and diffuse panicles are ornamental and lasting; it is a subject which may be grown in almost any part of the garden, and hardly seem misplaced, notwithstanding its height of 3ft., because only the slender stems, furnished with their minute flowers, rise above the ground, and from the cloud-like effects more dwarf flowers can be easily seen, even when behind them. In many such cases, therefore, this gauzy-flowered Sea-lavender proves of advantage.

The bloom is lilac-coloured, each flower being very small. The stout scape at a short distance above the ground becomes much branched; the branchlets, as already indicated, are slender, and furnished with the soft blue bloom. The leaves are radical, and arranged in somewhat rosette form, and for the most part prostrate; many of them are quite a foot long and 5in. broad, or long egg-shaped; they are wavy, of leathery substance, and a dark shining green colour.

Of all the genus, this is, perhaps, the most useful of the hardy species. Either in a growing or cut state, the flowers are much admired; cut, they need not be placed in water; and for a year, until the plant yields fresh supplies, they will remain presentable and even bright. Its culture is simple, though there are positions where I have found it to simply exist, viz., on rockwork, unless it was given a part where moisture would be abundant about the roots, in search of which its long woody roots go deeply; if planted in deep loam of a light nature, there will be little fear as to its thriving, but if well manured and mulched, specimens would grow to nearly double size. Propagated by root division. But often the crowns are all on one stout root, and then it is not a safe or ready operation; still, with a sharp knife, the woody root may be split its whole length—this should be done in spring, when the divisions can begin to grow at once. Another and safer plan would be to divide the root for an inch or more from the crowns downwards, insert a few pebbles to keep the parts open, and put back the specimen in freshly dug earth, where, during a season of growth, the cut parts would produce vigorous roots.

Flowering period, August to October.

## Statice Profusa.
PROFUSE SEA-LAVENDER; *Nat. Ord.* PLUMBAGINACEÆ.

A HYBRID hardy form, not to be confounded with the hairy-leaved and tender kind commonly grown under glass, which has the same name. All the Sea-lavenders are profuse blooming, but the one now under notice is more especially so, as may be seen by the illustration (Fig. 100). The seed of this genus is prolific in varieties, and, although the name of this variety, or even the plant, may not be generally known, and the parentage, perhaps, untraceable, it appeared to such advantage, when grown by the side of such species as *S. bellidifolia, S. echioides, S. gmelina, S. incana, S. latifolia, S. sereptana, S. speciosa, S. tatarica, S. tormentilla, S. virgata, and S. Wildenovi*, that I considered it worth a short description, more especially as the object of this book is to speak of subjects with telling flowers or attractive forms. It is well known that the Statices have insignificant blossoms, taken individually, though, from their great profusion, they have a singular beauty. The variety now under notice, at the height of 2ft., developed a well branched panicle about the latter end of August; gradually the minute flowers expanded, when, in the middle of September, they became extremely fine, the smaller stems being as fine as horsehair, evenly disposed, and rigid; the head being globular, and supported by a single stem.

The flowers are of a lively lilac, having a brownish or snuff-coloured spiked calyx, the effect being far prettier than the

FIG. 100. STATICE PROFUSA.
(One-tenth natural size.)

description would lead one to imagine. The leaves are radical, 6in. to 8in. long, oval, or somewhat spathulate, waved, leathery, shining and dark green, the outer ones prostrate, the whole being arranged in lax rosette form.

The flowers are very durable, either cut or in the growing state; they may be used to advantage with dried grasses, ferns, and "everlastings;" or the whole head, when cut, is a good substitute for gold-paper clippings in an unused fire grate; our people have so used one for two years, and it has still a fresh appearance. It needs no words of mine to explain that such a plant as is represented by the illustration will prove highly decorative in any part of the flower garden. There is nothing special about the culture of the genus. All the Sea-lavenders do well in sandy loam, enriched with stable manure. Some sorts, the present one included, are not very readily propagated, as the crowns are not on separate pieces of root, but often crowded on a woody caudex. I have, however, sometimes split the long root with a sharp knife, and made good plants; this should only be done in spring, when growth can start at once.

Flowering period, August to frosts.

## Stenactis Speciosus.

*Syn.* ERIGERON SPECIOSUS; SHOWY FLEABANE; *Nat. Ord.* COMPOSITÆ.

THIS has not long been cultivated in this country; but though a native of the warm climate of California, it proves to be one of the most hardy of herbaceous perennials; it begins to flower in early summer, but August is the heyday of its showiness, and it continues at least a month longer. Its more recent name, *Stenactis*, is, according to Paxton, a happy and appropriate derivation, and tends much to explain the form of flower, "*Stene*, narrow, and *aktin*, a sunbeam, from the narrow and sunlike rays of the expanded flower." It belongs to a genus of "old-fashioned" flowers, which, moreover, is that of the most modern fashion in flowers. As a garden plant it is not only effective, but one of that class which will put up with the most off-hand treatment; tenacious of life, neither particular as to soil nor position, constant in fair and foul weather, and doing duty alike in town or suburban garden, these qualities go to make it a worthy subject. Whilst it is nearly related to, and much resembles, the starworts or Michaelmas daises, it far exceeds in beauty the best of them, with only a third of their ungainly length of stem.

The flowers are fully two inches across, of a light purple colour; the disk is somewhat large and of a greenish yellow; the florets of the ray are numerous, full, narrow, and slightly uneven at their points, giving the otherwise dense ray a feathery appearance. These large flowers are produced in bunches of six or ten on each branch, at the height of about eighteen inches; there are many stems, and each one is well branched, the species being very floriferous; the leaves are herb-like, lance-shaped, pointed, amplexicaul, and smooth; root-leaves spathulate.

This plant needs no cultural care; its only requirements are a place in the garden and some one to appropriate its beaming crop of flowers, which cannot fail to be serviceable. As a border plant, among suitable companions, bold clumps are fine, especially when seen by twilight; in lines, too, it may be profitably used. Propagated by division of the roots at any time.

Flowering period, June to September.

## Stokesia Cyanea.
### JASPER-BLUE STOKESIA, or STOKES' ASTER; *Nat. Ord.* COMPOSITÆ.

THIS handsome, hardy, herbaceous perennial was brought from Carolina in the year 1766. It is the only species known of the genus, and was named after Jonathan Stokes, M.D., who assisted Withering, the botanist, in his arrangement of British plants. The order which includes it is a very extensive one, and it may be useful to add that it belongs to the sub-order *Carduaceæ*, or the Thistle family. The mention of this relationship may not help our subject much in the estimation of the reader, but it must be borne in mind that in plant families as well as others, there are individual members that often contrast rather than compare with their relatives, and so it is in the Thistle family, for it embraces the gay Doronicums, silky Gnaphaliums, shining Arnica, and noble Stobæa and Echinops. But the relationship will, perhaps, be better understood when it is stated that as a sub-order the *Carduaceæ* stand side by side with that of the *Asteraceæ*, which includes so many well-known and favourite flowers. Let me now ask the reader to glance at the illustration (Fig. 101), and he will, I think, see marks of affinity with both the thistle and the aster; the few thorny teeth at the base of the larger leaves, and the spines on the smaller divisions of the imbricate calyx, are clearly features of the former, whilst the general form of the plant and flowers are not unlike the aster.

Of all herbaceous plants, this is one of the latest to bloom; in favourable situations it will begin in October, but often not until November and December in northern parts of the country; and, I hardly need add, unless severe frosts hold off, it will be cut down before its buds expand. There is much uncertainty about its flowering, when planted in the ordinary way, so that, fine as its flowers are, the plant would scarcely be worth a place in our gardens, if there were no means by which such uncertainty could be at least minimised; and were it not a fact that this plant may be bloomed by a little special treatment, which it justly merits, it would not have been introduced in this book, much less illustrated. The plant itself is very hardy, enduring keen frosts without apparent damage, and the bloom is also durable, either cut or on the plant.

I scarcely need further describe the flowers, as the form is a very common one. It has, however, a very ample bract, which supports a large imbricate calyx, the members of which have stiff bristle-like hairs. Each flower will be 2in. to 3in. across, and of a fine blue colour. The leaves are aranged on stout round stems, 18in. high, being from 2in. to 6in. long, somewhat lobed and toothed at the base, the teeth rather spiny; their

Fig. 101. Stokesia Cyanea.
(One-sixth natural size.)

shape varies very much, but generally they are lance-shaped, concave, often waved at the edges, and otherwise contorted. The foliage is more thickly furnished at the upper part of the plant, it has a glaucous hue, is of good substance, smooth and shining, like many of the gentians. It will, therefore, be seen that this is far from a weedy-looking subject, and throughout the season has a tidy and shrub-like appearance, but it grows top-heavy, and, unless supported, is liable to be snapped off at the ground line by high winds.

In order to get it to bloom before the frosts cut it, the soil and situation should be carefully selected; the former cannot be too sandy if enriched with manure, whilst cold, stiff soil is quite unsuited to it. The position should not only have the sunniest possible aspect, but be at the base of a wall that will ward off the more cutting winds. In such snug quarters many things may be had in bloom earlier, and others kept in flower through the winter, as violets; whilst fuchsias, crinums, African and Belladonna lilies, and similar roots, that would perish in more exposed parts, will live from year to year in such situations. Unless the subject now under consideration can have these conditions, it is useless to plant it—not that its hardiness is doubtful, but because its blooming period should be hastened. Its propagation may be by division of the roots after it has flowered, or in spring.

Flowering period, October to December.

## Symphytum Caucascium.

CAUCASIAN COMFREY; *Nat. Ord.* BORAGINACEÆ.

A COMPARATIVELY modern species in English gardens, belonging to a genus well represented by native species, from which this differs mainly in being less tall and hairy, and otherwise less coarse. The erect habit, and abundant azure flowers produced in pendent form, which, moreover, last for several weeks, go to make this a capital border plant. If not an old species, from its resemblance to some which are so, it is rendered a suitable companion to "old-fashioned" subjects. The plant grows to a height of nearly 2ft., is of dark greyish-green colour, from being thickly covered with short, stiff hairs, on every part, including the calyx.

The flowers are more than $\frac{1}{2}$in. long, produced in elongated clusters, opening three or four at a time, and just before expansion they are of a bright rose colour, but afterwards turn a fine blue; calyx five-parted, as also is the corolla, the segments being drawn in at the mouth. The entire flower is long and bell-shaped; the pendent clusters of bloom are well held out from the main stem by leafy branches, each being terminated by two racemes. The leaves of the root are large and stalked, oval, lance-shaped, and wrinkled; those of the stems are stalkless, and so attached as to give the stems a winged appearance near their junction.

The plant will thrive in any kind of soil, but it likes shade and moisture, and a specimen grown under such conditions will be found to be much superior in every way. A position under fruit trees suits it admirably, and for such thoughtful planting it will well repay the lover of flowers for vase decoration. It also makes a good subject for large or rough rockwork, on which, however, it should be sheltered from the midday sun. Its propagation may be carried out at any time by dividing the roots, but autumn is the preferable period.

Flowering period, April to June.

## Tiarella Cordifolia.
### *Nat. Ord.* SAXIFRAGACEÆ.

THE illustration (Fig. 102), together with the order given to which it belongs, will convey a fair idea of the style and habit of the plant, but its exquisite flowers must be seen to be appreciated,

FIG. 102. TIARELLA CORDIFOLIA.
(One-fifth natural size; *a*, flower, natural size.)

and hardly could they appear to more advantage than in a growing state, the rich foliage forming their most natural and effective ground. This hardy herbaceous perennial has been known to English gardens for 150 years, and was introduced from North America, where it grows in glorious masses, but common as it is in its native country, and long as it has been grown in this, I scarcely know a flower respecting which so many have been in error as regards the true species. I have had all sorts of things sent to me under the name, and, after all, it is easy to be wrong with it unless the amateur has either closely noted its distinctions or grown it for a year at least. Heucheras are similar in habit and shape of foliage, and are often confounded with it, though otherwise very distinct. *Tellima grandiflora*, when in its young state, is very like it, but the strong crowns should be noted—they are twice the strength of *T. cordifolia*, and develope foliage more than double its size, whilst the flowers are on stems 3ft. high, nearly green, and might easily be taken for seed pods.

The Mitellas, however, are much more puzzling, the distinctions being finer and mostly of a botanical character. Still, in May and June, when all are in flower, the identification of our subject is not difficult, more especially if the other species of the same order are near for comparison.

*T. cordifolia* grows to the height of 9in. to 12in.; the flowers are composed of a calyx (five-parted) and five petals, which are entire, evenly set in the calyx. The ten stamens are prominent; each flower has a stout pedicel, which holds out the pretty white blossom in a nearly horizontal way. There is nothing of a bell-shape character about the flower, as in its nearest relative the Mitella. The flower stem is erect and round, being evenly furnished with flowers, for a length of 4in. to 6in.; the flowers are very lasting. The leaves are heart-shaped, acutely lobed, denticulate, slightly wrinkled, hairy on both sides, and more or less spotted or splashed with brown spots on the main ribs; the leaf stalks are long, and carry the foliage gracefully. The whole plant has a neat habit, and, when in vigorous health, sends out surface creepers.

It enjoys moist quarters and slight shade, though it is grown as seen in the drawing in an exposed part. The soil is good, but otherwise there is nothing special about its culture. If this little spring flower can be made more known, it will be sure to be more widely cultivated; for covering the bare parts of lawn shrubberies it would form a pleasing subject, and might be mixed with the scarlet ourisia and the finer sorts of myosotis; these would make an excellent blend, all flowering together, and lasting for a long time, besides being suitable otherwise for such shady positions. When increase is desired strong plants may be divided at any time, soon after flowering being the best; if the season be dry, the young stock should be shaded by a leafy branch and kept well watered.

Flowering period, May and June.

## Trientalis Europæa.

EUROPEAN WINTERGREEN, *or* STAR-FLOWER; *Nat. Ord.* PRIMULACEÆ.

SOME may say, "Why, this is a common British plant;" and so it is in some parts, but for all that there are many who have never seen it. In no way does the mention here of this lovely little flower need an apology: the best possible reasons for growing and recommending it are in the facts that it is very beautiful and greatly admired (see Fig. 103).

The flowers, which are ¾in. across, are salver-shaped, pure white, excepting for a day or two when newly opened, then they are stained with a soft pink; the calyx has eight handsome light green, shining, awl-shaped sepals; the corolla has five to nine petals, equal in size, flatly and evenly arranged, their pointed tips forming the star-like appearance from which

FIG. 103. TRIENTALIS EUROPÆA.
(Plant, one-third natural size; blossom, full size.)

the flower takes one of its common names; the flower stalks are exceedingly fine—thready—but firm, from 1in. to 3in. long, and each carries but one flower; they issue from the axils of the leaves, which are arranged in whorls of five or seven, and nearly as many blossoms will be produced from the whorl, but seldom more than one, and hardly ever more than two, flowers will be open together, when they occupy the central position of the foliage, which gives the plant an elegant appearance. The leaves are of a pale green colour, sometimes a little bronzed at the tips, veined, entire, bald, lance-shaped,

U

and, as before hinted, verticillate; they vary much in size, being from 1in. to 3in. long and ½in. to 1in. broad. The stems are round, reddish, slender, and naked, with the exception of two or three minute round leaves, borne distantly apart; the stems, too, like the leaves, vary in length; sometimes they grow 8in., while others equally floriferous are not above 3in. high; the root is creeping, and somewhat tuberous. A colony of this plant has the appearance of a miniature group of palms, bedecked with glistening stars at the flowering time, and it is one of the most durable flowers I know; so persistent, indeed, are they, that botanical descriptions make mention of it.

In a cut state they equal either violets or snowdrops, from the beautiful combination of flowers and foliage, and it is a pity that it is not grown in sufficient quantities for cutting purposes. Its culture is very easy, but to do it well it may be said to require special treatment; in its wild state it runs freely, and the specimens are not nearly so fine as they may be had under cultivation with proper treatment. It should have moist quarters, a little shade, light vegetable soil, and confinement at the roots. I ought, perhaps, to explain the last-mentioned condition. It would appear that if the quick-spreading roots are allowed to ramble, the top growths are not only straggling, but weak and unfruitful. To confine its roots, therefore, not only causes it to grow in compact groups, but in every way improves its appearance; it may be done by planting it in a large seed pan, 15in. across, and 4in. or 6in. deep. Let it be well drained; over the drainage place a layer of lumpy peat, on which arrange another of roots, and fill up with leaf soil and peat mixed with sand; this may be done any time from September to February; the pan may then be plunged in a suitable position, so as to just cover the rim from sight, and so do away with artificial appearances; but if it is sunk too deep, the roots will go over the rim and all the labour will be lost. So charming is this plant when so grown, that it is worth all the care. A well-known botanist saw such a pan last spring, and he could hardly believe it to be our native species. Pans at two years old are lovely masses, and very suitable for taking as grown for table decoration. The outer sides of the pans should be banked down to the tray with damp moss, which could be pricked in with any soft-coloured flowers, as dog roses, pinks or forget-me-nots.

I will only add that, unless the root confinement is effected either in the above or some other way, according to my experience, the plant will never present a creditable appearance as a cultivated specimen; at the same time, this somewhat troublesome mode of planting it is not in proportion to the pleasure it will afford and certainly ought not to prevent its introduction into every garden.

Flowering period, May and June.

## Trillium Erectum.

ERECT WOOD-LILY; *Nat. Ord.* MELANTHACEÆ.

A HARDY, tuberous perennial, from North America, whence most, perhaps all, the species of this genus are imported. The peculiar form of the plants gives rise to the generic name. A flowering specimen has on one stem three leaves, three sepals, and three petals; the specific name is in reference to the more erect habit of this species compared with others. Of *T. erectum* there are several varieties, having different-coloured flowers; the

FIG. 104. TRILLIUM ERECTUM.
(One-half natural size.)

specimens from which the drawing (Fig. 104) was taken have rich brown or dark maroon flowers. Little groups have a rather quaint look, they being very formal, the flowers curiously placed, and of unusual colour. The flowers are fully 2in. across, or much more, if the petals did not reflex almost their whole length. The sepals of the calyx are exactly alternate with the petals, and remain erect, giving the flower a characteristic quality; and, let me add, they are far more pleasing to the eye than to the sense of smell. The leaves are arranged in threes on the main stem, and that number constitutes the entire foliage of the plant; they are stalkless, oval, but pointed, entire, smooth, and of a shining dark green colour. The specimens from which the illustration was made are 5in. to 6in. high, but their height differs very much with the positions in which they are grown, shade and moisture inducing taller growths. The roots, which are tuberous, are of unusual form—soft swollen rootstocks may be more descriptive of them. Trilliums are now in much favour, and their quiet beauty is likely to create a genuine love for them. Moreover, the different species are distinct, and if grown in cool, shady quarters, their flowers remain in good form and colour for a long time. They are seen to most advantage in a subdued light, as under the shade of rather tall but not too thickly grown trees. They require vegetable soil, no matter how light it may be, provided it can be maintained in a moist state, the latter condition being indispensable. Trilliums are capable of taking a good share towards supplying shade-loving subjects. How finely they would mix with anemones, violets, *Paris quadrifolia*, hellebores, and such like flowers! Colonies of these, planted so as to carpet small openings in shrubberies, would be a clear gain in several ways to our gardens; to many they would be a new feature; more showy flowers would not have to be given up for such an arrangement, but, on the other hand, both would be more enjoyed by the contrast. Trilliums increase slowly; propagation may be carried out by the division of the roots of healthy plants.

Flowering period, May and June.

## Triteleia Uniflora

*Sometimes called* MILLA UNIFLORA; ONE-FLOWERED TRITELEIA, *or* SPRING STAR FLOWER; *Nat. Ord.* LILIACEÆ.

THIS is a favourite flower, and in some soils increases very fast; it is the commonest species of the very limited genus to which it belongs; was brought from South America only so recently as 1836, and it is already extensively grown in this country, and as a trade article is very cheap indeed, thanks to its intrinsic worth. Though small, its star-like form gives it a lively and effective appearance in the borders. It is much used by the Americans as a window and greenhouse plant, notwithstanding that it is a wild flower with them, and its pretty shape and lovely hues render it eligible for such uses, but on account of the esteem in which is held the odour of garlic, I should not like to recommend it for such close associations. The flower in shape is, as the generic name implies, like the Trillium, formed of three, or rather threes; the divisions are arranged in threes, or triangularly; the two triangles, being crossed, give the flower a geometrical and star-like effect. The flowers, which are 1in. to 2in. across, are borne on slender stems, 4in. to 6in. long. They are nearly white, but have various tints, bluish reflections, with a line of blue in each petal. The leaves resemble those of the snowdrop when overgrown and turning flabby, and have a somewhat untidy and sprawling habit; they are abundantly produced from the rather small cocoon-shaped bulbs. On the whole, the plant is very ornamental when in flower, and the bloom is produced more or less for many weeks; at any rate, it is an early flower, and if it cannot be used indoors

FIG. 105. TRITELEIA UNIFLORA.

(One-fourth natural size.)

it should be extensively planted amongst border subjects, than which there are few more hardy or reliable. Propagated by divisions of the crowded bulbs every other year, during late summer.

*T. u. lilacina* (the Lilac-coloured Star Flower) is a most handsome variety, having, as implied by the name, a richly coloured flower. I am indebted to a lady for roots and flowers recently sent me; so far as I know, it is not yet generally distributed. It is very distinct from the type in having smaller parts throughout, and a more highly coloured bloom, with the outer surface of the shining tube of a darker or brownish-green colour. I have seen a mauve coloured form, but this is much more pronounced and effective. The chief recommendation of this otherwise desirable flower, to my thinking, is its rich new-mown hay scent; in this it differs much from the parent form.

Flowering period, March to May.

## Tritoma Uvaria.

GREAT TRITOMA ; *Common Names*, FLAME-FLOWER, RED-HOT POKER; *Nat. Ord.* LILIACEÆ-HEMERO-CALLIDEÆ.

THIS is one of our finest late-flowering plants; it has, moreover, a tropical appearance, which renders it very attractive. It is fast becoming popular, though as yet it is not very often seen in private gardens; it comes from the Cape of Good Hope, its year of introduction being 1707. In this climate, when planted in well-exposed situations and in sandy loam, it proves hardy but herbaceous; if protected it is evergreen; and I ought to add that if it is planted in clay soil, or where the drainage is defective, it will be killed by a severe winter; but when such simple precautions as are here indicated will conduce to the salvation of a somewhat doubtful plant, it may be fairly termed hardy. According to my experience during severe winters, plants in wet stiff loam were all killed, but others of the same stock, in light sandy earth, did not suffer in the least. I have also made similar observations outside my own garden.

The stout scapes or stems sometimes reach a height of 4ft., and are topped with long or cocoon-shaped spikes of orange and red flowers; the flowers are tubular and small, closely arranged, and drooping; each will be about an inch long, and the spikes 6in. to 8in. long. The leaves are narrow, 2ft. to 3ft. long, keeled, channelled, and rough on the edges, of a dark green colour and prostrate habit. Either amongst trees or in more conspicuous positions this flower proves very effective, whilst in lines it is simply dazzling; when grown in quantity it may be cut for indoor decoration, than which few large flowers are more telling.

Cultural hints have already been given in speaking of its hardiness, but I may add that where the soil is naturally light and dry a liberal dressing of well-rotted manure may be dug in with great benefit to the flowers. It is readily propagated by division of the roots every third year; the young stock should be put in rows, the earth having been deeply stirred and well broken; this may be done in late autumn or spring—if the former, a top dressing of leaves will assist root action.

This bold and brilliant flower appears in September, and is produced in numbers more or less to the end of the year, provided the season does not set in very severe.

## Tropæolum Tuberosum.
TUBEROUS TROPÆOLUM; *Nat. Ord.* TROPÆOLACEÆ.

ALL the species of this genus are highly decorative garden subjects, including the annual varieties, and otherwise they are interesting. They are known by various names, as Trophy-plant, Indian Cress, and Nasturtium, though the latter is only applicable strictly to plants of another order. The plant under notice is a climber, herbaceous and perennial, having tuberous roots, whence its specific name; they much resemble small potatoes, and are eaten in Peru, the native country of the plant. It has not long been grown in this country, the date of its introduction being 1836; it is not often seen, which may be in part owing to the fact of its being considered tender in this climate. But let me at once state that under favourable conditions, and such as may easily be afforded in any garden, it proves hardy. As a matter of fact, I wintered it in 1880-1, and also in 1881-2, which latter does not signify much, as it proved so mild; but it must be admitted that the first-mentioned winter would be a fair test season. The position was very dry, viz., on the top of a small bank of earth, against a south wall; the soil was sandy loam, and it was overgrown with ivy, the leaves of which would doubtless keep out many degrees of cold, as also would the dryness of the soil; another point in favour of my specimen proving hardy, would be the fact of its exposure to the sun, by which the tubers would be well and duly ripened. It is one of the handsomest trailers or climbers I know for the herbaceous garden; a free grower, very floriferous, bright, distinct, and having a charming habit. The illustration (Fig. 106) can give no idea of the fine colours of its flowers, or richly glaucous foliage. One specimen in my garden has been much admired, thanks to nothing but its own habit and form; under a west wall, sheltered from the strong winds, it grows near some *Lilium auratum*; after outgrowing the lengths of the stems, and having set off to advantage the lily bloom, it caught by its tendril-like shoots an apricot tree on the wall, and then reached the top, being furnished with bloom its whole length. The flowers are orange and scarlet, inclining to crimson; they are produced singly on long red stalks, which spring from the axils of the leaves; the orange petals are small and overlapping, being compactly enclosed in the scarlet calyx; the spur, which is also of the same colour, is thick and long, imparting a pear-like form to the whole flower, which, however, is not more than 1½in. long. The leaves are nearly round in outline, sub-peltate, five, but sometimes only three-lobed; lobes entire, sometimes notched, smooth and glaucous; the leaf-stalks are long and bent, and act as tendrils. The plant makes rapid growth, the stems going out in all directions, some trailing on the ground.

It is a good subject for the drier parts of rockwork, where a twiggy branch should be secured, which it will soon cover. It is also fine for lattice work, or it may be grown where it can appropriate the dried stems of lupine and larkspurs. For all such situations it is not only showy, but beautiful. The flowered sprays are effective in a cut state, especially by gaslight; they come in for drooping or twining purposes, and last a long time in water.

If grown as a tender plant its treatment is as simple as can be; the tubers may be planted in early spring in any desired

Fig. 106. Tropæolum Tuberosum.
(One-fifth natural size.)

situation, and when the frosts at the end of the season have cut down the foliage, the tubers may be taken up and stored in sand; but if it is intended to winter it out the situation should be chosen for its dryness, and the soil should be of a sandy nature, in which the tubers ought to be placed 5in. or 6in. deep. It is self-propagating, the tubers being numerously produced; and like "potato sets," the larger ones may be cut in pieces; if, however, numbers are not the object they are better left uncut. Caterpillars are fond of this plant; at the first sight of an eaten leaf, they should be looked for and destroyed.

It begins to flower in the latter part of summer, continuing until stopped by frosts.

## Umbilicus Chrysanthus.
### *Nat. Ord.* CRASSULACEÆ.

THIS is a very pretty and distinct subject, and never fails to flower very late in the year. It is a plant having the appearance of being tender, and is not often seen growing fully exposed in the garden; it is, however, perfectly hardy, enduring any amount of cold; it suffers more from wet. It is also evergreen. Its soft dull or greyish-green rosettes are in marked

FIG. 107. UMBILICUS CHRYSANTHUS.
(One-half natural size.)

contrast with the rigid and shining sempervivums, in the company of which it is frequently placed. It is an alpine subject, and comes from the mountains of Asiatic Turkey, being also found more west. Not only is it interesting, but its pretty form and habit are qualities which render it very useful in a garden, more especially for dry parts, such as old walls and rockwork.

It grows 6in. high, the older rosettes elongate and form leafy flower stalks, which are topped by drooping panicles of flowers, somewhat bell shaped; each flower is ¾in. long, of a yellowish white colour; the petals are finely pointed, and well supported by a fleshy calyx; the bloom is slowly developed and very enduring, even when the worst weather prevails. The leaves are arranged in flat rosette form (the rosettes from 1in. to 2in. across), lower leaves spathulate, those near the centre more oval.

All are fleshy, covered with short hairs, and somewhat clammy to the touch. Its habit is neat, and it adorns such situations as otherwise suit it, viz., banks or risen beds, and such other positions as have already been named.

Its culture is easy, but it ought to have the compost it most enjoys—peat and grit—and it should be sheltered from the strong winds, otherwise its top-heavy flower stalks will be laid prostrate. When it once finds a happy home it increases fast; the thick stalks are procumbent and emit roots. These may either be left to form large specimens or be taken off during the growing season for stock. Excessive wet is its greatest enemy. For such subjects, the wire and glass shelters are not only a remedy, but very handy.

Flowering period, summer, until stopped by frosts.

## Vaccinium Vitis-Idæa.

RED WHORTLE-BERRY; *sometimes called* COW-BERRY;
*Nat. Ord.* VACCINACEÆ.

ALTHOUGH a native evergreen, and in some parts occurring extensively, it proves to be both decorative and useful as a garden subject; as a neat evergreen it is worthy of a place, especially when it is not to be found near in a wild state. It is seldom seen without either its waxy and pink-tinted white flowers or its bright clusters of red berries, but in October it carries both, which, together with the fine condition of the foliage, renders the shrub most attractive. It grows 6in. to 9in. high under cultivation.

In form the flowers somewhat resemble the lily of the valley, but they are closely set in the stems and partly hidden, owing to the shortness and drooping character of the racemes; not only are the flowers pleasingly tinted, but they exhale a full and spicy odour; the buds, too, are tinted with a lively pink colour on their sunny sides. The berries are quickly developed, being nearly the size of the holly berry, but a more bright red. The leaves are stout, shining, and leathery, and ofttimes pleasingly bronzed. They are over ½in. long and egg-shaped, being bent backwards. The stems are furnished with short hairs, are much branched, and densely foliaged. This compact-growing shrub would make a capital edging, provided it was well grown in vegetable soil. It would go well with *Erica carnea* to form a double line, either to a shrubbery or permanent beds of dwarf flowering trees. Now that berries are so much used for wearing about the person and for indoor decoration, those of this shrub may become useful. A dishful of sprigs in October proves pleasant both to the sight and smell, the flowers and fruit being charmingly blended.

*V.v.-i. major* is a variety which is simply larger in all its parts; it is, however, rather more bronzed in the foliage. I daresay by

FIG. 108. VACCINIUM VITIS-IDÆA.
(Natural size.)

many it would be preferred to the typical form, both for its robust and decorative qualities. It is nearly twice the size of the type.

As may be inferred, both from the order to which this shrub belongs and the localities where it occurs in its wild state, a peaty or vegetable soil will be required. I find the species grow most freely in a mixture of leaf soil and sand, the position being moist but exposed. It does not object to a little shade, but then its useful berries are neither so numerously produced nor so well coloured.

It is easily propagated by division at almost any time.

Flowering period, May to October.

## Veronica Gentianoides.
*Syn.* V. GENTIANIFOLIA; GENTIAN-LEAVED SPEEDWELL;
*Nat. Ord.* SCROPHULARIACEÆ.

THIS is a distinct and pleasing species, viewed as a garden plant. It is very hardy, and one of the herbaceous kinds; it has been grown in English gardens nearly 150 years, and came originally from the Levant. It is pretty widely used, but it deserves a place in every garden; not only are its tall spikes of flowers effective during their season, but the foliage, compared with other Veronicas, is of a bright and plump character. The newly-formed tufts, which are somewhat rosette-shaped, have a fresh appearance throughout the winter, it being one of the few herbaceous subjects in which the signs of life are so visible in this climate.

The flowers are small—$\frac{1}{4}$in. in diameter—numerously produced on spikes 18in. high. They are blue, striped with light and dark shades; both calyx and corolla, as common to the genus, are four-parted, petals of uneven size. The flower spikes are finely developed, the flowers and buds occupying 12in. of their length, and tapering off to a point which bends gracefully. The buds are not less pretty than the flowers, resembling as they do turquoise in a deep setting of the calyx. The leaves are smooth, shining, and of much substance, 3in. to 6in. long, and 1in. to 2in. broad, lance-shaped, serrated, and sheathing. They are of a somewhat clustered arrangement close to the ground. Good pieces of this plant, 1ft. to 2ft. across, are very effective, and flower for a good while.

The rich and graceful spikes are of great value for vase decoration, one or two sufficing in connection with other suitable flowers.

There is a lovely variety of this species called *V. g. variegata*; in shape and habit it resembles the type though scarcely as vigorous, but not at all "miffy." The leaves are richly coloured pale green, white, and pink; and the flowers, as seldom occurs in variegated forms, are larger and more handsome than in the parent; in all respects, it is as useful, and, for forming an edging, perhaps more suitable than the common form.

Both kinds like a good fat loam and a moist situation; they may be grown either in borders or on rockwork, but specimens on the latter compare poorly with those grown otherwise; either they are too dry, or the soil gets washed from them, so that the new roots, which strike down from the surface-creeping stems, do not find the needful nourishment. Their increase is easily effected by division of the rooted stems any time after they have done flowering. If the season is droughty, they should be well watered.

Flowering period, May to July.

## Veronica Pinguifolia.

FAT-LEAVED SPEEDWELL; *Nat. Ord.* SCROPHULARIACEÆ.

THIS is a rather uncommon species, being of the shrubby section, but unlike many of its relative kinds, it is perfectly hardy, also evergreen and very dwarf; a specimen three or four years old is but a diminutive bush, 18in. through and 8in. high. The habit is dense, the main or old branches are prostrate, the younger wood being erect and full of very short side shoots.

The flowers are produced on the new wood; the chubby flower-spikes issue from the axils of the leaves near the leading shoot; in some cases there are three, in others four, but more often two. Each flower spike has a short, stout, round stem, nearly an inch long, and the part furnished with buds is nearly as long again. At this stage (just before they begin to open) the buds are rice-shaped, snow white, waxy, and arranged cone form. They are, moreover, charmingly intersected with the pale green sepals in their undeveloped stage. The little bunches of buds are simply exquisite. The flowers are small, pure white, waxy, and twisted in the petals. The two filaments are longer than the petals, having rather large anthers, which are bright purple. This pleasing feature, together with the young shoots in the midst of the blossoms, which have small stout glaucous leaves tipped with yellow—nearly golden—give the clusters a bouquet-like appearance. The leaves are small—little more than half an inch long—and ovate, slightly cupped, stem-clasping, and opposite. They are a pale glaucous hue, and closely grown on the stems; they greatly add to the rich effect of the flowers.

This shrub is a most fitting subject for rockwork, and it would also make an edging of rare beauty, which, if well grown, no one could but admire. It seems to enjoy loam and leaf soil in a moist but sunny situation. It may be propagated by cuttings, taken with a part of the previous year's wood.

Flowering period, May to July,

## Veronica Prostrata.

PROSTRATE SPEEDWELL; *Nat. Ord.* SCROPHULARIACEÆ.

THIS is sometimes confounded with *V. repens*, I presume from the slight distinction in the specific names, but so different are the two species that no one who has seen them can possibly take one for the other. *V. repens* is herb-like; it creeps and roots, and has nearly white flowers in April; but *V. prostrata* is a deciduous trailer, and the more common and best form has fine gentian-blue flowers; it is a capital rock plant, being most effective when hanging over the face of large stones. The flowers are small, and produced in rather long sprays, which are numerous, so that little else than flowers can be seen for two or three weeks.

It will grow and flower freely in any soil, but the aspect should be sunny; it is easily increased by division or rootlets. I may add that the very long stems of this prostrate plant (when in bloom) are well adapted for indoor decoration. Where pendent, deep blue flowers are needed, there are very few good blues so suitable.

Flowering period, May to July.

## Vesicaria Græca.
### *Nat. Ord.* CRUCIFERÆ.

THIS beautiful, diminutive, hardy evergreen shrub comes to us from Switzerland, being an alpine species (see Fig. 109).

When in flower it does not exceed the height of 6in. or 8in.,

FIG. 109. VESICARIA GRÆCA.
(One-third natural size; 1, full size.)

at which time it is very showy, covered, as it is, with flowers of the brightest golden yellow, surpassing the golden alyssum, which in some respects it resembles, being half woody, possessing greyish leaves, and dense heads of flowers, which, however, are arranged in small corymbs, and being also much larger. The leaves of the flower stalks resemble lavender leaves in general appearance; those of the unproductive stems are larger, and arranged sparingly in rigid rosette form, such unproductive stems being few.

The neat and erect habit of the plant renders it most suitable for rockwork or edgings, and otherwise, from its long continued flowering, which will exceed a month in moderate weather, it is one of the most useful spring flowers; whilst, for cutting purposes, it cannot but rank with the more choice, as, combined with extra bightness of colour, it exhales a rich hawthorn perfume. To all who have a garden, big or little, I would say, grow this sweet little shrub. It has never failed to do well with me in any situation that was fully exposed; it flowers freely in a light dry bed, but on rockwork it is most at home. The quickest way to prepare plants of flowering strength is to divide strong pieces; but this interferes with the larger specimens, which are by far the best forms in which to grow and retain it. Another mode is to cut off all the flowers nearly down to the old wood; side shoots will thus be induced to grow earlier than otherwise, so that in late summer they may be taken off as slips, and there will still be plenty of time to strike them like wallflower slips, and get plenty of roots to them before the cold weather sets in. The plant also produces seed freely in its inflated pods, which affords another, but more tedious, way of increasing it.

Flowering period, April to June.

## Viola Pedata.

### PEDATE-LEAVED or BIRD'S-FOOT VIOLET; Nat. Ord. VIOLACEÆ.

OVER a hundred years ago this hardy herbaceous violet was introduced from North America; still, it is not largely grown, though it is now becoming quite a favourite. As may be seen by the illustration (Fig. 110), it is distinct in general appearance, more especially in the foliage, which in its young state is bird-foot-shaped, whence the appropriateness of its specific name; it should perhaps be explained that the leaves are very small compared with the flowers when the plant first begins to bloom, but later they increase very much in size. There are several characteristics about this species which render it desirable, and no choice collection should be without either this (the typical form) or some of its varieties. Deep cut, shining, dark green foliage, very bright blue flowers, and pleasing habit are its most prominent features; its blooming period is prolonged, and it has a robust constitution, which further commends it to lovers of choice flowers, and if once planted in proper quarters it gives no further trouble in the way of treatment.

The flowers are nearly an inch across, bright purple-blue, produced on stalks of varying lengths, but mostly long; the leaves are many parted, segments long, narrow and lance-shaped, some being cut or toothed near the tips; the crown of the root is rather bulky; the roots are long and fleshy.

The following are varieties; all are handsome and worth growing: *V. p. alba*, new; flowers white, not so robust as the type. *V. p. bicolor*, new; flowers two colours. *V. p. flabellata* (syn. *V. digitata*); flowers light purple. *V. p. ranunculifolia* (syn. *V. ranunculifolia*); flowers nearly white.

As this plant requires a moist and partially shaded situation, it is not eligible for doing duty indiscriminately in any part of

Fig. 110. VIOLA PEDATA.
(Two-thirds natural size.)

the garden; still, it will thrive under any conditions such as the well-known violets are seen to encounter. On the north or west side of rockwork, in dips or moist parts, it will be found to do well and prove attractive.

The propagation of all the kinds may be carried out by allowing the seed to scatter itself, and, before the winter sets in, a light top-dressing of half rotted leaves and sand will not only be a natural way of protecting it until germination takes place, but will also be of much benefit to the parent plants. Another mode of increase is to divide the roots of strong and healthy specimens; in this way only can true kinds be obtained; seedlings are almost certain to be crossed.

Flowering period, May and June.

## Viola Tricolor.

THREE-COLOURED VIOLET, PANSY, *or* HEARTSEASE;
*Nat. Ord.* VIOLACEÆ.

THIS well known herbaceous perennial is a British species. It has long been grown in gardens, where, by selection and crossing, innumerable and beautiful kinds have been produced, so that at the present time it is not only a "florist's flower," but a general favourite. Besides the above-mentioned common names, it has many others, and it may not be uninteresting to repeat them—"Love in Idleness," "Call me to you," "Kiss me

FIG. 111. VIOLA TRICOLOR.

(One-third natural size.)

ere I rise," "Herb Trinity," and "Three Faces under one Hood." Although this plant is herbaceous, the old stems remain green until the new growths come into flower, and, in many varieties, by a little management in plucking out the buds during summer, flowers may be had in the autumn and well into winter. If, also, from other plants early cuttings have been taken, and become well rooted, they will produce large flowers very early in spring,

X

and so the Pansy may be had in flower nearly the year round. Any description of this well-known plant would be superfluous to an English reader.

The wild *V. tricolor* is, however, a very different plant and flower to its numerous offspring, such as the illustration (Fig. 111) depicts, and in which there is ever a tendency to "go back." It is only by constant care and high cultivation that the Pansy is kept at such a high standard of excellence, and one may add that such labour is well repaid by the results. With no flower more than the Pansy does all depend on the propagation and culture. Not the least reliance can be placed on seeds for producing flowers like those of the parent. Cuttings or root divisions should be made in summer, so as to have them strong, to withstand the winter. They enjoy a stiffish loam, well enriched. And in spring they may be lifted with a ball and transplanted into beds, borders, lines, or irregular masses, where they are equally effective, and no flower is more reliable for a profusion of bloom.

## Yucca Filamentosa.

THREADY-LEAVED YUCCA; *Nat. Ord.* LILIACEÆ.

THIS is of a more deciduous nature than *Y. gloriosa*, reclothing itself each spring more amply with foliage. In December, however, it is in fine form, and though it is a better flowering species than most of its genus, and to a fair extent valuable for its flowers, it will be more esteemed, perhaps, as a shrub of ornamental foliage. It came from Virginia in the year 1675.

The flowers are pretty, greenish-white, bell-shaped, and drooping: they are arranged in panicles, which, when sent up from strong plants, are, from their size, very attractive; but otherwise they are hardly up to the mark as flowers. The leaves in form are lance-shaped, concave, reflexed near the ends, and sharp-pointed. The colour is a yellowish-green, the edges are brown, and their substance is split up into curled filaments, which are sometimes 9in. or more long, and are blown about by every breeze. From these thready parts the species takes its name. It is seldom that this kind grows more than 4ft. high, but a greater number of offsets are produced from this than from any other of our cultivated Yuccas.

I know no better use for this kind than planting it on the knolly parts of rockwork, positions which in every way suit it, for it enjoys a warm, dry soil.

*Y. f. variegata*, as its name implies, is a form with coloured foliage. In the north it proves to be far from hardy, and therefore cannot be recommended for culture in the open garden. My reasons for mentioning it are that it is convenient to do so when the typical form is under notice, and that it is frequently spoken of as hardy. Subjects needing well selected positions, protection, and a mild winter in order to keep them alive from autumn to spring, can in no sense be considered hardy, even though they may be planted out of doors.

Flowering period, August to October.

## Yucca Gloriosa.

GLORIOUS YUCCA, ADAM'S NEEDLE; *Nat. Ord.* LILIACEÆ.

A HARDY evergreen shrub which has long been grown in England, but for all that is not often met with in private gardens. It is a native of South America, and was brought to our shores in 1596. The genus is remarkable for not flowering constantly in our climate, and also for slow growth; fortunately, both these drawbacks, if one may term them such, are counterbalanced by the handsome foliage of the various species, mostly of an evergreen and very durable nature, and also by the bold and symmetrical arrangement of the same. This Yucca flowers in the autumn, but it may be considered more especially a foliage subject, as the bloom is insignificant compared with the leaves and is not produced more than once in four years as a rule. The leaves assume their richest hues and become thoroughly matured about the end of the year; and when the ground is covered with a thick coat of snow, their rigid forms are amongst the very few of any note that can be seen. In any garden, no matter how large or how small, a Yucca imparts a style or character to it which scarcely any other subject can give. It may not be so easy to explain this, but the fact is recognised by the most casual observer at first sight. If I say the effect is tropical, noble, rich, and sometimes graceful, a partial idea of its ornamental qualities may be conveyed; but to know its value and enjoy it, it should be grown. The species under consideration has many forms, some differing rather widely from the type, so much so that these varieties are honoured with specific names. First may be given a brief description of the parent form.

It grows from 3ft. to 6ft. high, according to the more or less favourable conditions. These dimensions apply to blooming specimens; but shrubs, three to six years old, if they have never bloomed, may not exceed 1ft. to 2ft. in height, and about the same in diameter. The flowers, as may be gathered from the order to which the genus belongs, are lily-like, or bell-shaped; they are of a greenish white colour, arranged in lax clusters on stoutish stalks. The leaves are 12in. to 2ft. long, 3in. or more broad in their widest parts, concave or boat-shaped, sharp pointed, glaucous, sometimes slightly plicate, rigid, and leathery.

The habit, after flowering, is generally to form offsets, when the plant loses much of its former boldness and effect. From the lateness of its blooming period, and a lack of suitable conditions, it does not ripen seed in our climate, and it must of necessity be raised from seed ripened in more favourable climes.

The following are said to be some of its varieties, bearing useful descriptive names: *Y. g. pendula*, having a pendulous habit or reflexed leaves; *Y. g. plicata*, having plaited leaves; *Y. g. minor*, a lesser form in its various parts. There are other reputed varieties of more doubtful descent.

For cultivation see *Y. recurva*.

## Yucca Recurva.

RECURVE-LEAVED YUCCA; *Common Name*, WEEPING YUCCA; *Nat. Ord.* LILIACEÆ.

THIS is a charming species, perfectly hardy and evergreen; it was brought from Georgia about ninety years ago.

The flowers are a greenish-white, and undesirable where the shrub is grown for the sake of its ornamental qualities; fortunately they are far from being constant in their appearance. September is its blooming period in our climate. The leaves are its main feature; with age it becomes rather tall, 6ft. to 9ft. high, having a woody bole or caudex, which is largely concealed by the handsome drooping foliage; a few of the youngest leaves from the middle of the tuft remain erect. The whole specimen is characterised by its deep green and glossy foliage, combined with a most graceful habit. Few things can be planted with such desirable effect as this shrub; it puts a stamp on the landscape, parterre and shrubland, and when well grown forms a landmark in the most extensive garden.

For all the species and varieties of Yucca the mode of culture is not only similar but simple. They have long roots of a wiry texture. These denote that they require deep soil, light, and rather dry. Sandy loam, light vegetable soil, or marl and peat grow them well. Raised beds or borders, the higher parts of rockwork, or any open position, thoroughly drained, will not only be conducive to their health, but also prove fitting points of vantage. In planting Yuccas it must never be forgotten that perfect drainage is the all important requisite, and if it is not afforded the stock will never thrive, but ultimately die from rot or canker. Another matter, when referred to, will perhaps complete all that is special about the culture, or rather planting, of Yuccas. Begin with young stuff; I know nothing that

OLD-FASHIONED GARDEN FLOWERS. 309

transplants worse than this class of shrubs after they have become considerably grown. Their spare, wiry roots, when taken

FIG. 112. YUCCA RECURVA (one-eighteenth natural size).

out of a sandy soil, do not carry a "ball," and from the great depth to which they run they are seldom taken up without more than ordinary damage. Young specimens, 6in., 9in., or not more than 12in. high, should be preferred, and of these sizes the least will prove the safest. Yuccas are readily propagated at the proper season; and in specifying the season it is needful to point out that of offsets, from which young stock is soonest obtained, there are two kinds. Some spring from immediately below the earth, and may more properly be termed suckers; the others grow on the visible part of the stem or caudex, often close to the oldest leaves; these should be cut off with a sharp knife, in early summer, and if they have a little of the parent bark attached to them all the better. If they are planted in a shady place, in sweet sandy loam, they will make good roots before winter, and may be allowed to make the following summer's growth in the same position. In the succeeding autumn it will be a good plan to put them in their permanent places. The suckers will be found to have more or less root; they should be taken in spring from the parent specimen, the roots should be carefully preserved, and the pushing parts planted just level with the surface.

# FLOWERING PERIODS.

As an aid to readers desirous of making a selection of plants which will secure a succession of bloom the year through, we here give a list of those described in the preceding pages, arranged according to their average periods of flowering.

## January.

Anemone fulgens, Aralia Sieboldi, Bulbocodium vernum, Cheiranthus Cheiri, Crocus medius, Eranthis hyemalis, Helleborus abchasicus, H. antiquorum, H. Bocconi, H. colchicus, H. cupreus, H. fœtidus, H. guttabus, H. niger, H. orientalis, H. olympicus, Jasminum nudiflorum, Petasites vulgaris, Saxifraga Burseriana.

## February.

Anemone blanda, A. fulgens, A. stellata, Arabis lucida, A. Sieboldi, Bellis perennis, Bulbocodium trigynum, B. vernum, Cheiranthus Cheiri, Corydalis solida, Daphne Mezereum, Eranthis hyemalis, Erica carnea, Galanthus Elwesii, G. Imperati, G. nivalis, G. plicatus, Helleborus abchasicus, H. antiquorum, H. Bocconi, H. colchicus, H. cupreus, H. dumetorum, H. fœtidus, H. guttabus, H. niger, H. odorus, H. orientalis, H. olympicus, H. purpurascens, Hepatica angulosa, H. triloba, Jasminum nudiflorum, Petasites vulgaris, Polyanthus, Primula acaulis, Saxifraga Burseriana.

## March.

Anemone blanda, A. fulgens, A. Pulsatilla, A. stellata, Arabis lucida, Aralia Sieboldi, Bellis perennis, Bulbocodium trigynum, B. vernum, Cheiranthus Cheiri, Chionodoxa Luciliæ, Corydalis solida, Daphne Mezereum, Dentaria digitata, Doronicum caucasicum, Epigæa repens, Erica carnea, Erythronium dens-canis, Galanthus Elwesii, G. Imperati, G. nivalis, G. plicatus, G. Redoutei, Helleborus abchasicus, H. antiquorum, H. Bocconi, H. colchicus, H. cupreus, H. dumetorum, H. fœtidus, H. guttabus, H. niger, H. odorus, H. orientalis, H. olympicus, H. purpurascens, Hepatica angulosa, H. triloba, Jasminum nudiflorum, Leucojum vernum, Muscari botryoides, M. racemosum, Narcissus minor, Omphalodes verna, Orobus vernus, Phlox frondosa, Polyanthus, Primula acaulis, P. Cashmeriana, P. denticulata, P.

marginata, P. purpurea, P. Scotica, Pulmonarias, Puschkinia scilloides, Saxifraga Burseriana, S. ciliata, S. cordifolia, S. coriophylla, S. ligulata, S. oppositifolia, S. Rocheliana, Sisyrinchium grandiflorum, Soldanellas, Triteleia uniflora.

## April.

Alyssum saxatile, Andromeda tetragona, Anemone Apennina, A. fulgens, A. Pulsatilla, A. stellata, Arabis lucida, Bellis perennis, Calthus palustris flore-pleno, Cheiranthus Cheiri, Chionodoxa Luciliæ, Corydalis nobilis, C. solida, Daphne cneorum, D. Mezereum, Dentaria digitata, D. Jeffreyanum, D. Meadia, Dondia Epipactis, Doronicum caucasicum, Epigæa repens, Erica carnea, Erysimum pumilum, Erythronium denscanis, Fritillaria armena, Galanthus nivalis, G. plicatus, G. Redoutei, Gentiana verna, Helleborus antiquorum, H. colchicus, H. orientalis, H. purpurascens, Hepatica angulosa, H. triloba, Houstonia cœrulea, Jasminum nudiflorum, Leucojum vernum, Muscari botryoides, M. racemosum, Narcissus minor, Omphalodes verna, Orobus vernus, Phlox frondosa, Polyanthus, Primula acaulis, P. capitata, P. Cashmeriana, P. denticulata, P. farinosa, P. marginata, P. purpurea, P. Scotica, P. vulgaris flore-pleno, Pulmonarias, Puschkinia scilloides, Ranunculus acris florepleno, R. amplexicaulis, R. speciosum, Sanguinaria canadensis, Saxifraga Burseriana, S. ciliata, S. cordifolia, S. ligulata, S. oppositifolia, S. purpurascens, S. Rocheliana, S. Wallacei, Scilla campanulata, Sisyrinchium grandiflorum, Soldanellas, Symphytum caucasicum, Tritelia uniflora, Vesicaria græca.

## May.

Alyssum saxatile, Anchusa Italica, A. sempervirens, Andromeda tetragona, Anemone Apennina, A. coronaria, A. decapitate, A. fulgens, A. nemorosa flore-pleno, A. Pulsatilla, A. stellata, A. sulphurea, A. sylvestris, A. vernalis, Arabis lucida, Bellis perennis, Calthus palustris flore-pleno, Cheiranthus Cheiri, C. Marshallii, Corydalis lutea, C. nobilis, C. solida, Cypripedium calceolus, Daphne cneorum, Dentaria digitata, Dianthus hybridus, Dodecatheon Jeffreyanum, D. Meadia, Dondia Epipactis, Doronicum caucasicum, Erysimum pumilum, Fritillaria armena, Gentiana acaulis, G. verna, Geranium argenteum, Heuchera, H. Americana, H. cylindrica, H. Drummondi, H. glabra, H. lucida, H. metallica, H. micrantha, H. purpurea, H. ribifolia, H. Richardsoni, Houstonia cœrulea, Iberis corresefolia, Leucojum æstivum, Lithospermum prostratum, Muscari botryoides, M. racemosum, Omphalodes verna, Orchis fusca, Orobus vernus, Ourisia coccinea, Papaver orientale, Phlox frondosa, Podophyllum peltatum, Polyanthus, Primula acaulis, P. capitata, P. Cashmeriana, P. denticulata, P. farinosa, P. marginata, P. Scotica, P. vulgaris flore-pleno, Pulmonarias, Puschkinia scilloides, Ramondia pyrenaica, Ranunculus aconitifolius, R. acris flore-pleno, R. amplexicaulis, R. speciosum, Sanguinaria canadensis, Saponaria ocymoides, Saxifraga cæsia, S. ciliata, S. cordifolia, S. ligulata, S. paradoxa, S. pectinata, S. purpurascens, S. tuberosa, S.Wallacei, Scilla campanulata, Sisyrinchium grandiflorum, Soldanellas, Spiræa ulmaria variegata, Symphytum caucascium, Tiarella cordifolia, Trientalis europæa, Trillium erectum, Triteleia uniflora, Vaccinium Vitis Idæa, Veronica gentianoides, V. pinguifolia, V. prostrata, Vesicaria græca.

## June.

Acæna Novæ Zealandiæ, Achillea ægyptiaca, A. filipendula, A. millefolium, A. Ptarmica, Allium Moly, A. neapolitanum, Anchusa italica, A. sempervirens, Anemone alpina, A. coronaria, A. decapitata, A. fulgens, A. stellata, A. sulphurea, A. sylvestris, A. vernalis, Anthericum Liliago, A. Liliastrum, Anthyllis montana, Arabis lucida, Arisæma triphyllum, Arum crinitum, Aster alpinus, Bellis perennis, Calthus palustris flore-pleno, Campanula grandis, C. latifolia, C. speciosa, Centaurea montana, Centranthus ruber, Cheiranthus Cheiri, C. Marshallii, Cornus canadensis, Corydalis lutea, C. nobilis, Cypripedium calceolus, Dianthus deltoides, D. hybridus, Dodecatheon Jeffreyanum, D. Meadia, Doronicum caucasicum, Erigeron caucasicus, E. glaucum, Erysimum pumilum, Festuca glauca, Funkia albo-marginata, Gentiana acaulis, G. Burseri, G. cruciata, G. gelida, G. verna, Geranium argenteum, Gillenia trifoliata, Hesperis matronalis flore-pleno, Heuchera, H. Americana, H. cylindrica, H. Drummondi, H. glabra, H. lucida, H. metallica, H. micrantha, H. purpurea, H. ribifolia, H. Richardsoni, Houstonia cœrulea, Iberis corræfolia, Iris fœtidissima, Kalmia latifolia, Lathyrus grandiflorus, L. latifolius, Leucojum æstivum, Lithospermum prostratum, Lychnis chalcedonica, L. Viscaria flore-pleno, Margyricarpus setosus, Mazus pumilio, Melittis melissophyllum, Morina longifolia, Œnothera speciosa, Œ. taraxacifolia, Ononis rotundifolia, Onosma taurica, Orchis foliosa, O. fusca, Ourisia coccinea, Papaver orientale, Pentstemons, Physalis Alkekengi, Podophyllum peltatum, Polyanthus, Pratia repens, Primula acaulis, P. capitata, P. farinosa, P. sikkimensis, P. vulgaris flore-pleno, Ramondia pyrenaica, Ranunculus aconitifolius flore-pleno, R. acris florepleno, R. speciosum, Saponaria ocymoides, Saxifraga cæsia, S. longifolia, S. Macnabiana, S. mutata, S. paradoxa, S. pectinata, S. peltata, S. purpurascens, S. pyramidalis, S. umbrosa, S. Wallacei, Scilla campanulata, Sempervivum Laggeri, Spiræa ulmaria variegata, S. venusta, Stenactis speciosus, Symphytum caucasicum, Tiarella cordifolia, Trientalis europæa, Trillium erectum, Vaccinium Vitis-Idæa, Veronica gentianoides, V. pinguifolia, V. prostrata, Vesicaria græca.

## July.

Acæna Novæ Zealandiæ, Achillea ægyptiaca, A. filipendula, A. millefolium, A. Ptarmica, Allium Moly, A. neapolitanum, Anchusa Italica, A. sempervirens, Anthericum Liliago, A. liliastrum, Anthyllis montana, Arisæma triphyllum, Arum crinitum, Aster alpinus, Bellis perennis, Calystegia pubescens flore-pleno, Campanula grandis, C. latifolia, C. persicifolia, C. pyramidalis, C. speciosa, C. Waldsteiniana, Centaurea montana, Centranthus ruber, Coreopsis lanceolata, Cornus canadensis, Corydalis lutea, Dianthus deltoides, D. hybridus, Doronicum caucasicum, Edraianthus dalmaticus, Erigeron caucasicus, E. glaucum, Erysimum pumilum, Festuca glauca, Funkia albo-marginata, F. Sieboldi, Galax aphylla, Galega officinalis, G. persica lilacina, Gentiana acaulis, G. asclepiadea, G. Burseri, G. cruciata, G. gelida, Geranium argenteum, Gillenia trifoliata, Hesperis matronalis flore-pleno, Heuchera, H. americana, H. cylindrica, H. Drummondi, H. glabra, H. lucida, H. metallica, H. micrantha, H. purpurea, H. ribifolia, H. Richardsoni, Houstonia cœrulea, Hydrangea paniculata grandiflora, Hypericum calycimum, Iris fœtidissima, Isopyrum gracilis, Kalmia latifolia, Lathyrus grandiflorus, L. latifolius, Leucojum æstivum, Lithospermum prostratum, Lychnis chalcedonica, L. Viscaria florepleno, Lysimachia clethroides, Margyricarpus setosus, Mazus pumilio, Melittis melissophyllum, Monarda didyma, M. fistulosa, M. Russelliana, Morina longifolia, Muhlenbeckia complexa, Nierembergia rivularis, Œnothera speciosa, Œ. taraxacifolia, Ononis rotundifolia, Onosma taurica, Orchis foliosa, Ourisia coccinea, Pentstemons, Physalis Alkekengi, Polygonum cuspidatum, Potentilla fructicosa, Pratia repens, Primula sikkimensis, Ramondia pyrenaica, Ranunculus aconitifolius flore-pleno, Rudbeckia californica, Saponaria ocymoides, Saxifraga longifolia, S. Macnabiana, S. mutata, S. pyramidalis, S. umbrosa, S. Wallacei, Sempervivum Laggeri, Spiræa palmata, S. ulmaria variegata, S. venusta, Stenactis speciosus, Umbillicus chrysanthus, Vaccinium Vitis-Idæa, Veronica gentianoides, V. pinguifolia, V. prostrata.

## August.

Acæna Novæ Zealandiæ, Achillea ægyptiaca, A. filipendula, A. millefolium, A. Ptarmica, Aconitum autumnale, Allium Moly, A. neapolitanum, Anchusa italica, A. sempervirens, Anemone japonica, Apios tuberosa, Asters, A. ptarmicoides, Bocconia cordata, Calystegia pubescens flore-pleno, Campanula persicifolia, C. pyramidalis, C. Waldsteiniana, Centaurea montana, Centranthus ruber, Chrysanthemum, Cichorium Intybus, Clethra alnifolia, Coreopsis auriculata, C. grandiflora, C. lanceolata, C. tenuifolia, Cornus canadensis, Corydalis lutea, Dianthus deltoides D. hybridus, Edraianthus dalmaticus, Erigeron caucasicus, E. glaucum, Eryngium giganteum, Erysimum pumilum, Festuca glauca, Funkia albo-marginata, F. Sieboldi, Galax aphylla, Galega officinalis, G. persica liliacina, Gentiana asclepiadea, G. Burseri, G. gelida, Gillenia trifoliata, Gynerium argenteum, Harpalium rigidum, Helianthus multiflorus, Hesperis matronalis flore-pleno, Heuchera, H. americana, H. cylindrica, H. Drummondi, H. glabra, H. lucida, H. metallica, H. micrantha, H. purpurea, H. ribifolia, H. Richardsoni, Hydrangea paniculata grandiflora, Hypericum calycinum, Iris fœtidissima, Isopyrum gracilis, Kalmia latifolia, Lathyrus grandiflorus, L. latifolius, Linum flavum, Lobelia cardinalis, Lychnis chalcedonica, L. Viscaria flore-pleno, Lysimachia clethroides, Margyricarpus setosus, Mazus pumilio, Melittis melissophyllum, Monarda didyma, M. fistulosa, M. Russelliana, Muhlenbeckia complexa, Nierembergia rivularis, Œnothera speciosa, Œ. taraxacifolia, Ononis rotundifolia, Onosma taurica, Ourisia coccinea, Pentstemons, Phlox, Physalis Alkekengi, Polygonum Brunonis, P. cuspidatum, P. filiformis variegatum, P. vaccinifolium, Potentilla fruticosa, Pratia repens, Pyrethum uliginosum, Rudbeckia californica, Saponaria ocymoides, Saxifraga mutata, S. Wallacei, Sedum Sieboldi, S. spectabile, Sempervivum Laggeri, Senecio pulcher, Spiræa palmata, S. ulmaria variegata, S. venusta, Statice latifolia, S. profusa, Stenactis speciosus, Tropæolum tuberosum, Umbilicus chrysanthus, Vaccinium Vitis-Idæa.

### September.

Acæna Novæ Zealandiæ, Achillea ægyptiaca, A. filipendula, A. millefolium, Aconitum autumnale, Anchusa italica, A. sempervirens, Anemone japonica, Apios tuberosa, Asters, A. ptarmicoides, Bocconia cordata, Calystegia pubescens flore-pleno, Campanula persicifolia, C. pyramidalis, Centaurea montana, Centranthus ruber, Chrysanthemum, Cichorium Intybus, Clethra alnifolia, Colchicum autumnale, C. variegatum, Coreopsis auriculata, C. grandiflora, C. lanceolata, C. tenuifolia, Cornus canadensis, Corydalis lutea, Cyananthus lobatus, Daphne cneorum, Dianthus deltoides, Dianthus hybridus, Echinacea purpurea, Erigeron caucasicus, E. glaucum, Eryngium giganteum, Erysimum pumilum, Festuca glauca, Funkia Sieboldii, Galega officinalis, G. persica liliacina, Gynerium argenteum, Harpalium rigidum, Helianthus multiflorus, H. orygalis, Hydrangea paniculata grandiflora, Hypericum calycinum, Lactuca sonchifolia, Lilium auratum, Linum flavum, Lobelia cardinalis, Lysimachia clethroides, Margyricarpus setosus, Mazus pumilio, Monarda didyma, M. fistulosa, M. Russelliana, Ononis rotundifolia, Onosma taurica, Origanum pulchellum, Ourisia coccinea, Phlox, Physalis Alkekengi, Polygonum Brunoni, P. filiformis variegatum, P. vaccinifolium, Potentilla frusticosa, Pratia repens, Pyrethrum uliginosum, Rudbeckia californica, R. serotina, Salix reticulata, Sedum Sieboldi, S. spectabile, Senecio pulcher, Statice latifolia, S. profusa, Stenactis speciosus, Tritoma uvaria, Tropæolum tuberosum, Umbilicus chrysanthus, Vaccinium Vitis-Idæa.

### October.

Achillea millefolium, Aconitum autumnale, Anemone japonica, Apios tuberosa, Asters, A. ptarmicoides, Campanula pyramidalis, Chrysanthemum, Colchicum autumnale, C. variegatum, Coreopsis lanceolata, Cornus canadensis, Corydalis lutea, Cyananthus lobatus, Dianthus deltoides, Echinacea purpurea, Erigeron caucasicus, E. glaucum, Erysimum pumilum, Gynerium argenteum, Helianthus orygalis, Lactuca sonchifolia, Lilium auratum, Lobelia cardinalis, Onosma taurica, Origanum pulchellum, Phlox, Physalis Alkekengi, Polygonum Brunonis, P. filiformis variegatum, P. vaccinifolium, Potentilla fruticosa, Pratia repens, Primula vulgaris flore-pleno, Rudbeckia serotina, Salix reticulata, Saxifraga Fortunei, Sedum spectabile, Senecio pulcher, Statice latifolia, S. profusa, Stokesia cyanea, Tritoma uvaria, Tropæolum tuberosum, Umbilicus chrysanthus, Vaccinium Vitis-Idæa.

### November.

Achillea millefolium, Anemone japonica, Aralia Sieboldi, Asters, Chrysanthemum, Lilium auratum, Origanum pulchellum, Petasites vulgaris, Physalis Alkekengi, Primula vulgaris flore-pleno, Saxifraga Fortunei, Stokesia cyanea.

### December.

Aralia Sieboldi, Eranthis hyemalis, Helleborus fœtidus, H. niger, H. orientalis, H. olympicus, Jasminum nudiflorum, Petasites vulgaris, Physalis Alkekengi, Stokesia cyanea.

# COLOURS OF FLOWERS.

The following list will be found useful to those who wish to select flowers of any particular colour:—

**Blue** (including some of the shades inclining to Purple).
Aconitum autumnale, 5.
Anemone Apennina, 12; A. blanda, 12; A. coronaria, 13; A. japonica vitifolia, 16.
Anchusa italica, 8; A. sempervirens, 9.
Campanula grandis, 49; C. latifolia, 50; C. persicifolia, 50; C. pyramidalis, 51.
Centaurea montana, 54.
Chionodoxa Luciliæ, 58.
Cichorium Intybus, 61.
Cyananthus lobatus, 74.
Eryngium giganteum, 96.
Galega officinalis, 110.
Gentiana acaulis, 111; G. cruciata, 114; G. verna, 115.
Hepatica triloba, 140.
Houstonia cœrulea, 146.
Lactuca sonchifolia, 158.
Lithospermum prostratum, 165.
Muscari botryoides, 179; M. racemosum, 180.
Omphalodes verna, 185.
Orobus vernus, 192.
Primula, 212; P. capitata, 213.
Pulmonarias, 224; P. azurea, 225.
Scilla campanulata, 267
Soldanella alpina, 276; S. montana, 276.
Stokesia cyanea, 284.
Symphytum caucasicum, 286.
Veronica gentianoides, 300; V. prostrata, 301.

BLUE (*continued*).
Viola pedata, 303; V. tricolor, 305.

**Brown.**
Cheiranthus Cheiri, 56.
Corydalis nobilis, 71.
Chrysanthemum, 59.
Gillenia trifoliata, 117.
Orchis fusca, 189.
Trillium erectum, 291.

**Green.**
Helleborus abchasicus, 126; H. Bocconi, 128; H. dumetorum, 131; H. fœtidus, 131; H. odorus, 136; H. orientalis elegans, 138.
Heuchera Richardsoni, 146.
Margyricarpus setosus, 171.

**Lilac.**
Asters or Michaelmas daisies, 37.
Bulbocodium trigynum, 45; B. vernum, 46.
Campanula Waldsteiniana, 53.
Crocus medius, 74.
Erigeron glaucum, 94.
Erythronium dens canis, 98.
Funkia albo-marginata, 102; F. Sieboldii, 103.
Galega persica liliacina, 110.
Phlox, 202.
Statice latifolia, 280; S. profusa, 281.
Triteleia uniflora liliacina, 293.
Helleborus cupreus, 130.

**Pink** (including shades of Blush and Rose).
Achillea millefolium, 4.
Anemone japonica, 16.
Calystegia pubescens flore-pleno, 48.
Centaurea montana, 54.
Centranthus ruber coccinea, 56.
Chrysanthemum, 69.
Daphne cneorum, 78.
Dianthus deltoides, 81, 152; D. hybridus, 82.
Geranium argenteum, 116.
Helleborous orientalis, 137.
Hepatica triloba, 140.
Heuchera glabra, 144.
Lathyrus grandiflorus, 159; L. latifolius, 160.
Lychnis Viscaria flore-pleno, 170.
Melittis Melissophyllum, 174.
Morina longifolia, 176.
Origanum pulchellum, 191.
Phlox, 202.
Polygonum Brunonis, 207; P. vaccinifolium, 209.
Primula denticulata amabilis, 217.
Pulmonarias, 224; P. saccharata, 225.
Saponaria ocymoides, 237.
Saxifraga cordifolia, 245; S. ligulata, 249; S. peltata, 259; S. purpurascens, 261.
Scilla campanulata carnea, 268.
Sedum Sieboldi, 269; S. spectabile, 269.
Sempervivum Laggeri, 270.
Spring Beauty, 152.

**Purple** (including shades Lilac Purple, Rosy and Reddish Purple, Purple Blue, &c).
Anemone coronaria, 13; A. pulsatilla, 18; A. stellata, 20; A. vernalis, 24.
Anthyllis montana, 27.
Apios tuberosa, 27.
Arum crinitum, 35.
Aster alpinus, 37; A. Amellus, 37; A. Madame Soyance, 37.
Bulbocodium vernum, 46.

Purple (*continued*).
Campanula speciosa, 53.
Colchicum autumnale, 63; C. variegatum, 64.
Corydalis solida, 73.
Crocus medius, 74.
Chrysanthemum, 59.
Cyananthus lobatus, 74.
Daphne Mezereum, 79.
Dentaria digitata, 81.
Dodecatheon Meadia, 84; D. Meadia elegans, 85.
Echinacea purpurea, 87.
Edraianthus dalmaticus, 88.
Erica carnea, 92.
Erigeron caucasicus, 93.
Erythronium dens-canis, 98.
Gentiana gelida, 114.
Helleborus abchasicus, 126; H. A. purpureus, 126; H. colchicus, 129; H. olympicus, 136; H. purpurascens, 139.
Hepatica triloba, 140.
Hesperis matronalis flore-pleno, 141.
Heuchera americana, 143.
Melittis Melissophyllum, 174.
Monarda fistulosa, 176.
Orchis foliosa, 189; O. fusca, 189.
Primula cashmeriana, 214; P. denticulata, 216; P. farinosa, 217; P. purpurea, 219; P. Scotica, 220.
Prunella pyrenaica, 152.
Saxifraga oppositifolia, 255; S. purpurascens, 261.
Sisyrinchium grandiflorum, 274.
Soldanella Clusii, 276; S. minima, 276.
Stenactis speciosus, 283.
Viola pedata digitata, 304; V. p. flabellata, 304; V. tricolor, 305.

**Red** (including Ruby and shades of Crimson).
Bellis perennis fistulosa, 40.
Centranthus ruber, 55.
Daisy, Sweep, 40.

## COLOURS OF FLOWERS. 319

**Red** (*continued*).
Daphne Mezereum autumnale, 80.
Hepatica triloba splendens, 141.
Hesperis matronalis flore-pleno, 141.
Lobelia cardinalis, 166.
Lychnis Viscaria flore-pleno, 170.
Primula acaulis, 211.
Saxifraga mutata, 254.
Senecio pulcher, 272.
Spiræa palmata, 278; S. venusta, 280.
Tropæolum tuberosum, 295.

**Scarlet.**
Anemone coronaria, 13; A. fulgens, 15.
Dianthus hybridus, 82.
Lychnis chalcedonica, 168.
Monarda didyma, 175.
Ononis rotundifolia, 185.
Ourisia coccinea, 193.
Papaver orientale, 195.

**Striped.**
Anemone coronaria, 13; A. stellata, 20.
Arisæma triphyllum, 33.
Gentiana asclepiadea, 112.

**Violet** (including shades of Mauve).
Colchicum autumnale, 63.
Chrysanthemum, 59.
Hepatica angulosa, 139.
Mazus pumilis, 173.
Pratia repens, 210.
Primula, 211; P. capitata, 213; P. marginata, 218.
Pulmonaria angustifolia, 225.
Ramondia pyrenaica, 228.

**White** (sometimes with delicate edgings of colour, or with pale tints).
Achillea Ptarmica, 5.
Allium neapolitanum, 6.
Anemone coronaria, 13; A. decapetala, 15; A. japonica alba, 16; A. nemorosa flore-pleno, 17; A. stellata, 20; A. sylvestris, 22.

**White** (*continued*).
Anthericum liliago, 25; A. liliastrum, 25; A. l. major, 27.
Aralia Sieboldi, 30.
Aster alpinus albus, 39; A. ptarmicoides, 39.
Bellis perennis hortensis, 44.
Bocconia cordata, 42.
Campanula persicifolia, 50; C. pyramidalis alba, 53.
Centaurea montana, 54.
Centranthus ruber albus, 56.
Clethra alnifolia, 62.
Cornus canadensis, 68.
Daisy, Bride, 40.
Daphne Mezereum alba, 80.
Dianthus hybridus, 82.
Dodecatheon Meadia albiflorum, 85.
Epigæa repens, 90.
Erythronium dens canis, 98.
Galax aphylla, 108.
Galega officinalis alba, 110.
Helleborus antiquorum, 127; H. guttatus, 132; H. niger, 132; H. n. maximus, 134.
Hepatica triloba, 140.
Hesperis matronalis flore-pleno, 141.
Houstonia albiflora, 146.
Hutchinsia alpina, 147.
Hydrangea paniculata grandiflora, 148.
Iberis corresefolia, 151.
Kalmia latifolia, 157.
Lathyrus latifolius albus, 161.
Leucojum æstivum, 161; L. vernum, 162.
Lilium auratum, 162.
Lychnis, 168.
Lysimachia clethroides, 170.
Monarda Russelliana, 176.
Muhlenbeckia complexa, 178.
Muscari botryoides alba, 180.
Nierembergia rivularis, 181.
Œnothera speciosa, 182; Œ. taraxacifolia, 183.
Petasites vulgaris, 198.
Phlox divaricata, 202; P. glaberrima, 202; P. Nelsoni, 202.
Physalis Alkekengi, 203.

WHITE (continued).
Podophyllum peltatum, 205.
Polygonum cuspidatum, 208.
Pratia repens, 210.
Primula, 211.
Pulmonaria officinalis alba, 225.
Puschkinia scilloides, 225.
Pyrethrum uliginosum, 227.
Ranunculus aconitifolius, 229;
R. amplexicaulis, 231.
Sanguinaria canadensis, 235.
Saxifragia Burseriana, 238; S. cæsia, 238; S. ceratophylla, 240; S. ciliata, 242; S. coriophylla, 245; S. Fortunei, 247; S. Macnabiana, 253; S. oppositifolia alba, 256; S. pectinata, 258; S. Rocheliana, 265; S. Wallacei, 266.
Scilla campanulata alba, 268.
Sisyrinchium grandiflorum album, 276.
Tiarella cordifolia, 288.
Trientalis europæa, 288.
Tritelia uniflora, 292.
Umbilicus chrysanthus, 297.
Vaccinium Vitis-Idæa, 298.
Veronica pinguifolia, 301; V. repens, 301.
Viola pedata alba, 304; V. p. ranunculifolia, 304.
Yucca filamentosa, 306; Y. gloriosa, 307; Y. recurva, 308.

Yellow (all shades, from Cream to Deep Orange; also shades of Greenish Yellow).
Achillea ægyptiaca, 3; A. filipendula, 4.

YELLOW (continued).
Allium Moly, 6.
Alyssum saxatile, 7.
Anemone sulphurea, 21.
Calthus palustris flore-pleno, 47.
Cheiranthus Marshallii, 58.
Coreopsis auriculata, 65, 68.
Corydalis lutea, 70; C. nobilis,. 71.
Chrysanthemum, 59.
Cypripedium calceolus, 76.
Dondia Epipactus, 85.
Doronicum caucasicum, 86.
Eranthis hyemalis, 91.
Erysimum pumilum, 97.
Erythronium dens-canis, 98.
Fritillaria armena, 101. .
Gentiana Burseri, 113.
Harpalium rigidum, 121.
Helianthus multiflorus, 123 ; H. orygalis, 124.
Heuchera micrantha, 145.
Hypericum calycinum, 150.
Jasminum nudiflorum, 155.
Linum flavum, 164.
Narcissus minor, 180.
Onosma taurica, 187.
Potentilla fruticosa, 209.
Primula, 211; P. auricula marginata, 218; P. sikkimensis, 221; P. vulgaris flore-pleno, 223.
Ranunculus acris flore-pleno, 231; R. speciosum, 232.
Rudbeckia californica, 233; R. serotina, 234.
Saxifraga mutata, 254.
Tropæolum tuberosum, 295.
Vesicaria græca, 302.
Viola tricolor, 305.

# INDEX.

## A.

Acæna microphylla, 1.
    Novæ Zealandiæ, 1.
Achillea ægyptica, 3.
    filipendula, 4.
    millefolium, 4.
    ptarmica, 4.
    slvestris, 4.
Aconite, winter, 91.
Aconitum autumnale, 5.
    japonicum, 6.
Adamsia scilloides, 225.
Adam's needle, 307.
Alkanet, Italian, 8.
Allium Moly, 6.
    neapolitanum, 6.
Alum root, 142.
Alyssum saxatile, 7.
Anchusa italica, 8.
    sempervirens, 9.
Andromeda tetragona, 10.
Anemone alpina, 11.
    apennina, 12.
    apiifolia, 21.
    blanda, 12.
    blue Grecian, 12.
    coronaria, 13.
    decapetala, 15.
    double-wood, 17.
    fulgens, 15.
    geranium-leaved, 12.
    Honorine Jobert, 16.
    hortensis, 15, 20.
    japonica, 16.
    nemorosa flore-pleno, 17.
    pavonina, 15.
    pulsatilla, 18.
    snowdrop, 22.

Anemone stellata, 20.
    sulphurea, 21.
    sylvestris, 22.
    triloba, 140.
    vernalis, 23.
Anthericum liliago, 25.
    liliastrum, 25.
    liliastrum major, 27.
Anthyllis montana, 27.
Apios Glycine, 27.
    tuberosa, 27.
Apple, May, 205.
Aralia Sieboldi, 30.
Arabis alpina, 29.
    lucida, 29.
    l. variegata, 29.
Arisæma triphyllum, 33.
    zebrinum, 33.
Arum crinitum, 35.
    hairy, 35.
    three-leaved, 33.
    triphyllum, 33.
Asters, 37.
    alpinus, 37.
    amellus, 37.
    diversifolius, 37.
    dumosus, 37.
    ericoides, 37.
    grandiflorus, 37.
    Mdme. Soyance, 37.
    pendulus, 37.
    ptarmicoides, 39.
    Stokes', 284.
Astrantia Epipactis, 85.

## B.

Bachelor's buttons, 229.

# INDEX.

Bachelor's buttons, yellow, 231.
Balm, bee, 175.
   large-flowered bastard, 174.
Bay, dwarf, 79.
Bellflower, broad-leaved, 50.
   peach-leaved, 50.
   great, 49.
Bellis perennis, 40.
   p. aucubæfolia, 40.
   p. prolifera, 40.
Bergamot, wild, 176.
Bloodroot, 235.
Blandfordia cordata, 108.
Bluebell, 267.
Bluebottle, large, 54.
Bluets, 146.
Bocconia cordata, 42.
Borago sempervirens, 9.
Bruisewoorte, 42.
Buglossum sempervirens, 9.
Bulbocodium, spring, 46.
   trigynum, 45.
   vernum, 46.
Butterbur, common, 198.

## C.

Calthus palustris flore-pleno, 47.
Calystegia pubescens flore-pleno, 48.
Campanula, chimney, 51.
   glomerata dahurica, 53.
   grandis, 49.
   latifolia, 50.
   muralis, 54.
   persicifolia, 50.
   pulla, 49.
   pyramidalis, 51.
   speciosa, 53.
   Waldsteiniana, 53.
   Zoysii, 54.
Candytuft, everlasting, 151.
Cardinal flower, 166.
Cassiope tetragona, 10.
Catchfly, 168.
   German, 170.
Centaurea montana, 54.
Centranthus ruber, 55.
Chaixia Myconi, 228.
Cheiranthus Cheiri, 56.

Cheiranthus Marshallii, 58.
Cherry, winter, 203.
Chicory, 61.
Chionodoxa Luciliæ, 58.
Chrysanthemum, 59.
Cichorium Intybus, 61.
   perenne, 61.
   sylvestre, 61.
Cinquefoil, shrubby, 209.
Claytonia, 151.
Clethra, alder-leaved, 62.
   alnifolia, 62.
Colchicum autumnale, 63.
   caucasicum, 45.
   variegatum, 64.
Comfrey, Caucasian, 286.
Cone-flower, Californian, 233.
   late, 234.
Convolvulus, double, 48.
Conyza, chilensis, 94.
Coreopsis auriculata, 65.
   ear-leaved, 65.
   grandiflora, 66.
   lanceolata, 66.
   large-flowered, 66.
   slender-leaved, 67.
   spear-leaved, 66.
   tenuifolia, 67.
Cornell, Canadian, 68.
Cornflower, perennial, 54.
Cornus canadensis, 68.
   suecica, 67.
Corydalis lutea, 70.
   noble or great-flowered, 71.
   nobilis, 71.
   solida, 73.
Coventry bells, 18.
Cowberry, 298.
Cowslip, 206, 211.
   American, 84.
Crane's-bill, silvery, 116.
Crocus, 202.
   autumnal, 63.
   medius, 74.
Crowfoot, aconite-leaved, 229.
   double acrid, 231.
   English double white, 229.
Cup, white, 181.
Cypripedium calceolus, 76.
Cyananthus lobatus, 74.
Cynoglossum omphalodes, 185.

## D.

Daffodil, smaller, 180
Daisy, blue, 37.
   common perennial, 40.
   double, 40.
   Hen and Chickens, 40.
   little, 42.
   Michaelmas, 37.
Daphne Cneorum, 78.
   mezereum, 79.
   m. alba, 80.
   m. autumnale, 80.
   m. trailing, 78.
Dentaria digitata, 81.
Dianthus barbatus, 82.
   deltoides, 81, 152.
   hybridus, 82.
   multiflorus, 82.
   plumarius, 82.
Dodecatheon Jeffreyanum, 83.
   meadia, 74.
   m. albiflorum, 85.
   m. elegans, 85.
   m. giganteum, 85.
Dogwood, 68.
Dondia Epipactis, 85.
Doronicum caucasicum, 86.
   orientale, 86.
Dragon's mouth, 35.
Duck's foot, 205.

## E.

Easter flower, 18.
Echinacea purpurea, 87.
Edraianthus dalmaticus, 88.
Epigæa repens, 90.
Eranthis hyemalis, 91.
Erica carnea, 92, 166.
Erigeron caucasicus, 93.
   glaucum, 94.
   speciosus, 283.
Eryngium giganteum, 96.
Eryngo, great, 96.
Erysimum pumilum, 97.
Erythronium dens-canis, 98.
Euonymus japonicus radicans variegata, 99.
Everlasting pea, large-leaved, 160.
   large-flowered, 159.

EVERGREENS:—Achillea ægyptica, 3; Alyssum saxatile, 7; Anchusa sempervirens, 9; Andromeda tetragona, 10; Aralia Sieboldi, 30; Campanula grandis, 49; Cheiranthus Cheiri, 56; Daphne Cneorum, 78; Dianthus hybridus, 82; Epigæa repens, 90; Erica carnea, 92; Erigeron glaucum, 94; Euonymus japonicus radicans variegata, 99; Galax aphylla, 108; Gentiana acaulis, 111; Hedera conglomerata, 122; Helleborus abchasicus, 126; H. fœtidus, 131; H. niger, 132; Heuchera, 142; Houstonia cœrulea, 146; Hutchinsia alpina, 147; Iberis correæfolia, 151; Iris fœtidissima, 153; Kalmia latifolia, 157; Lithospermum prostratum, 165; Margyricarpus setosus, 171; Saxifraga Burseriana, 238; S. ceratophylla, 240; S. purpurascens, 261; S. Rocheliana, 265; Umbillicus chrysanthus, 297; Vaccinium vitis-idæa, 298; Veronica gentianoides, 300; V. pinguifolia, 301; Vesicaria græca, 302; Yucca gloriosa, 307; Y. recurva, 308.

## F.

February, Fair Maids of, 106.
Felwoth, spring alpine, 115.
Festuca glauca, 101.
Feverfew, marsh, 227.
Flame-flowers, 294.
Flaw flower, 18.
Flax, yellow, 164.
Fleabane, Caucasian, 93.
   glaucous, 94.
   showy, 283.
Flower, milk, 107.
FOLIAGE PLANTS:— Achillea ægyptica, 3; Arabis lucida variegata, 29; Aralia Sisboldi,

30; Arisæma triphyllum, 33; Bocconia cordata, 42; Cornus canadensis, 68; Corydalis lutea, 70; C. nobilis, 71; C. solida, 73; Dodecatheon Jeffreyanum, 83; Erica carnea, 92; Euonymus japonicus radicans variegata, 99; Festuca glauca, 101; Funkia albo-marginata, 102; F. Sieboldii, 103; Galax aphylla, 108; Galega officinalis, 110; Gentiana asclepiadea, 112; G. Burseri, 113; Geranium argenteum, 116; Gynerium argenteum, 119; Hedera conglomerata, 122; Helleborus fœtidus, 131; Heuchera, 142; H. glabra, 144; H. metallica, 145; H. purpurea, 145; Iris fœtidissima, 153; Isopyrum gracilis, 153; Lactuca sonchifolia, 158; Lysimachia clethroides, 170; Ononis rotundifolia, 185; Ourisia coccinea, 193; Podophyllum peltatum, 205; Polygonum Brunonis, 207; P. cuspidatum, 208; P. filiformis variegatum, 209; Statice latifolia, 280; Saxifraga Burseriana, 238; S. cæsia, 238; S. ceratophylla, 240; S. ciliata, 242; S. ligulata, 249; S. longifolia, 250; S. Macnabiana, 253; S. paradoxa, 257; S. pectinata, 258; S. peltata, 259; S. purpurascens, 261; S. pyramidalis, 262; S. Rocheliana, 265; S. umbrosa variegata, 265; Sempervivum Laggeri, 270; Spiræa ulmaria variegata, 279; Tiarella cordifolia, 287; Yucca gloriosa, 308.

Forget-me-not, creeping, 185.
Fritillaria armena, 101.
Fumitory, 73.
   "hollowe roote," 71, 73.
   yellow, 70.
Funkia albo-marginata, 102.
   Sieboldii, 103.

## G.

Galanthus Elwesii, 105.
   folded, 107.
   imperati, 105.
   nivalis, 106.
   plicatus, 107.
   redoutei, 107.
Galax aphylla, 108.
   heart-leaved, 108.
Galega officinalis, 110.
   persica liliacina, 110.
Garland flower, 78.
Garlic, large yellow, 6.
Gentian, Burser's, 113.
   cross-leaved, 114.
   ice-cold, 114.
   lithospermum, 165.
   swallow-wort leaved, 112.
Gentiana acaulis, 111.
   asclepiadea, 112.
   Burseri, 113.
   cruciata, 114.
   gelida, 114.
   verna, 115.
Gentianella, 111.
Geranium argenteum, 116.
Gillenia trifoliata, 117.
Gilloflower, 107.
   Queene's, 141.
   stock, 142.
   wild, 81.
Gillyflower, 57.
Gladdon or Gladwin, 153.
Glory, Snowy, 58.
Goats-rue, officinal, 110.
Golden drop, 187.
Goose-tongue, 4.
Grandmother's frilled cap, 51.
Grass, blue, 101.
   pampas or silvery, 119.
Gromwell, prostrate, 165.
Groundsel, noble, 272.
Gynerium argenteum, 119.

## H.

Hacquetia Epipactis, 85.
Harebell, showy, 53.
Harpalium rigidum, 121.

Heath, winter, 92.
Hedera conglomerata, 122.
Helianthus multiflorus, 123.
   m. flore-pleno, 124.
   orygalis, 124.
   rigidus, 121.
Heliotrope, winter, 198.
Hellebore, abchasian, 126.
   ancient, 127.
   black, 132, 138.
   Boccon's, 128.
   bushy, 131.
   Colchican, 129.
   coppery, 130.
   eastern, 137.
   officinalis, 137.
   Olympian, 136.
   purplish, 139.
   spotted, 132.
   stinking, 131.
   sweet-scented, 136.
Helleborus abchasicus, 126.
   a. purpureus, 126.
   antiquorum, 127.
   Bocconi, 128.
   B. angustifolia, 129.
   colchicus, 129.
   cupreus, 130.
   dumetorum, 131.
   fœtidus, 131.
   guttatus, 132.
   hyemalis, 91.
   multifidus, 128.
   niger, 132, 138.
   n. angustifolius, 134.
   n. maximus, 134.
   odorus, 136.
   olympicus, 136.
   orientalis, 137.
   o. elegans, 138.
   purpurascens, 139.
Hepatica, anemone, 140.
   angulosa, 139.
   triloba, 140.
   t. splendens, 141.
Herb, Christ's, 132.
Hesperis matronalis flore-pleno, 141.
Heuchera, 142, 288.
   americana, 143.
   currant-leaved, 145.

Heuchera cylindrica, 143.
   cylindrical-spiked, 143.
   Drummondi, 144.
   glabra, 144.
   lucida, 144.
   metallica, 145.
   micrantha, 145.
   purpurea, 145.
   ribifolia, 145.
   Richardsoni, 146.
   shining-leaved, 144.
   small-flowered, 145.
   smooth, 144.
Hill tulip, 18.
Houseleek, Lagger's, 270.
Houstonia albiflora, 146.
   cœrulea, 146.
Hutchinsia alpina, 147.
Hyacinth, 267.
   grape, 179.
Hydrangea, large-flowered, 148.
   paniculata grandiflora, 148.
Hypericum calycinum, 150.


I.

Iberis corrææfolia, 151.
Indian cress, 295.
Iris fœtidissima, 153.
Isopyrum gracilis, 153.
   slender, 153.
Ivy, conglomerate, 122.


J.

Jack in the pulpit, 33.
Jasminum nudiflorum, 155.


K.

Kalmia, broad-leaved, 157.
   latifolia, 157.
Knapweed, mountain, 54.
Knotweed, 207, 209.
   cuspid, 208.
   vaccinium-leaved, 209.

## L.

Lactuca sonchifolia, 158.
Lathyrus grandiflorus, 159.
  latifolius, 160.
  l. albus, 161.
Laurel, creeping or ground, 90.
Leopard's bane, 86.
Lepidium alpinum, 147.
Lettuce, sow thistle-leaved, 158.
Leucojum æstivum, 161.
  vernum, 162.
Lilium auratum, 162.
Lily, erect wood, 291.
  golden-rayed or Japanese, 162.
  rush, 274.
  St. Bernard's, 25.
  St. Bruno's, 25.
  Siebold's plantain-leaved, 103.
  white-edged, plantain-leaved, 102.
Lilywort, 226.
Linaria pilosa, 237.
Linum flavum, 164.
  narbonnense, 165.
  perenne, 165.
Lithospermum fruticosum, 165.
  prostratum, 165.
Lobelia cardinalis, 166.
  pratiana, 210.
  repens, 210.
Loosestrife, clethra-like, 170.
Lungworts, 224.
Lychnis chalcedonica, 168.
  scarlet, 168.
  viscaria flore-pleno, 170.
Lysimachia clethroides, 170.

## M.

Macleaya cordata, 42.
Madwort, rock, or golden tuft, 7.
Margyricarpus setosus, 171.
Marigold, double marsh, 47.
Marjoram, beautiful, 191.
Mazus, dwarf, 173.
  pumilio, 173.
" Meadow bootes," 47.
Meadowsweet, 279.
Meadows, Queen of the, 279.

Megasea ciliata, 242, 249.
  cordifolia, 245.
  ligulata, 249.
  purpurascens, 261.
Melittis grandiflorum, 174.
  melissophyllum, 174.
Merendera caucasicum, 45.
Mertensia, 224.
Mezereon, 79.
Milfoil, common, 4.
Milla uniflora, 292.
Mitella, 288.
Monarda affinis, 176.
  altissima, 176.
  didyma, 175.
  fistulosa, 176.
  kalmiana, 175.
  media, 176.
  oblongata, 176.
  purpurea, 176.
  rugosa, 176.
  Russelliana, 176.
Monk's-hood, autumn, 5.
Morina elegans, 176.
  longifolia, 176.
Moss, silver, 238.
Muhlenbeckia complexa, 178.
Mullien, 228.
Muscari botryoides, 179.
  b. alba, 180.
  racemosum, 180.

## N.

Narcissus minor, 180.
Nasturtium, 295.
Nierembergia rivularis, 181.
  water, 181.
Nightshade, red, 204.

## O.

Œnothera speciosa, 182.
  taraxacifolia, 183.
Omphalodes verna, 185.
Ononis rotundifolia, 185.
Onosma taurica, 187.
Orchis, brown, 189.
  foliosa, 189.
  fusca, 189.

Orchis, leafy, 189.
   militaris, 189.
   soldier or brown man, 189.
Origanum pulchellum, 191.
Orobus vernus, 192.
Oswego tea, 175.
Ourisia coccinea, 193.
Oxlips, 211.

P.

Paigles, 211.
Pansy, 306.
Papaver bracteatum, 195.
   orientale, 195.
Pasque-flower, 18.
Passe-flower, 18.
Peachbels, 50.
Pearl-fruit, bristly, 171.
Peaseling, 192.
Pellitory, wild, 4.
Pentstemons, 197.
Petasites vulgaris, 198.
Phlox, 199.
   decussata, 199.
   early and late flowering, 199.
   frondosa, 201.
   omniflora, 200.
   ovata, 200.
   paniculata, 200.
   procumbens, 200.
   stolonifera, 200.
   suffruticosa, 199.
Physalis Alkekengi, 203.
Pinguicula vulgaris, 173.
Pink, maiden, 81, 152.
   mule, 82.
Pinke, maidenly, 81.
   virgin-like, 81.
Podophyllum peltatum, 205.
Polyanthus, 206.
Polygonum Brunonis, 207.
   cuspidatum, 208.
   c. compactum, 208.
   filiformis variegatum, 209.
   vaccinifolium, 209.
Poppy, oriental, 195.
Potentilla fruticosa, 209.
Prairie, Queen of the, 280.
Pratia, creeping, 210.
   repens, 210.

Primrose, Cashmere, 214.
   dandelion-leaved evening, 183.
   double-flowered, 223.
   margined, 217.
   mealy or bird's-eye, 217.
   Scottish, 220.
   showy evening, 182.
Primula acaulis, 211.
   Allioni, 213.
   amœna, 213.
   auricula, 213.
   a. marginata, 218.
   capitata, 213.
   carniolica, 213.
   cashmeriana, 124.
   crenata, 217.
   decora, 213.
   denticulata, 213, 216.
   d. amabilis, 217.
   d. major, 217.
   d. nana, 217.
   elatior, 211.
   farinosa, 213, 217, 220.
   glaucescens, 213.
   glutinosa, 213.
   grandiflora, 211.
   grandis, 213.
   latifolia, 213.
   longifolia, 213.
   luteola, 213.
   marginata, 213, 217.
   minima, 213.
   nivalis, 213.
   purple-flowered, 219.
   purpurea, 219.
   round headed, 213.
   scotica, 213, 220.
   sikkimensis, 221.
   sinensis, 213.
   spectabilis, 213.
   sylvestris, 211.
   tyrolensis, 213.
   toothed, 216.
   veris, 206, 211.
   villosa, 213.
   viscosa, 213.
   vulgaris, 211.
   v. flore-pleno, 223.
   Wulfeniana, 213.
Prunella pyrenaica, 152.
Ptarmica vulgaris, 4.

Pulmonarias, 224.
   maculata, 225.
   mollis, 225.
   officinalis, 225.
Puschkinia libanotica, 225.
   scilla-like, 225.
   scilloides, 225.
   s. compacta, 226.
Pyrethrum uliginosum, 227.

### R.

Ramondia pyrenaica, 228.
Ranunculus aconitifolius, 229.
   acris flore-pleno, 231.
   albus multiflorus, 229.
   amplexicaulis, 231.
   speciosum, 232.
   stem-clasping, 231.
Red-hot poker, 294.
Rest-arrow, round-leaved, 185.
Rocket, double sweet, 141.
ROCKWORK PLANTS:—Acæna Novæ Zealandiæ, 1; Alyssum saxatile, 7; Andromeda tetragona, 10; Anthyllis montana, 27; Arabis lucida, 29; Aralia Sieboldi, 30; Aster alpinus, 37; Campanula Waldsteiniana, 53; Cardamine trifolia, 70; Colchicum variegatum, 64; Cornus canadensis, 68; Corydalis nobilis, 71; C. solida, 73; Cyananthus lobatus, 74; Dentaria digitata, 81; Dodecatheon Jeffreyanum, 83; Dondia Epipactis, 85; Doronicum caucasicum, 86; Edraianthus dalmaticus, 88; Erica carnea, 92; Erigeron glaucum, 94; Erysimum pumilum, 97; Festuca glauca, 101; Funkia Sieboldii, 103; Galax aphylla, 70, 108; Gentiana acaulis, 111; G. Burseri, 113; G. gelida, 114; G. verna, 115; Geranium argenteum, 116; Hedera conglomerata, 122; Houstonia cœrulea, 146; Iberis corresæfolia, 151; Linum flavum, 164; Lithospermum prostratum, 165; Lychnis Viscaria flore-pleno, 170; Margyricarpus setosus, 171; Muhlenbeckia complexa, 178; Nierembergia rivularis, 181; Onosma taurica, 188; Origanum pulchellum, 191; Orobus vernus, 192; Phlox, 202; Polygonum vaccinifolium, 209; Pratia repens, 210; Primula, 213, 216, 218, 222; Pyrola rotundifolia, 70; Ramondia pyrenaica, 228; Ranunculus amplexicaulis, 231; Salix reticulata, 70, 235; Saponaria ocymoides, 237; Saxifraga Burseriana, 238; S. cæsia, 238; S. ceratophylla, 240; S. ciliata, 242; S. coriophylla, 246; S. Fortunei, 247; S. longifolia, 250; S. mutata, 254; S. oppositifolia, 255; S. paradoxa, 257; S. pectinata, 258; S. pyramidalis, 262; S. umbrosa variegata, 265; S. Wallacei, 266; Sedum spectabile, 269; Sempervivum Laggeri, 270; Symphytum caucasicum, 286; Tropæolum tuberosum, 295; Umbilicus chrysanthus, 297; Veronica pinguifolia, 301; V. prostrata, 301; Vesicaria græca, 302; Viola pedata, 303; Yucca filamentosa, 306.
Rose, Christmas, 132, 138.
   lenten, 137.
   of Sharon, 150.
Rudbeckia californica, 233.
   purpurea, 87.
   serotina, 234.
Rues, maidenhair-like, 153.

### S.

Saffron, meadow, 63.
   spring, 46.
Saint John's Wort, cup, 150.
   large calyxed, 150.
Salix reticulata, 235.
Sanguinaria canadensis, 235.

Saponaria ocymoides, 237.
   ocymoides splendens, 237.
Satin-flower, 274.
Saxifraga Aizoon, 258, 259.
   alpina ericoides flore cœruleo, 255.
   australis, 257, 258.
   Burseriana, 238, 246.
   cæsia, 238.
   carinthiaca, 257, 258.
   ceratophylla, 240.
   ciliata, 242, 249.
   cordifolia, 245, 261.
   coriophylla, 245.
   cornutum, 241, 266.
   cotyledon, 253, 254, 262.
   crassifolia, 261.
   crustata, 257.
   fortunei, 247.
   geranioides, 266.
   japonica, 247.
   ligulata, 242, 249, 257.
   longifolia, 250, 254, 257.
   macnabiana, 253.
   mutata, 254.
   nepalensis, 253.
   oppositifolia, 246, 255.
   o. alba, 256.
   paradoxa, 257.
   pectinata, 258.
   peltata, 259.
   pentadactylis, 240, 266.
   pryamidalis, 262.
   purpurascens, 261.
   rocheliana, 265.
   umbrosa, 265.
   variegata, 265.
   sarmentosa, 243.
   Wallacei, 266.
Saxifrage, blue, 255.
   Burser's, 238, 246.
   Fortune's, 247.
   grey, 238.
   hairy margined, 242.
   horn-leaved, 240.
   large-leaved purple, 261.
   long-leaved, 250.
   Mac Nab's, 253.
   opposite-leaved, 255.
   paradoxical, 257.
   purple mountain, 255.

Saxifrage, Queen of, 250.
   Rochel's, 265.
Scilla, bell-flowered, 267.
   campanulata, 267.
Sea lavender, broad-leaved, 280.
   profuse, 281.
Sedum Fabarium, 269.
   spectabile, 269.
   Sieboldi, 269.
Self heal, 152.
Sempervivum Laggeri, 270.
Senecia pulcher, 272.
Sibthorpia europæa, 237.
Sisyrinchium grandiflorum, 274.
   Grandiflorum album, 276.
Slipper, English lady's, 76.
Sneezewort, 4.
Snowdrop, common, 106.
   Elwes's, 105.
   imperial, 105.
Snowflake, spring, 162.
   summer, 161.
Soapwort, basil-leaved, 237.
   rock, 237.
Solanum Halicacabum, 204.
Soldanella alpina, 276.
   Clusii, 276.
   minima, 276.
   montana, 276.
Speedwell, fat-leaved, 301.
   gentian-leaved, 300.
   prostrate, 301.
Spikenard, 94.
Spindle tree, variegated, rooting, 99.
Spiræa odorata, 279.
   palmata, 278.
   palm-like, 278.
   trifoliata, 117.
   triloba, 117.
   ulmaria variegata, 279.
   venusta, 280.
Spring beauty, 152.
Spurge-flax, 79.
   German olive, 79.
   wort, 153.
Squill, striped, 225.
Star-flower, 288.
   lilac, 293.
Star-flower, spring, 292.
Star, shooting, 84.
Starwort, 37, 283.

Starwort, alpine, 37.
  bouquet, 39.
Statice latifolia, 280.
  profusa, 281.
  varieties of, 281.
Steeple-bells, 50.
Stenactis speciosus, 283.
Stokesia, jasper blue, 284.
  cyanea, 284.
Stonecrop, showy, 269.
  Siebold's, 269.
Succory, wild, 61.
Sunflower, graceful, 124.
  many-flowered, 123.
  rigid, 121.
Symphytum caucasicum, 286.

T.

Teazel, 176.
Thistle, 284.
Tiarella cordifolia, 287.
Tirentalis europæa, 288.
Toothwort, 81.
Treacle-mustard, dwarf, 97.
Trillium erectum, 291.
Triteleia, one-flowered, 292.
  uniflora, 292.
  u. liliacina, 292.
Tritoma, great, 294.
  uvaria, 294.
Tropæolum tuberosum, 295.
  tuberous, 295.
Trophy plant, 295.
Tussilago fragrans, 198.
  petasites, 198.

U.

Umbillicus chrysanthus, 297.

V.

Vaccinium Vitis-Idæa, 298.
Valerian red, 55.
Valeriana ruber, 55.
Verbascum Myconi, 228.
Veronica gentianoides, 300.

Veronica pinguifolia, 301.
  prostrata, 165, 301.
  repens, 301.
Vesicaria græca, 302.
Vetch, mountain kidney, 27.
  spring bitter, 192.
Viola pedata, 303.
  pedata bicolor, 304.
  tricolor, 305.
Violet, Dame's, 141.
  dog's tooth, 98.
  early bulbous, 106.
  pedate-leaved, or bird's-foot, 303.

W.

Wallflower, common, 56.
  fairy, 97.
  Marshall's, 58.
Whorl flower, 176.
Whortleberry, red, 298.
Willow, wrinkled or netted, 235.
Windflower, 141.
  alpine, 11.
  double, 17.
  fair, 12.
  Japan, 16.
  mountain, 12.
  poppy-like, 13.
  shaggy, 23.
  shining, 15.
  star, 20.
  stork's-bill, 12.
  sulphur-coloured, 21.
Wintergreen, English, 288.

Y.

Yarrow, Egyptian, 3.
  wild, 4.
Yucca filamentosa, 306.
  filamentosa variegata, 306.
  gloriosa, 307.
  recurva, 308.
  thready-leaved, 306.
  weeping, 308.

www.ingramcontent.com/pod-product-compliance
Lightning Source LLC
Chambersburg PA
CBHW021156230426
43667CB00006B/416